Hampshire Record Series Volume VII

The Register of William Edington Bishop of Winchester 1346–1366

PART 1

Edited by Dom S. F. Hockey, F.R.Hist.S.

Hampshire Record Office for
Hampshire County Council, 1986

Contents

Acknowledgements v
Introduction vii
1 Biographical vii
2 Diocesan administration viii
3 The manuscripts xvi
4 Editorial note xviii
References to Introduction xviii
Abbreviations xxi
Itinerary xxiii
The Calendar 1
Notes 254
Index of persons and places 280

ACKNOWLEDGEMENTS

Thanks are due to a large circle of friends who have helped to solve difficulties. For their advice and encouragement, I would mention especially the late Professor Walter Ullmann, Professor C. R. Cheney, Mrs. Dorothy Owen and Dr. R. N. Swanson. For detailed questions concerning the medieval churches of Winchester, I would like to thank Mrs. B. Carpenter-Turner. Miss R. C. Dunhill, the County Archivist and her staff have always given me every assistance. Working from a microfilm has great advantages, but it is impossible to compare one page with another. Fortunately Miss M. E. Cash, lately County Archivist, who has acted as General Editor for this volume, volunteered to undertake the task of checking the edition with the original: for this I am deeply grateful. The shortcomings of this edition remain my own.

The section of the introduction describing the manuscripts was written by C. M. Woolgar of Southampton University and Paul Morgan of the Bodleian Library Oxford.

Part of the cost of this edition was met by a grant from the Pantin Charitable Trust. This is warmly acknowledged.

Quarr Abbey, Isle of Wight

INTRODUCTION

1. BIOGRAPHICAL

William Edington, whose register as Bishop of Winchester forms the text of this volume, was a native of Edington in Wiltshire, from which his name derived. He is remembered there for a "wonderful and highly important church",[1] remaining from his foundation of a college in 1351, later to be converted into a monastery of Bonhommes. The church was consecrated in 1361; we find in the *Register* documents dated from Edington, 23–27 July 1361, which would be the time of the consecration. One other visit is similarly recorded for 28–29 August 1362. Then on 9 February 1364 the church of Newton Valence was appropriated to the brethren to increase their endowment (i, 1612). The *Register* has nothing more to offer concerning the foundation.

After his studies, possibly at Oxford, Edington joined the *familia* of Adam Orleton, to be clerk to the household of the bishop of Worcester by 1332. With most of Orleton's staff he moved with the bishop to Winchester in 1333, to become master of St Cross in 1335 and rector of Cheriton in that same year. For him as for the other members of the *familia*, Orleton secured canonries—Lincoln (1342), Salisbury (1343) and Hereford (1344), which he was to vacate when a bishop himself.[2] Meantime he was advancing along the normal stages of a permanent royal official: king's clerk by 1335, keeper of the wardrobe by 1341, then to be treasurer of the exchequer from 1344 to 1356, before becoming lord chancellor from 1356, until he resigned that office in 1363. His reform of the currency was an outstanding achievement. "Something of the anonymity of the model civil servant still clings to him."[3] The *Register* records an episcopate of twenty years, with a bishop much preoccupied with affairs outside his diocese. It is true that he resided almost continually at his manor of Southwark with only the Thames to separate him from Westminster, and a barge to convey him. Still the question must arise: what are we to make of his episcopate? Let us say at once that the *Register* gives evidence of full activity, with ordinations normally celebrated by the bishop himself, in spite of the disorganisation and stress of the Black Death. But there is little sign of pastoral activity or of visitations. The essentials of the diocesan administration were carried out by the official, the commissary-general and the sequestrator-general, but always, it would seem, with a clear direction from the bishop.

Edington had been coadjutor to Orleton, who had become almost blind at the time of his death at Farnham castle, 17 July 1345. With him were several who had also come from Worcester, ready to work with him as we shall see. On the death of Orleton the monks of St. Swithun,

Winchester, received a licence to elect a successor on 26 July,[4] but this was revoked on 27 July by a royal writ. However, within that short interval the monks had elected Nicholas Devenish from their community, as a result of which the prior with another monk were ordered to appear in chancery on 5 August. Edington became bishop of Winchester by papal provision at the request of Edward III, 9 December 1345.[5] We need not therefore be surprised at the absence of any sign of cordiality between bishop and monks, or at his rare appearances in the cathedral. When later we discover that at the beginning of 1362 the bishop quashed the election of a prior by the community, and provided Hugh de Basyng in his stead (i, 1493), we need not be surprised at an atmosphere of cold officialdom.

Edington died on 7 or 8 October 1366 at Bishops Waltham, where he had been since the beginning of August. He was buried in his cathedral in the earliest of the chantry chapels, beneath a recumbent effigy of simple alabaster. His will is dated 11 September 1366 and has been printed in full Latin text in *Wiltshire Notes and Queries,* iii (1899–1901), 214–221. There is a long list of bequests, after which the residue was left for completing the building of the cathedral nave which Edington had begun. He nominated as his executors his faithful officials: John de Blebury, Thomas de Hungerforde, Walter de Sevenhampton and John Corfe, who all figure prominently in the *Register.* William Edington cannot exactly be considered an absentee prelate; he was generally present in his diocese, though acting usually through his officials.

2. DIOCESAN ADMINISTRATION

a. *Officials*

The diocese was divided into two archdeaconries: Winchester and its ten deaneries and Surrey with three. The new bishop inherited a dispute of long standing with the archdeacon of Surrey as to what were the precise boundaries between episcopal and archidiaconal jurisdiction. Two earlier attempts at reaching a settlement are entered into the *Register of John de Pontissara*[6] at its very beginning. M. William Inge had been archdeacon of Surrey since 1320 and had been publicly insulting to bishop Adam Orleton. To the new bishop he took the oath of obedience, but through his official, M. John de Aumbresbury; the bishop seized the occasion to underline that his jurisdiction in the archdeaconry must not be infringed (i, 63). Inge died in 1347 (ii, 91), but in the preceding year his goods had been sequestrated, since he had so often ignored citations to appear before the king's justices (ii, 50, 610–11, 613, 618). The bishop called upon the archbishop of Canterbury to act as arbitrator on the issue of jurisdiction between himself and the new archdeacon, M. Richard Vaghan. These important documents (i, 84–5) were so frequently consulted that the pages are today difficult to decipher. It is not necessary to discuss the agreement here, as its terms are perfectly clear and the differences between the bishop of Winchester and his archdeacon were thereby smoothed out.

M. Richard Vaghan was a Welshman from the diocese of St. David's who had studied at Oxford, becoming doctor of common law. He was a man of distinction, having served as the king's orator at the Roman Curia and as envoy to France. By 1344 he was treasurer of St. Paul's, accumulating the usual canonries: St. Paul's, Abergwili and Wells all in 1346, and St. David's in 1352. It was by papal provision that he was appointed archdeacon, but within a few years he took the monastic habit at Canterbury.[7] He was succeeded as archdeacon in 1351 by John Edington, destined to remain in office for over forty years. A nephew of the bishop, he had been master of the *Domus Dei,* Portsmouth, then in 1349 master of St. Cross, with a seven year leave for study. Another relative was Thomas Edington, canon of Salisbury and Chichester, aged 17, who received dispensation to hold another benefice.[8]

The main administration of the medieval diocese was effected through the official, the commissary-general and the sequestrator-general. The *Register* tends to name them by their canonry rather than by their office, but it will be of particular interest here to note how many of the episcopal staff had previously worked with Orleton, even at Worcester. The chancellor was M. John de Wolveley, rector of Arreton, Isle of Wight, and canon of Salisbury. He was to be succeeded in that office by M. Thomas de Enham and later by M. Walter Benyt. The official figures very much in the *Register*; he dealt with most diocesan business, presiding over enquiries about elections or appropriations. M. John de Usk was a native of the diocese of Llandaff and as a canon lawyer had served at Worcester as commissary. At Winchester he was the official of Orleton and the vicar-general, while his predecessor in office, M. John de Lech, doctor of canon law, is found assisting him occasionally (i, 562, 916). M. John de Boys had been chancellor under Orleton, whose physician he was also. He died as rector of Brighstone, Isle of Wight, in 1347, and the *Register* records his disputed will. M. John de Nubbelaye had been treasurer of Wolvesey; he had come from Worcester and for a few years continued at the treasury, for we have his final account on relinquishing his office at the beginning of 1349 (ii, 570). M. Nicholas de Caerwent had been treasurer of Orleton's household at Winchester after serving at Worcester. As notary-public he had been a sequestrator and figures considerably in the *Register*; he lived on until 1381, dying at Crondall. As registrar, M. John de Beautre, a native of the Worcester diocese, appears throughout the *Register*, much of it being, as he frequently reminds us, written by his own hand. M. Adam Wambergh and M. Thomas de Enham who had served under Orleton, appear first as sequestrators or commissaries, often inducting to benefices, under Edington. It will therefore be clear that the bishop of Winchester had from the start a group of highly qualified men around him to carry out all the diocesan business. The *Register* is full of commissions to one or the other. To these men he was able to add other masters of the schools, such as Walter Benet from the diocese of Salisbury to whom the bishop gave permission for absence for seven years of study. He was a *magister* by 1350, holding livings in the Isle of Wight with canonries at Wells and Salisbury. Appointed chancellor in 1361, we find him being commissioned frequently by the bishop for important business. He died in late 1364 or at the beginning of 1365 (i, 1666).

b. *Diocesan clergy*

Edington had been consecrated by the archbishop of Canterbury. He himself was to consecrate nine bishops, beginning with the archbishop of Dublin, 14 February 1350; then John Sheppey for Rochester, 10 March 1353, Michael Northburgh for London and Michael Mackenlagh for Whithorn, 12 July 1355, Thomas Percy for Norwich, 3 January 1356, Adam Houghton for St David's, 2 January 1362, John Barnet for Worcester and Simon Langham for Ely at St Paul's, 2 March 1362, and finally John de Bukyngham for Lincoln, 25 June 1363. Percy was consecrated at Waverley abbey; while Thomas Percy was still bishop-elect at Norwich, Edington celebrated an ordination of seventeen candidates for his diocese, probably at St Mary, Southwark (ii, 863). This explains the large number of place-names of Norfolk and Suffolk to be found in the index.

As bishop of Winchester for 20 years Edington celebrated 64 ordinations for his diocese, not counting those in which there were less than five ordinands, which were no doubt of a more private nature. Nine ordinations were celebrated in his absence either by the bishops of Worcester and Rochester, or by the suffragan bishop, Benedict of Sardica, who had been prior of the Austin Friars in Norwich. We have excluded the granting of first tonsure for which there are very long lists (ii, 941, 950). The bishop's last ordination was the first tonsure of 13 young men at Wolvesey. We are bound to say that this is a good record: 64 ordinations in an episcopate of 20 years. Almost always they were held at the traditional times, Ember-days, or the Saturday before Passion Sunday (*Sitientes*), and 50 were celebrated in his minor chapels. If from the dating of the *Register* we consider his itinerary, we note that he did not go far from Southwark and the manors of his bishopric—Farnham, Bitterne, Highclere, Marwell, Bishops Waltham and Bishops Sutton, then Downton in Wiltshire, Brightwell and Wargrave in Berkshire and Witney in Oxfordshire; he does not seem ever to have visited Taunton. As we consider the ordination lists, if these seem to contain an unusual proportion from other dioceses, this is perhaps to be explained by proximity to the capital.

Turning now to the relations of the bishop with the clergy, we are certainly struck by the large number of dispensations for absence. The constitution of Boniface VIII of 1298 had given bishops the authority to grant leave of absence for study at some university, commonly referred to as *Cum ex eo*, though the reference does not regularly appear. This could be granted for a period of up to seven years, but on three conditions: that substitutes were provided for the *cura animarum*; that within a year of the date of the licence the cleric would seek ordination to the subdiaconate; that a year after returning to his parish he would be ordained to the priesthood. These rules seem to have been properly kept, with only occasional permissions to live from the fruits of the benefice during the study period. The university is only twice named, once as Oxford (i, 718a), once as Cambridge (i, 1668). There are just over 110 of these licences, two or three times for two years, once for three years, five times for seven years. By exception, we find licences granted to a deacon (i, 1615) and to priests (i, 119, 132). By the side of the clerical education, which *Cum ex eo* certainly helped, was the problem of absenteeism. It seems clear that Edington kept a watch on the student clergy, even when he was ready to renew the licence for one year's absence; this is seen in the case of William Boulge, rector of Farnborough (i, 53, 94, 164). He was prepared to dispute publicly with John Edington his nephew, absent on leave for seven years, insisting that he should return to Ringwood (i, 1062). Just after the Black Death the bishop addressed a general admonition against non-residence (i, 233). It was found that William Elyot, rector of Farleigh Wallop was absent without leave and with his whereabouts unknown: he was to return within a month (ii, 236). But the *Register* contains over 70 licences for absence at the service of notables—from the king or the Black Prince to a bishop or an abbess, almost without exception for people of title. Almaric de Pontiliaco began with a licence to be at the service of William de Cusancia, keeper of the wardrobe. Then he had leave to study for a year, renewed for a second year; and again renewed, with a proviso that immediately after the end of the year he must be back in residence or be penalized. During these years he had exchanged his benefice of Baddington for Baughurst (i, 216, 706, 878, 880). The perpetual vicars, i.e. with a perpetual endowment, were far less a cause of anxiety; they took the oath to reside continually according to the constitutions of the legates Otto and Ottobon. The oath so regularly accompanies the admission to a vicarage, that the names of the legates have been omitted in this edition and signs of neglect of the oath have not been noticed. The vicars could not normally use the licence *Cum ex eo,* as they were sworn to reside.[9]

Every candidate for ordination by a bishop other than his diocesan had to present letters dimissory to prove that he was of good living and worthy of advancement to holy orders, usually but not always issued for one order only. The *Register* normally indicates by an abbreviation that these letters have been presented. Only when some unusual element appears is this fact noted here. Furthermore the candidate had to show his title to some revenue or benefice which would enable him to enjoy a secure income and live as befitted his orders. All these are set out in this edition, as they show a large range of religious houses which were prepared to grant this title. The members of religious houses did not require this; their order or their community guaranteed their maintenance. The exact significance of these titles, even their honesty, is much disputed.[10] Here very few seek ordination on their own patrimony. One candidate adds to this a corrody in Winchester Cathedral (ii, 782): another presents himself on his own pension (ii, 722). The grant from the priory of Newark (Novo Loco) of five marks from a chantry at Ashtead appears under three names (ii, 735, 738, 903)—five marks being considered the standard rate. An annual pension of 100s. from the bishop of Worcester (ii, 836, 843) must indicate some link with the ordinand. At times the personal link is clear, through a local association of some kind:

> John le Greyn of Breamore *ad titulum* the prior of Breamore
> Walter Fabri of Cerne Abbas, *ad tit.* the abbot of Cerne

Severin de Tyntagel, *ad tit.* the prior of Launceston
Many more similar cases must be hidden under the names of villages in the vicinity of religious houses, though very few of the major abbeys appear in the lists. But above and beyond any such personal contact stands the very large number receiving their title from insignificant communities, which cannot have had many benefices to offer. For this *Register* the most prominent examples are the churches of St Mary Kalendar and St Peter in the centre of the city of Winchester. The donors can hardly have been more than confraternities attached to these city churches. Yet St Mary Kalendar granted no less than 52 titles within seven years—and seven titles for the bishop's first ordination, 10 June 1346. One next wonders what can be the significance of the fact that in an episcopate from 1346 to 1366, the name of St Mary Kalendar does not appear after 1353 (ii, 843). Does this indicate the closure of an agency or clearing-house? We should perhaps add here that several bishops are stated to have retained the original document of grant in their registry: the entry of this fact into the Winchester register seems to have been considered as sufficient proof of title. This evidence from Edington's register may have something to contribute to the continuing debate as to titles, though it is more likely to confirm the general situation for the middle of the fourteenth century.

The episcopate of Edington was marked by the scourge of the Black Death and his register has been carefully scrutinised by the historians of the plague.[11] The first mention of the scourge is the mandate from the bishop appealing for penance and prayer (ii, 166). The plague struck the diocese of Winchester with special violence; 48.8% of all beneficed clergy died, a figure not exceeded in any other diocese of England.[12] It can be argued that the clergy were more exposed to contagion because of their pastoral duties in administering the last sacraments and conducting funerals; the episcopal register demonstrates how many benefices had to be filled. The register began by stating that the benefice was vacant by reason of the death of its occupant, but it will be noted that after April even this is omitted. We have calculated from the register the entries for the three years under review here. The norm had been one institution per month; allowing for the gap between a death and the succession the critical period would be March and April 1349; the year 1350 still shows high figures, no doubt caused by the general weakness from which the whole population suffered. There may be a margin of error in our figures of one or two—natural causes, old age—but the record remains very impressive. The bishop had to fill the gap from the unbeneficed clergy, but the ordination lists after the plague years shows a marked increase in those who had been clerks holding high office, now advancing to the priesthood. We cannot here deal systematically with the effect of the pestilence on the religious houses; let it be sufficient to point out two examples of the lesser houses for which the loss of just a few members could create a crisis. At the hospital of St Mary Magdalen, Sandon in Surrey, all the brethren died; the bishop was obliged to find a custodian (i, 554). St Thomas hospital, Southwark, had given the bishop much concern, which can be followed up in the *Register,* but by the end of 1361 all the brethren save one were dead (i, 1426). Among the other side

REGISTER OF EDINGTON Vacant benefices			
	1348	1349	1350
January	—	11	3
February	1	20	7
March	3	40	4
April	—	64	7
May	1	56	4
June	1	35	1
July	1	25	3
August	—	13	3
September	1	15	7
October	1	16	6
November	—	7	4
December	3	13	5
	12	315	54

effects of the pestilence are the delays in payments of levies and requests for exemption from payment of tenths (ii, 429). However, in these cases the pestilence is not usually alleged as the direct cause of distress, but rather misrule.

c. *Other aspects*

During most of Edington's episcopate Edward III was at war, compelled to defend his claims in France, as the *Register* puts it, 16 March 1346, requesting prayers and processions for the safety of the country and for success at arms (i, 47). Edward invaded Normandy in July 1346, captured Caen and won the battle of Crecy, 26 August; the following year Calais surrendered, 4 August, and the truce which followed, 28 September, necessitated the bishop's presence at Calais, 24 November to 12 December 1348. But the war was to be renewed in 1355 by the raiding campaign of the Black Prince, which called for another mandate for prayers (ii, 311, 376). Thanksgiving services were ordered for his victory at Poitiers, 19 September 1356, and the capture of the French king. At the peace of Bretigny, 8 May 1360, a heavy ransom was laid down for King John's release; (this ransom appears in the *Register* in another context). The bishop on this occasion had a longer stay in Calais, 24 August to 6 November, when the peace was ratified, 24 October. The expedition of the Black Prince to Aquitaine called for more prayers in the spring of 1363. One consequence of these military expeditions was the pressure on aliens holding benefices in England; they were to be listed with the valuation of their benefices (ii, 609). The alien priories suffered from the sequestration of their goods and taxation (ii, 502, 599).

Money was urgently needed for the war and the *Register* has its series of appeals through convocation to secure the co-operation of the bishops in raising funds from the beneficed clergy, according to the assessment of 1291. From Calais, 28 December 1346, the king ordered the payment of the biennial tenth to be advanced in view of the serious situation (ii, 619). The reluctance or the poverty of some of the clergy can be judged by the arrears still being collected from the triennial tenth of 1337 (ii, 624), of the triennial tenth of 1344 (ii, 633, 641) and of 1342 (ii, 635). From St Paul's, as was customary, convocation granted another biennial tenth, 14 May 1347 (ii, 636) and yet another grant, for which the mandate for the first year was issued 1 September 1351 (ii, 665). Payments were staggered and as usual collected by archdeaconries. The mandate for the second year of the grant is dated 20 October 1352 (ii, 670). In view of the dangerous situation of the country, the king appealed through convocation, by a royal brief of 22 April 1360, for a tenth, to be made in two payments. The *Register* contains a list of poor benefices appealing for a reduction in the tax, 29 June 1361 (ii, 681). But in November of 1364 efforts were still being made to round up those who had not yet fully paid; there is a list of these (ii, 685) with entries concerning special cases.

Until after the treaty with France at Calais in 1362 no pope had levied an aid from the clergy of England for over thirty years; hence the murmuring aroused by the bull of Innocent VI requesting the grant of a tenth, 1 April 1362 (ii, 422). Instead of paying a tenth for two years, the bishops offered an aid of 100,000 florins. By an ingenious arrangement this money was paid into the English exchequer as part of the ransom of King John of France.

The numerous documents concerning procurations to cardinals constitute the most complicated section of those dealing with finance. Cardinals on mission to England were granted these procurations to cover their expenses, calculated at a farthing to the pound on the assessed value of ecclesiastical benefices (i, 39, 81). These payments were much resented; hence the postponements, the part-payments, the arrears which complicate all these entries. The work of W. E. Lunt, *Financial Relations of the Papacy with England, 1327–1534*, makes it possible to put some order into what at first sight seems so chaotic. First, we can extract the special peace mission of a bishop and the abbot of Cluny (ii, 328) and then we must reverse the order of the register to reach the chronological order of ii, 628; ii, 518; ii, 335ff. Annibaldus, bishop of Tusculum, and Stephen of St John and St Paul, on their way to England, were ordered to await the crossing of the king on his way to invade Normandy. They met him and claimed from the English clergy procurations for their stay in France, but the parliament of 11 September 1346 had forbidden this. When in the spring they sent proctors to collect their procurations, these were again forbidden by a royal mandate of 2 April 1347 (ii, 628). However, by August 1348 such payments were permitted and by 20 October of that year the bishop of Winchester had paid part-payments for two years (ii, 518). Next we have the two cardinals Talleyrand de Perigord, bishop of Albano, and Nicholas Capocci, bishop of Urgel, who began their embassy, 21 June 1356;[13] hence the mention of the first year of the nunciature in 1357 (ii, 335), the second (ii, 337) and the third (ii, 351). As a result during 1357 the English clergy paid almost two procurations; the rate is not usually given, but is known to vary from diocese to diocese and from year to year. Each cardinal had his own receiver, Pontius de Vereriis for Talleyrand, Luke de Tholomeis for Nicholas. When the cardinals ordered the payment for the second year in September 1357, they also demanded the arrears of the first year; the bishop of Winchester will be found receiving the arrears of two years in November 1358 (ii, 362). The number of these documents with part-payments and repeated arrears gives ample proof of the burden on the clergy of these cardinals working for a truce between England and France.[14]

Of unusual interest is a series of nine items (between ii, 639 and 661), dated 1347–1348, concerning the Augustinian priory of Bustlesham or Bisham in Berkshire, which William de Montecute, first earl of Salisbury, had founded by a charter dated 1337. It is clear that, though lands had been granted in various counties (Berkshire, Buckinghamshire, Somerset, Wiltshire and Hampshire) the priory was insufficiently endowed. Adam Orleton had approved the appropriation of the church of Kingsclere (i, 46, 189), to which were to be added Curry Rivel in Somerset, August 1398, and East Claydon, Bucks., in 1409. In 1398 the bishop of Bath and Wells stated that the priory was burdened with debt, its rents were diminished through the pestilence and the church was still not finished. The earl of Salisbury had been prevented by death (1344) from completing the endowment of his foundation.[15]

The prior, Thomas de Wiltshire, had been borrowing money on a considerable scale; from William de la Pole, a merchant of Hull and baron of the exchequer, £400 (ii, 639 etc.); from Berard de la Bret, a Gascon, £2,400 (ii, 645 etc.); and from Walter de Wyville, treasurer of Salisbury, 1,000 marks (ii, 646, 661). In 1347 Sir William de la Pole was still living, but the others were dead. The share of the whole debt for the diocese of Winchester was 200 marks for Sir William de la Pole, £500 for the executors of Sir Berard de la Bret and 300 marks for the executors of Walter de Wyville. The executors of Sir Berard were Reginald de Pontibus and his wife Joan, a sister of Berard de la Bret, with six others—all Gascons from places in the Gironde and Charente-Inferieure. His will was proved, 4 May 1347, at St Paul's;[16] the king ordered the plea pending between the executors and the prior of Bisham to proceed, i.e. concerning £500 in a debt of £2,400. Since the loan had been taken in the names of Thomas, the prior, with Edward de Montecute and Simon, bishop of Ely, brothers of the earl of Salisbury,[17] these acknowledged that they were bound to Berard, and the repayment of the £500 was due for Michaelmas.[18] But the bishop of Ely was dead by 20 June 1345.

As for the money due from the executors of Walter de Wyville—300 marks in four payments (ii, 661), the executors were Robert de Wyville, bishop of Salisbury and William de Weston. When the prior failed to repay Sir William de la Pole the debt of 200 marks, the bishop was ordered to sequestrate his ecclesiastical goods (but, as so frequently in the *Register*, purchasers could not be found for sequestrated goods (ii, 639)).

The *Register* contains a certain amount of testamentary business, but no wills. It is abundant and full in recording exchanges of benefices and careful in questions of appropriation of churches to religious houses. Licences to dispense from illegitimacy of birth are in one case mathematically checked. There is the usual matrimonial business. Disputed elections were always carefully examined, if not by the bishop himself. There are a few cases of clergy involved in violence, to place by that of the Austin Friars in Winchester. The bishop was generous in granting licences for the sick or elderly to hear Mass in their homes. One misses the presence of any visitation records, but the licences for study show a real effort to promote a growth in the academic quality of the clergy. There is no reference anywhere to heresy.

3. THE MANUSCRIPTS

William Edington's register is now bound in two volumes, deposited among the diocesan records in the Hampshire Record Office, A/1/8 and A/1/9. Both volumes contain parchment leaves which measure approximately 245 × 375 mm, and both have the same binding. The second register is the better preserved; the first was rebacked in the nineteenth century. The volumes are bound in brown, smooth tanned leather commonly used in England from c.1460 onwards. The covers are blind-tooled in an all-over diaper pattern that came to England with Caxton's binder and was copied successively in Cambridge, London, Winchester and Oxford, c.1488–1500. The presence of the remains of metal clasps hinged to the upper cover confirms the English origin, as European bindings have clasps hinged to the lower cover. The pastedowns give no clues to the origin of the bindings. Though very worn, the tools can safely be ascribed to a craftsman known as the Greyhound Binder who worked somewhere in England at the end of the fifteenth and beginning of the sixteenth century. This could have been at Oxford, Winchester or London; Richard Fox (d.1528), Bishop of Winchester, owned six volumes surviving at Corpus Christi College, Oxford, bound in a similar pattern with the same tools as Edington's registers, but as Fox is known to have bought books in London as well as Oxford, it is not possible to fix a definite location. Besides these six volumes at Corpus, other examples of this binder's work are at Merton and Magdalen Colleges, Oxford, Worcester Cathedral, and Pembroke College, Cambridge. Another three of the Winchester episcopal registers, the two for William of Wykeham and that of Cardinal Beaufort, have the same binding.[19] It is unfortunate that the spine of both the Edington volumes is so damaged that it is impossible now to determine whether the head-bands were plaited with pink cord or not, as this was a distinctive feature of the Greyhound Binder's technique; the plaiting is present, however, on Beaufort's register. The tool with a greyhound, after which the binder is named, is not present on Edington's registers. The Greyhound Binder had 15 tools in all available, but only a selection was used on each volume. The bindings of Edington's registers are specimens of late fifteenth or early sixteenth century English binding in blind-tooled tanned leather by the Greyhound Binder.[20]

The two volumes of Edington's register have been paginated consecutively (pp. 1–270 and 271–528) and are referred to in this edition by this pagination. The earliest numbering present is a series of Roman numerals of the mid to late fourteenth century in the bottom right hand corner of the first folio of many of the gatherings. The earliest foliation present is in Arabic numerals in a hand of the early sixteenth century, possibly contemporary with the binding of the registers, which continues as far as page 394 in the second volume. A hand of the late seventeenth century or early eighteenth century has continued the foliation to page 428 and has lettered the remaining folios. The first volume contains Edington's register as bishop elect, and the register of presentations, collations, institutions, inductions, processes, dispensations and licences for the remainder of his episcopate. The second volume contains, firstly, commissions, inquisitions, procurations, licences and other letters; secondly, bulls and other papal letters and processes; thirdly, temporal letters writs and other royal letters; and fourthly, letters dimissory and ordinations or commissions to celebrate ordinations. Each of the sections in the second volume, together with Edington's register as bishop elect, was originally in unbound quires or *quaterni*. The start of the two sections in the first volume and of each of the four sections in the second volume (pp. 3, 31, 273, 381, 395, 429) is marked *quarternus primus*. Both volumes are principally arranged in gatherings of four bifolia. The first volume is made up of 19 gatherings: pp. 1–2, 3–18, 19–28, 29–30, 31–46, 47–63, 64–78, 79–94, 95–110, 111–26, 127–42, 143–58, 159–74, 175–90, 191–206, 207–22, 223–38, 239–54, 255–70. Pages 3–28 are Edington's register as bishop elect, to which a singleton has been added at the front. Pages 29–30 may be an early sixteenth century insertion: the heading ''Edyndon'' is written on page 29 in a hand of this date, as a title page. The main register follows. The second volume is less regularly grouped in 23 gatherings: pp. 271–2, 273–88, 289–304, 305–20, 321–36, 337–50, 351–66, 367–80 (and two unnumbered stubs), 381–94 (and one unnumbered stub), 395–412, 413–26, 427–8 (and one unnumbered stub), 429–44, 445–8, 449–56, 457–60, 461–76, 477–80, 481–4, 485–8, 489–504, 505–20, 521–8 (and several stubs, unnumbered, pasted to the back cover). There have been excisions from both volumes: text is missing on pages 183–4 and 337–42.

The pages are well laid out, each having a margin of about 15 mm at the binding, 20 mm at the top, 80 mm at the foot and 65 mm on the remaining side. On the earliest pages the margins have been ruled off in pencil; on later pages in ink, or by folds. A number of hands wrote the volumes. The first hand in each of the main sections of the register is the same accomplished charter hand; and a sequence of similar business hands were employed to write the remainder of the text. Entries were made in the registers at intervals ranging from one or two days to several months, presumably from rough notes.[21] The first clerk envisaged a lavish decoration for the volumes: the initial letters of the first words of the principal sections of the register still await embellishment. In the margin next to each entry a very short summary of its contents was entered.

The margins of the volumes also contain notes by later clerks, to draw attention to particular entries.

4. EDITORIAL NOTE

The title of this edition bears the bishop's name in the spelling of the placename from which it derives; the bishop's registrars always wrote *Edyndon*, and this is followed in the calendar. No personal name has been omitted: each has been printed as found entered in the register. Place-names have all been recorded and are given in their modern spelling, where available. The medieval spelling is to be found in the index. Every effort has been made to reduce unnecessary punctuation. The index includes personal names and placenames. A subject index to cover volumes 1 and 2 will appear in volume 2.

REFERENCES TO INTRODUCTION

1. N. Pevsner *The Buildings of England: Wiltshire* (Harmondsworth, 1963) 208
2. R. M. Haines *The Church and Politics in Fourteenth-Century England: the Career of Adam Orleton, c.1275–1345* (Cambridge, 1978)
3. M. McKissack *The Fourteenth Century* (Oxford, 1959) 213
4. *CCIR 1343–1346* 590
5. *Reg. Com. Seal* 195, n. 5. For the fate of the Devenish, see W. A. Pantin *The English Church in the Fourteenth Century* (Cambridge, 1955) 57
6. *Reg. Pont.* i, 1–4
7. *Emden: History of the University of Oxford* I, ed. J. I. Catto (Oxford, 1984) 579
8. *C.Pap.L.* iii, 386
9. "The Constitution *Cum ex eo* of Boniface VIII" in L. E. Boyle *Pastoral Care, Clerical Education and Canon Law, 1200–1400* (London, 1981)
10. For the most recent discussion, see R. N. Swanson "Titles to Orders in English Episcopal Registers" in *Studies in Medieval History Presented to R. H. C. Davis* ed. H. Mayr-Harting and R. I. Moore (London, 1985) pp. 233–45
11. F. A. Gasquet *The Black Death of 1348–9* (London, 1908); P. Ziegler *The Black Death* (London, 1969)
12. Ziegler, 145
13. cf. *Chart. Winch. Cath.* 164–5
14. *Lunt* chapter 3
15. *VCH Berkshire* ii, 82
16. *CCIR 1346–1349* 364; *CPR 1345–1348* 287, 331, 427
17. *Complete Peerage* ix, 82n
18. There is a different date in ii, 645
19. Hampshire Record Office, Winchester Diocesan Records, A/1/10–12
20. J. B. Oldham *English Blind-Stamped Bindings* (Cambridge, 1952) 8, 21, 59 and plate xv (tools 136, 141, 145); G. Pollard, "The Names

of some English Fifteenth-Century Binders'', *The Library* 5th series, 25 (1970) 197, 199–204, 213 and plates 6–7; G. D. Hobson *English Binding before 1500* (Cambridge, 1929) 24

21. D. M. Smith *Guide to Bishop's Registers of England and Wales: a Survey from the Middle Ages to the Abolition of Episcopacy in 1646* (London, 1981) ix

ABBREVIATIONS

CClR	*Calendar of Close Rolls*
C.FineR	*Calendar of Fine Rolls*
Chart. Winch.	*Chartulary of Winchester Cathedral* ed. A. W. Goodman (Winchester, 1927)
Cath.	
C.Inquis.	*Calendar of Inquisitions Miscellaneous*
C.Pap.L.	*Calendar of Papal Letters*
C.Pap.Pet.	*Calendar of Papal Petitions*
C.Pap.R.	*Calendar of Papal Registers*
CPR	*Calendar of Patent Rolls*
Complete Peerage	G. E. Cocayne *The Complete Peerage* ed. V. Gibbs et al. (12 vols. in 13, London, 1910–59)
DNB	*Dictionary of National Biography*
Dugdale	W. Dugdale *Monasticon Anglicanum* ed. J. Caley, H. Ellis and B. Bandinel (6 vols. in 8, London, 1817–30)
Emden	*A Biographical Register of the University of Oxford to A.D. 1500* ed. A. B. Emden (3 vols., Oxford, 1957–9)
Inquis.p.m.	*Calendar of Inquisitions post mortem*
Insula Vecta	S. F. Hockey *Insula Vecta: the Isle of Wight in the Middle Ages* (London, 1982)
Le Neve	J. Le Neve *Fasti Ecclesiae Anglicanae 1300–1541* (Institute of Historical Research, London, 1962–7)
Lunt	W. E. Lunt *Financial Relations of the Papacy with England 1327–1534* (Cambridge, Massachusetts, 1962)
Lunt Acc.	W. E. Lunt *Accounts rendered by Papal Collectors in England 1317–1378* (Philadelphia, 1968)
Med. Rel. Houses	D. Knowles and R. H. Hadcock *Medieval Religious Houses: England and Wales* (revised edition, London, 1971)
Oxf. Place Names	E. Ekwall *The Concise Oxford Dictionary of English Place-Names* (fourth edition, Oxford, 1960)
Reg. Com. Seal	*The Register of the Common Seal of the Priory of St. Swithun, Winchester* ed. J. Greatrex (Hampshire Record Series, 2; 1979)
Reg. Pont.	*Registrum Johannis de Pontissara, Episcopi Wyntoniensis, 1282–1304* ed. C. Deedes (Canterbury and York Society, 19, 30; 1915–24)
RS	*Rolls Series*
Stow	*Stow's Survey of London* ed. H. B. Wheatley (London, 1912, reprinted 1970)

Stubbs	W. Stubbs *Registrum Sacrum Anglicanum: an Attempt to Exhibit the Course of Episcopal Succession in England* (second edition, Oxford, 1897)
Taxatio	*Taxatio Ecclesiastica Angliae et Walliae Auctoritate P. Nicholai IV circa A.D.1291* (Record Commission, London, 1802)
VCH	*Victoria County History*
Wyk. Reg.	*Wykeham's Register* ed. T. F. Kirby (2 vols., Hampshire Record Society, 1896–9)

ITINERARY

1346

May 14. Otford
August 28. Bishops Waltham
September 28. Bishops Waltham

1347

March 1. Esher
March 28–April 1. Esher
September 22. Marwell
September 24, 25. Wolvesey
September 28. Marwell
September 30. Farnham

1348

January 5. London
March 26. Esher
April 1. Esher
May 12. Esher
June 8, 13–15. Esher
June 16. London
June 21. Chertsey
August 15. Esher
August 16–21. Farnham
August 23–25. Bishops Waltham
September 7. Houghton
September 8, 9. Bishops Waltham
September 11. Hambledon
September 13. Bitterne
September 13, 14. Beaulieu
September 15. Wells near Romsey
September 17–19. Highclere
October 1. Farnham
November 24. Departure to Calais
December 12. Return from Calais

1349

January 1, 2. Esher
January 5–11. Farnham
January 14. Esher
January 16, 18. Farnham

January 22–March 19. Esher,
  visiting Cobham, March 7
March 19–April 18. Farnham,
  visiting Newark, March 20
  visiting Winchester, April 13
April 26, 27. Farnham
May 12–19. Esher
May 21–June 14. Esher
  visiting Sandon, June 6
June 23–25. Esher
July 12–26. Highclere
July 28, 29. Marwell
August 1, 2, 6. Marwell
August 8–11. Hursley
September 3. Fareham
September 3, 4. Bitterne
September 7. Downton
September 15–20. Bishops
  Waltham
December 28–31. Farnham

1350

January 1–6. Farnham
March 13. Kingston
March 16–28 Esher
July 24. Esher
August 13. Highclere
August 17, 29. Bishops Waltham
September 4, 5. Bishops Waltham
September 5. Sutton
September 12. Esher
September 14, 18–20. Highclere
September 22. Sutton
September 26. Wargrave
September 26, 27. Esher
October 11. Esher
December 26–30. Esher

1351

March 29–April 2. Esher
April 14–18, 24. Esher

May 8. Esher
August 21. Esher
October 6. Farnham
October 9. Esher
October 21. Farnham
December 14–19. Kimpton, Herts
December 20. Overton
December 24–29. Esher

1352

February 24, 29. Esher
April 2, 4. Esher
April 7, 11. Farnham
May 31. Esher
June 1. Farnham
June 16. Esher
September 18, 19. Wolvesey
September 27. Overton
December 21–31. Esher

1353

March 25, 30. Esher
May 5, 14. Esher
July 31–August 3. Farnham
August 16, 22, 28. Bishops
    Waltham
September 1. Bishops Waltham
September 18. Esher
September 22. Bishops Waltham
December 19. Esher
December 21, 22, 30, 31. Farnham

1354

January 4. Farnham
January 18. Esher
April 8–28. Farnham
May 5. Esher
July 11. Bishops Waltham
August 1, 2. Downton
August 31. Bishops Waltham
September 2. Hambledon
September 4. Sutton
September 20. Esher
December 20, 28. Bishops
    Waltham

1355

January 1, 7, 8. Bishops Waltham
January 9. Farnham

March 28–30. Esher
April 4, 10. Esher
August 7, 17, 23, 30. Farnham
September 5. Highclere
September 17. Sutton
December 15, 16. Esher

1356

January 3. Waverley
March 25. Esher
April 2, 6, 10, 13, 26. Esher
June 13. Stratfield Saye
September 11, 18. Marwell
September 25. Farnham
September 29. Esher
October 10. Westminster

1357

[all dating for every month is from
    Southwark]

1358

March 24–26. Esher
April 4–6. Esher
August 25. Farnham
September 28. Farnham
September 30. Esher

1359

April 20. Farnham
December 7. Sutton

1360

April 23. Windsor
August 7. Marwell
August 9. Sutton
August 10, 11. Farnham
August 24. Departure for Calais
November 6. Return from Calais
December 12. Wolvesey
December 31. Farnham

1361

January 1–10. Farnham
May 13, 20, 21. Esher
June 14. Esher
June 17, 18. Farnham
June 20. Esher

July 4–7. Esher
July 18. Wargrave
July 21. Brightwell
July 22. Buckland
July 23–27. Edington
August 6–16. Highclere
August 18–30. Bishops Waltham
September 1–16. Farnham
September 17–29. Wargrave
   visiting Esher 23

1362

February 1. Farnham
February 18. Sutton
February 20. Southwick
February 22–24. Bishops Waltham
February 25. Marwell
February 26. Hursley, Wolvesey
February 27, 28. Highclere
March 2. London, St Pauls
April 16, 23. Farnham
July 24, 30. Esher
August 18. Witney
August 28, 29. Edington
September 10–12. Highclere
September 17–20. Farnham
September 23–25. Esher
December 14–15. Esher
December 27–31. Farnham

1363

January 1–5. Farnham
January 12. Esher
February 23, 24. Esher
March 5–24. Esher
April 1, 12, 16, 26, 28. Esher
May 2, 9, 10. Esher
May 28, 29. Highclere
June 1. Highclere
June 3. Wolvesey
June 6. Winchester
June 8. Wargrave
June 8, 9. Highclere
June 25, 28. Wargrave
July 5–9, 19. Wargrave
July 28, 29. Farnham
August 8. Farnham
August 16. Wolvesey
August 27. Bishops Waltham

August 29. Marwell
August 29. Edington
September 1. Marwell
September 15. Compton
September 23, 28. Esher
November 4, 9. Esher
December 9. Esher
December 12. Highclere
December 18. Esher
December 18. Newark
December 21. Overton
December 21–29. Highclere

1364

January 2–6. Highclere
January 12. Esher
February 13, 14. Esher
February 29. Farnham
March 9, 23–30. Bishops Waltham
April 2, 4. Bishops Waltham
April 8. Farnham
May 6, Wolvesey
May 6, 11–28. Wargrave
June 15. Wargrave
July 1. Wargrave
July 12. Esher
August 4. Coleshill
August 5, 9. Highclere
August 16. Bishops Waltham
August 18. Bitterne
August 24. Bishops Waltham
August 29. East Meon
September 2. Marwell
September 10, 17. Downton
September 20. Esher
October 20. Dummer
November 4, 21, 29. Farnham
December 20, 21. Farnham

1365

January 1–4. Farnham
January 9. Highclere
January 12, 13. Wolvesey
January 16. Farnham
February 21–23. Farnham
March 4–9. Highclere
March 16, 27–31. Bishops
   Waltham
April 12, 18. Bishops Waltham

April 25, 26. Farnham
May 2, 9. Farnham
May 13. Bishops Waltham
May 15, 23–25. Farnham
May 27. Wargrave
June 3–8, 21. Wargrave
June 22. Esher
June 30. Wargrave
July 4. Wargrave
July 8, 12, 16. Witney
July 18. Hursley
July 19. Witney
July 20. Hartley Wintney
July 28. Wargrave
August 17–19. Hursley
September 6, 14. Bishops Waltham
September 20. Sutton
October 2–5. Esher
November 3, 10, 15, 24. Farnham
December 15–19. Farnham
December 26. Highclere

1366

January 3–5. Highclere
January 24. Farnham
January 25. Highclere
February 3–10. Highclere
February 20–29. Wolvesey,
  visiting St Elizabeth, 28
March 1, 21–25. Wolvesey,
  visiting St Elizabeth, 21
March 29, 30. Hursley
April 1. Hursley
May 4, 15, 18. Esher
May 18. Wargrave
May 20. Esher
May 25, 26. Reigate
May 28. Esher
June 1, 5, 6. Esher
June 30. Wargrave
July 2, 3, 14. Wargrave
August 5, 6. Highclere
August 18, 20, 25, 29. Bishops
  Waltham
September 8, 15, 16, 20, 26.
  Bishops Waltham
October 2, 6. Bishops Waltham.

THE REGISTER OF BISHOP EDINGTON

1,2   Blank

3   **1**. Register of the Reverend Father in Christ William de Edyndon by the grace of God elect of Winchester, now confirmed. When he was Treasurer of England he received the apostolic bulls concerning his provision to the see of Winchester from the Apostolic See at London, 14 February 1345. In virtue of these bulls the temporalities of the bishopric of Winchester were conferred upon him at Westminster by the King of England on February 21.

2. First quire of apostolic bulls, royal letters and writs, collations, institutions and inductions to churches, also dispensations, letters dimissory, licences for study and oratories, with commissions and other letters.

3. BULL of Clement [VI] addressed to King Edward [III]. The pope intending in his prudence to provide a suitable person to govern the church of Winchester, had, while Adam [de Orleton] was still holding the see, reserved the nomination of a successor to himself, declaring any other to be null and void, by whatever authority conferred. Now at the death of Adam, he appoints William de Edyndon, clerk of Winchester and canon of Salisbury, to be bishop and pastor of Winchester—a man of learning and experience in spiritual and temporal affairs, able to govern and defend his church. In this the royal favour will support him. May all reverence and obedience be shown him.

Avignon, 9 December 1345

[There follow six more bulls, all with essentially the same text and with the same date, with slightly adapted conclusion.]

4   **4**. BULL of Clement VI to [John Stratford] archbishop of Canterbury.

5. BULL of Clement VI to William de Edyndon, clerk.

5   **6**. BULL of Clement VI to the chapter of Winchester.

7. BULL of Clement VI to the clergy of the city and diocese of Winchester.

6   **8**. BULL of Clement VI to all the vassals of the church of Winchester.

7   **9**. BULL of Clement VI to the people of the city and diocese of Winchester.

10. BULL of Clement VI to William, elect of Winchester. Since the pope had specially reserved nomination to the see of Winchester to himself, so that it might no longer suffer from the inconveniences of a vacancy, he now turns to William de Edyndon, providing him to the see, bidding him care for it in temporal and spiritual matters, that it may prosper under his government.

Avignon, 9 December 1345

[*Margin*] Received on Christmas Eve, 1345.

11. MANDATE from John Stratford, archbishop of Canterbury, to the official and commissary of the diocese of Winchester. The archbishop has learned from the pope that William de Edyndon, canon of Salisbury, has been provided to the see of Winchester. He orders them to allow the bishop to exercise his authority, handing over to him the consistorial registers with other books and seals concerning the spirituality of the city and diocese which are in their custody.

Croydon, 15 February 1346

8   **12.** ANNOUNCEMENT that the bishop has appointed M. Adam de Wamberghe, rector of the church of Ashbury in the diocese of Salisbury, to be his proctor, granting him full powers to be in charge of the consistory seal and register, or others concerning spiritual matters; to seek and receive acquittances and to do whatever may seem necessary and opportune.

London, 16 February 1346

13. MANDATE to M. Adam de Wamberghe. The bishop, having full confidence in Adam, requests him to publish the apostolic bulls concerning the bishop's provision in the city and diocese. Also, to receive the canonical obedience of all and singular abbots, priors, deans, rectors, vicars of churches and other holders of ecclesiastical benefices or spiritual offices in the diocese, from whom it is customary and legitimate to receive obedience.

London, 16 February 1346

14. MANDATE to the archdeacon, to his official and the deanery of Winchester. The bishop wishes them to summon all abbots, priors, guardians of communities and colleges, deans, rectors, vicars holding ecclesiastical benefices, whether exempt or not from archidiaconal jurisdiction, with other religious and seculars who are to swear obedience to the bishop. Those who are thus cited will appear before the bishop or his commissary in the cathedral church of Winchester, 21 February next, to hear the apostolic mandate concerning his provision and to tender canonical obedience.

London, 16 February 1346

15. MANDATE to summon the clergy of the other deaneries of the archdeaconry of Winchester.

16. MANDATE to the archdeacon of Surrey. The bishop greets the archdeacon and his official. He bids him summon all who hold ecclesiastical benefices, whether exempt from archidiaconal jurisdiction or not, religious or secular of the archdeaconry of Surrey to tender obedience, whether by custom or by right. Those from the deaneries of Guildford and Farnham for the first law-day after the 2nd Sunday in Lent in the church of the Holy Trinity at Guildford; those from the deanery of Ewell for the second law-day after the said Sunday in the parish church of Kingston; those of Southwark for the third law-day after that Sunday in St Margaret's church in Southwark. They are to appear before the bishop to hear the apostolic bulls concerning the provision; they will tender him obedience. The archdeacon will have the names of those taking the oath appended to the mandate.

London, 24 February 1346

9

17. COMMISSION to M. Adam de Wamberghe, rector of Ashbury. The bishop entrusts to him the responsibility for hearing and terminating causes and other business in the consistory; for revoking or approving wills with the distribution of the goods and recording this; also for correcting and punishing the excesses of his subjects and dealing with appeals and complaints, with powers of coercion, in the absence of the official.

London, 16 February 1346

18. MANDATE to enquire into the vacancy of a church. Sir W[illiam] Trussel of Cubblesdon has presented Robert de Souky clerk to the church of Abbotstone vacant. He presents by reason of the minority of Edmund, son and heir of Hugh de Sancto Johanne, deceased, whose lands are entrusted by the king to William until Edmund comes of age. Enquiry is to be made whether the church is vacant and since when; by whom the last presentation was made; whether the church is subject to charges of any kind and how much. The names of those taking part in the enquiry will be included in a sealed document.

London, 17 February [1346]

19. ADMISSION AND INSTITUTION of Robert de Souky to be rector of Abbotstone, presented by sir William Trussel, patron for this one turn. [The other details are identical with those in 18 above.]

London, 26 February 1346

Under the same date the archdeacon of Winchester was notified for the induction of Robert.

20. ADMISSION AND INSTITUTION of John Godman priest as rector of St Martin *pargamenorum* in the city of Winchester, vacant after the death of William de Stok'. The patrons are the abbess and convent of Wherwell. The official of the archdeacon and the dean were jointly notified for his induction.

London, 19 February 1346

21. APPOINTMENT OF A CONFESSOR addressed to Thomas de Berton' monk of Winchester. Commission to act in the place of the bishop to hear the confessions of his fellow-monks and of any in the diocese who wish to confess their sins in those cases especially reserved to the bishop; to grant absolution and impose salutary penance. Certain matters (*named*) are reserved to the bishop.

London, 24 February

Similar commission to John Clifford monk of the same church.

London, 4 March 1346

22. Similar commission to friar Richard de Guldeforde of the Guildford Dominican friary for the archdeaconry of Surrey and to the rector of Gatcombe in the Isle of Wight, except that the clause for monks is omitted from the commission.

10   **23.** LETTERS DIMISSORY from the bishop elect for ordinations by any catholic bishop:
to Robert de Pernycote rector of Mickleham for the priesthood.

London, 26 February 1346

24. to the abbot of Chertsey, on behalf of William de Frome and Henry de Bruynton for the diaconate; Hugh de Blaby and John de Otery for the priesthood, all monks of Chertsey.

London, 4 March 1346

25. to M. Thomas de Paxton rector of Bedhampton for minor orders.

London, 3 March 1346

26. to Henry le Cartere rector of Chilcomb for the priesthood.

London, 2 March 1346

27. to fr. Thomas de Gormecester canon of Merton, for the diaconate and priesthood.

London, 2 March 1346

28. to Thomas le White of Romsey, for the priesthood.

London, 3 March 1346

29. to Thomas de Forde, Robert de Burgate, Walter de Mulleforde for minor orders; Ralph de Donniton and John de Osmencon for the priesthood; Richard de Merwelle and Robert de Melkesham for both diaconate and priesthood, all monks of Winchester.

London, 26 February 1346

30. to William de Chuddene rector of Froyle for the diaconate and priesthood.

London, 4 March 1346

31. to John Pravis of Selbourne for the diaconate.

London, 4 March 1346

32. to fr. Thomas de Croyndon for the diaconate; John de Wycumbe for the priesthood, canons of Tandridge.

London, 9 March 1346

11   **33**. to John atte Crouche for the diaconate.

London, 9 March 1346

34. LICENCE FOR STUDY to M. John de Wolveleye, rector of Arreton in the Isle of Wight, to absent himself for two years; he may receive the revenue of his benefice, provided that divine service, the cure of souls, almsgiving and the maintenance of the rectory-house are diligently cared for.

London, 1 March 1346

35. LICENCE FOR A PRIVATE ORATORY. Notification to the rector of [East] Woodhay. The bishop elect has granted to Edward atte Ok' of that parish, on account of his blindness and old age, permission for himself and his household to hear divine service in his private oratory and have Mass said there by a suitable priest; on major feasts both Edward and the household will resort to the mother-church.

London, 6 March 1346

36. APPOINTMENT of M. John de Ware as sequestrator for the archdeaconry of Winchester, with power to prohibit or invalidate wills in all cases reserved to the bishop.

London, 19 February, 1346

37. NOTIFICATION to all knights and free-holders that the bishop elect has appointed John de Nubbeleye and John Payn to receive the fealty due to himself.

London

38. NOTIFICATION that the bishop elect has appointed Thomas Cary to be constable of the castle of Taunton and bailiff of his lands and franchises, during pleasure [*in French.*]

London, 20 March 1346

12   **39**. MANDATE for payment of procurations to Nicholas, archbishop of Ravenna, sent on difficult business to Edward III. Delivered to him by pope Clement VI, dated Avignon, 7 September 1345. The pope requests a levy of 15 papal florins (*florentis auri*) towards his expenses and safe-conduct. Penalties permitted for defaulters.
Nicholas gave the mandate to John Stratford archbishop of Canterbury, indicating that it was still bearing its leaden seals and above suspicion. He said he had been already 55 days in England and would spend some time longer, hence the total of procurations would be £138 2s. 6d. There

would also be a portion to meet the archbishop's expenses in collection. Dated London, 6 January 1346.

13   The archbishop of Canterbury paid the sum from his own treasury (*de nostro erario*) and wrote to the bishops authorizing a levy from the beneficed clergy of a farthing for every pound in their assessment for the tenth. The mandate was to be published within 15 days and the money paid within one month to the collector. The total receipts were to be sent to the dean of St Paul's in London, the principal receiver, with the customary statement and list of defaulters, within 20 days. Dated Croydon, 17 February 1346.

14   The bishop-elect of Winchester deputed the abbot of Hyde to collect the sums due from the archdeaconry of Winchester within 15 days and to deliver the money within 12 days at the bishop's house in London, with the customary lists.

London, 26 February 1346

40. ACQUITTANCE OF PROCURATIONS. The bishop elect received the archbishop's letter of 26 February; it was published 13 March. The farthings were ordered to be paid to the sub-collectors within the prescribed period. He now sends the money due from the ecclesiastical goods and benefices, together with the names of defaulters and the lists of benefices.

Southwark, 27 April 1346

41. ADMISSION of Robert de Wolverton', acolyte, to the chapel of Limerstone in the Isle of Wight, vacant by the resignation of the last chaplain, M. Nicholas Haghman, and at the presentation of Roger de Ticheborne, patron and guardian of the chapel. The rector of Brighstone has received written notice for his induction.

London, 15 March 1346

42. GRANT OF FACULTY FOR ORDINATIONS to Ralph [Kelly, o.carm.], archbishop of Cashel, to confer orders on the candidates as in the appended list, on Ember Saturday of the first week in Lent, that is 11 March, in any suitable place within the diocese.

London, 10 March 1346

43. ORDINATIONS conferred in the conventual church of St Mary, Southwark, 11 March 1346.
Acolytes: fr. Roger de Bernak', John de Bonterwyk', Robert de Bromore, John de Cauleston', friars minor; fr. Robert de Leyre, John de Berkhamsted, Thomas de Cantuar', John Fenglesham, Peter Martini, carmelites; fr. Reginald atte Wode, augustinian canon of Lesnes in the diocese of Canterbury; M. John de Irford, rector of Oddingley in the diocese of Worcester; William Scarle, rector of Skinnand in the diocese of Lincoln.
Subdeacons: fr. Robert Wyle, John Rydden', Henry Knolle, John Gyles, friars minor; fr. John Spirk', Richard Hoo, John Maideston', John de Hertford, carmelites; fr. John de Newport, monk of Bermondsey.

15 *Deacons*: fr. William de Maydeston', Adam de Maydeston', Thomas de Wylkham, John de Stammpes, Alexander Dabetor, carmelites; John atte Crouche of Ringwood *ad titulum* of the priory of Ivychurch; fr. Geoffrey de Sutton', friar minor; Geoffrey de la Leye of Tonbridge *ad ecclesiam romanam nullo medio pertinente*, of the diocese of Rochester; fr. Thomas de Gormecestre, canon of Merton; William Trewelove, canon of Leeds. *Priests*: fr. William Folevyle, Thomas de Sansted', John Oxewyk, John de Crondale, friars minor; fr. Judacus de Isendyk', carmelite; fr. William Eyr of Leeds, canon of Leeds.

44. GRANT OF FACULTY to Ralph, archbishop of Cashel, to consecrate portable altars (*altaria viatica*) for the holy Sacrifice. He may do this on the second Sunday in Lent in any suitable place within the diocese.

London, 11 March 1346

45. PUBLICATION OF ROYAL WRIT from Edward [III] to the bishop elect. For reasons touching the safety and defence of the realm of England, the king wishes to confer with all those aliens holding ecclesiastical benefices in England, or with the procurators, farmers or bailiffs of aliens living outside the kingdom but holding benefices which have not been taken into the king's hands. He orders that all such aliens beneficed in the diocese, or their procurators, farmers and bailiffs, under threat of forfeiture, with no excuses permitted, shall appear in person before the king and his council in London on Monday of the first week in Lent, there to confer concerning the safety of the realm and to hear what he and his council shall expound. The bishop is to declare to the chancery the names of all he has thus forewarned. Dated, Westminster, 12 February 1346.

Therefore the bishop orders those who receive his mandate to forewarn all aliens holding ecclesiastical benefices within the archdeaconry of Winchester, or, in their absence, their procurators, farmers or bailiffs, that they are to appear in person before the king and his council on the day, and in the place mentioned, to learn what shall be done. The names of all such aliens are to be forwarded three days before the date prescribed.

London, 20 February 1346

16 **46.** ACQUITTANCE from John le Dyare of Wight, perpetual vicar of Kingsclere, of 4 marks sterling for the Ladyday term of 1346 (according to the reckoning of the English church), being the annual pension to the bishop from the vicar, for reasons set out in the documents concerning the appropriation of the said church to the prior and convent of Bisham in the diocese of Salisbury, now fully paid for the year.

London, 16 March 1346

47. ROYAL WRIT forwarded by the bishop elect to the prior and chapter of the church of Winchester.

The bishop will know how since his accession the king has been continually harassed by wars. After the truce in Brittany when peace could have been hoped for, suddenly this was ended by a dreaded storm.

Philip de Valois broke the truce by striving to overthrow the English nation under cover of that truce, hence the king is compelled to resume the war for the defence of the church and the realm and for the recovery of his hereditary rights beyond the seas, which Philip is unjustly and craftily violating. To this end the king requests the prayers of clergy and people that, as they lift up their hands to God the just judge, so the king may prevail over his enemies.

Westminster, 27 February 1346

Responding to this humble and just request of the king, the bishop asks that this holy season of Lent should inspire special prayers in the daily masses, devout processions and sermons, especially on Sundays and Fridays, so that united with the religious, the clergy and the people of the city and outskirts of Winchester, all may pray for the safety of the realm, the success of the army and the blessings of peace.

London, 16 March 1346

48. MANDATE to the archdeacon of Winchester or his official.
The bishop has received this brief from the king: Edward etc. Referring to his previous writ, he asks that as speedily as possible all abbots, priors etc. holding benefices, with the priests and people of the archdiaconate of Winchester, by virtue of obedience and in the spirit of Lent, offer prayers in daily masses, processions and sermons, especially on Sundays and Fridays, or on market-days going around the church or through the market-place, as weather permits; when the people will take part praying for the Church universal and particularly for the English Church, for the tranquillity of the realm and the success of the expedition. To further this end, John, archbishop of Canterbury, grants to all the penitent taking part in masses or processions and prayers an indulgence of 40 days—to those absent with legitimate cause who recite 5 times the Lord's prayer and the *Ave Maria* 30 days indulgence. To this the bishop adds a similar indulgence. Given.
[*Margin*] Date as in preceding mandate. Similar instructions sent to the archdeacon of Surrey.

49. MANDATE CONCERNING WOOL the king to the bishop elect:
On 28 August 1340 Robert de Watford and Stephen de Bicerle, sergeant (*serviente nostro*)—since dead under arms—were nominated to superintend and check all the wools in Southampton and the other ports of the county which had been removed from or brought there, so that the captors deputed by the king could have them taken and seized for delivery to the customs' collectors in that port and to the mayor and bailiffs of Southampton through the Jews; also to enquire into the wools in the port concealed and hidden in the port as also for their delivery to the said collectors and mayor in the same way. Since the said Robert is a beneficed clerk in the diocese of Winchester, holding no lay fee by which he could be distrained as has been sufficiently testified to the treasurer and barons of the Exchequer, the king orders that the said Robert be distrained through the ecclesiastical goods and benefices he may have in the diocese, in such a way that he may appear before the

barons at Westminster in the fortnight from Easter Sunday to certify to the treasurer and barons of the Exchequer, as also with the heirs and executors of the tenements and lands of the said Stephen at that time, to certify concerning the wools taken by the said Robert and Stephen and delivered to the collectors and mayor and to render account as required, bringing this writ.

Witness: R' de Sadyngton', Westminster, 23 February 1346

The bishop has warned Robert de Watford' clerk that he is to appear before the king at the place and time set out in the mandate.

50. ADMISSION of John Heynot of Nuneaton, acolyte, to the church of Chalton in the diocese of Winchester, vacant, at the presentation of the prioress and convent of Nuneaton, of the order of Fontevrault, diocese of Coventry and Lichfield, patrons of the said church. He has been canonically instituted as rector. The archdeacon of Winchester and his official have been informed for his induction.

London, 17 March 1346

51. LICENCE FOR STUDY granted to John Heynot, rector of Chalton, for one year from this date to pursue the study of letters, granting absence from personal residence, during which time he may receive minor orders up to the subdiaconate, but without obligation.

London, 18 March 1346

52. LICENCE TO ELECT A PRIOR granted to the convent or conventual church of St Peter, Taunton, augustinian, in the diocese of Bath and Wells. The vacancy follows the death of Robert de Messyngham, late prior, as the bishop has learned from fr. Thomas Cook', one of the canons, requesting that to avoid a long vacancy with dilapidations permission be granted to elect a suitable person as prior. Since the custody of the priory during a vacancy belongs to the bishop, he replies favourably to their petition, detailing the proper dispositions for proceeding to an election.

London, 21 March 1346

53. LICENCE FOR STUDY granted to William Boulge, rector of the church of Farnborough in the diocese of Winchester, for one year from this date to pursue the study of letters; he will not be bound to be personally resident, nor to advance to major orders.

London, 21 March 1346

54. ORDER TO SEARCH A REGISTER, the king to the bishop elect:
Wishing to ascertain who and how many vicars have been admitted to the church of Kingston on Thames in the diocese of Winchester from the beginning of the king's 13th regnal year, also at whose presentation and by what title, when and for what reasons, the king orders search to be made in the register of the late bishop Adam [de Orleton], which is in the bishop's custody, so that the information may reach the chancery clearly and without delay.

Westminster, 24 February 1346

Having searched the register of the late bishop Adam, it was found that Humphrey de Wakefeld' was admitted to the vicarage of Kingston, 25 March 1339, at the resignation of Henry de Trencham, vacant by reason of an exchange of benefices, at the presentation of the prior and convent of Merton, patrons of the vicarage. Afterwards, 14 June 1341, Nicholas de Lomis was admitted to the vicarage at the resignation of the said Humphrey, vacant by reason of an exchange between himself and the said Nicholas, at the presentation of Merton priory. Subsequently Maurice Barnabas de Botykesham was admitted, 12 April 1342, to the said vicarage, vacant at the death of the said Nicholas, presented by the same patrons.

55. DETENTION OF GOODS DUE FOR DISTRIBUTION UNDER A WILL, to the RECTORS AND VICARS OF THE DIOCESE:
The bishop has received the grave complaint from the executors of Rose, once the wife of sir John de Montegomeri, that certain evil persons whose names are unknown have taken the goods of the deceased and are concealing them, so that they cannot be administered according to the wishes of the deceased for the good of her soul. For this they incur *ipso facto* the sentence of excommunication for impeding the last wishes of the dying. The bishop orders the clergy in their churches on Sundays and feast-days when there is the greatest concourse of people publicly and privately to admonish the illegal holders and concealers of these goods; they are to restore them within 20 days, otherwise they are to be solemnly denounced until they make satisfaction and seek absolution. The names of those found guilty and their part in the deed are to be duly certified to the bishop.

London, 24 March 1346

19   56. Second quire for the time of William by the grace of God elect of Winchester, confirmed.

57. MANDATE FOR CONVOKING THE BISHOPS, from Ralph [Stratford] bishop of London to William, elect of Winchester:
The bishop has received a mandate from John, archbishop of Canterbury, containing as follows:
In his meditations the archbishop is daily infuriated at the insidious machinations of laymen in these days, subverting the rights and liberties of the Church in England and of the clergy. To safeguard the honour of God and of his Church, he wishes to call together all his fellow-bishops for a deliberation on the matter. Therefore he charges the bishop to summon his suffragans of the Canterbury province, or else their vicars-general, to meet in the church of St Paul in London on the nearest law-day after the feast of the Finding of the Cross, to take counsel for the urgent business of the Church.

Croydon, 23 February 1346

The bishop charges his suffragans to appear at St Paul's at the date fixed or to explain their absence.

Hadham, 12 March 1346

58. THIS 25TH DAY OF MARCH BEGINS THE YEAR OF OUR LORD 1346.

59. CERTIFICATION by William, bishop elect, to John, archbishop of Canterbury, that he has received the letter of Ralph, bishop of London, of 23 March *ut supra*, with which he fully agrees and will comply.

Southwark, 2 May 1346

20 **60**. COMMISSION to fr. John de Lecchelade, subprior of the conventual church of Southwark, to act as penitentiary for the archdeaconry of Surrey; in form it is the same as that given to Thomas de Berton', monk of the cathedral church of Winchester, except that in this commission no mention is made of monks or other religious.

London, 2 March 1346

61. PRESENTATION by the bishop elect to Robert, bishop of Salisbury, by letters patent in the customary form, of John Payn, priest, requesting his admission and institution into the church of Broad Hinton, in the diocese of Salisbury, vacant; the right of presentation belongs to the bishop.

London, 30 March 1346

62. COMMISSION by the bishop elect to fr. Thomas, subprior of St Denys at Southampton, to receive in his stead the oath of obedience for the office of penitentiary in the archdeaconry of Winchester, until this faculty is withdrawn.

London, 2 April 1346

63. GRANT OF PROCURATION FOR OATHS by M. William Inge, archdeacon of Surrey, to M. John de Aumbresbury, his official. M. John will take the oath of obedience for him to whatever ordinary he is bound by law or custom to swear an oath, whenever it is useful or required, and for whatever is necessary or opportune; he constitutes M. John his true and legitimate procurator.
In the chapel of the manor of Southwark before William bishop elect and touching the gospels, he swore canonical obedience in the name of the archdeacon in all things licit and canonical. Afterwards the same M. John, in his own name as official of Surrey, similarly swore obedience. Then the bishop enjoined them that they should not usurp his jurisdiction in the archdeaconry of Surrey, but keep the synodal statutes of the bishopric as they have hitherto been observed. Were present at the oath-taking and at the injunction M. John de Usk', rector of the church of Burghclere, M. Richard de Hyde, John de Boxgrave, Thomas de Durlee, John de Chitterne and John de Beautre, public notary.

Southwark, 3 April 1346

64. ALTERATION OF A PRESENTION by the prior and convent of St Mary of Southwark, augustinians. They had presented to the bishop elect William son of William Peender of Winchester, chaplain, for the perpetual vicarage of the parish church of Reigate, vacant and of their patronage. At the enquiry into the vacancy ordered by the bishop,

William was found unworthy of the said benefice for definite reasons expressed at the enquiry, which the said William publicly admitted, whereas the bishop had intended to provide as a suitable person for the vicarage John Coleman, priest, of Chitterne. The prior rejected the claim that he had knowingly presented someone unworthy, which would incur devolution for this turn; he now presents the said John, begging the bishop to admit him to the vicarage and to institute him canonically. To this request the prior and convent have set their seals.

21

Southwark, 3 April 1346

65. ADMISSION of John Coleman of Chitterne priest to the vicarage of Reigate, vacant, at the presentation of the prior of Southwark, after an enquiry ordered by the bishop elect. He took the oath on his admission as perpetual vicar with the obligation of residence and ministry. The archdeacon and his official were informed for his induction.

Southwark, 5 April 1346

66. PRESENTATION by the prior and convent of Leeds, augustinian canons, to William bishop elect for the vicarage of the church of Leatherhead; the church has been appropriated to the priory by apostolic authority and the vicar's portion ordained by John, archbishop of Canterbury. The vicar pays all the dues and receives the offerings and whatever is bequeathed or left to the rector of the church, as also all the tithes (16 titheable entities listed); it has been estimated by an enquiry at £14 2s. in annual value. For this vicarage, newly ordained and apportioned for the church of Leatherhead, vacant, the prior presents William de Harple, chaplain, begging the bishop to admit him with obligation of residence and to institute him canonically.

Leeds, in the chapter-house, under the common seal, 22 March 1346

67. CERTIFICATION OF AN ENQUIRY into the presentation for Leatherhead. The bishop elect to the archdeacon of Surrey:
The prior and convent of Leeds in the diocese of Canterbury has presented a perpetual vicar to the church of Leatherhead, appropriated to them, as they assert, with a vicar's portion recently ordained, as they assert. The bishop orders the archdeacon to enquire: if the church is vacant and since when it has been appropriated; when and how the vicarage became vacant, have others been presented to it; by whom and how was the vicarage ordained, in what portions, to what annual value; what are the charges on the vicar; is the vicarage litigious or pensionary; what is the age and character of the presentee, does he hold another benefice etc. The enquiry is to be held in the chapter-house of the deanery where the church is situated. A sealed report is to be presented.

London, 29 March 1346

68. Enquiry held at Ewell. Were present: John rector of Long Ditton, John rector of Sanderstead, Thomas rector of Coulsdon, Walter vicar of Horley, Richard vicar of Malden, Thomas vicar of Banstead, Roger vicar of Carshalton, Baldwin vicar of Morden, Hugh vicar of Mitcham, William vicar of Cuddington, John vicar of Epsom, John vicar of Farley.

22 They said that the church of Leatherhead was appropriated to the religious by royal collation and provided by the apostolic see, 15 September in the 4th year of Clement VI[1345]; it was granted to its last rector John Claver, who resigned voluntarily, 15 November 1345. The church came into the possession of the religious 19 March next following and the vicarage was newly ordained by John, archbishop of Canterbury, 10 February, with the offerings and the tithes; it is assessed at £10—what will be its true value in the future, they say they do not know, but, before the archbishop, it was valued at £14 2s. These are the charges on the vicarage: he will pay royal and papal tenths and other taxes at the rate of his assessment; he will pay a pension of 13s. 4d. annually to the bishop of Winchester; to the archdeacon at Martinmas a pension of 13s. 4d.; to the same archdeacon 2s. 1d. for his ordinary dues; to the same for procurations at visitation 7s. 7½d.; he will meet the expenses of the archdeacon's chaplains; he will see to the repair of service-books and vestments entrusted to competent seniors by the religious; he will pay 20s. to a clerk serving the church; he will find bread and wine and lights for the church. The said vicarage is not litigious, nor portionary, but pensionary. The presentee is virtuous, aged 42 years and over; he is free, legitimate and in holy orders, of good living and character; he is not beneficed elsewhere, as far as they know. To this they have appended their seals.

Sutton, 3 April 1346

69. ADMISSION of Hamund de Chikkewell' clerk to the church of Wisley in the diocese of Winchester, vacant at the presentation of prince Edward as patron. He has been canonically instituted and the archdeacon of Surrey has been informed for his induction.

Southwark, 30 April 1346

70. MANDATE FOR AN ENQUIRY addressed by the bishop elect to Adam de Wamberghe, rector of Ashbury in the diocese of Salisbury. He is to conduct a canonical enquiry into the title of John Thomas called Lecest' de Thresk' to the prebend of Itchen which the bishop has heard he has occupied and still occupies. He will forward the whole process to the bishop.

Southwark, 26 April 1346

71. GRANT OF FACULTY to Benedict, bishop of Cahors, to reconcile the churchyard of Kingston after bloodshed.

Southwark, 3 April 1346

72. INTIMATION OF THE ELECTION of a prior for the canons of Taunton, diocese of Bath and Wells, on the death of fr. Robert de Messyngham, after licence granted by the bishop elect. Robert the subprior announces the election of Thomas called Cooke. The assent of the bishop is sought, **23** requesting him to write to Ralph, bishop of Bath and Wells, the customary letters required by his pastoral office.

Taunton, the chapter-house, 30 March 1346

73. ASSENT TO THE ELECTION of Thomas Cooke as prior of Taunton in the place of Robert de Massyngham deceased, granted by the bishop elect of Winchester as patron. He now requests Ralph, bishop of Bath and Wells, to proceed as is customary for this worthy man.

Southwark, 4 April 1346

74. DIMISSORIAL LETTERS granted to John Heynot, rector of the church of Chalton, to receive the minor orders he has not yet been given and the other holy orders.

Southwark, 5 April 1346

75. ADMISSION TO THE PERPETUAL VICARAGE of Leatherhead, newly ordained by apostolic authority, of William de Harple, at the presentation of the prior and convent of Leeds, with obligation of residence and ministry. He has taken the oath on admission and been instituted. The archdeacon of Surrey has been informed for his induction.

Southwark, 12 April 1346

76. DIMISSORIAL LETTERS granted by the bishop elect to Nicholas de Langeford subdeacon, rector of Chale in the Isle of Wight, to receive the diaconate.

Southwark, 13 April 1346

77. ADMISSION of Walter de Depham clerk to the church of Elden, in the diocese of Winchester, vacant by the death of the last rector, Robert de Rombrigge, at the presentation of Laurence de Brembelschete. He has been canonically instituted as rector. The archdeacon of Winchester has been informed for his induction.

Southwark, 14 April 1346

78. APPOINTMENT OF PUBLIC NOTARY. The bishop elect to William de Cevere, styled Waverleye.
The bishop has received a bull from pope Clement VI, outlining the purpose of the office of notary and authorizing him to appoint six clerks, neither married nor in holy orders. Before assuming the office, they will take the usual oath (the lengthy formula is set out) of loyalty to the **24** Holy See and scrupulous honesty in handling and copying documents.

Avignon, 2 January 1346

The bishop has found William de Cevere suitable for the office of public notary; he therefore appoints him, investing him with the traditional inkwell, pen and charter. Through John de Beautre, public notary by apostolic authority.

Southwark, in the bishop's house, 17 April 1346

John de Beautre, of the diocese of Worcester, public notary, has been entrusted with the examination of William de Cevere, conferring the office after receiving the oath. He did this in the presence of M. John de Usk', rector of Burghclere, and George Vincent of the diocese of Salisbury.

17 May 1346

79. OFFICE OF PUBLIC NOTARY conferred by the bishop elect on William de Tyrinton, clerk, neither married nor in holy orders. After diligent examination he was found suitable, took the prescribed oath and was invested. Were present personally as witnesses M. John de Usk' rector of Burghclere, John de Bosegrove, Thomas de Coleshull', Nicholas le Chamberlain, William de Bradeley and M. John de Beautre, public notary.

Southwark, in the bishop's house, 6 May 1346

80. DISPENSATION granted by the bishop elect to John de Ichenestok', rector of the church of Abbots Worthy, deacon, to study for one year from this date in view of ordination to the priesthood, without obligation of residence.

Southwark, 22 April 1346

81. ACQUITTANCE FOR PROCURATIONS from Gilbert, dean of London, to the bishop and clergy of the diocese of Winchester. The procurations are to be conveyed to Nicholas, archbishop of Ravenna, papal nuncio to England, by John, archbishop of Canterbury. William de Meone, rector of Compton, by Winchester, handed to the dean £11 4s. 9d. from the farthings per pound (*quadrantibus librealibus*) due from spiritual and temporal income; 62s. ½d. being the bishop's portion and £8 2s. 8½d. that of the clergy.

London, 30 April 1346

82. COMMISSION OF THE BISHOP'S OFFICIAL. The bishop has been assured of the loyalty, wisdom and industry of John de Usk', rector of Burghclere, whom he appoints with canonical authority in the bishop's pleasure, to hold consistories, hear cases and business concerning diocesans and in due course to terminate them.

Southwark, 20 April 1346

83. LICENCE FOR STUDY granted by the bishop elect to Henry Mayner, rector of Worplesdon, for one year from this date for reasons of study. He is not bound to reside in the parish.

Southwark, 9 May 1346

84. COMPOSITION between the bishop of Winchester and the archdeacon of Surrey as to the exercise of jurisdiction.
John, archbishop of Canterbury, to avoid the strife and discord of former times has been requested to arbitrate between William bishop of Winchester and M. Richard Vaghan archdeacon of Surrey, in order to reach an amicable agreement on the points at issue. The archbishop has heard and examined the matter and through M. John de Usk' has set out the process:
DEPOSITION of the points of discord between the bishop and M. William Inge, deceased: the ordering and disposal of the goods of those dying intestate in the archdeaconry; the appointment and removal of commissaries, rural deans and apparitors; the probate and annulment of the wills of those dying within the archdiaconate or outside, with the

25

administration of the goods through executors delivering a statement; the mode of exercising jurisdiction in the archdeaconry; the cases of offenders with their correction and punishment in matters appertaining to ecclesiastical jurisdiction; the collection and disposal of the profits from churches and vicarages during vacancy, which had by custom been divided between the bishop and the archdeacon; the nomination of sequestrators; the annual pension of 20 marks by ancient custom due to the bishop for the synodals, Peter's pence and St Swithun's farthings collected by the archdeacon; M. Richard asserts that the late M. William declared that all moneys, synodals, with those called *paschales*, *martinales*, Peter's pence and St Swithun's farthings from all churches and parishoners, were collected by the archdeacon from the incumbents for his own purposes, provided that the portions for the nuncio and the farthings for the sacrist of the cathedral were paid by the archdeacon annually at the customary amount, the imposition and lifting of sequestration and ecclesiastical censures.

RECOMMENDATIONS of the archbishop as arbitrator. He has secured agreement between the parties and pronounces that: the bishop shall dispose of the goods of the intestate, whether lay or clerical and the archdeacon shall not intervene without a mandate; the archdeacon may

26 nominate and dismiss his officials, rural deans etc. as it is expedient; these officials on appointment will take the oath of obedience to the bishop; the two apparitors will not interfere with the bishop's officials; the sequestrators in the archdeaconry will deal with the goods of those dying intestate, also with the execution of all royal writs involving levies on the goods and revenues of the secular clergy and vicars; as for the fruits of churches during vacancy, one half shall belong to the bishop and one half to the archdeacon as it pleases him to employ it; the bishop, his official or the president of the consistory may depose a dean or apparitor, when the archdeacon will appoint suitable successors; questions of probate and executions of wills outside the time of visitation are to be settled by the archdeacon, unless appeal is made by executors to the bishop; the administration of the wills of the clergy or of the bishop's household staff belongs to the bishop, not to the archdeacon; disputes over wills may be heard by the bishop or the archdeacon; offenders, as hitherto, may be corrected by the archdeacon; he may deal with offences between parents and children, unless thay are heard during the bishop's annual visitation; matters reserved for the visitation do not concern the archdeacon, whose jurisdiction lapses during any visitation; delays in hearing enquiries and making known the results must not exceed six

27 weeks; unless advised beforehand to the contrary, the archdeacon may correct offenders; they may be heard before the bishop during visitation; as for the moneys collected, next after the portions to the nuncio and the cathedral sacrist, the archdeacon will arrange for the pensions to be paid to the bishop; every Easter he will pay 20 marks to the bishop; all the synodals etc. from the parishes the archdeacon may employ without and direction from the bishop; any cessation of payment of the 20 marks' pension will entail sequestration of the fruits of the archdiaconate; likewise the deacon himself may employ censures and sequestration to secure payment from the parishes.

In all this the archbishop does not intend to derogate from the rights of the bishop or the archdeacon, but to confirm them.
(The last ten lines are illegible, except that the document was written by M. John de Beautre; some nine or ten witnesses to the composition held at the chapel at Maidstone, two of whom can be recovered: John Wolveleye of Atherton [Arreton in the Isle of Wight] and William Serle of Baddesley Clinton in the diocese of Coventry and Lichfield. 1348).

85. NOTARIAL ATTESTATION to the submissions and promises made by the bishop of Winchester and the archdeacon of Surrey as they are set out above, with the proceedings and ordinances of the archbishop of **28** Canterbury which the bishop and archdeacon have promised to observe. John de Beautre of the diocese of Worcester, notary public, was present and wrote out the archbishop's mandate with his own hand: he is responsible for the two erasures in the text. Date and place as above.
Nicholas de Yfeele of the diocese of Lincoln, notary public, attests that he also was present among the witnesses and notaries, with the said John de Beautre, at the submissions and promises and set his seal to the instruments. Same date.

RATIFICATION OF THE COMPOSTITION by the prior and convent of the cathedral church of Winchester, who had carefully considered beforehand in chapter the proposals for putting an end to the dissensions and found them according to reason.

Winchester, in the chapter-house, 29 June 1348.

SIMILAR RATIFICATION by the prior and convent of Christchurch, Canterbury, who approve the definitive statutes laid down, saving the rights and dignity of the metropolitan see of Canterbury.

Canterbury, in the chapter-house, 3 August 1348.

29   EDINGTON

30   Blank
31   Register of William de Edyndon, consecrated by apostolic authority bishop of Winchester by John [Stratford] archbishop of Canterbury, primate of all England, assisted by Ralph [Stratford] bishop of London and Robert [Stratford] bishop of Chichester in the chapel of the archbishop's manor of Otford.

14 May 1346.

87. First quire of presentations, collations, institutions and inductions, of proceedings as to vacancies and elections, of dispensations and licences for absence and study.

88. CONSENT TO AN EXCHANGE OF BENEFICES. William bishop of Winchester informs Robert bishop of Salisbury that Hamo de Chickewelle rector of Wisley in the diocese of Winchester has sought permission to exchange benefices with M. William Graspays rector of Fonthill [Bishop] in the diocese of Salisbury. The bishop of Winchester who has the right to present, consents to the exchange; he requests the bishop of Salisbury to institute him as rector.

Southwark, 23 May 1346.

89. PROCEDURE FOR EXCHANGE OF BENEFICES. The archbishop of Canterbury informs the bishop of Winchester that William le Taillour vicar of Selling in his diocese desires to exchange benefices with Richard de Langeford rector of Rotherhithe in the diocese of Winchester. The archbishop has held the customary enquiry, since the vicarage is at the presentation of the prior and convent of St Augustine, Canterbury. The archbishop forwards the results of the enquiry for the consideration of the bishop, in view of accepting the resignation of William and admitting Richard to the vicarage with obligation of residence.

Croydon, 23 May 1346.

32

The bishop replies to the archbishop that he has examined the results of the enquiry and authorizes the exchange of benefices in the person of his proctor, William de Thorne.

Southwark, 26 May 1346.

90. In his reply the archbishop, having considered the whole question, authorizes the exchange and admits Richard, in the person of William de Thorne, chaplain, to the vicarage of Selling, instituting him canonically.

Date as above.

91. ADMISSION of William le Taillour priest to be rector of the church of Rotherhithe on the resignation of Richard de Langeford, following an exchange of benefices for the vicarage of Selling in the diocese of Canterbury. To the rectory he had been presented by the prior and convent of Bermondsey. Sealed with the seal in use before the bishop's consecration. The same day a letter was sent to the archdeacon of Surrey for the induction.

Southwark, 25 May 1346.

92. ADMISSION of William Randulf priest to the church of Dogmersfield, vacant, to the evident benefit of that church, with the consent of Ralph [of Shrewsbury] bishop of Bath and Wells, the patron. The bishop of Winchester commends this, following the regulation of Gregory X at the council of Lyons. Letter sent the same day to the archdeacon of Winchester for the induction.

Southwark, 18 May 1346

93. ADMISSION AND INSTITUTION of Adam de Thorpe priest to be rector of Abbotstone after the voluntary resignation of Robert de Soukey the last rector and at the presentation of William Trussel of Cubblesdon, by reason of the minority of Edmund, son and heir of Hugh de Sancto Johanne, deceased, patron by royal grant until Edmund comes of age. Letter to the archdeacon of Winchester for the induction.

Southwark, 27 May 1346

94. DISPENSATION granted to William Boulge rector of the church of Farnborough, to be absent for study from this date until the Purification (2 Feb.) in view of receiving holy orders, without obligation of residence or of proceeding to orders.

Southwark, 15 May 1346

33   **95.** CERTIFICATION OF AN ENQUIRY into a proposed exchange of benefices. Letter from Thomas bishop of Lincoln to the bishop:
Since John Coleman of Chitterne vicar of Reigate in the diocese of Winchester and Richard de Redegrave rector of Fleet Marston in the diocese of Lincoln desire to exchange benefices, after a careful enquiry by the archdeacon of Buckden, the bishop is prepared to institute him. The patron is John Neirunt, knight, and the church is vacant after the resignation of the said Richard. The bishop of Lincoln awaits the results of the process from Winchester in order to proceed to the induction.

Buckden, 23 May 1346

After examining and approving the exchange, the customary certification was sent to the bishop of Lincoln.

Southwark, 30 May 1346

96. ADMISSION of Richard de Redegrave to the vicarage of Reigate, at the resignation of John Coleman and at the presentation of the prior and convent of St Mary of Southwark, patrons; with obligation of residence according to the constitutions of the legates Otto and Ottobon with the prescribed oath. The archdeacon of Surrey has been informed for the induction.

Southwark, 23 May 1346

97. DISPENSATION granted to Thomas de Paxton rector of Bedhampton, subdeacon, to be absent for one year from this date in view of study at some *studium generale*. He will farm out the church to some suitable person who will reside in the parish. He is not obliged to proceed to further orders, according to the constitutions of Boniface on this matter.

Southwark, 1 June 1346

98. ADMISSION of Thomas de Heyton' clerk to the church of Ewell at the presentation of the abbot and convent of Chertsey, patrons, for which the bishop has ordered an enquiry.

Southwark, 18 June 1346

MANDATE for an enquiry to be held by the archdeacon of Surrey into the vacancy of the benefice, to discover if the church is truly vacant, and if it is litigious, portionary or pensionary. Also to inquire into the person of the incumbent presented. This enquiry must be held in the same deanery.

Southwark, 9 June 1346

INQUISITION held in the name of the archdeacon of Surrey by John rector of Sanderstead, M. William de Wantynge proctor for the rector of

Sutton, John rector of Long Ditton, Walter de Aston' proctor for the rector of Woodmansterne, John Horwode proctor for the rector of Burgh, John Morle proctor for the rector of Ashstead, Maurice vicar of Kingston, Thomas vicar of Banstead, William vicar of Leatherhead, Ranulf vicar of Ashstead, John vicar of Farley, Baldwin vicar of Morden, Hugh vicar of Mitcham. They say that the church of Ewell is vacant by the death of John Dunsteple the last rector, 5 June last. The church is at the presentation of the abbey of Chertsey; it is not litigious, but is pensionary by 40 marks to that abbey. The presentee is free and legitimate, being age 24 or above, of commendable living and good character. He has received the tonsure and holds no benefice. Sealed etc.

Ewell, 14 June 1346

99. INSTITUTION of Thomas de Heyton' clerk to be rector of the church of Ewell, at the presentation of the abbot and convent of Chertsey on the authority of the above enquiry.

Southwark, 18 June 1346

100. MANDATE to M. John de Aumbresbury, official of the archdeacon of Surrey. The bishop orders him, in virtue of obedience, to induct Thomas de Heyton' into the rectory of Ewell.

Date as above.

101. INSTITUTION of John Payn priest as rector of South [Bishop's] Waltham, vacant; at the collation of the bishop. Same day a letter was sent to M. John de Ware, sequestrator-general for the archdeaconry of Winchester, for his induction.

Southwark, 20 June 1346

102. DISPENSATION FOR STUDY granted to Thomas de Heyton clerk for 2 years from this date, in view of minor orders and the subdiaconate within one year, without obligation of residence.

Southwark, 22 June 1346

103. LICENCE granted to John de Wylie rector of Walton [-on-Thames] to be absent from his parish at the service of Edward de Kendale, knight.

Southwark, 23 June 1346

104. CONSENT TO AN EXCHANGE OF BENEFICES. Letter from Thomas bishop of Ely to the bishop of Winchester concerning an exchange between John de Camera rector of Mapledurham in the diocese of Winchester and Thomas de Brayles rector of Tydd St Giles in the diocese of Ely. The bishop of Ely approves the exchange and requests the bishop of Winchester to enquire into the matter with a certification.

Doddington, 14 June 1346

After examining the causes for the exchange the bishop approves of the resignations, consents to the exchange and authorizes John to take an oath of obedience to the bishop of Ely. A letter has been sent to the archdeacon of Winchester for the induction of Thomas to Mapledurham.

Southwark, 24 June 1346

105. LICENCE granted to Thomas de Brayles to be at the service of Thomas earl of Warwick for one year.

Southwark, 27 June 1346

106. AUTHORIZATION OF AN EXCHANGE OF BENEFICES. The bishop has received from Robert bishop of Salisbury his approval of the exchange between Hamo de Chikewell' rector of Wisley and William Graspais rector of Fonthill Bishop; he has sent a copy of the process which he had ordered, to assist the bishop of Winchester to accept the resignation of William from Fonthill and to admit Hamo.

Doddington, 17 June 1346

After discussing the matter the bishop authorizes the resignation and the presentation to Fonthill, which is of his patronage. The proceedings have been forwarded to the registrar (*certificator*) of the bishop.

Southwark, 1 July 1346

107. INSTITUTION OF William Graspeis to the church of Wisley, by an exchange of benefices with Hamo de Chikewell' rector of Fonthill, of the patronage of the bishop of Winchester. Prince Edward is the patron of the church of Wisley, now vacant. After the customary enquiry the bishop canonically institutes William as rector.

Southwark, 1 July 1346

108. MANDATE from the bishop to M. John de Ambresbury, official of the archdeacon of Surrey, to induct William with the formula used for the rector of Ewell.

Same date.

109. EXCHANGE OF BENEFICES between Thomas de Okham priest rector of Wolverton in the diocese of Winchester and Geoffrey de Kedyngton' vicar of Wigton in the diocese of York, concerning which the bishop has received letters from the chapter of St Peter, York. The conclusions of the enquiry are sent under the prebendal seal of Wigton etc. The vicarage has been resigned by Geoffrey, and Thomas has taken his oath of obedience before institution, the induction being specially reserved.

York, 6 June 1346

The bishop has examined the process, acknowledges the resignation by Thomas of the rectory and approves the exchange through M. Thomas de la Mare prebendary of Wigton and patron of the vicarage. The bishop admits Geoffrey to the rectory of Wolverton, sending a certificate of the process under the same date to the chapter.

Southwark, 4 July 1346

110. INSTITUTION of Geoffrey de Kedyngton' to the church of Wolverton at the resignation of Thomas de Okham after an exchange with the vicarage of Wigton. The rectory is at the presentation of Matthew Fitz Herbert, knight, the patron. A letter has been sent to the archdeacon of Winchester for his induction.

Southwark, 4 July 1346

111. ENQUIRY INTO AN EXCHANGE OF BENEFICES. A commission has been received from John archbishop of Canterbury concerning an exchange between Bartholomew Bradele perpetual vicar of Bersted in the deanery of Pagham, of the immediate jurisdiction of the archbishop, and William de Canmell rector of the church of Shalden in the diocese of Winchester. The archbishop consents to this exchange at the presentation of M. Raymond Pelegrini, acting as proctor for Gaucelin, cardinal bishop of Albano and rector of Pagham with the chapel of Bersted; the cardinal has power to present suitable persons to the vicarage and the dean of Pagham has carried out the necessary enquiry, the conclusions of which, duly sealed, the archbishop transmits for the bishop's examination, seeking his authorization of the exchange. The resignation from the vicarage of Bersted has been accepted and the archbishop admits William to the perpetual vicarage with obligation of residence.

Maidstone, 1 July 1346

The bishop has examined the request for the exchange and accepts the authority of M. Raymond Pelegrini to present as proctor for cardinal Gaucelin, patron of the vicarage. The bishop institutes Bartholomew to the church of Shalden, at the presentation of the patrons, the prior and convent of Southwick, sending a letter to the archdeacon of Winchester for the induction.

Southwark, 5 July 1346

112. ADMISSION of Thomas Duryval of Bishop's Lavington priest to the church of Quarley in the diocese of Winchester, vacant by the resignation of William de Peveseye, the last rector. This is at the presentation of Richard de Beusevall', prior of Ogbourne, by reason of the spiritualities and temporalities of the abbey of Bec-Herluin, the prior holding all its English advowsons by commission of the king of England. Following the enquiry made by the prior, the bishop institutes Thomas, writing to the archdeacon of Winchester for the induction.

Southwark, 8 July 1346

113. APPOINTMENT TO THE OFFICE OF DEACON in the chapel of St Elizabeth near Winchester. Peter de Fyndon' priest is collated by the bishop to the office, vacant by the death of Thomas de Dounton', and confirmed in his office in accordance with the ordinances of bishop John de Pontissara, the founder of the chapel.

Southwark, 12 July 1346

114. INDUCTION of Peter de Fyndon' to the office of *prepositus* of the chapel of St Elizabeth; the bishop confers the office of deacon with its stipends and other rights.

date as above

115. ADMISSION of John de Hyda of Newton Toney priest to the perpetual vicarage of the church of Itchen Stoke, vacant by the death of John de Stratton', the patrons being the abbess and convent of Romsey. An enquiry was ordered by the bishop before the admission. The vicar has the obligation of residence and ministry. John has taken the canonical oath; the archdeacon has been informed for the induction.

Southwark, 20 July 1346

116. ADMISSION of John called Ranulf de Coleshull' priest to the church of Dogmersfield, vacant and at the presentation of Ralph bishop of Bath and Wells as patron. Letter to the archdeacon of Winchester for the induction.

Southwark, 21 July 1346

38 **117.** NOMINATION OF A NUN by the bishop, by reason of his consecration, to Maud, abbess of Our Lady of Winchester. In virtue of his rights and prerogatives as of the church of Winchester, the abbess will receive and veil as a nun Maud Palmere, duly accepting her as a sister.

Southwark, 22 July 1346

118. ADMISSION of John de Broughton' priest to the church of Chawton in the diocese of Winchester, vacant at the death of Thomas de Saxlingham the last rector, at the presentation of Henry Coyne, attorney for William Trussel of Cubblesdon, knight, custodian of the lands of the late Hugh de Sancto Johanne by royal grant. Letter sent to the archdeacon of Winchester for the induction.

Southwark, 1 August 1346

119. DISPENSATION for reasons of study granted to John de Broughton, rector of Ashstead priest for one year from this date.

Southwark, 2 August 1346

120. ADMISSION of Thomas de Whitcherche priest to the church of Wisley, vacant, at the presentation of Edward prince of Wales. He has been canonically instituted and the archdeacon of Surrey has been informed for the induction.

Southwark, 1 August 1346

121. EXCHANGE OF BENEFICES. The bishop has received a letter from Roger bishop of Coventry and Lichfield concerning the request for an exchange between Hugh Alayn perpetual vicar of the prebendal church of Hurstbourne in the diocese of Winchester and Philip de Boketon vicar of Wormleighton in the diocese of Coventry and Lichfield. An enquiry has been held by the archdeacon of Coventry, the results of which are now sent to the bishop of Winchester, requesting him to accept this commission and inform the bishop of Coventry and Lichfield of his process.

Coventry, 13 July 1346

Having examined the request received, the bishop authorizes the admission of Philip to the perpetual vicarage of Hurstbourne, with

39   obligation of residence and ministry. The vicarage of Wormleighton is
at the presentation of the prior and canons of Kenilworth.

                                        Southwark, 4 August 1346

Under the same date a certificate of the process has been sent to Coventry.

122. ADMISSION of Philip de Boketon to the vicarage of Hurstbourne,
vacant by the resignation of Hugh Aleyn, with obligation of residence.
Philip was presented by M. John de Whitcherch' canon and prebendary
of Burbage and Hurstbourne. Letter sent to the archdeacon of Winchester
for his induction.

                                        Southwark, 4 August 1346

123. EXCHANGE OF BENEFICES. Letter to Robert bishop of Salisbury
concerning an exchange between Philip de Weston' rector of Cheriton,
in the diocese and of the collation of the bishop of Winchester and M.
Peter de Inkepenn', canon of the conventual church of Wherwell and
prebendary of Middleton in the Winchester diocese, and rector of
Portland, in the Salisbury diocese but of the patronage of the bishop of
Winchester. The bishop consents to the presentation to Portland and
asks the bishop of Salisbury to admit and institute Philip canonically
into the church of Portland.

                                        Southwark, 3 August 1346

124. AUTHORIZATION OF THE EXCHANGE. The bishop writes to the bishop
of Salisbury that he has considered the exchange, accepts the resignations
of Philip from the church of Cheriton and of Peter from his prebend.
He admits Philip into the canonicate and into the prebend of Middleton
in the church of Wherwell after due enquiry by the archdeacon of
Winchester, of which details are sent to Salisbury. The oaths of both are
reserved to the bishop of Winchester who forwards his certificate.

                                        Southwark, 6 August 1346

125. MANDATE TO ACCEPT A NUN. Letter from the bishop to the abbess
and convent of Romsey that by reason of his recent episcopal consecration
they are to receive Isabella daughter of Margery Seymor among their
sisters.

                                                Same date

(Margin) This letter was afterwards revoked by the bishop.

40   **126.** ADMISSION of William Boun priest to the chapel of Yaverland, Isle
of Wight, at the presentation of Alianora wife of Theobald Russel knight,
deceased, patroness and vacant by the resignation of William de la
Chapelle, the last rector. Letter sent to the archdeacon of Winchester
for the induction.

                                        Southwark, 12 August 1346

127. DISPENSATION granted to Symon de Geynesburgh rector of
Winchfield priest to be at the service of William de Clynton', earl of
Huntingdon for two years from this date, without obligation of residence.

                                        Southwark, 12 August 1346

128. DISPENSATION granted to M. John de Hegham rector of Millbrook, of absence for study for one year from this date, at the request of Queen Philippa, without obligation of residence.

Southwark, 24 August 1346

129. DISPENSATION granted to William de Walyngford rector of Chipstead for one year from this date for study.

Southwark, 6 October 1346

130. DISPENSATION granted to John de Tygehale rector of Blendworth, subdeacon, to study for one year, without obligation of residence or of proceeding to further orders.

Same date

131. DISPENSATION granted to William de Swanebourne rector of Hambledon to be absent for one year from this date at the service of the prioress of Amesbury, provided that he arranges for the care of his parish.

Same date

132. DISPENSATION granted to Nicholas de Langeford rector of Chale, priest, to study for one year.

Southwark, 16 October 1346

133. DISPENSATION granted to M. Peter de Hope rector of Alverstoke priest and to Thomas Creue rector of Fawley to be absent for study for one year. With special licence to let the church at farm to a suitable person.

Southwark, 19 October 1346

134. ADMISSION of John de la Vyne clerk to the church of Chaldon vacant by the death of John de Werdon', the last rector. The patron was John de Couer, knight. The canonical institution has taken place and the archdeacon of Surrey has been informed for the induction.

Southwark, 20 October 1346

135. CONFIRMATION OF A DISPENSATION granted by his predecessor Adam de Orleton to M. William Joce rector of Crawley to be absent for study for seven years. He may continue these studies. Were present M. John de Usk' chancellor, William de Waverleye clerk and John de Beautre the bishop's secretary.

Southwark, 22 September 1346

41   **136.** LETTERS PATENT to the bishop of Salisbury, presenting William de Farlegh' clerk to the church of Bishopstone in the diocese of Salisbury, but of the patronage and presentation of the bishop of Winchester.

Southwark, 6 October 1346

137. ADMISSION of William de Waverleye clerk to the chapel of Standen in the Isle of Wight, vacant at the death of William de Staunden the last rector, and at the presentation of Thomas Haket the patron. A letter has been sent to the archdeacon of Winchester for the induction.

Southwark, 26 October 1346

138. CERTIFICATE OF EXCHANGE OF BENEFICES. The bishop has received certificatory letters from the bishop of Ely.

Southwark, 26 October 1346

He has received letters from the bishop of Winchester concerning the proposed exchange of benefices between Robert de Stonch vicar of Chertsey and John Arlich perpetual vicar of the churches of Barton and Great Eversden in the diocese of Ely. Desiring to show his approval of the exchange, the bishop of Winchester accepts the resignation of Robert from the vicarage of Chertsey and admits John Arlich to Chertsey, relying on the enquiry made by the official of the archdeacon of Surrey, held by mandate of the bishop. John will have the obligation of residence and ministry.

Southwark, 19 October 1346

Having examined the process sent by the bishop of Ely, he approves the resignation of Robert de Stonch from the vicarage of Chertsey and institutes John Arlich to the perpetual vicarage. Mandate of the same date to the archdeacon of Surrey for the induction.

Hadham, 26 October 1346

139. LETTERS CONCERNING EXCHANGE OF BENEFICES. The bishop writes to Robert de Killum clerk. He has received letters from Thomas bishop of Lincoln concerning the proposed exchange of benefices between Geoffrey de Kyllum rector of Calcott in the diocese of Lincoln and Robert de Killum rector of Havant in the diocese of Winchester. At the enquiry held by the archdeacon of Huntingdon, it was made clear that Robert had been presented to Calcott by King Edward, as custodian of the lands and of the heir of Edmund earl of Kent, deceased, lands which had been held by tenure *in capite*. Robert was admitted at the resignation of Geoffrey from the church of Calcott, induction and oath being specially reserved. The bishop requests the process for certification.

Stow, 29 September 1346

42

Having examined the matter, the bishop approves the resignation of Geoffrey from Calcott and the admission of Robert.

Southwark, 27 October 1346

Certificate of the process sent that day to the bishop of Ely.

140. COLLATION of the church of Havant to Geoffrey de Kyllum, vacant by the resignation of Robert de Killum its last rector, after an exchange for Calcott in the diocese of Lincoln. A letter has been sent to M. Adam de Wambergh', the commissary general, for induction.

Southwark, 27 October 1346

141. LETTERS CONCERNING AN EXCHANGE OF BENEFICES. The bishop has received letters from Robert bishop of Salisbury concerning an exchange between Philip de Weston' rector of Cheriton and M. Peter de Ingepenn' canon of Wherwell, prebendary of Middleton and rector of Portland. After due consideration he approves the exchange and the necessary resignations, admitting M. Peter to Cheriton and Philip to the canonicate and to the prebend of Middleton in the church of Wherwell. An enquiry had been held by the archdeacon of Winchester. The oaths of both are specially reserved. The bishop requests a certificate from the bishop of Salisbury.

Southwark, 3 August 1346

Having discussed the matter on 8 August, the bishop instituted Philip through his proctor to the canonicate of Wherwell with the prebend of Middleton. Peter was inducted to the church of Cheriton 9 August.

At our park of Ramsbury, 12 August 1346

43 **142.** INSTITUTION of Roger Fitz Hugh (*Filius Hugonis*) of Doun priest to the perpetual vicarage of Cuddington in the diocese of Winchester, vacant, with obligation of residence and ministry according to the constitution. The vicarage was at the presentation of King Edward by reason of the priory of Merton, lately vacant and in the king's hands. Letter sent to the archdeacon of Surrey for the induction.

Southwark, 31 October 1346

143. DISPENSATION granted to John de Pembrok rector of Thruxton for one year from this date to be at the service of Margaret countess of Kent, by special permission.

Same date

144. DISPENSATION granted according to the constitutions of Boniface to John atte Vyne rector of Chaldon, clerk, for one year for study, with no obligation of residence, but he is to proceed to the subdiaconate within a year.

Southwark, 8 December 1346

145. RESIGNATION into the bishop's hands by Thomas de Haydon' rector of the church of Ewell, in the presence of John Beautre public notary, fr. John le Archer hospitaler and John de Haydon' father of the said Thomas, all personally present as witnesses (formula in full).

Southwark, 10 December 1346

146. DISPENSATION granted to John de Salyngg' rector of Mottisfont for one year from this date for study, without obligation of residence.

Southwark, 29 December 1346

147. PRESENTATION by the bishop by letters to Robert bishop of Salisbury of Edward Chaumberleyn rector of the church of Drexthorpe in the diocese of Lincoln to the church of Portland in the diocese of Salisbury, but of the patronage of the bishop of Winchester. This follows upon the exchange with Philip de Weston', who had been rector of the same church of Portland.

Same date

148. NOMINATION OF A NUN by sealed mandate from the bishop to the abbess of Wherwell. She will receive Elizabeth daughter of Peter de la Mare into her house as a sister and nun.

Southwark, 23 January 1347

149. COMMISSION FOR VICARIOUS AUTHORITY IN THE BISHOP'S ABSENCE. To the religious of the cathedral church of Winchester and to M. John de Usk' rector of Burghclere, chancellor.

Since the bishop must at times be absent about the business of the king or the realm, he ordains them to be his general vicars for the spirituality of his bishopric: to authorize elections to prebends and to confirm those elected; to confirm the elections held in certain monasteries subject to the bishop, or to annul them; to admit suitable persons to vacant benefices; to institute canonically those presented to benefices and to induct them; to authorize exchanges of benefices; to act in testamentary matters; to grant dispensations for non-residence; to punish non-residence canonically; to grant aid to infirm clerics; to grant dismissory letters; to act in matters of sequestration, even when specially reserved to the bishop; to question any bishop or dignatory from the Holy See before he exercises his official duties, as may be expedient; to execute business which concerns the bishop's external jurisdiction according to custom or law, with coercive powers.

44

Southwark, 12 December 1346

Vicariate: M. John de Usk' rector of Burghclere, general vicar for spiritualities.

150. INSTITUTION of John de Skyvyngton priest to the chapel of St Leonard, Standen, Isle of Wight, vacant, at the presentation of Thomas Haket, patron. Sealed with the seal of the diocesan official. Letter to the archdeacon of Winchester for the induction.

Southwark, 12 December 1346

151. DIMISSORIAL LETTERS to fr. Richard de Chiriton', William Hakat, Nicholas Rannvill', John de Lech' and Nicholas Gifferd, cannons of Southwich priory: Richard for the priesthood, William, Nicholas and John for the diaconate, and Nicholas Gifferd for minor orders.

Southwark, 19 December 1346

152. INSTITUTION of William Cevere called Waverlee to the church of Ewell vacant, at the presentation of the abbot and convent of Chertsey as patrons, with John de Chitterne rector of Marston in the diocese of Lincoln acting as William's proctor. Letter sent to the archdeacon of Surrey for the induction.

Southwark, 19 December 1346

End of vicariate.

153. INSTITUTION of Roger de Eston' priest to the perpetual vicarage of Odiham, at the presentation of Elias de Sancto Albano, chancellor of Salisbury cathedral, who holds the rectory of Odiham as part of the chancellorship. Roger has taken the oath obliging him to residence and ministry. Letter to the archdeacon of Winchester for the induction.

Southwark, 30 January 1347

154. COLLATION of the parochial church of Froyle to M. Thomas de Enham, the presentation devolving to the bishop for this once by lapse. Letters to the archdeacon of Winchester and to the dean of Alton for the induction.

Southwark, 29 January 1347

155. DISPENSATION granted to John Heynote subdeacon, rector of Chilbolton to study for one year.

Southwark, 5 February 1347

156. DISPENSATION granted to Thomas le Blount clerk, rector of All Saints Southampton, for one year for study and to proceed to minor orders and to the subdiaconate.

Southwark, 8 January 1347

45 **157.** COMMISSION entrusted by the bishop to John de Usk' chancellor, Roger de Fulford doctor at law and John de Wolveley rector of Arreton, to enquire into the election of fr. John de Benham monk of Chertsey, o.s.b., vacant by the death of John de Retherwyk' the last abbot; to be held today Friday, the third law-day after SS. Vedast and Amandus [6 Feb.].

Southwark, 9 February 1347

158. ACTA OF THE COMMISSION of enquiry into the Chertsey election, before the aforesaid sitting as a tribunal in the conventual church of St Mary of Southwark. Fr. John de Wylton monk of Chertsey acted as proctor for the newly elect. The customary documents were exhibited with a certificate from the prior of Newark. One day's delay was required to consider any possible objectors on canonical grounds. The commissioners drew up a decree of the election with the letters and instruments shown by the proctor, while the two *instructores* viz. fr. Richard de Dumbeliton', John de Hurlee monks of Chertsey, with two other witnesses, Richard rector of Clandon and Thomas atte Vyne, drew up the *instructio* to be presented to the bishop on Saturday morning, 10 Februrary, in the chapel of his manor at Southwark, to carry through the necessary formalities.

On the said day the elect with the aforesaid appeared before the bishop. The matter was expounded by M. Thomas de Enham and discussed by legal experts, as also the person and character of the elect. He was declared to be of good reputation, learned and mature, and so the final pronouncement was drawn up. The bishop declared the election to have been canonically correct and entrusted to abbot John the spiritual care and the administration of the abbey. Immediately the bishop intoned the Te Deum, *sonore voce*, recited a solemn prayer over the abbot lying prostrate.

11 February in the chapel at Mass, the new abbot was blessed, renewing his profession and canonical obedience (formula in full).

46 **159.** CONFIRMATION of the election granted to abbot John of Chertsey, with cure of souls and administration, saving the rights of the bishop and the church of Winchester.

Southwark, 11 February 1347

160. COMMENDATION of the new abbot to the monks of Chertsey. He will be their pastor and adminstrator; they will render him all reverence, as devoted sons to a father.

Same date

161. MANDATE to the archdeacon of Surrey to put the new abbot into corporal possession of the conventual church of Chertsey, to induct him, leading him to his stall in choir and to his place in the chapter-house.

Same date

162. NOTIFICATION TO KING EDWARD. Since the election of John de Benham requires the royal assent, the bishop informs the king that he has this day canonically confirmed the election and begs the king to bestow the favour.

Same date

163. DISPENSATION granted to William de Malmesbury rector of Knight's Enham, for one year's absence as executor and administrator of the will of John de Handlo, knight, deceased.

Southwark, 8 February 1347

164. DISPENSATION to M. William Boulge rector of Farnborough, priest, to be absent for study for one year.

Southwark, 27 February 1347

165. GRANT OF CUSTODY. Since the custody of vacant benefices belongs to the bishop by custom and by canon law, he entrusts to Thomas de Crosse priest the custody of the precentorship of the church of St Mary, Southampton, now vacant—in spiritualities and temporalities for the duration of the vacancy, at the bishop's pleasure.

Southwark, 18 February 1347

47 **166.** EXCHANGE OF BENEFICES between M. Reymund Pelegrini, Master of the Hospital of St Cross, Winchester, and Richard de Lusteshull prebendary of the prebendal church of Gillingham in the conventual church of Shaftesbury, at the presentation of the abbess and convent. From Robert bishop of Salisbury the bishop has learned of the proposed exchange and of the enquiry held. The bishop of Salisbury is ready to consent and to accept the resignation of Richard from the prebendal church of Gillingham, to admit Raymond or his proctor, and to induct him to that church, reserving the oath of obedience.

at his park at Ramsbury, 14 February 1347

The bishop of Winchester having examined the matter grants his approval and authorizes the exchange, accepting the resignation of Richard de Lusteshull through his proctor John de London', rector of Esher. He admits M. Raymond to the rectory of Gillingham under the patronage of the abbess and institutes him as prebendary—with the reservation as before.

Southwark, 21 February 1347

167. CERTIFICATE OF THE EXCHANGE from the bishop to the bishop of Salisbury. Having considered the matter and found all in order, he authorizes the exchange, accepts the resignation of John de London' as proctor for Richard de Lusteshull', admits M. Raymond Pelegrini to the prebendal church under the patronage of the abbey of Shaftesbury and institutes him canonically.

Date as above

168. INSTITUTION of Richard de Lusteshull' to the mastership (*custos*) of the Hospital of St Cross at Winchester. From time out of mind this benefice without cure of souls (*beneficium non curatum*) has been granted to members of the secular clergy. It is vacant at the resignation of M. Raymond Pelegrini by exchange for the prebendal church of Gillingham and granted, in the person of John de London', to Richard de Lusteshull'.

Southwark, 21 February 1347

M. Adam de Wambergh, commissary-general and master (*prepositus*) of the chapel of St Elizabeth will induct Richard or his proctor.

48 **169.** LETTERS CONCERNING EXCHANGE OF BENEFICES. The bishop has received information from the bishop of Norwich concerning the exchange between Robert Doget rector of Waltham in the diocese of Winchester and William Tirwhit rector of Bedfield in the diocese of Norwich. The bishop of Norwich has examined the matter through an enquiry carried out by the archdeacon of Suffolk, of which he sends a transcript. He is prepared to admit Robert to the church of Bedfield and to institute him canonically after receiving the resignation of William from that church, with the oath of obedience reserved. He requests a certificate from the bishop of Winchester.

Norwich, 5 February 1347

The bishop has examined the matter; he notes that the patron of the church of Bedfield is the king, by reason of the alien priory of Eye being in his hands on account of war, but that the presentation has been entrusted to the bishop. He therefore approves the admission of Robert to the church of Bedfield.

Southwark, 23 February 1347

Under the same date a certificate of the process was sent to the bishop of Norwich.

170. ADMISSION of William Tirwhit priest to the church of Waltham, vacant by the resignation of Robert Doget, through an exchange with the church of Bedfield in the diocese of Norwich. The patron of Waltham is John, earl of Warenne, Surrey and Strathern, lord of Bromfield and Yale. Letter sent to the archdeacon of Surrey for the induction.

Same date

171. COLLATION to Henry de Assh', priest, of the chantry chapel of Mapledurwell, vacant. The bishop canonically institutes Henry as perpetual chaplain.

Southwark, 6 March 1347

Letters sent to the archdeacon of Winchester and the dean of Basingstoke for the induction, The chantry was vacant by the resignation of Eh'e de Chakynden' the last chaplain.

Southwark, 6 March 1347

He freely and absolutely resigned in the presence of John de Beautre, notary, M. Thomas de Enham rector of Froyle and Thomas de Beautre as witnesses.

172. DISPENSATION granted to William Smyth rector of Burgh to be at the service of Henry earl of Lancaster for one year.

7 March 1347

173. DISPENSATION for study granted to William de Walyngford priest, rector of Chipstead for one year.

20 March 1347

49   **174.** COLLATION by the bishop of the church of Brighstone, Isle of Wight, to Richard de Norwico priest, vacant by the death of John de Boys the last rector. He has been canonically instituted and a letter of the same date sent to the rector of Calbourne or his proctor for his induction into this parochial chapel.

Esher, 1 April 1347

175. COLLATION of the vicarage of Sopley to John Heryng' 'poor clerk' of Winterbourne Herringston in the diocese of Salisbury, the bishop acting as sole executor for the apostolic see providing John with a benefice, with or without cure of souls, at the presentation of the Augustinian canons of Christchurch Twynham. The perpetual vicarage was vacant by the death of Roger de Ware. The bishop instituted John as perpetual vicar after taking the oath.

Southwark, 23 March 1347

Under the same date letters were sent under the same apostolic authority to Thomas rector of Minstead and Hugh 'poor vicar' of Ellingham for the induction to Sopley.

176. EXCHANGE OF BENEFICES within the diocese. The bishop has approved the exchange requested between William de Meone priest, rector of Compton and Nicholas de Wynton rector of the church of Houghton. He institutes William to Houghton.

Southwark, 25 April 1347

Letter under the same date to Adam de Wambergh commissary-general for the induction.

177. COLLATION of the church of Compton vacant by the resignation of William de Meone, last rector, to Nicholas de Wynton after an exchange of benefices. He is canonically instituted.

Same date

Letter to Adam the commissary-general for the induction.

178. TESTIMONIAL LETTER from John, archbishop of Canterbury. Examining in the register of a predecessor, Walter [Reynolds], the will of Thomas Romayn, late of the city of London, he has discovered this clause:
I bequeath to John de Bureford and Roysia his wife the 6 marks of annual quit-rent which I have had from their feoffment from a certain tenement in the parish of St Thomas in London, to be held for John and Roysia and their heirs during the life-time of Juliana my wife. And after the death of the said Juliana, I grant those 6 marks of annual quit-rent for the maintenance of a chaplain to celebrate divine service every year in the church of Clapham for the above mentioned souls. And I entrust the bishop of Winchester for the time being with the presentation of the chaplain to this chantry for ever.
This extract the archbishop testifies by his seal.

Lambeth, 23 April 1347

179. COLLATION TO THE CHANTRY of Clapham of John son (*nato*) of John de Toucestr' to the chantry set up in accordance with the will of Thomas Romayn [detail as above]. The bishop institutes John as perpetual chaplain.

Southwark, 28 April 1347

Under same date a letter to the rector of Clapham that he is to permit John to celebrate in the church according to the pious wishes of Thomas Romayn.

180. CERTIFICATE FOR AN EXCHANGE OF BENEFICES from William Bachiler, canon and official of Lincoln, *sede vacante*. The bishop has received the letter and replies to the official of Lincoln. Since William le Coupere vicar of the church of Shirburn in the diocese of Lincoln and Walter de Depham rector of the church of Elden seek to exchange benefices, the bishop on his part has enquired into the reasons. Finding them legitimate, he approves the exchange, after the enquiry held by the archdeacon of Winchester, the results of which have been forwarded to Lincoln. At the presentation of Laurence de Brembelshet', he will institute William to the church of Elden after the resignation of Walter from the church of Elden.

Esher, 29 March 1347

The official of Lincoln has received the letter and the process, all of which he approves. The bishop may admit William to the church of Elden in the person of John de Depham his proctor.

Lincoln, 4 April 1347

The certificatory letter has been received by the bishop; at once he requested the archdeacon of Winchester to induct William or his proctor to the church of Elden.

181. REQUEST FOR AN EXCHANGE OF BENEFICES. The bishop writes to Richard de Redegrave, priest, vicar of the church of Reigate that he has received the letter of Robert bishop of Chichester, concerning his desire to exchange benefices with Richard Consande vicar of Arlington in the diocese of Chichester, under the patronage of the bishop. The bishop of Chichester approves of the resignation of the vicar of Arlington and will admit Richard de Redegrave to that perpetual vicarage, relying on the enquiry of which he sends a copy to Winchester. He will institute and induct him and requests from the bishop a letter accepting what has been done.

Drungewick, 30 April 1347

51 The bishop accepts the proposals of the bishop of Chichester for the resignation of Richard Consande from the church of Arlington and admits Richard de Redegrave to that vicarage, noting the approbation of M. Richard de Seffold rector of the prebendal church of Arlington. There will be obligation of residence and ministry.

Southwark, 2 May 1347

Under the same date a certificate of the whole process was sent to Chichester.

182. INSTITUTION of Richard Consande to the vicarage of Reigate, vacant by the resignation of Richard de Redegrave, at the presentation of the prior and convent of St Mary of Southwark, patrons.

Same date

Letter to the archdeacon of Surrey for the induction.

183. DISPENSATION for absence granted to Henry Maygn' rector of Worplesdon to be at the service of Laurence earl of Pembroke for one year.

Southwark, 7 May 1347

THE SECOND YEAR OF WILLIAM BISHOP OF WINCHESTER BEGINS 1347

184. ADMISSION of John Mareschal of Wield priest to the vicarage of the prebendal church of Wherwell, vacant by the death of Adam, perpetual vicar there, at the presentation of Nicholas Talemache, prebendary of the prebendal church, with obligation of residence and ministry. Letter sent to the archdeacon of Winchester and to the dean of Andover for the induction.

Southwark, 14 May 1347

185. DISPENSATION for study granted to Thomas de Paxton' rector of Bedhampton subdeacon, for 1 year at some *studium generale*, without obligation of residence or of proceeding to major orders.

Southwark, 29 May 1347

186. DISPENSATION granted to John de Wylie rector of Walton in the diocese of Winchester, to be at the service of Edward de Kendale knight.

Southwark, 29 May 1347

187. LICENCE granted to Nicholas de Wynton rector of Compton to be absent for legitimate reasons and to lease the church at farm.

Southwark, 1 May (*sic*) 1347

188. DISPENSATION from residence for study granted to M. John de Hegham rector of Millbrook.

Southwark, 9 June 1347

52 **189.** LICENCE granted by the bishop to the prior and convent of Bisham (Montagu) in the diocese of Salisbury to lease a church at farm for a period. After the transfer of the profits of the church of Kingsclere in the diocese of Winchester to the monastery by appropriation, the canons find that rather than deal with bailiffs, it would be better to lease the church to some suitable person. The bishop grants the request on condition that in the meantime a suitable proctor be found to rebuild the buildings of the rectory, do general repairs, care for the poor of the parish and pay all ecclesiatical dues.

Southwark, 10 July 1347

190. COLLATION of the church of Kingston to Hugh de Rothewelle rector of half of the church of Isham. The church of Kingston is vacant by the resignation into the hands of the bishop of the perpetual vicarage by Maurice Barnabas de Batykesham (Bottisham). This will be to the evident benefit of the church and follow the constitutions of John XXI in the council of Lyons.

Southewark, 16 July 1347

Letter to the archdeacon of Surrey for the induction of Hugh or his proctor.

191. CERTIFICATE CONCERNING AN EXCHANGE OF BENEFICES. The bishop writes to John bishop-elect of Lincoln concerning the exchange proposed between M. John de Bokyngham rector of the church of Bramdean in the collation of the bishop and in his diocese of Winchester and William Knyght perpetual vicar of the church of Langford near Bampton in the diocese of Lincoln. The bishop has considered the matter and approves the resignation of M. John from the church of Bramdean; he will admit William Knyght to that church and canonically induct him. Reserving the oath to the bishop-elect of Lincoln, he asks to have a copy of the process.

Southwark, 13 July 1347

The bishop-elect, having considered the matter, will carry out everything as the bishop of Winchester has set out.

Bedwyn, 21 July 1347

On receiving the certificate, a mandate was sent to the archdeacon of Winchester for the induction of William Knyght to the church of Bramdean.

Southwark, 24 July 1347

53   **192.** COLLATION of the church of Brighstone, Isle of Wight, vacant by the resignation of William Jolyf, acting as proctor for M. John le Yonge the last rector, exchanging benefices for the church of Dunton Waylett in the diocese of London. The bishop confers this church on Richard de Norwico priest, in the person of Walter de Berneye his proctor, and institutes him canonically.

Southwark, 1 July 1347

Under the same date a letter to the dean of the Island for the induction of Roger de Beautre proctor for Richard de Norwico.

193. ADMISSION of Robert de Swanlond acolyte, in the person of William de Ilkeston' rector of Stowe his proctor, to the church of Wotton in the diocese of Winchester, at the presentation of Phillippa, queen of England and duchess of Acquitaine, patron. He is canonically instituted.
A letter sent to the archdeacon of Surrey for the induction.

Southwark, 3 August 1347

194. EXCHANGE OF BENEFICES. Robert, bishop of Salisbury has received the bishop's letter concerning the proposed exchange between Walter Waleys rector of Shalfleet, Isle of Wight, and John de Wynkeleye, prebendary of the prebend of Burton, of the church of Salisbury and in the diocese of Worcester. He has examined the matter and approves, accepting the resignation of Walter from Shalfleet, to which chuch he will admit John de Wynkeleye. The king presents as custodian of the lands of William de Monteacuto earl of Salisbury, deceased, and so as patron. An enquiry had been held by the archdeacon of Winchester, a copy of which has been sent to Salisbury. The bishop will arrange for the induction and receive the oath of obedience.

Southwark, 22 July 1347

The bishop acknowledges this from his manor of Sonning

2 August 1347

The certificatory letter was received 4 August, on which day a letter was sent to the dean of the Island for the induction of John to the church of Shalfleet.

54   **195.** COLLATION OF A PENITENTIARY for South Malling. The bishop writes to Robert de Chilberton' priest that he has received a letter from John, archbishop of Canterbury. John Bray penitentiary of the collegiate church of South Malling, of the archbishop's patronage and immediate jurisdiction, wishes to exchange benefices with Robert de Chilberton' perpetual vicar of Walkhamstead in the diocese of Winchester. The archbishop has ordered the customary enquiry and sends the process; he accepts the resignation of John and will collate the penitenciary on Robert. He requests the bishop's certificate.

Croydon, 4 [August] 1347

The bishop, having examined the matter, consents to the exchange.

Southwark, 6 September 1347

Under the same date a certificatory letter was sent to the archbishop.

196. INSTITUTION of John Bray to the perpetual vicarage of Walkhamstead, vacant by the resignation of Richard de Chilberton' by reason of an exchange. The patrons who present are the prior and convent of Tandridge, for this once on account of the exchange. There is obligation of residence.

Same date

197. INDUCTION by John de Wolveleye rector of Arreton, deputizing in the vacancy of the archdeaconry of Surrey, of John Bray to the perpetual vicarage of Walkhamstead, after an exchange with the penitentiary of South Malling in the diocese of Canterbury.

Same date

198. CERTIFICATE OF THE PROCESS OF EXCHANGE sent to Robert bishop of Salisbury concerning Thomas de Brailles of Mapledurham and Peter de Dene of Brightwell in the diocese of Salisbury. The bishop approves and will admit Peter to the church of Mapledurham and accept his oath.

55   Southwark, 22 July 1347

Having examined the matter, the bishop of Salisbury approves the resignation of Thomas from Mapledurham and the admission of Peter.

Sonning, 20 September 1347

Memorandum that after the dispatch of the letter, the archdeacon of Winchester was informed for the induction of Peter and for receiving his oath on behalf of the bishop.

Marwell, 22 September 1347

199. CERTIFICATE FOR AN EXCHANGE OF BENEFICES. Ralph bishop of London informs the bishop that he has the received the letter concerning the exchange of benefices between Reginald de Leghton rector of Limpsfield and Walter de Merstham rector of St Nicholas of Coldabbey in the city of London. The bishop accepts the resignation of Reginald from Limpsfield and will admit Walter, relying on the inquiry held by the bishop's authority during the vacancy of the archdeaconry, of which he sends a certificate. He will arrange for the induction and requests a similar certificate of the process.

Southwark, 13 September 1347

The bishop of London will authorize the admission of Walter to Limpsfield.

[Bishops] Stortford, 15 September 1347

Mandate to M. John de Wolveleye, holding the jurisdiction of the archdeaconry of Surrey as deputy during the vacancy, to induct Walter de Merscham to the church of Limpsfield. The same day Walter took the oath of obedience to the bishop.

Marwell, 22 September 1347

200. DISPENSATION for study granted to Walter de Merstham for one year in preparation for the diaconate.

Southwark, 11 October 1347

201. INSTITUTION to the perpetual vicarage of Kingston of William de Burstall' deacon, following the free resignation of Maurice Barnabas at the presentation of the king, by reason that the priory of Merton is in the king's court pending a decision as to the recovery of its court (*per condiderationem curie recuperationis.*). Letter sent to the official of the archdeacon of Surrey for the induction.

Southwark, 3 October 1347

56   **202.** TESTIMONIAL LETTER ON THE ADMISSION AND INSTALLATION of the archdeacon of Surrey, addressed to all deans, rectors, etc. The bishop has admitted to his stall in choir and seat in chapter M. Richard Vaughan, with the rights of the archdeaconry.

Wolvesey, 24 September 1347

203. OATH OF CANONICAL OBEDIENCE pronounced by Adam Cissor priest as proctor for M. Richard Vaughan archdeacon of Surrey, in the presence of M. John de Usk' chancellor, John de Beautre, Richard de Dorsete public notaries, William Chuere priest and William Jolyf as witnesses. He took the oath kissing the Gospels.

Wolvesey, 24 September 1347

204. OATH OF THE ARCHDEACON'S COMMISSARY pronounced by William Chuere priest and commissary of M. Richard archdeacon of Surrey in the presence of M. John de Usk' chancellor, John de Beautre public notary, with Thomas de Beautre as witnesses.

Southwark, 3 October 1347

205. DISPENSATION FOR STUDY granted to M. Thomas Enham rector of Froyle deacon, for seven years at some *studium generale*.

Southwark, 5 October 1347

206. LICENCE for absence granted to Peter de Dene rector of Mapledurham to be at the service of Ralph bishop of London, with exemption from residence.

Southwark, 9 October 1347

207. DISPENSATION FOR STUDY granted to Walter Noht rector of Lainston subdeacon, to be at some *studium generale* for a term (*per terminum*).

Wolvesey, 25 September 1347

208. DISPENSATION FOR STUDY granted for one year to M. William Joce of Crawley and Thomas Sadok' of South Warnborough, rectors and priests, without obligation of residence.

Southwark, 3 October 1347

209. LICENCE granted to William de Swanebourne rector of Hambledon to be at the service of Isabella prioress of Amesbury, leasing the church meanwhile to some suitable person.

Southwark, 18 October 1347

210. DISPENSATION FOR STUDY granted to John de Tygehale rector of Blendworth, priest.

Southwark, 20 October 1347

211. LICENCE to lease at farm the fruits and revenues of the church of Brading, Isle of Wight, for five years granted to the prior and convent of Breamore, to whom the church is appropriated. They may lease it to M. Walter de Peveseye clerk, who will arrange for a suitable procurator responsible for buildings and the care of the poor.

Southwark, 24 October 1347

212. INSTITUTION to the church of Dunton Waylett by exchange. The bishop informs M. John le Yonge clerk that he has received a letter from Ralph bishop of London concerning the desire to exchange benefices between Richard de Norwico of Dunton Waylett of his diocese and M. John le Yonge of Brighstone, Isle of Wight. The bishop of London has considered the facts presented by the bishop, approves the exchange of rectories and is ready to induct John to the church of Dunton; he requests a certificate.

Orsett, 31 July 1347

Having discussed the matter and accepted the resignation of Richard de Norwico in the person of Walter de Berneye his proctor from the church of Dunton Waylett, which is at the presentation of the prior of Ogbourne, as proctor for the abbot of Bec Helewin in England—now in the hands of the king on account of the war. The prior had held the customary enquiry at the bishop's mandate through the official of the archdeacon of Essex. The bishop institutes M. John le Yonge to the church of Dunton.

Southwark, 29 October 1347

213. COLLATION of the church of Brighstone, Isle of Wight, to Richard de Norwico after an exchange and the resignation of M. le Yonge in the person of Walter de Berneye his proctor. The bishop institutes him canonically.

Southwark, 29 October 1347

Under the same date the dean of the Island was informed for the induction.

214. ADMISSION of Robert de Wilford clerk to the church of Niton, Isle of Wight, vacant by the death of Robert de Maydenwelle the last rector, at the presentation of king Edward, patron by reason of the priory of Carisbrooke being in the king's hands because of the war. The archdeacon of Winchester has been informed for the induction.

Southwark, 24 November 1347

215. LETTER CONCERNING AN EXCHANGE OF BENEFICES from the bishop to the dean of Hereford cathedral. William de Dymmok' rector of the church of St Anastasius in the 'suburb' of the city of Winchester and Roger de Oleton rector of the church of St Andrew without St Andrew's gate in the city of Hereford seek to exchange benefices. The bishop accepts the resignation of William and is prepared to admit Roger to the church of St Anastasius. He requests a certificate.

Southwark, 30 August 1347

The dean of Hereford approves the exchange.

Hereford, 2 November 1347

On receiving the certificate the bishop ordered the archdeacon of Winchester to induct Roger.

Southwark, 5 December 1347

216. DISPENSATION granted to Almaric de Pontaliaco rector of Beddington to be at the service of William de Cusancia clerk for one year, with permission to lease the church at farm during that period.

Southwark, 9 November 1347

217. LETTER CONCERNING AN EXCHANGE OF BENEFICES from Robert bishop of Salisbury, to the bishop. Peter de Fyndon' priest, deacon of the chapel of St Elizabeth outside Winchester and Walter de Compton' rector of Chalbury in the diocese of Salisbury wish to exchange benefices. The bishop of Salisbury sends a copy of the enquiry he had ordered, approving the exchange and requesting the certificate from Winchester.

at his park of Ramsbury, 14 December 1347

The bishop having examined the matter, accepts the resignation of Walter from Chalbury to which he had been presented by Nicholas Devenish and in view of the enquiries held, he approves the exchange.

59

Southwark, 21 December 1347

Under the same date a certificatory letter sent to the bishop of Salisbury.

218. COLLATION OF THE OFFICE OF DEACON in the chapel of St Elizabeth, vacant by the resignation of Peter de Fyndon', at the exchange with the church of Chalbury, upon Walter de Compton' priest—keeping the regulations laid down by John de Pontissara, founder of the chapel. The bishop institutes him to this perpetual office.

Southwark, 21 December 1347

A letter sent to the *prepositus* of the chapel for the admission of Walter to the office.

219. COLLATION OF THE OFFICE OF PRIEST in the chapel of St Elizabeth, vacant by the death of Robert de Sarum, upon John Yongwyne of Boxgrave priest; he is ordained as its perpetual chaplain according to the founder's regulations. He is instituted canonically and the *prepositus* has been informed for his installation.

Southwark, 1 January 1348

220. INSTITUTION of John Yongwyne of Boxgrave to the perpetual vicarage of Kingsclere, vacant by the resignation of John called le Dyare of the Island, by exchange with the office of priest of the chapel of St Elizabeth. The vicarage of Kingsclere is at the presentation of the prior and convent of Bisham. The bishop admits John to the vicarage with the obligation of ministry.

Southwark, 12 January 1348

Under the same date a letter to the archdeacon of Winchester for the induction.

221. COLLATION OF THE OFFICE OF PRIEST to the chapel of St Elizabeth conferred upon John called le Dyare, vacant by the resignation of John Yongwyne of Boxgrave, following an exchange with the vicarage of Kingsclere.

Same date

Letter to the *prepositus* of the chapel to admit John to the office which he is to administer.

222. DISPENSATION FOR STUDY granted to John de la Vyne rector of Chaldon subdeacon, for one year to study at some *universitate generali*.

Southwark, 7 December 1347

223. LICENCE granted to Blasius prior of Carisbrooke to lease at farm half of all the lesser tithes and offerings of the church of Chale, excepting those from the house once belonging to Hugh Gernon, as well as from a certain croft in the parish. He will lease this to William de Twyford priest for a period of five years.

London, 5 January 1348

60   **224.** LICENCE granted to William de Walyngford rector of Chipstead to be at the service of Ralph de Stafford knight, for one year.

Southwark, 16 January 1348

225. LETTER CONCERNING AN EXCHANGE OF BENEFICES from John archbishop of Canterbury to the bishop. Thomas Plomer vicar of South Bersted in the diocese of Canterbury and William de Harpele vicar of Leatherhead desire to exchange benefices. The enquiry showed that the vicarage of Leatherhead is at the presentation of the prior and convent of Leeds and a copy of the process has been sent to the bishop. If no obstacle intervenes, the archbishop approves and will institute William to the vicarage of Bersted with obligation of residence. He requests the certificate of the bishop.

Lambeth, 18 January 1348

The bishop having examined the matter authorizes the exchange and approves the admission of William to the vicarage of Bersted.

Southwark, 25 January 1348

Under the same date a certificatory letter was sent to the archbishop.

226. ADMISSION of Thomas Plomer priest to the perpetual vicarage of Leatherhead, vacant by the resignation of William de Harpele, at the presentation of the prior and convent of Leeds, after an exchange. There is obligation of residence.

Same date

Letter to the archdeacon of Surrey for the induction.

227. ADMISSION of John Seys clerk to the church of Shalfleet, Isle of Wight, vacant by the death of M. John de Wynkele and at the presentation of the king as custodian of the lands of William de Montecuto, earl of Salisbury, deceased. Letter sent to the archdeacon of Winchester for the induction.

Southwark, 27 January 1348

228. LICENCE granted to William de Benacre rector of Mottistone, Isle of Wight, to be for one year at the service of Isabella of Lancaster, prioress of Amesbury.

Southwark, 1 February 1348

61   **229.** ELECTION OF A PRIOR for [Monk] Sherborne. To the archdeacon of Winchester the bishop writes that he has received letters from the abbot and convent of St Vigor of Cerisy, o.s.b., in the diocese of Bayeux in Normandy, announcing that the priory of Sherborne, dependent or annexed to that abbey, was vacant by the death of fr. Thomas le Galobre, on Monday after the feast of St John at the Latin Gate, viz, 9 May 1345. The abbot of Cerisy fixed the date for the election, held by custom on some solemn feast, for Thursday before the feast of St John Baptist, viz 23 June. The convent elected from their own body fr. Robert Corbel; Robert gave his assent and the patron, William Trussel of Cubblesdon, accepted him. For various reasons there was a delay in presenting him to the bishop for confirming the election. The bishop therefore asks the archdeacon to make an enquiry to see if there is any opposition or contradiction to the election and to order any such opponents to appear before the bishop or his commissary in the church of St Mary of Southwark, on the first law-day after the feast of St Thomas the Apostle. The archdeacon will inform the bishop of the names of those wishing to be heard.

Southwark, 6 December 1347

230. PROCESS OF THE ENQUIRY INTO THE ELECTION at Sherborne, before John de Usk' rector of Burghclere, deputed to hear the case of the election of Robert Corbel, monk of St Vigor as prior, held in the church of St Mary, Southwark. The tribunal inspected the decree and papers which the prior-elect showed; the certificate of the archdeacon of Winchester was read, calling on those opposed to the election to appear at the church door. When these did not appear, the tribunal proceeded the same day to conclude the proceedings at the manor chapel of Southwark, before M. Richard Drax, advocate of the court of Canterbury. He found the prior-elect to be mature and of praiseworthy repute, and pronounced the confirmation (formula set out).

Southwark, 22 December 1347

62   **231.** CONFIRMATION OF THE ELECTION by the bishop, who has examined the conduct of the election of Robert Corbel as prior of Sherborne St John and found it canonically celebrated; he confirms the election and entrusts to the prior the cure of souls and the administration.

Southwark, 22 December 1347

232. RECOMMENDATION TO THE COMMUNITY. The bishop announces to the prior and convent of Sherborne St John that he has examined the conduct of the election and confirms it; he establishes fr. Robert as prior and pastor, trusting that by his circumspection and industry he will prove worthy of the reverence and obedience of the brethren.

Same date

233. MANDATE TO THE ARCHDEACON OF WINCHESTER for the induction of prior Robert with all the rights customary to his office, assigning him to his stall in choir and seat in chapter.

Same date

234. THE KING IS ADVISED. Since the priory of Sherborne St John is in the king's hands on account of the war, the bishop informs the king

that he has confirmed the election of Robert Corbel as prior in succession
to fr. Thomas le Galoberr' deceased.

Same date

235. LETTER CONCERNING AN EXCHANGE OF BENEFICES. The bishop informs
Robert bishop of Salisbury that Walter de Kemeseye, perpetual vicar of
Milford of his diocese, and Thomas de Manndevill' rector of Buckhorn
Weston of the diocese of Salisbury seek to exchange benefices. The
rectory of Buckhorn Weston is at the presentation of Christchurch
Twynham. Relying on the enquiry of the archdeacon of Winchester,
63   conducted at his mandate, the bishop is prepared to authorize the
exchange and induct Thomas to the vicarage of Milford, with obligation
of residence. He requests the certificate of the bishop of Salisbury.

Southwark, 27 January 1348

The bishop of Salisbury approves the exchange, accepting the resignation
of Walter from Milford, and will institute Walter with obligation of
residence.

from his park at Ramsbury, 30 January 1348

236. MANDATE TO THE ARCHDEACON of Winchester for the induction of
Thomas de Mandeville, sent on receipt of the certificatory letter from
the bishop of Salisbury.

Southwark, 3 February 1347

237. LICENCE granted to the prior and convent of St Mary, Southwark,
to lease at farm, rather than to collect the fruits and revenues from
appropriated churches through bailiffs. This will be for three years and
the lessees must be suitable persons. The convent will appoint suitable
procurators to be responsible for the rectory and buildings, as well as
the care of the poor.

Southwark, 1 February 1348

238. LETTER CONCERNING A EXCHANGE OF BENEFICES received by the
bishop from John bishop of Hereford, concerning the wish of M. Thomas
de Bokenhull' rector of Eastnor in his diocese and William de Marcle
rector of Farleigh [Wallop] near Basingstoke to exchange. The bishop
approves and accepts the resignation of M. Thomas and is ready to
admit William, to receive his oath and to induct him to the church of
Eastnor. He requests a certificate.

Finsbury near London, 2 February 1348

The bishop having considered the matter, approves of the exchange,
64   accepts the resignation of M. Thomas de Bokenhull' from Eastnor and
admits him in the person of Thomas de Wyrecestr' his proctor, reserving
the oath.

Southwark, 9 February 1348

Under the same date a certificate of the process was sent to the bishop
of Hereford.

239. INSTITUTION to the church of Farleigh [Wallop], vacant by the resignation of M. William de Marcle, of M. Thomas de Bokenhull', in the person of Thomas de Wyrecestr' his proctor, after an exchange with the church of Eastnor in the diocese of Hereford. Robert la Zouche, lord of the manor of Farleigh, presented him.

Southwark, 9 February 1348

Under same date a letter sent to the archdeacon of Winchester for the induction.

240. INSTITUTION OF A VICAR BY EXCHANGE OF BENEFICES. The bishop has received letters from John bishop of Lincoln concerning the exchange proposed between John Russell, priest, rector of Sanderstead and John Stanfeld vicar of Chalfont St Peter in the diocese of Lincoln. The bishop of Lincoln, relying on the enquiry, of which he sends a copy, is ready to admit John Russel to the vicarage of Chalfont St Peter. He requests a certificate.

The Old Temple, London, 14 February 1348

The bishop having considered the request authorizes the exchange, accepting the resignation of John de Stanfeld from Chalfont St Peter and the admission to that vicarage of John Russel, at the presentation of the abbot and convent of Missenden, patrons—he now admits John de Stanefeld to Sanderstead with obligation of residence.

Southwark, 17 February 1348

Under the same date the certificate of the process was sent to the bishop of Lincoln.

241. INSTITUTION of John Stanefeld' to the church of Sanderstead, vacant by the resignation of John Russel after an exchange of benefices with the vicar of Chalfont St Peter. The patrons are the abbot and convent of Hyde.

Same date

65 The archdeacon of Surrey was informed for the induction.

242. INSTITUTION OF THE PRIOR OF ELLINGHAM. The bishop informs fr. Galvanus de Hambeya. o.s.b., professed monk and priest of St Sauveur-le-Vicomte in the diocese of Coutances, that he has been presented by his monastery as prior of Ellingham, now vacant. In the customary manner the bishop admits him canonically as prior.

Southwark, 22 February 1348

Under the same date the archdeacon of Winchester was informed for the induction.

243. INSTITUTION of Philip de Alba Marlea clerk to the free chapel of Alverstone, Isle of Wight, vacant, at the presentation of William de Umframvile, patron. The bishop canonically institutes him.

Southwark, 23 February 1348

Under the same date letter to the archdeacon for induction.

244. LICENCE granted to William de Kyfthill' rector of the church of St Peter Whitbread in Winchester to be absent for one year at the service of John Darcy, lord of Knaith, while still receiving the profits from the church by special permission.

Southwark, 22 February 1348

245. LICENCE granted to John Seys rector of Shalfleet, Isle of Wight, to be absent for one year only at the service of Guy Brian knight, while still receiving the profits from the church, or leasing it at farm by special permission.

Southwark, 23 February 1348

246. ADMISSION of William de Peyce priest to the church of Buckland, vacant, at the presentation of Eleanor Ferris, patron for this turn. He was instituted canonically as rector.

Southwark, 8 March 1348

Letter to the archdeacon of Surrey for induction.

247. LICENCE granted to Nicholas Talemache, prebendary of the prebend of Wherwell, to lease at farm his prebend for one year to John de Frollebury and John de Boxgrove of Kingsclere, perpetual vicars.

Southwark, 25 March 1348

248. DISPENSATION granted to Thomas le Blount rector of All Saints, Southampton, subdeacon, to be absent for one year for study without obligation of proceeding to higher orders.

Southwark, 11 January 1348

249. COLLATION of John de Edyngton clerk to the custody of the Hospital of St Nicholas at Portsmouth, vacant and at the collation of the bishop since its foundation.

Southwark, 12 March 1348

Letter to Robert called le Clerc, rector of Meonstoke, and William de Wygynton', rector of Bishopstoke, for his induction.

250. COLLATION conferred upon John de Edyndon' clerk of the church of Cheriton, vacant by the death of M. Peter Ingepenne last rector. He was instituted canonically.

Southwark, 14 March 1348

Under the same date a letter was written to the rector of the church of Alresford or his parochial chaplain for the induction of John or his proctor.

66 **251.** COLLATION of the church of Cheriton, vacant by the resignation of John de Edyngdon', late rector, to John de Usk' by exchange for the church of Burghclere—both of the bishop's collation.

Esher, 26 March 1348

Under same date letter for the induction sent to the official of Winchester, the rectors of Alresford and Hinton [Ampner] and to their parish chaplain.

252. COLLATION, similar to the preceding, to John de Edyndon' clerk, of the church of Burghclere. Letters written to the rectors of [East] Woodhay and Highclere and their chaplains for the induction to the church, vacant by the resignation of M. John de Usk', by exchange.

26 March 1348

253. COLLATION of the church of Cheriton, which M. John de Usk' for certain reasons had resigned into the hands of the bishop and the bishop had accepted, was afterwards conferred upon him anew.

Same date

Letter to those mentioned above for the induction.

254. LICENCE granted to John Heynote rector of Chalton to be absent for study for one year.

Southwark, 27 March 1348

255. LICENCE TO LEASE AT FARM the church of Laverstoke for one year, granted to Edmund de Chynham.

7 April 1348

256. LICENCE granted to Robert de Swanlond', rector of Wotton, to be absent for one year at the service of Richard, earl of Arundel.

7 April 1348

257. LICENCE granted to John Puppe rector of Puttenham to be absent for one year at the service of Gilbert de Imworth, knight, and to lease the church at farm to some suitable person.

Southwark, 8 April 1348

258. LICENCE to be absent for one year for study granted to Henry Maign' rector of Worplesdon.

Southwark, 15 April 1348

259. ADMISSION of Roger de Toneton' acolyte to the church of Tunworth, vacant by the resignation of Richard de Chilewell' and at the presentation of John de Grey, lord of Codnor, knight, patron. He was canonically instituted. Letter sent to the archdeacon of Winchester for the induction.

Southwark, 16 April 1348

67 **260**. ADMISSION after an exchange of benefices of John le Mareschal priest to the rectory of Cliddesden vacant by the resignation, through his proctor William de Colton', of John Palfreour late rector. This was by an exchange with the perpetual vicarage of the prebendal church of Wherwell. The patron of the church of Cliddesden was John Valence. The bishop admits to the rectory.

Southwark, 23 April 1348

Under the same date a letter was written to John le Palfreour for his institution to the vicarage of Wherwell. Also to the archdeacon of Winchester for the induction.

261. INDUCTION OF A GUARDIAN for the hospital of St John of Fordingbridge. The office which is of the bishop's collation, vacant by the resignation of Thomas de la More of Finchampstead into the hands of John de Beautre notary public, with Hugh de Neovill knight, M. William de Wyrkynton' and Richard de Derby clerk as witnesses, was conferred on Richard de Mora priest and he was instituted.

Southwark, 1 May 1348

Letter to the dean of Fordingbridge and to the perpetual vicar for the induction.

262. RESIGNATION OF THE PRIOR OF CARISBROOKE. In the presence of the bishop in the greater hall (*maiori camera*) at Southwark, fr. Peter le Seneschal, acting as proctor for fr. Blaise Doublel late prior of St Mary, Carisbrooke, freely resigned the office into the bishop's hands, in the presence of John de Beautre, John de Usk', John de Wolveleye as witnesses. In the name of fr. Blaise, the bishop accepted a written resignation (text given) from fr. Peter (both being monks of the abbey of Lyre).

Southwark, 4 May 1348

263. INSTITUTION OF THE PRIOR OF CARISBROOKE. Letter from the bishop to fr. John Pepyn, professed monk of Lyre abbey in the diocese of Evreux, admitting him to the office of prior of St Mary Carisbrooke, to which he was presented by M. John de Wolveleye rector of Arreton and fr. Peter Seneschal, constituted as proctors with authority to present. He institutes him canonically as prior.

Southwark, 5 May 1348

Under the same date letter to the archdeacon of Winchester to induct the prior according to the usages of the priory. On the same day fr. John Pepyn took the oath of obedience to the bishop.

68 **264**. APPOINTMENT of a locum tenens FOR AN ABSENTEE. Letter to John le Walshe priest saying that Walter Douk' of Fenny Stratford, perpetual chaplain of the chapel of St Mary Magdalen of Kingston, had for a long time been absent without licence or reasonable excuse and without finding a substitute, leaving the chapel without divine service. He had not replied to any admonition. The bishop now entrusts the chapel which has suffered much harm to John, recommended to the bishop by John Lovekyn, parson of the chapel, until such time as the said Walter returns, or the situation is canonically clear.

Southwark, 6 May 1348

265. INSTITUTION of Peter Travers as perpetual vicar of Thorley, Isle of Wight, vacant by the death of Thomas de Stanesmour and at the presentation of the prior and convent of Christchurch Twynham as patrons—with obligation of residence. Letter to the archdeacon of Winchester for the induction.

Esher, 11 May 1348

266. DISPENSATION for study granted for one year to M. Thomas de Paxton' rector of Bedhampton subdeacon.

Southwark, 20 May 1348

267. DISPENSATION granted to John de Leycestr' rector of Hartley Mauditt to be at the service of Henry earl of Lancaster for one year.

Southwark, 28 May 1348

268. APPROBATION OF AN EXCHANGE OF BENEFICES. The bishop accepts the resignations of Thomas de Durleye rector of St Faith near Winchester and of Hugh de Pebworth rector of Binstead, Isle of Wight, in view of a mutual exchange. He canonically institutes Hugh to the church of St Faith and writes to Richard de Lusteshull, master of St Cross and Henry *prepositus* of the chapel of St Elizabeth for the induction. Were present at the resignations M. John de Usk' chancellor, J' de Wolveleye, Thomas de Enham and John de Beautre notary public.

The manor chapel of Southwark, 29 May 1348

269. INSTITUTION AFTER EXCHANGE OF BENEFICES. Robert bishop of Salisbury writes to the bishop that John le Rede perpetual vicar of Epsom in the diocese of Winchester and Roger de Gotham perpetual vicar of the prebendal church of Bishopstone in the diocese of Salisbury seek to exchange benefices. He has held an enquiry into Bishopstone through the dean of Salisbury and transmits the data. If the bishop approves, the bishop of Salisbury will accept the resignation of Roger from Bishopstone **69** and institute John, with obligation of residence. He asks for a certificate from the bishop.

Chardstock, 28 May 1348

The bishop, having examined the process and accepted the resignation of Roger, authorizes the admission of John le Rede to the prebendal church of Bishopstone, at the presentation of Raymond Pelegrini, acting as proctor for Peter Reymundi of Ropistagno, prebendary of the prebendal church and patron of the vicarage. He admits him with the obligation of residence.

Southwark, 2 June 1348

Under same date a certificate of the process sent to the bishop of Salisbury.

270. INSTITUTION to the perpetual vicarage of Epsom of Roger de Gotham, vacant by the resignation of John le Rede, by exchange of benefices with the prebendal church of Bishopstone and at the presentation of the abbot and convent of Chertsey, patrons. He has the obligation of residing.

Southwark, 2 June 1348

Letter same date to the archdeacon of Surrey for the induction.

271. INSTITUTION to the vicarage of the parish church of Titchfield of fr. William de Wollop canon regular of St Mary's abbey, Titchfield, presented by fr. Peter, the elect of the abbey. The bishop admits him according to the *indulgentia* granted by the Holy See, with the obligation of residence. The bishop gives him charge of the parish, provided he has another canon to help him.

Esher, 8 June 1348

Same date letter to the archdeacon of Winchester for the induction.

272. ABBATIAL BLESSING of fr. Peter de Wynton canon regular of the monastery of Titchfield, according to the privileges of the order, in the parish church of Esher during pontifical Mass.

Feast of Pentecost, 8 June 1348

273. ADMISSION OF A NUN. The bishop orders a letter to be written to the abbess and convent of Romsey in the customary form, requesting that they receive into their community Joan daughter of Isabella de Cormailles as a nun.

Southwark, 8 June 1348

274. MANDATE FOR INDUCTION sent to the archdeacon of Winchester for Walter de Farndale to the church of Blendworth, on receipt of a letter from Robert bishop of Chichester concerning the proposed exchange of benefices between M. Walter de Farndale rector of Upmarden in the diocese of Chichester and John de Tygehale rector of Blendworth. The process of the enquiry accompanied the letter. The bishop will admit M. Walter to Blendworth.

Southwark, 20 May 1348

Having discussed the matter and approving the resignation from Blendworth, the bishop of Chichester admits the new rector of Upmarden.

Ferring, 2 June 1348

275. MANDATE FOR THE INDUCTION of Hugh de Neeuton' to the church of Morestead, vacant by reason of an exchange for the church of Tugford in the diocese of Hereford, entrusted to the rectors of Bishopstoke,

Chilcombe and St Maurice of Winchester. This follows the receipt of the certificatory letter from the bishop of Hereford given below.

Esher, 13 June 1348

276. LETTER CONCERNING AN EXCHANGE OF BENEFICES from John bishop of Hereford, who acknowledges the bishop's letter concerning the exchange sought by John de Middleton' rector of Morestead and Hugh de Neeuton rector of Tugford. The bishop of Winchester approved the exchange and was prepared to admit Hugh as rector of Morestead.

Southwark, 20 May 1348

The bishop of Hereford has examined the matter and the resignation of John from the church of Morestead. Hugh will be admitted to Morestead in the person of his proctor Richard de Tymberlake.

Goldhill, 1 July 1348

277. PRESENTATION to the church of [East] Orchard. Letter to Ralph bishop of Bath and Wells: the church of Orchard in that diocese is vacant, but of the presentation of the bishop of Winchester by reason of the custody of the heir and lands of Thomas de Orchard' deceased, lord of the manor or hamlet of Orchard and patron of the church. The bishop presents Walter de Haulo to the bishop requesting him to institute him as rector and arrange for the induction.

London, 16 June 1348

71   **278.** LICENCE FOR STUDY for one year granted to M. William Joce rector of Crawley priest.

Southwark, 26 June 1348

279. LICENCE FOR STUDY granted to William Knyt rector of Bramdean for one year.

Southwark, 26 June 1348

280. ADMISSION of John le Walssh priest to the chapel of St Mary Magdalen near Kingston, vacant by the free resignation of Walter Tonk' of Fenny Stratford its last perpetual chaplain. At the presentation of John Lovekyn citizen of London, John is instituted as perpetual chaplain. Letter sent to the archdeacon of Surrey for his induction.

Southwark, 30 June 1348

281. COLLATION to the parish of Binstead, Isle of Wight of Ralph de Suthfeld clerk in the person of M. Peter de Normanby his legally constituted proctor. The rectory was vacant by the resignation of Hugh Broun of Pebworth.

Southwark, 8 July 1348

282. EXCHANGE OF BENEFICES between Binstead, as above, and Brighstone, both in the Isle of Wight. Richard de Norwico resigned Brighstone into the bishop's hands and was instituted to Binstead. Ralph de Suthfeld was collated to Brighstone and instituted in the person of M. Peter his proctor. Letter sent to the rector of Calbourne and to its chaplain for the induction of Ralph.

Southwark, 8 July 1348

283. DISPENSATION granted to Roger de Toneton' rector of Tunworth acolyte to be absent for one year for study without obligation of residence or of advancing beyond the subdiaconate, in accordance with the constitution of Boniface.

Southwark, 11 July 1348

284. DISPENSATION granted to John Heynote rector of Chalton subdeacon to be absent for study for one year without obligation of residence or of proceeding to higher orders, according to the constitution *Cum ex eo*.

Southwark, 3 July 1348

285. LICENCE granted to M. John de Asshton' rector of Stratfieldsaye to be absent for one year at the service of Edmund de Bereford.

Southwark, 18 July 1348

286. LICENCE granted to M. Walter de Farnedale rector of Blendworth priest to be for one year at the service of Ralph bishop of London.

Southwark, 21 July 1348

287. LICENCE TO LEASE AT FARM to a suitable person the profits of the church of Farnham and the chapels annexed thereto granted to Richard Vachan archdeacon of Surrey.

Southwark, 1 July 1348

288. Repetition of 286

289. MANDATE TO RECEIVE A NUN. Letter from the bishop to the prioress and convent of Wintney that they are to receive Isabella daughter of Roger Gervais as a sister and nun in their house. The bishop nominates her by reason of his elevation to the see. They will send the customary certificate.

[Bishop's] Waltham, 23 August 1348

290. DISPENSATION to be absent for study granted for one year to Thomas Creue rector of Fawley.

Southwark, 26 August 1348

291. ADMISSION of Robert atte Gate priest to the vicarage of Brading, Isle of Wight, vacant by the resignation of John de Hunnyngton' lately perpetual vicar, following an exchange of benefices with the vicar of [South] Stoneham. The patrons are the prior and convent of Breamore. As perpetual vicar Robert will have the obligation of residence according to the constitutions. A letter sent to the archdeacon of Winchester for the induction.

Bitterne, 13 September 1348

292. ADMISSION of John de Hunnyngton' to the vicarage of [South] Stoneham, vacant by the resignation of Robert atte Gate by way of exchange. The church is at the presentation of the precentor of St Mary Southampton as patron. As perpetual vicar John will have the obligation of residence and he took the oath at his institution. Letter sent to the precentor for his induction.

Bitterne, 13 September 1348

293. INSTITUTION of Thomas Tourgys clerk to the church of Stratfield Turgis, vacant by the death of Thomas Ladde, at the presentation of John Turgys patron. Letter sent to the archdeacon of Winchester for his induction.

Southwark, 23 September 1348

294. DISPENSATION granted to Bugonus Mauduyt rector of Deane to be at the service of Robert de Bury knight and during that time to lease his church at farm to any suitable person, so that divine service may be maintained.

Southwark, 23 September 1348

295. LICENCE to be absent for study for one year granted to M. John de Hegham rector of Millbrook.

Southwark, 25 September 1348

296. DISPENSATION granted to John de Wilie rector of Walton to be for one year at the service of Edward de Kendale, knight.

Southwark, 26 September 1348

297. MANDATE to the archdeacon of Winchester to induct Adam de Wynchyndon' to the perpetual vicarage of Hurstbourne [Tarrant], vacant by the resignation of Philip de Buketon, following an exchange of benefices with the vicar of Little Yarmouth in the diocese of Norwich. The patron of Hurstbourne is M. John de Whitchurch, prebendary of the same.

Southwark, 30 August 1348

298. ADMISSION of William de Engulby clerk to the rectory of Wotton, vacant by the resignation of Robert de Swanlond, at the presentation of Philippa queen of England and duchess of Aquitaine, patron for this turn as custodian of the lands and tenements of William Latimer, deceased. Letter to the archdeacon of Surrey for the induction.

Southwark, 8 October 1348

299. LICENCE to be absent for study for one year granted to Thomas Blount rector of All Saints Southampton, without obligation of residence or of proceeding to higher orders according to the constitutions.

Southwark, 16 October 1348

73   **300.** DISPENSATION granted to William de Swanebourne rector of Hambledon to be for one year at the service of Isabella of Lancaster prioress of Amesbury. He may lease his church at farm to a suitable person.

Southwark, 17 October 1348

301. DISPENSATION granted to William de Kyftbill rector of the church of Whitbread in Winchester to be absent for one year at the service of John Darcy lord of Knaith.

Southwark, 29 October 1348

302. ADMISSION of Richard de Sutton' vicar of Arreton, Isle of Wight, to the chapel of Knighton, Isle of Wight, vacant by the death of John Russel, last chaplain, at the presentation of Theobald de Gorges, knight, patron. He was canonically instituted. Letter sent to the archdeacon of Winchester for his induction.

Southwark, 13 November 1348

303. LETTER CONCERNING AN EXCHANGE OF BENEFICES from John bishop of Lincoln on behalf of Thomas de Croxford' rector of Farnham in the diocese of Lincoln and William de Burstall' perpetual vicar of Kingston. The archdeacon of Buckingham has held an enquiry, the results of which the bishop of Lincoln now transmits. The church of Farnham is at the presentation of Elizabeth de Burgo, the lady of Clare and the bishop is prepared to admit William de Burstall' to the church of Farnham on the resignation of Thomas. The bishop of Lincoln asks for a certificate from the bishop.

Old Temple, London, 6 November 1348

The bishop institutes William de Burstall' to the church of Farnham.

Southwark, 14 November 1348

Under the same date a certificate of the process was sent to the bishop of Lincoln.

304. ADMISSION of Thomas de Croxford' to the vicarage of the parish church of Kingston, vacant by the resignation of William de Burstall' on account of an exchange with the church of Farnham in the diocese of Lincoln. This is at the presentation of the king, the priory of Merton being in his hands. There will be obligation of residence, which Thomas has sworn to keep on his admission. The archdeacon of Surrey was informed for the induction.

Southwark, 14 November 1348

305. LICENCE granted to the prior and convent of Reigate to lease at farm the church of Dorking to Giles rector of Nutfield and Warner rector of Weston Colville in the diocese of Ely.

Southwark, 20 November 1348

74   **306.** COLLATION of Robert de Bosewyne of Orton, poor priest of the diocese of Lincoln, by provision of the apostolic see and at the presentation of the abbot and convent of Chertsey, to the perpetual vicarage of Egham in the diocese of Winchester, vacant by the death of Nicholas de Stokebysshop'. He will have the obligation of residence and ministry which he swore to maintain at his institution.

Southwark, 12 December 1348

Letters sent to the vicar of Weybridge and to the parish priest of Chertsey for his induction.

307. EXCHANGE OF BENEFICES WITHIN THE DIOCESE: John called the Mareschal priest becomes rector of Eversley at the resignation of Gilbert atte Mulle. John had been presented to Cliddesden at the presentation of M. Nicholas Haghema patron.
Similarly at that date Gilbert was admitted to the church of Cliddesden, vacant at the resignation of John, exchanging for Eversley at the presentation of John de Valoyns, patron. Letters to the archdeacon [of Winchester] for the induction.

Southwark, 16 December 1348

308. ADMISSION of Thomas atte Berton' deacon to the chapel of Frobury at the free resignation of John called the Mareschal of Frobury, the last rector. The chapel is at the presentation of Henry de Loksele, patron. Letter sent to the archdeacon of Winchester for the induction.

Southwark, 16 December 1348

309. ADMISSION of M. Edmund Morteyn priest, in the person of John Philip rector of the church of Langton in the diocese of Lincoln his proctor, to the church of Fordingbridge, vacant by the death of Baldwin de Mohann and at the presentation of Ralph baron of Stafford, patron. Letter sent to the archdeacon of Winchester for the induction.

Southwark, 21 December 1348

310. DISPENSATION to be absent for study granted for one year to Ralph de Gatesbury rector of Ockham with licence to lease at farm the fruits of the church.

Southwark, 18 December 1348

311. COMMENDATION of the church of Hursley for its evident benefit to William de Bathe priest, in whom the bishop has full confidence.

Southwark, 14 December 1348.

Letter to M. John de Ware sequestrator-general for the induction.

312. PRESENTATION of M. John de Ware clerk by the bishop to the church of Bishopstone in the diocese of Salisbury, with the customary letter to the bishop of that diocese.

Southwark, 22 December 1348

313. COMMENDATION of the church or precentory of St Mary Southampton, of the bishop's collation now vacant, for its evident benefit, to John Payn priest, in whose industry the bishop has full confidence.

Southwark, 23 December 1348

Letter to John de Ware sequestrator and to the dean of Southampton for the induction.

75   **314.** ADMISSION of Adam de Derneford' priest to the parish church of Peniton Mewsey vacant by the death of its last rector, at the presentation of John de Wynton', patron. Letter for the induction written to the archdeacon of Winchester.

Southwark, 25 December 1348

315. ADMISSION of John de Sandfeld clerk to the parish church of Elden at the presentation of Laurence de Brembeschete, patron. Letter to the archdeacon of Winchester for the induction.

Farnham, 5 January 1349

316. ADMISSION of John Devercy priest to the vicarage of the chapel in Carisbrooke Castle, Isle of Wight, at the presentation of the abbot and convent of Quarr. He will be a perpetual vicar with obligation of residence according to the constitutions. Letter to the archdeacon of Winchester for the induction.

Farnham, 7 January 1349

317. INSTITUTION of Thomas de Stannford' clerk to be rector of St Pancras, Winchester, of the bishop's collation. Letter written to M. John de Ware sequestrator-general and Thomas rector of St Maurice in the city of Winchester for the induction.

Farnham, 7 January 1349

318. MEMORANDUM. INSTITUTION to the rectory of Binstead, Isle of Wight, of the bishop's collation, of Madoc de Cheddarne of Usk, priest.

Farnham, 1 October 1348

Under that date a letter was written to the rector of Newchurch and to the dean of the Island for the induction.

319. EXCHANGE OF BENEFICES WITHIN THE DIOCESE: To the church of Rowner vacant by the resignation of David Boun, the bishop admits Richard de Louth, rector of the church of Hambledon. The patron of Rowner is Maurice de Breon, knight.

Farnham, 8 January 1349

Letter sent to the archdeacon of Winchester for the induction.

320. COLLATION of the vicarage of Hambledon, vacant by the resignation of Richard de Louth, to David Boun by way of exchange for the church of Rowner. He took the oath for residence.

Farnham, 8 January 1349

Letter sent to the rector of Meonstoke for the induction.

321. LETTER CONCERNING AN EXCHANGE OF BENEFICES sent to Robert bishop of Salisbury. William de Farlee rector of Steeple Langford, in the diocese of Salisbury, and William de Meone rector of Houghton wish to exchange benefices. The bishop of Winchester approves and is prepared to admit William de Farlee to the church of Houghton, reserving to himself the induction and the oath.

Southwark, 16 December 1348

76

The bishop of Salisbury has examined the case, accepts the resignation of William de Farlee and confers the church on William de Meone.

Ramsbury, 22 December 1348

Letters sent to M. John de Ware, sequestrator, and Thomas de Houleston' rector of St Maurice, Winchester, for the induction.

Southwark, 26 December 1348

322. COLLATION of the church of Houghton by way of exchange. Henry de Forde is collated to the church of Houghton, vacant by the free resignation of William de Farlee, with the provostship of the chapel of St Elizabeth near Winchester. The bishop institutes Henry canonically to the church of Houghton.

Esher, 1 January 1349

Letter to M. John de Ware, sequestrator-general, and Thomas de Houleston' rector of St Maurice for the induction.

323. COMMENDATION of the provostship of the chapel of St Elizabeth, for its evident benefit, to Henry de Forde rector of Houghton in whose loyalty and prudence the bishop has every confidence.

Esher, 1 January 1349

Letters to M. John the sequestrator and the above-mentioned rector for the induction.

324. COLLATION to William de Farlee priest of the church of Hursley, vacant by the death of Hugh de Welewyk, last rector. He was canonically instituted.
Letters to M. John de Ware sequestrator and to M. Thomas de Houleston for the induction.

Esher, 2 January 1349

325. ADMISSION of Geoffrey de Brokhampton acolyte to the church of Steventon, vacant by the resignation of Thomas de Insula. The patron is Joan widow of John de Roches, knight. He was canonically instituted.
Letter sent to the archdeacon of Winchester for the induction.

Farnham, 10 January 1349

326. ADMISSION of William de Wranby priest to the church of All Saints in the Vines (*de vineis*) near Winchester at the presentation of the abbess and convent of Winchester. He was canonically instituted and a letter was sent to the archdeacon of Winchester for the induction.

Farnham, 16 January 1349

327. ADMISSION of John de Merewe priest to the church of Peper Harrow, vacant by the death of Hugh de Mursele. The patron is Andrew Braunche, knight. He was canonically instituted and a letter written to the archdeacon of Surrey for the induction.

Farnham, 18 January 1349

328. ADMISSION of M. Walter de Sevenhampton clerk to the church of Baughurst, vacant by the death of M. Roger de Breynton'. He was instituted and a letter was written to the parish priest of Baughurst for the induction of M. Walter.

Farnham, 5 January 1349

329. COLLATION of the church of Baughurst to Richard de Hampton' priest, vacant by the resignation of M. Walter de Sevenhampton, by exchange for the church of Worting. Letter to the parish priest of the same place for the induction.

Farnham, 10 January 1349

330. ADMISSION of M. Walter de Sevenhampton clerk to the church of Worting, vacant by the resignation of Richard de Hampton' late rector, by exchange with the church of Baughurst. The patrons are the abbot and convent of Hyde. Walter was canonically admitted and the archdeacon of Winchester informed for the induction.

Farnham, 10 January 1349

331. ADMISSION of William de Ware clerk to the church of St Mary Magdalen, Bermondsey in the diocese of Winchester, vacant, at the presentation of the prior and convent of St Saviour, Bermondsey. He was canonically instituted; a letter was sent to the archdeacon of Surrey for the induction

Esher, 22 January 1349

332. WITH THE PRESENT INCREASING MORTALITY the bishop must provide for the needs of his flock. Knowing the prudence of Walter atte Hulle, the bishop entrusts to him the custody and care of the vicarage of Wandsworth, now vacant by the death of John de Langedon, until 1 February next.

Esher, 14 January 1349

333. DURING A VACANCY the bishop is custodian of churches and their revenues. The church of Fordingbridge is now vacant. By devolution the bishop collates the perpetual vicarage to Robert de Ruwe, with obligation of residence according to the constitutions.

Farnham, 9 January 1349

77

334. TO THE PRIORS OF MERTON AND SOUTHWARK the bishop states that in the register of the church of Winchester he finds that Adam de Orleton entrusted to Thomas de Bradwardyn, then chancellor of St Paul's, London, the provision by apostolic authority for William son of (*nato*) Richard de Wynewyk, poor priest of the diocese of Lincoln, of an ecclesiastical benefice with or without cure of souls, at the collation of the priory of Bermondsey. At an enquiry William was declared to be of praisworthy life, as the rescript demands, deserving of a benefice when vacant.

Farnham, 29 March 1345

Since M. Thomas was prevented from executing this commission, the bishop now entrusts this mandate, in virtue of obedience to the apostolic see, to the priors of Merton and Southwark.

Farnham, 8 January 1349

335. COLLATION of the church of St Martin outside Westgate in Winchester to Mielus son of John Boger of Usk. He was canonically instituted and a letter was written to the archdeacon of Winchester for the induction.

Farnham, 12 January 1349

336. ADMISSION of Geoffrey Stibb priest to the vicarage of the parish of Farnham, vacant by the death of James, the last vicar, at the presentation of M. Richard Vacham archdeacon of Surrey the perpetual vicar. He took the oath of residence at his canonical institution. The dean of Farnham was informed for his induction.

Esher, 26 January 1349

78   **337.** COLLATION BY APOSTOLIC AUTHORITY of William Gaterugg' of Alresford, poor clerk of the diocese, at the presentation of the abbot and convent of Hyde, to the perpetual vicarage of Alton. He will have the obligation of residence for which he has taken the oath.

Esher, 29 January

Letters sent to the dean of Alton and the rector of Chawton for the induction.

338. INSTITUTION of Bartholomew Bradele priest to the perpetual vicarage of Farnham, vacant after the free resignation of Geoffrey Stibb, by exchange for the vicarage of Shalden. M. Richard Vacham, archdeacon of Surrey is the patron. There will be obligation of residence, which he swore to keep at his canonical institution.

Esher, 30 January 1349

339. ADMISSION of Geoffrey Stibb priest to the church of Shalden, vacant by the resignation of Bartholomew Bradele, by exchange for Farnham. The patrons are the prior and convent of Southwark. The archdeacon of Winchester has been informed for the induction.

Esher, 30 January 1349

340. INSTITUTION of Philip Payn priest to the vicarage of the prebendal church of Wherwell, at the presentation of Nicholas Talemache prebend of the prebendal church. There will be obligation of residence, for which Philip has taken the oath. The archdeacon of Winchester has been informed for the induction.

Esher, 31 January 1349

341. COLLATION of the chantry in the abbey church of St Mary in Winchester to Walter de Edyndon' priest by M. Robert de Wambergh, lately archdeacon of Wells. He will become the perpetual chaplain according to the constitutions of the chantry.

Esher, 1 February 1349

342. ADMISSION of Thomas Daniel priest, in the person of John Wyn his proctor, to the vicarage of St Bartholomew *in atrio* of the monastery of Hyde, patrons. There will be obligation of residence according to the constitutions which Thomas swore to keep. Letter to the archdeacon of Winchester for the induction.

Esher, 2 February 1349

343. MANDATE TO THE PRIOR OF THE CATHEDRAL CHURCH of Winchester to effect the collation or presentation of a benefice by the abbot and convent of Hyde, to John Bysshop', poor clerk of the diocese, as provided by the apostolic see and directed to Adam de Orleton, late bishop. He had ordered an enquiry into the life of John, which found him to be of good and praiseworthy living. By virtue of obedience to the apostolic authority, he should be provided for, the bishop giving full powers of canonical coercion.

Esher, 5 February 1349

344. INSTITUTION of M. Henry Nuggh' priest to the church of West Tytherley, vacant by the death of Thomas de Escote, at the presentation of Hugh de Escote knight, patron. Letter to the archdeacon of Winchester for the induction.

Esher, 5 February 1349

79   **345.** COLLATION BY APOSTOLIC AUTHORITY of the church of Clapham, vacant, to Peter son of John at the Spring (*nato Johannis ad fontem*), poor priest, at the presentation of the prior and convent of Merton. Letter to John de Stratton' rector of the church of St Olave near the Tower of London and to Ralph Aleyn and Stephen Wyle priests for the induction.

Esher, 2 February 1349

346. ADMISSION of John de Baddeby priest to the church of Woodmansterne, vacant by the death of John de Dallynge last rector, at the presentation of the prior and convent of Southwark, patrons. Letter for the induction to the archdeacon of Surrey.

Esher, 7 February 1349

347. ADMISSION of Robert de Kynebell' priest to the chapel of Pittleworth *curata*, vacant by the death of Symon last rector, at the presentation of Nicholas de Haywode patron for this turn. Letter to the archdeacon of Winchester for the induction.

Esher, 7 February 1349

348. ADMISSION of Richard de Foncel priest to the perpetual vicarage of the church of Nether Wallop, vacant by the death of the last vicar, at the presentation of Henry de Fulham, rector of Wallop and patron of the vicarage; with residence according to the constitutions, which he swore to keep. Letter to the archdeacon of Winchester for the induction.

Esher, 7 February 1349

349. ADMISSION of Hugh Lysewy clerk to the chapel of the Holy Trinity at Knighton, Isle of Wight, vacant at the death of Richard Cristyan last rector, at the presentation of Theobald de Gorges patron. Letter for the induction to the archdeacon of Winchester.

Esher, 9 February 1349

350. COLLATION of the vicarage of St Mary Bourne and Prior's Hurstbourne, vacant by the death of the last vicar to Walter Passelewe priest, with obligation of residence according to the constitutions which he swore to keep. Letter to the vicar of Whitchurch and to the parochial chaplain of that place for the induction.

Esher, 9 February 1349

351. ADMISSION of Thomas de Eykeryng' acolyte, to the church of Abbotts Ann, vacant by the death of Reginald the last rector, at the presentation of the abbot and convent of Hyde, patrons. Letter for the induction to the archdeacon of Winchester.

Esher, 11 February 1349

352. ADMISSION of Richard le Feure priest to the parochial church of Monxton, vacant by the death of Robert last rector, at the presentation of Richard de Beausenall', prior of Ogbourne, patron by grant of the king on account of the war. Letter sent to the archdeacon of Winchester for the induction.

Esher, 10 February 1349

353. COMMISSION TO ENQUIRE INTO AN EXCHANGE OF BENEFICES from John archbishop of Canterbury. Thomas de Subbay of the church of Leaveland in the diocese of Canterbury and John Whiterik' of Eston' near Stannford, vicar of the church of Camberwell in the diocese of Winchester seek to exchange benefices. The archbishop approves; John was presented to the church of Leaveland by King Edward; the customary enquiry has been held and the process sent for the bishop's consideration, with the resignation of Thomas, and in the event to approve of John Whiterik' for the church of Leaveland. The bishop will sent the customary certificate.

London, 8 February 1349

80

The bishop sends his approbation of the exchange, with oath and induction reserved.

Esher, 15 February 1349

354. INSTITUTION of Thomas de Subby' priest to the vicarage of Camberwell, at the presentation of the prior and convent of St Saviour of Bermondsey, patrons, to be perpetual vicar with obligation of residence for which he took the oath. Letter to the archdeacon of Surrey for the induction.

Esher, 15 February 1349.

355. BY EXCHANGE OF BENEFICES the bishop confers on John le Diare priest the 'priestly office' in the chapel of St Elizabeth near Winchester, vacant by the resignation of John de Bexgrave, by exchange for the vicarage of Kingsclere, which John had first obtained. Letter to Henry de Forde provost of the chapel to install him according to the directions of John de Pontissara, the founder.

Southwark, 11 January 1349.

356. ADMISSION of Thomas de Heyford priest to the church of Tatsfield, vacant by the death of Thomas de Hoo last rector, at the presentation of Thomas Recher knight, patron. Letter for the induction sent to the archdeacon of Surrey.

Esher, 17 February 1349

357. LETTER from John bishop of Lincoln to Robert Thursteyn priest. By commission of the bishop of Winchester he confers on Robert the perpetual office of subdeacon in the chapel of St. Elizabeth near Winchester, vacant by the resignation of John de Sidebrok', by reason of an exchange for the vicarage of Leigh in the diocese of Lincoln. By the authority of the bishop of Winchester, he accepts the resignation and institutes him.

Fingest, 28 January 1349

Letter to the commendatory of the chapel for the admission of Robert de Thurstayn.

Esher, 30 January 1349

358. INSTITUTION of Henry de Schitlyngton' priest of the vicarage of Banstead, vacant by the death of Thomas the last vicar, at the presentation of the prior and convent of Southwark, patrons, with obligation of residence. Letter sent to the archdeacon of Surrey for the induction.

Esher, 17 February 1349

359. INSTITUTION of Walter Passelewe priest to the vicarage of Fordingbridge, vacant at the resignation of Robert Rue last vicar, by exchange with the vicarage of St Mary Bourne and Priors Hurstbourne, which Walter had first obtained at the presentation of Edmund Morteyn rector of the church of Fordingbridge; with obligation of residence which

Walter swore to keep. Letter to the archdeacon of Winchester for the induction.

Esher, 18 February 1349

360. COLLATION of the vicarage of St Mary Bourne and Priors Hurstbourne, vacant by the resignation of the said Walter by exchange, to Robert Rue priest, with obligation of residence according to the constitutions, which Walter swore to keep. Letter to the vicar of Whitchurch for the induction.

Esher, 18 February 1349

81

361. AS CUSTODIAN OF VACANT BENEFICES in the archdiaconate of Winchester, the bishop confers on John le Queor priest the rectory of the parish church of Botley, vacant, in the bishop's custody through the vacancy of the provostship of the chapel of St Elizabeth. He institutes him canonically.

Esher, 18 February 1349

Letter for the induction to the archdeacon of Winchester.

362. COLLATION BY APOSTOLIC AUTHORITY of William de Wortynge poor clerk of the diocese to the church of Wymering, at the presentation of the prior and convent of Southwick, by apostolic provision. Letters for the induction sent to Stephen de Lekford subprior of Southwick and to Robert rector of Wellsworth.

Esher, 20 February 1349

363. ADMISSION of Erard de Pratell', alien, to the parish church of St George next the Bar, Southwark, vacant by the death of William the last rector, at the presentation of the prior and convent of St Saviour, Bermondsey, patrons. Letter to the archdeacon of Surrey for the induction.

Esher, 20 February 1349

364. ADMISSION of Peter Morteyn priest to the church of Bedhampton, at the presentation of King Edward as guardian of the heir of Edward earl of Kent, deceased. Letter to the archdeacon of Winchester for his induction, or else M. John Trigontras his proctor.

Esher, 23 February 1349

365. ADMISSION of Henry de Guldeford' priest to the vicarage of St Mary, Porchester, vacant by the death of Richard Baron last vicar, at the presentation of the prior and convent of Southwick, patrons. The perpetual vicar has the obligation of residence according to the constitutions, for which he has taken the oath. Letter to the archdeacon of Winchester for the induction.

Esher, 27 February 1349

366. ADMISSION of William Gurgan priest to be perpetual chaplain of Freefolk Syfrewast, at the presentation of Henry Husee, knight, patron. Letter to the archdeacon of Winchester for the induction.

Esher, 26 February 1349

367. COLLATION BY APOSTOLIC AUTHORITY of the vicarage of Egham, vacant, on Adam atte Lythe priest, at the presentation of the abbot and convent of Chertsey. Letter to the vicar of Chertsey for the induction.

Esher, 25 February 1349

368. COLLATION BY APOSTOLIC AUTHORITY of the church of East Clandon on Robert de Schire poor priest of the diocese, at the presentation of the abbot and convent of Chertsey. Letter to the dean of Guildford for the induction.

Esher, 28 February 1349

369. COLLATION of the church of Cheriton on John de Edyngdon' clerk. The church is vacant by the death of M. John de Usk' last rector. Letters to Henry de Forde rector of Houghton for his induction or his proctor.

Esher, 2 March 1349

82   **370.** INSTITUTION of John de Dorkecestria priest to the vicarage of the prebendal church of Longparish, vacant by the death of Robert le Veysi last vicar, at the presentation of Philip de Weston' prebendary of the prebend of Middleton in the monastery of the nuns of Wherwell. He will be perpetual vicar with obligation of residence according to the constitution which John swore to keep. Letter to the archdeacon of Winchester for the induction.

Esher, 27 February 1349

371. ADMISSION of Ralph Tristram acolyte to the church of Greatham, vacant by the death of the last rector, at the presentation of Nicholas Devenisch', patron. Letter sent to the archdeacon of Winchester for the induction.

Esher, 2 March 1349

372. ADMISSION of William de Walcote priest to the church of St George in the city of Winchester, vacant by the death of Roger Iwon the last rector, at the presentation of the abbot and convent of Hyde, patrons. Letter to the archdeacon of Winchester for the induction.

Esher, 2 March 1349

373. ADMISSION of Symon Michel priest to the vicarage of the church of Hayling, vacant by the death of Richard de Heselerton' last vicar; at the presentation of King Edward, patron on account of the war for the priory of Hayling. As perpetual vicar he will have the obligation of residence according to the constitutions which he swore to keep at his institution. Letter to the archdeacon of Winchester for the induction.

Esher, 3 March 1349

374. ADMISSION of M. Henry de Lutegarshale acolyte to the church of South Tidworth, vacant by the death of Richard the last rector, at the presentation of Roger Normannd', knight, patron. Letter to the archdeacon of Winchester for the induction.

Esher, 3 March 1349

375. ADMISSION of Robert Ballok priest to the vicarage of the prebendal church of Goodworth Clatford, vacant, at the presentation of John de Shaftebury, canon of the prebendal church of Wherwell and prebendary of the church of Goodworth as patron. He will have the obligation of residence according to the constitutions, for which he took the oath. Letter to the archdeacon of Winchester for the induction.

Esher, 4 March 1349

376. ADMISSION of Alan de Notyngham priest to the vicarage of Crondall, vacant by the death of Hugh the last vicar, at the presentation of Raymond Pelegrini, rector of the church of Crondall, patron. He will be perpetual vicar with obligation of residence according to the constitutions, for which he took the oath. Letter for the induction to the archdeacon of Winchester.

Esher, 7 March 1349

377. ADMISSION of John de Toneton' priest to the church of Tunworth, vacant by the death of M. Roger de Toneton' last rector, at the presentation of John de Grey of Codnor, knight, patron. Letter to the archdeacon of Winchester for the induction.

Esher, 6 March 1349

378. ADMISSION of Robert de Hampton' clerk to the church of St Laurence in the city of Winchester, vacant, at the presentation of the abbot and convent of Hyde, patrons. Letter for the induction to the archdeacon of Winchester.

Esher, 8 March 1349

379. PRESENTATION to the church of Bleadon, in the diocese of Bath and Wells, of Thomas de Bokenhulle priest, the bishop of Winchester being the patron.

Esher 7 March 1349

380. INSTITUTION of John de Monlisch' priest to the vicarage of Shorwell, Isle of Wight, vacant by the death of Richard de Upton, at the presentation of Reginald de Wylinton rector of Shorwell. He will have the obligation of residence according to the constitutions for which he took the oath. Letter for the induction to the archdeacon of Winchester.

Esher, 9 March 1349

381. INSTITUTION of John Groyn priest to the vicarage of Whitsbury, at the presentation of the prior and convent of Breamore, patrons. He will be the perpetual vicar with obligation of residence according to the constitutions, for which he took the oath. Letter to the archdeacon of Winchester for the induction.

Esher, 7 March 1349

83   **382.** ADMISSION of John le Frye clerk to the chapel of Yaverland, Isle of Wight, vacant by the death of William, last rector, with cure of souls at the presentation of Alianora widow of Theobald Russel, knight, patron. Letter sent to the archdeacon of Winchester for the induction.

Esher, 10 March 1349

383. ADMISSION of M. John de Neuport acolyte to the church of Puttenham, vacant by the death of John Puppe, last rector, at the presentation of the prior and convent of St Mary without Bishopsgate, London. Letter for the induction to the archdeacon of Surrey.

Esher, 10 March 1349

384. ADMISSION of William de Bokkebrugg' clerk to the church of Farley Chamberlayne, vacant by the death of Robert Froumond last rector, at the presentation of Mary de Langressch' patroness. Letter to the archdeacon of Winchester for the induction.

Esher, 10 March 1349

385. ADMISSION of Ralph de Fernham priest to the vicarage of Monk Sherborne, vacant by the death of Henry last vicar, at the presentation of King Edward, the priory of Sherborne being in his hands on account of the war. He will be perpetual vicar with obligation of residence, in accordance with the constitutions, which he swore to keep. Letter for the induction to the archdeacon of Winchester.

Esher, 11 March 1349

386. ADMISSION of Adam de Sunnynges priest to the church of Holy Cross, Southampton, vacant, at the presentation of the king, the priory of St Denys being vacant. Letter to the archdeacon of Winchester for his induction.

Esher, 12 March 1349

387. ADMISSION of John de Hursele priest to the vicarage of East Wellow, vacant, at the presentation of the abbot and convent of Netley, patrons. He will be perpetual vicar with obligation of residence according to the constitutions which he has sworn to keep. Letter for the induction to the archdeacon of Winchester.

Esher, 16 March 1349

388. ADMISSION of Reginald de Goderynton' *in forma immediata prescripta* to the vicarage of the church of Leatherhead, vacant by the death of Thomas last vicar, at the presentation of the prior and convent of Leeds, patrons, to be perpetual vicar with obligation of residence. Letter to the archdeacon of Surrey for the induction.

Esher, 16 March 1349

389. PROVISION BY APOSTOLIC AUTHORITY of a benefice for Robert Henry de Bukyngham, poor priest of the Lincoln diocese, at the presentation of the prior and convent of St Mary Spital without Bishopsgate, London. The bishop entrusts the matter to the official of Winchester, in obedience to the apostolic see. The inquisition had been ordered by Adam de

Orleton, late bishop, and carried through by M. William de Bergeveny, late chancellor of Oxford.

Southwark, 16 March 1349

390. ADMISSION of Roger de Wyke priest to the church of St Mary of Burgh, in the diocese of Winchester, vacant by the death of William de Fairford last rector, at the presentation of the prior and convent of Southwark patrons. Letter for the induction to the archdeacon of Surrey.

Southwark, 17 March 1349

391. ADMISSION of Richard de Guldeford' to the vicarage of the church of Kingsclere, vacant, at the presentation of the prior and convent of Bisham, patrons—to be perpetual vicar with obligation of residence according to the constitutions, for which he took the oath at his institution. Letters to the archdeacon of Winchester and to the dean of Basingstoke for the induction.

Southwark, 17 March 1349

84 **392.** INSTITUTION of William de Blytheworth' priest to the perpetual chantry established in honour Of Our Lady in the parish church of Lambeth by Thomas Romayn late of the city of London. There is an annual rent of 6 marks from certain tenements as endowment. At the presentation of John, archbishop of Canterbury, patron as ordained in the will of the deceased founder. William is canonically instituted as perpetual chaplain. Letter to the prior and subprior of St Mary, Southwark, and to the vicar of St Olave for the induction.

Esher, 18 March 1349

393. INSTITUTION of Henry de Forde priest to the church of Freshwater, Isle of Wight, vacant by the resignation of John de Beautre last rector, by exchange for the church of Houghton, which Henry had first obtained, at the presentation of the king, holding the temporalities of the abbot of Lyre on account of the war. Letter to the archdeacon of Winchester and to the dean of the Island for the induction.

Esher, 18 March 1349

394. COLLATION of the church of Houghton on John de Beautre priest, vacant by the resignation of Henry de Forde, by exchange of benefices. Letter to the archdeacon of Winchester and to the dean of Somborne for the induction.

Esher, 18 March 1349

395. ADMISSION of John de Boxgrave priest to the church of Kimpton, vacant, at the presentation of John de Edyngdon' patron. Letter to the archdeacon of Winchester and to the dean of Andover for the induction.

Esher, 18 March 1349

396. ADMISSION of Roger de Kerselawe priest to the vicarage of Egham, vacant by the death of Adam Sare, at the presentation of the abbot and convent of Chertsey, patrons, to be perpetual vicar with obligation of residence, for which he took the oath. Letter for the induction to the archdeacon of Surrey.

Esher, 19 March 1349

397. ADMISSION of M. William de Polinorva deacon to the church of Witley, at the presentation of Philippa the queen, patron. Letter for the induction to the archdeacon of Surrey.

Esher, 19 March 1349

398. ADMISSION of Richard de Weston' clerk to the church of West Clandon, vacant by the death of John le Wyse, last rector, at the presentation of Margery widow of William de Weston, patron. Letter for the induction to the archdeacon of Surrey.

Priory of *Novi Loci*, 20 March 1349

399. ADMISSION of Adam de Offham priest to the perpetual vicarage of Amport, vacant by the death of William de Stedeham the last vicar, at the presentation of the dean and chapter of Chichester, patrons. He took the oath of obligation to residence. Letter for the induction to the archdeacon of Winchester.

Farnham, 21 March 1349

400. COLLATION on William Wolf' of Edington clerk the sacerdotal office in the chapel of Marwell by the bishop, who instituted him into the perpetual office. Letter to Henry de Forde rector of Freshwater for the induction.

Farnham, 22 March 1349

401. ADMISSION of Hugh Broun priest to the church of East Clandon vacant, at the presentation of of the abbot and convent of Chertsey, patrons. Letter to the archdeacon of Surrey for the induction.

Farnham, 24 March 1349

402. ADMISSION of William Elyot priest to the church of Cliddesden, vacant by the death of Gilbert the last rector, at the presentation of John de Valoyns, patron. Letter to the archdeacon of Winchester for the induction.

Farnham, 22 March 1349

85 **403.** ADMISSION of William de Melton' priest to the church of Streatham, vacant, at the presentation of fr. Richard de Beausenall', prior of Ogbourne, procurator of the abbey of Bec Helewyn, diocese of Rouen, holding at farm by grant of the king. Letter for the induction to the archdeacon of Surrey.

Farnham, 24 March 1349

404. ADMISSION of Thomas de Eltesle priest to the church of Lambeth, vacant by the death of John de Colonia' last rector, at the presentation of John de Offord' archbishop confirmed of Canterbury, patron of the church of Lambeth. Letter to the archdeacon of Surrey for the induction.

Farnham, 24 March 1349

405. ADMISSION of Walter de Freland clerk to the church of Ockham, vacant by the death of Ralph de Gatesbury last rector, at the presentation of Ralph baron of Stafford, patron. Letter for the induction to the archdeacon of Surrey.

Farnham, 25 March 1349

406. COLLATION of William Wolf de Edyngdon clerk to the church of Houghton, vacant by the resignation of John de Beautre, by exchange of benefices for the chapel of Marwell, which he had first obtained. Henry de Forde was requested for the induction.

Same date, collation of John de Beautre to the sacerdotal office at Marwell. Letter for induction to the same Henry.

Farnham, 25 March 1349

407. ADMISSION of Robert de Offynton priest to the vicarage of the church of Addington, vacant, at the presentation of the prior and convent of Southwark, patrons, to be perpetual vicar with obligation of residence, for which he took the oath. Letter for the induction to the archdeacon of Surrey.

Farnham, 25 March 1349

408. ADMISSION of Hugh Corteys priest to the church of Rowner, vacant, at the presentation of Maurice de Bruyn, patron. Letter to the archdeacon of Winchester for the induction.

Farnham, 28 March 1349

409. COLLATION of the church of Burghclere to John de Beautre priest, by exchange, vacant at the resignation of William Jolyf' who takes the chapel of Marwell. Letter for the induction to Henry de Forde, rector of Freshwater.

Farnham, 28 March 1349

410. ADMISSION of Nicholas Waspail clerk to the church of Hartley Wespall, vacant, at the presentation of John Waspail, patron. Letter for the induction to the archdeacon of Winchester.

Farnham, 28 March 1349

411. ADMISSION of M. John de Totteford' clerk to the church of Long Ditton, vacant, at the presentation of the prior and convent of Merton, patrons. Letter for the induction to the dean of Ewell.

Farnham, 28 March 1349

412. ADMISSION of John Abban priest to the vicarage of Milford, vacant, at the presentation of the subprior and convent of Christchurch Twynham, who are without a prior. He will be perpetual vicar with obligation of residence which he swore to keep. Letter to the archdeacon of Winchester for the induction.

Farnham, 29 March 1349

413. ADMISSION of Philip de Nassyngton priest to the church of Faringdon, vacant, at the presentation of John bishop of Exeter. Letters for the induction to the archdeacon of Winchester and to the dean of Alton.

Farnham, 31 March 1349

86   **414.** ADMISSION of Henry atte Dene clerk to the church of Winslade, vacant, at the presentation of M. Nicholas Hagheman, patron. Letter for the induction to the archdeacon of Winchester and to the dean of Basingstoke.

Farnham, 31 March 1349

415. INSTITUTION of William Danndely priest to the vicarage of the church of Portsea, vacant, at the presentation of the prior and convent of St Mary, Southwick, patrons. To be perpetual vicar with obligation of residence, for which he took the oath. Letter for the induction to the archdeacon of Winchester.

Farnham, 1 April 1349

416. COLLATION by the bishop of the guardianship of the hospital of St John of Fordingbridge, vacant, on William Wyse priest. Letters for the induction to the rector and perpetual vicar of Fordingbridge.

Farnham, 28 March 1349

417. ADMISSION of Richard de Polyngfold priest to one half of the church of Abinger, vacant by the death of William de Jarpenvill' last rector, at the presentation of Thomas de Jarpenville patron of the said half. Letter for the induction to the archdeacon of Surrey.

Farnham, 1 April 1349

418. ADMISSION of Peter de Berondon' clerk to the half of the church of Abinger, vacant by the death of Richard de Folefenne last rector of the half, at the presentation of Thomas de Syndlesham, patron of the half. Letter to the archdeacon of Surrey for the induction.

Farnham, 2 April 1349

419. ADMISSION of John Husee priest to the church of Over Wallop, vacant, at the presentation of Richard de Wallop, patron. Letter for the induction to the archdeacon of Winchester.

Farnham, 2 April 1349

420. ADMISSION of John Kyng of Langley Marish deacon to the vicarage of Godshill, Isle of Wight, vacant, at the presentation of king Edward, the temporalities of the abbey of Lyre being in his hands on account of the war. To be perpetual vicar according to the constitutions, for which he took the oath. Letter for the induction to the archdeacon of Winchester.

Farnham, 3 April 1349

421. ADMISSION of Ralph de Stapenhull' priest to the church of St Laurence, Southampton, vacant, at the presentation of the prior and convent of St Denys, patrons. Letter to the archdeacon of Winchester for the induction.

Farnham, 4 April 1349

422. ADMISSION of William de Hayton' priest to the vicarage of Ashstead, vacant, at the presentation of John de Broughton', the rector. To be perpetual vicar with obligation of residence, for which he took the oath. Letter to the archdeacon of Surrey for the induction.

Farnham, 4 April 1349

423. ADMISSION of John de Childevill' priest to the vicarage of the church of Leatherhead, vacant, at the presentation of the prior and convent of Leeds, patrons. To be perpetual vicar with obligation of residence for which he took the oath. Letter to the archdeacon of Surrey for the induction.

Farnham, 4 April 1349

424. COLLATION by the bishop of the church or precentory of St Mary, Southampton, at his collation, on John Payn priest. Letter to M. John de Ware sequestrator of the archdeaconry of Winchester for the induction.

Farnham, 10 January 1349

87 **425.** PROCESS OF THE ENQUIRY INTO THE ELECTION of the prior of Christchurch Twynham, entrusted to M. John de Usk' chancellor, held in the church of Cobham. After hearing how fr. William Tyrenache, augustinian canon of Christchurch, was canonically elected prior, the bishop confirms the election, entrusting to him the administration of the priory.

Cobham, 7 March 1349

426. CONFIRMATION OF THE ELECTION of the new prior, vacant by the death of fr. Robert de Legh', addressed to fr. William de Tyrenache, granting him the cure of souls and the administration.

Cobham, 7 March 1349

427. TO THE SUBPRIOR AND CONVENT the bishop announces that he has confirmed the election; reminding the canons of the reverence and obedience now due to him and his orders.

Same date

428. TO THE NOBLE PATRONESS of the priory, Catherine, countess of Salisbury, the bishop announces his confirmation of the election.

Same date

429. TO THE ARCHDEACON OF WINCHESTER the bishop asks that the new prior be inducted to his stall in choir and his place in chapter, carrying out all that is customary.

Same date

430. PRESENTATION of M. Thomas de Bokenhull' to the church of Bleadon in the diocese of Bath and Wells, under the patronage of the bishop of Winchester.

Esher, 7 March 1349

88

431. MANDATE to the official of the archdeaconry of Winchester and the dean of Southampton to enquire into the manner of the election of fr. Richard de Stanfeld, canon of St Denys near Southampton, as prior and to cite those who may wish to object to appear in the conventual church of St Mary, Southwark, Monday after the 2nd Sunday of Lent, viz 9 March next. The bishop will be informed of the names of objectors.

Esher, 28 February 1349

432. PROCESS OF THE ELECTION TO THE CONVENTUAL CHURCH OF ST DENYS near Southampton. Before the bishop in the church of St Mary Southwark, M. John de Wolveleye chancellor reported his findings. The bishop then declared fr. Richard de Stannfeld to be canonically elected as successor to fr. William de Warham deceased. Confirming the election he entrusted the new prior with the care of souls and administration.
Notification of the confirmation sent to the subprior and convent of St Denys for their obedience and to the King as patron of the priory, as sent out for the election of the prior of Christchurch Twynham.

Southwark, 9 March 1349

433. COLLATION of the provostship of the chapel of St Elizabeth near Winchester, vacant by the resignation of John son of William Wodelok', after an exchange of benefices for the church of Upham, now conferred upon John de Overton' priest. Letter for the induction to Thomas de Wolveleye.

Farnham, 6 April 1349

434. COLLATION by the bishop of the church of Upham on John son of William Wodelok' clerk, vacant by the resignation of John de Overton', by exchange for the provostship of the chapel of St Elizabeth. Letter sent to Thomas de Wolveleye for the induction.

Farnham, 6 April 1349

435. COLLATION by the bishop of the priestly office in the chapel of St Elizabeth, first granted to John de Overton but vacant by his resignation, now to William de Draicote priest, following the ordinance of John de Pontissara the founder. Letter to John de Overton to admit William to the priestly office.

Farnham, 7 April 1349

436. ADMISSION of William son of Symon de Craneslee priest to the vicarage of Hound, at the presentation of the king, the priory of Hamble being in his hands on account of the war. He will be perpetual vicar, for which he has taken the oath. Letter to the archdeacon of Winchester for the induction.

Farnham, 4 April 1349

89 **437.** ADMISSION of Gregory de Stokebrugg' priest to the vicarage of the church of Basingstoke, vacant by the death of Thomas the last vicar, at the presentation of the prior and convent of Selborne, patrons. He will be perpetual vicar, for which he took the oath. Letter for the induction to the archdeacon of Winchester.

Farnham, 7 April 1349

438. ADMISSION of Robert de Tonge priest to the vicarage of the church of Andover, vacant, at the presentation of King Edward, the priory of Andover being in his hands on account of war. He will be perpetual vicar according to the constitutions. Letter for the induction to the archdeacon of Winchester.

Farnham, 8 April 1349

439. ADMISSION of Richard Palmer priest to the vicarage of the church of Great Bookham, vacant, at the presentation of the abbot and convent of Chertsey, patrons. He will be perpetual vicar according to the constitutions. Letter to the archdeacon of Surrey for the induction.

Farnham, 9 April 1349

440. ADMISSION of John de Kent priest to be vicar of the church of Kingston, vacant, at the presentation of the prior and convent of Merton, patrons. He will be perpetual vicar according to the constitutions. Letter for the induction to the archdeacon of Surrey.

Farnham, 9 April 1349

441. ADMISSION of John le Tannere priest to the free chapel of Briddlesford, [Isle of Wight], vacant, at the presentation of Elizabeth del Isle patron. He was instituted as perpetual chaplain. The archdeacon of Winchester was informed for the induction.

Farnham, 9 April 1349

442. ADMISSION of William de Twyford chaplain to the chapel of Kingston, Isle of Wight, with some cure of souls (*aliqualiter curata*) at the presentation of John de Kyngeston, knight, patron. He was instituted as perpetual chaplain, the archdeacon of Winchester being informed for the induction.

Farnham, 9 April 1349

443. ADMISSION of Philip de Hoo clerk to be chapel of Whipstrode, vacant, at the presentation of Joan, widow of John des Roches, patron. Letter to the archdeacon of Winchester for the induction.

Farnham, 9 April 1349

444. LETTER CONCERNING AN EXCHANGE OF BENEFICES from the bishop to M. John de Lech' clerk, doctor of the decretals, rector of Hardres in the diocese of London under the jurisdiction of the archbishop of Canterbury.

Recently the apostolic see allowed him to hold two benefices. He had been canonically instituted to the parish church of North Waltham. He now seeks to exchange this for the church of Arreton, Isle of Wight, with M. John de Wolveleye clerk, who has resigned Arreton for North Waltham. The bishop admits him to the church of Arreton, which is at the presentation of the king, the priory of Carisbrooke being in his hands because of the war. Letters for the induction to the archdeacon of Winchester and to the dean of the Island.

Farnham, 10 April 1349

90

445. ADMISSION of William de Hascombe priest as vicar for the church of Arreton, before the institution of M. John de Leche as rector. The vicarage was vacant and at the presentation of M. John de Wolveleye the former rector of Arreton; he will be perpetual vicar according to the constitutions, which he swore to maintain. Letter for the induction to the archdeacon of Winchester.

Farnham, 7 April 1349

446. ADMISSION M. Nicholas de Wambergh' deacon to the vicarage of Micheldever, vacant, at the presentation of the abbot and convent of Hyde, patrons, to be perpetual vicar according to the constitutions of the legates, for which he took the oath. Letter for the induction to the archdeacon of Winchester.

Farnham, 13 April 1349

447. DISPENSATION for study granted to Nicholas Waspayl rector of Hartley Wespall clerk, for one year at some *studium generale* to advance to the orders he has not yet received.

Farnham, 13 April 1349

448. COMMISSION to the official of Winchester to admit Richard de Wyschawe to the vicarage of Sutton as presented by the prior and convent of Merton, to be a perpetual vicar.

Farnham, 13 April 1349

449. DISPENSATION granted for one year to Thomas de Eykerynge rector of Abbots Ann priest, to be at the service of John de Maxfeld clerk of the Forest.

Farnham, 13 April 1349

450. DISPENSATION for study granted for one year to John de Westclendon' subdeacon, rector of West Clendon, without obligation to proceed to further orders.

Farnham, 11 April 1349

451. ADMISSION of John Banylon priest to the vicarage of Catherington, vacant, at the presentation of the prioress and convent of Nuneaton, order of Fontevrault, patrons. To be perpetual vicar according to the constitutions, for which he took the oath. Letter for the induction to the archdeacon of Winchester.

Farnham, 14 April 1349

452. COLLATION by the bishop of the church of St Mary de Vallibus near Winchester on Thomas de Stannford clerk as rector. Letter for induction to the official of Winchester.

Farnham, 15 April 1349

453. COLLATION by the bishop of the church of North Waltham on Stephen de Schirefeld' priest as rector. Letter for the induction to the official of Winchester.

Farnham, 15 April 1349

454. DISPENSATION for study granted for one year to M. William de Polinorva rector of Witley priest.

Farnham, 15 April 1349

455. INSTITUTION of William atte Bee priest to the vicarage of Wanborough, vacant, at the presentation of the abbot and convent of Waverley, patrons. To be perpetual vicar according to the constitutions for which he took the oath. Letter to the archdeacon of Surrey for the induction.

Farnham, 16 April 1349

456. ADMISSION of Richard de Wyschawe priest to the chapel of East Parley, at the presentation of Maurice Bruyn knight, patron of the chapel, to be rector. Letter for the induction to the archdeacon of Winchester.

Farnham, 16 April 1349

457. PRESENTATION of M. John de Wolveleye to the church of Elingdon in the diocese of Salisbury, of the patronage of the bishop of Winchester.

Farnham, 11 April 1349

458. DISPENSATION for study granted to Richard de Weston' rector of East Clandon for one year without obligation of residence or proceeding to further orders, according to the constitutions.

Farnham, 11 April 1349

91   **459.** LETTER OF PROCLAMATION to the official of the archdeacon of Winchester and the dean of Somborne in the matter of the recent election of fr. Robert de Brommore subprior of Mottisfont as prior. They are to certify their findings to the bishop in the cathedral church the next lawful day for business after the feast of St George.

Farnham, 17 April 1349

460. MANDATE to the prior of the cathedral church and to the official of the bishop to examine the process of the election at Mottisfont, with full canonical powers, and then to report to the bishop.

Farnham, 17 April 1349

461. COLLATION by the bishop of the church of Meonstoke, vacant by the death of Robert called Clerc, the last rector, on William called Wolf of Edington subdeacon. He was canonically instituted and a letter sent to the rector of the church of Droxford and his chaplain for the induction.

Farnham, 18 April 1349

462. COLLATION by the bishop of the vicarage of the church of Hambledon on Madec de Chiddarne of Usk, priest, vacant. He will be perpetual vicar according to the constitutions which he swore to maintain. Letter to the vicar of East Meon and his chaplain for the induction.

Farnham, 18 April 1349

463. COLLATION by the bishop of the parish church of Cheriton on John de Edyngdon subdeacon, vacant. He was canonically instituted. Letter for the induction to John de Nubbeleygh' rector of Alresford, treasurer at Wolvesey.

Farnham, 18 April 1349

464. COLLATION by the bishop of the hospital of St Cross near Winchester on John de Edyngdon, subdeacon, without cure of souls, customarily so granted to secular clerks by earlier bishops. He was canonically instituted to this perpetual benefice. Letter for the induction to J' de Nubbelegh' rector of Alresford and treasurer at Wolvesey.

Farnham, 18 April 1349

465. COLLATION by the bishop of the parochial church of Bishopstoke, vacant, on Robert de Aspale, clerk, as rector. Letter for the induction to the provost of the chapel of St Elizabeth.

Farnham, 18 April 1349

466. PRESENTATION of Nicholas de Kyngeston' priest to the church of Buttermere, vacant, in the diocese of Salisbury, of the bishop's patronage.

Farnham, 18 April 1349

467. COLLATION by the bishop of the church of St Faith in Winchester, vacant, on Nicholas de Kyngeston', priest, instituting him as rector and writing to J' de Nubbelegh' for the induction.

Farnham, 18 April 1349

468. COLLATION by the bishop of the perpetual chantry situated in the manor chapel of Roger de Ticheborne, lately deceased, in the parish of Cheriton, endowed with certain rents by the same Roger, vacant. It is at the bishop's collation, as guardian of the heir and the lands of the said Roger, for this one turn.

Farnham, 18 April 1349

92 **469.** ADMISSION of Henry de Chippenham', priest, as rector of the church of Holy Cross, Southampton, vacant, at the presentation of the prior and convent of St Denys, patrons, with letter to the archdeacon of Winchester for the induction.

Southwark, 22 April 1349

470. ADMISSION of Roger Biret, priest, as rector of Merrow, vacant, at the presentation of the prioress and convent of St Margaret, Ivinghoe, patrons. Letter for the induction to the archdeacon of Surrey.

Southwark, 22 April 1349

471. ADMISSION of Roger de Lokynton', priest, as rector of the church of St Peter upon Cheshull in Winchester, vacant, at the presentation of the prior and convent of St Denys, Southampton, patrons. Letter for induction to the archdeacon of Surrey.

Southwark, 22 April 1349

472. ADMISSION of John de Bromden' as rector of the church of Itchen Abbas, at the presentation of the abbess and convent of St Mary, Winchester, patrons. Letter to the archdeacon of Winchester for the induction.

Southwark, 22 April 1349

473. ADMISSION of Richard Wideman, priest, as rector of the church of Lasham, vacant, at the presentation of Ralph de Camoys, patron. Letters for the induction to the archdeacon of Winchester and to the dean of Alton.

Southwark, 22 April 1349

474. ADMISSION of William Tysour' of Carshalton, priest as perpetual vicar of the church of Effingham, vacant, at the presentation of the prior and convent of St Mary of Merton, patrons, with obligation of residence, for which William took the oath. Letter to the archdeacon of Surrey for the induction.

Southwark, 22 April 1349

475. MANDATE to M. John de Ware, sequestrator-general for the archdeaconry of Winchester to examine the presentation of William de Stafford, priest, to the church of St George in Winchester by the abbot and convent of Hyde, said to be vacant. With full powers to induct him to the church.

Southwark, 22 April 1349

476. ADMISSION of M. William de Ercheffonte, priest, as rector of the church of Abbots Ann, vacant, at the presentation of fr. Richard de Beausenall prior of Ogbourne, by commission of the king on account of the war. Letter to the archdeacon of Winchester for the induction.

Southwark, 24 April 1349

477. ADMISSION of John de Merlawe, priest, to the perpetual vicarage of Wotton, vacant, at the presentation of the prior and convent of the cathedral church of Winchester, patrons, with obligation of residence, for which he took the oath. Letter to the archdeacon of Winchester for the induction.

Southwark, 26 April 1349

478. ADMISSION of John de Renfeld of Burgh, priest, as perpetual chaplain of the chapel of St Mary Magdalen, Kingston, vacant, at the presentation of John Lovekyn of the city of London, patron. Letter for the induction to the archdeacon of Surrey.

Southwark, 26 April 1349

479. COLLATION by the bishop of the church of Compton, vacant, on John Lok' clerk. Letter for the induction to the official of Winchester and the treasurer of Wolvesey.

Southwark, 28 April 1349

93 **480.** COLLATION by the bishop of the vicarage of the church of Twyford, vacant, on William de Williamesthrop' priest. He will have the obligation of residence for which he took the oath. Letter for the induction to the official of Winchester and the provost of the chapel of St Elizabeth.

Farnham, 26 April 1349

481. COLLATION by the bishop of the church of Houghton, vacant, on John de Blebury clerk as rector. Letter for induction to the official of Winchester.

Farnham, 27 April 1349

482. MANDATE to the official of Winchester to examine the presentation of Thomas de Rouz clerk to the church of Whippingham [Isle of Wight] by the king and then to induct him, sending a certificate to the bishop.

Farnham, 27 April 1349

483. ADMISSION and institution of William de Calverton priest to the church of Tunworth, vacant, at the presentation of John de Grey, knight, lord of Codnor, patron. Letter for the induction to the archdeacon of Winchester.

Southwark, 28 April 1349

484. ADMISSION of Nicholas de Todysterne to the vicarage of the church of Carisbrooke at the presentation of the king, the temporalities of the priory being in his hands. To be perpetual vicar with obligation of residence according to the constitutions for which he took the oath. Letter for induction to the archdeacon of Winchester.

Southwark, 28 April 1349

485. ADMISSION of Richard atte Stokke priest to the church of Linkenholt, vacant, as rector at the presentation of the abbot and convent of Gloucester patrons. Letter for the induction to the archdeacon of Winchester.

Southwark, 28 April 1349

486. ADMISSION of Symon le Straunge priest to the vicarage of St Thomas the Martyr at Portsmouth, at the presentation of the prior and convent of Southwick, patrons. He will be perpetual vicar with obligation of residence according to the constitutions for which he took the oath. Letter for the induction to the archdeacon of Winchester.

Southwark, 29 April 1349

487. ADMISSION of Richard called Martyn of Chippenham to the church of Oxted, vacant, at the presentation of Robert de Stangrave, knight, patron. Letter for the induction to the archdeacon of Surrey.

Southwark, 29 April 1349

488. ADMISSION of Andrew son of John Bette priest to the vicarage of Andover, vacant, at the presentation of the king, the priory of Andover being in his hands on account of war. To be perpetual vicar with obligation of residence according to the constitutions which he swore on the gospels to keep. Letter for the induction to the archdeacon of Winchester.

Southwark, 29 April 1349

489. ADMISSION of Richard de Dorsete clerk to the church of Farleigh near Basingstoke, vacant, as rector, at the presentation of Robert la Zouche, lord of the manor of Farleigh, patron. Letter to the archdeacon of Winchester for the induction.

Southwark, 29 April 1349

490. ADMISSION of Richard de Weston' subdeacon to the church of Albury, vacant, as rector, at the presentation of William Dabernon, knight, patron. Letter for the induction to the archdeacon of Surrey.

Southwark, 30 April 1349

94   **491.** ADMISSION of John Godman priest to the perpetual chantry of the Holy Trinity in the cemetery of the monastery of St Mary Winchester, vacant, at the presentation of Robert de Ingepenne; he swore upon the gospels to keep all the articles set out by the founder. Letter to M. John de Ware sequestrator-general for the induction.

Southwark, 30 April 1349

492. ADMISSION of John Holewale priest to the custody of the chapel of the Holy Trinity in the cemetery of St Mary, Winchester, at the presentation of Robert de Ingepenne, citizen of Winchester patron. He will be perpetual guardian according to the ordination of the founder, which he swore to keep. Letter to the official of Winchester and to M. J' de Ware sequestrator-general for the induction.

Southwark, 30 April 1349

493. ADMISSION of John Gogh junior to the church of Ash, vacant, as rector, at the presentation of the abbot and convent of Chertsey patrons. Letter for the induction to the archdeacon of Surrey.

Southwark, 30 April 1349

494. ADMISSION of Robert de Lanynton' priest to the church of Bighton, vacant, as rector, at the presentation of the abbot and convent of Hyde patrons. Letter to the archdeacon of Winchester for the induction.

Southwark, 2 May 1349

495. ADMISSION of William de Northstok' priest to the church of Little Bookham, vacant, as rector, at the presentation of Thomas de Brewes, knight, patron. Letter to the archdeacon of Surrey for the induction.

Southwark, 3 May 1349

496. COLLATION by the bishop of the vicarage of Bourne and Hurstbourne on John le Frenssh' of Selborne priest. He took the oath to reside according to the constitutions. Letters for the induction to the archdeacon of Winchester and to the perpetual vicar of Whitchurch.

Southwark, 4 May 1349

497. ADMISSION of Richard de Byrlyngham priest to the vicarage of Ashley, vacant, at the presentation of the prior and convent of Mottisfont patrons. To be perpetual vicar with obligation of residence according to the constitutions for which he took the oath. Letter for induction to the archdeacon of Winchester.

Southwark, 5 May 1349

498. ADMISSION of Roger de Keteryng' priest as rector to the church of Hartley Wintney, vacant, at the presentation of Henry earl of Lancaster, patron. Letter for induction to the archdeacon of Winchester.

Southwark, 5 May 1349

499. ADMISSION of Richard called le Clerc as rector to the church of St Mary Guildford, vacant, at the presentation of the prior and convent of St Mary, Merton, patrons. Letter to the archdeacon of Surrey for the induction.

Southwark, 5 May 1349

500. ADMISSION of John de Faryndon' priest to the vicarage of the church of Warlingham, vacant, at the presentation of the prior and convent of St Saviour Bermondsey. To be perpetual vicar with residence according to the constitutions which he swore to keep. Letter for induction to the archdeacon of Surrey.

Southwark, 5 May 1349

501. ADMISSION of John Mygreyn subdeacon to the chapel of Henley, vacant at the presentation of Peter de Whatteford patron. Letter for induction to the archdeacon of Winchester.

Southwark, 6 May 1349

502. ADMISSION of Ralph Knyght of Sulthorn' priest to the vicarage of Weybridge vacant, at the presentation of the prior and convent of Newark patrons. To be perpetual vicar with residence for which he took the oath. Letter to the archdeacon of Surrey for the induction.

Southwark, 6 May 1349

503. COLLATION by the bishop of the church of North Waltham, vacant, on M. Walter atte Brugg' clerk as rector. Letters for the induction to the archdeacon of Winchester and to the chaplain of the parish church.

Southwark, 3 May 1349

95 **504.** DISPENSATION granted to Robert Aspale rector of the church of Bishopstoke to be absent for one year for legal service.

Southwark, 6 May 1349

505. PRESENTATION by the bishop of Hugh Loveday priest to the church of Buttermere in the diocese of Salisbury vacant.

Southwark, 7 May 1349

506. ADMISSION of Robert Everard priest to the vicarage of the parish church of Sherborne St John vacant, at the presentation of Robert de Jar' patron. To be perpetual vicar with obligation of residence for which he took the oath. Letter sent to the archdeacon of Winchester for the induction.

Southwark, 7 May 1349

507. INSTITUTION of John de Rympton clerk to the chapel of Wathe St Lawrence, Isle of Wight, vacant, at the presentation of Eleanor widow of Theobald Russel knight, patroness. Letter to the archdeacon of Winchester for the induction.

Southwark, 8 May 1349

508. ADMISSION of John de Kendale priest to the church of West Clandon as rector, vacant, at the presentation of Margery de Weston' patroness. Letter to the archdeacon of Surrey for the induction.

Southwark, 9 May 1349

509. ADMISSION of John Lumbard priest as rector to the church of Headley, vacant, at the presentation of Nicholas Placy knight, patron. Letter to the archdeacon of Surrey for the induction.

Southwark, 9 May 1349

510. ADMISSION of John de Bochardeston' clerk as rector to the church of Clanfield, vacant, at the presentation of the prioress of Nuneaton, order of Fontevrault, patroness. Letter to the archdeacon of Winchester for the induction.

Southwark, 9 May 1349

511. ADMISSION of Thomas de la Berton' priest to the vicarage of the parish church of Heckfield, vacant, at the presentation of John de la Berton' rector of the church of Heckfield, patron of the vicarage. To be

perpetual vicar with obligation of residence for which he took the oath.
Letter to the archdeacon of Winchester for the induction.

Southwark, 9 May 1349

512. ADMISSION of Walter atte Hulle priest to the vicarage of the church of Wandsworth, vacant, at the presentation of King Edward, the temporalities of the abbey of Westminster being in his hands during the vacancy. He will be perpetual vicar with obligation of residence for which he took the oath. Letter to the archdeacon of Surrey for the induction.

Esher, 12 May 1349

513. ADMISSION of William de Byketon' priest to the vicarage of the church of Overton, vacant, at the presentation of Nicholas de Wykewane rector of Overton. To be perpetual vicar with obligation of residence, for which he took the oath. Letter to the rector of Baughurst for the induction.

Esher, 12 May 1349

514. LETTER OF PROCLAMATION concerning the election of Joan Gervays as abbess of Romsey sent to the official of Winchester.

Southwark, 6 May 1349

515. ADMISSION of Robert de Kelleseye priest in the person of Walter de Wranghby as proctor, to the church of Stoneham Abbas vacant, to be rector, at the presentation of the abbot and convent of Hyde. Letter to the official of the archdeacon of Winchester for the induction.

Esher, 13 May 1349

516. ADMISSION of Walter de Maydene Wynterborne priest to the vicarage of the church of Froyle, vacant, at the presentation of M. Walter atte Brugge as proctor for M. Thomas de Enham, rector of Froyle and patron of the vicarage. To be perpetual vicar continuously residing for which he took the oath. Letters for the induction to the archdeacon of Winchester, his official, to the dean of Alton and the perpetual vicar of Farnham for the induction.

Esher, 13 May 1349

96 THE FOURTH YEAR OF WILLIAM BISHOP OF WINCHESTER BEGINS 14 MAY 1349

517. ADMISSION of William en le Hyle priest as rector to the church of West Deane, vacant, at the presentation of Laurence de Sancto Martino patron. Letter to the archdeacon of Winchester for the induction.

Esher, 14 May 1349

518. ADMISSION of Thomas Hert priest as rector of the church of All Saints, Walsworth, vacant, at the presentation of the prior and convent of Southwick, patrons. Letter for the induction to the archdeacon of Winchester.

Esher, 14 May 1349

519. ADMISSION of John de Upton' priest to the vicarage of the church of South Stoneham, vacant, at the presentation of John Payn precentor of St Mary, Southampton, patron. To be perpetual vicar continuously residing according to the constitutions, for which he took the oath. Letter to the precentor for the induction.

Esher, 19 May 1349

520. ADMISSION of John le Litherere priest as rector to the church of Chilton Candover, vacant, at the presentation of Philip Daundely knight, patron. Letter for the induction to the archdeacon of Winchester.

Southwark, 19 May 1349

521. ADMISSION of John de Tunbregg' as rector to the church of Oxted, vacant, at the presentation of Robert de Stangrave knight, patron. Letter for the induction to the archdeacon of Surrey.

Southwark, 19 May 1349

522. ADMISSION of Richard de Elyng' priest to the church of St Michael in Fleshmonger Street Winchester, vacant, at the presentation of the prior and convent of St Denys Southampton, patrons. Letter for the induction to the archdeacon of Winchester.

Southwark, 19 May 1349

523. ADMISSION of M. John de Cranborne clerk as rector of the church of Itchen, vacant, at the presentation of the abbess of St Mary Winchester, patrons. Letter to the archdeacon of Winchester and to the dean of Alresford.

Southwark, 19 May 1349

524. ADMISSION of Robert atte Church' priest to the vicarage of the church of Mitcham, vacant, at the presentation of the prior and convent of St Mary, Southwark, patrons. To be perpetual vicar with obligation of residence for which he took the oath. Letter for the induction to the archdeacon of Surrey.

Southwark, 20 May 1349

525. ADMISSION of John Cameros priest to the church of Kingsgate Winchester as rector, vacant, in the person of Thomas Folk' as proctor, at the presentation of M. Richard Vachan, archdeacon of Surrey, patron. Letter for the induction to the archdeacon of Winchester.

Esher, 21 May 1349

526. ADMISSION of William de Somborne priest to the church of Nately Scures as rector, at the presentation of John de Scures knight, patron. Letter for induction to the archdeacon of Winchester.

Esher, 22 May 1349

527. PRESENTATION by the bishop of M. William de Taunton', rector of the church of Minterne, diocese of Salisbury, to the church of Wyke of the bishop's patronage in the aforesaid diocese, by exchange with M. Walter de Schirborne, rector of Wyke.

Southwark, 20 May 1349

528. ADMISSION of John atte Welle of Fylbyng as rector to the church of 'Bursshele', vacant, at the presentation of Edward, prince of Wales, patron. Letter for induction to the archdeacon of Surrey.

Esher, 22 May 1349

529. ADMISSION of Andrew de Bekenesfeld as rector of the church of Wisley, vacant, at the presentation of Edward, prince of Wales, patron. Letter to the archdeacon of Surrey for the induction.

Esher, 22 May 1349

97 **530.** COLLATION by the bishop of the church of Highclere on Roger de Beautre clerk, vacant, instituting him canonically. Letter for the induction to the official of Winchester and to Hugh rector of Widley and to Nicholas vicar of Whitchurch.

Esher, 22 May 1349

531. COMMISSION addressed to M. John de Ware sequestrator-general for the archdeaconry of Winchester to examine, confirm or annul the election of Roger de Exon', also called Pope, as archpriest of the oratory of the Holy Trinity, Barton, Isle of Wight. Sending a certificate to the bishop.

Esher, 22 May 1349

532. ADMISSION of William de Blakelonde priest to the vicarage of the parish church of Dorking, vacant, at the presentation of the prior and convent of Reigate, patrons. To be perpetual vicar with residence according to the constitutions, for which he took the oath. Letter for induction to the archdeacon of Surrey.

Esher, 22 May 1349

533. ADMISSION of John de Kendale priest to the church of Fetcham, vacant, at the presentation of Adam de Swyneborne, by right of his wife Alice, late wife of John Dabernon, deceased, patron, vacant. Letter for the induction to the archdeacon of Surrey.

Esher, 22 May 1349

534. ADMISSION of Thomas Hardyng' priest to the vicarage of St Bartholomew at the gate of Hyde, vacant, at the presentation of the abbot and convent of Hyde, patrons. To be perpetual vicar, residing according to the constitutions, for which he took the oath. Letter for induction to the archdeacon of Winchester.

Esher, 22 May 1349

535. ADMISSION of Symon le Carpenter of Papenham priest as rector of the church of Albury, vacant, at the presentation of William Dabernon, patron. Letter to the archdeacon of Surrey for the induction.

Esher, 22 May 1349

536. ADMISSION of John atte Wode as rector of the church of Chaldon, vacant, at the presentation of John de Conert, knight, patron. Letter for the induction to the archdeacon of Surrey.

Esher, 24 May 1349

537. ADMISSION of Roger de Sancto Albano to the vicarage of the parish church of Sherborne St John's, vacant, at the presentation of Robert de Jar', rector of the same church, patron of the vicarage. To be perpetual vicar with residence according to the constitutions, for which he took the oath. Letter for the induction to the archdeacon of Winchester.

Esher, 24 May 1349

538. ADMISSION of William Richeman of Southflete, priest, as rector of Worplesdon, vacant, at the presentation of John de Cobeham knight, patron. Letter for the induction to the archdeacon of Surrey.

Esher, 25 May 1349

539. ADMISSION of William de Dodyngton' priest as rector of the church of North Charford, near Fordingbridge, vacant, at the presentation of Philip de Thame, prior of St John of Jerusalem in England, patron. Letter to the archdeacon of Winchester for the induction.

Esher, 26 May 1349

98 **540.** MEMORANDUM that after receiving the certificate from Ralph, bishop of London, to whom the bishop had entrusted the process, the exchange between Walter de Farndale, rector of Blendworth and Thomas de Clopton' rector of the free chapel at the entrance to the palace of the bishop of London in the city of London, is approved. Letter for the induction written to the archdeacon of Winchester.

Esher, 23 May 1349

541. ADMISSION of John Cameros priest to the vicarage of the church of Farnham, vacant, at the presentation of M. Richard Vacham archdeacon of Surrey, parton of the vicarage. To be perpetual vicar, residing according to the constitutions for which he took the oath. Letter to the archdeacon of Surrey and the dean of Farnham for the induction.

Esher, 27 May 1349

542. COLLATION by the bishop of the church of St James, Winchester, vacant, on John called Wyn of Alton accolyte, who was canonically instituted. Letters for the induction to the official of Winchester and the rector of St Martin outside Westgate for the induction.

Esher, 27 May 1349

543. CERTIFICATE FOR THE ELECTION of the prior of Mottisfont. Mandate from the bishop to the prior of Winchester cathedral and the official to examine the election of fr. Robert de Brommore, subprior, as prior, with full powers to confirm or annul.

Farnham, 17 April 1349

They find the election canonically correct and have confirmed it, entrusting the prior with the care of souls and of the temporalities. They send their certificates.

Winchester, 13 May 1349

544. CERTIFICATE FOR THE ELECTION of the abbess of Romsey. Mandate to the prior of the cathedral church and to the official to examine the election of Joan Gervays as abbess of Romsey, with power to confirm it or annul.

Southwark, 8 May 1349

They have confirmed the election and granted to the abbess powers of administration in spirituals and in temporals.

Winchester, 15 May 1349

545. LICENCE TO ELECT A PRIOR granted to the subprior and convent of St Mary, Southwark, augustinian canons, at the death of fr. Robert de Welles, late prior, stressing what should be the dispositions of the electors.

Esher, 24 May 1349

546. ADMISSION of Robert de Childecote priest as rector of West Clandon, vacant, at the presentation of Margery, widow of William de Weston, patroness. Letter for the induction to the archdeacon of Surrey.

Esher, 28 May 1349

547. (in French) LETTER from sir John Pultenoie begging the bishop to present a chaplain to the chapel of Corpus Christi in London, since the former chaplain was called from this life the morrow of Lady Day. He should be of good disposition, able to read and sing well and take charge as soon as convenient.

Poplar, Sunday 29 March 1349

548. ADMISSION of William de Tamworth' clerk as rector of the church of Silchester, vacant, at the presentation of King Edward, as custodian of the heir of William de Cusancia, knight, deceased. Letter for the induction to the archdeacon of Winchester.

Esher, 29 May 1349

549. ADMISSION of Richard de Norwico clerk to the prebend of Leckford in the church of St Mary, Winchester, vacant, at the presentation of the king, by reason of the vacancy of the abbey. He was instituted as prebendary. Letter for the induction to the archdeacon of Winchester, who will assign him to his stall in choir and place in chapter.

Esher, 29 May 1349

550. ADMISSION of Thomas Folk' clerk as rector of the church of Kingsgate, Winchester, vacant, at the presentation of M. Richard Vaghan archdeacon of Surrey, patron. Letters for the induction to the archdeacon and to the dean of Winchester.

Esher, 30 May 1349

551. ADMISSION of John Ferour priest to the vicarage of Cuddington, at the presentation of the prior and convent of Merton, patrons, with obligation of residence. Letter for the induction to the archdeacon of Surrey.

Esher, 30 May 1349

552. ADMISSION of Henry de Ticynge priest to the vicarage of St Martha, vacant, at the presentation of the prior and convent of Newark, patrons. To be perpetual vicar according to the constitutions. Letters for the induction to the archdeacon of Surrey and the dean of Guildford.

Esher, 30 May 1349

553. ADMISSION of John Chalkeberd priest as rector of the church of St Michael in Jewry Street, vacant, at the presentation of the abbot and convent of Hyde, patrons. Letter for induction to the archdeacon of Winchester.

Esher, 1 June 1349

100 **554.** LETTER from the bishop to M. William de Coleton' priest. Since all the brethren of the hospital of St Mary Magdalen of Sandon, now vacant, have died during the mortality of England and that the hospital is now destitute after the death of its last warden or prior, fr. John de Askam, the bishop, to whom the custody devolves, sets M. William over the hospital, the right of electing another warden in the future being reserved.

Esher, 1 June 1349

555. MANDATE to M. Robert de Pernicote, sequestrator-general for the archdeaconry of Surrey and John rector of Esher to induct M. William de Coleton', whom the bishop entrusts with the administration of the aforesaid hospital, except for the rights reserved, but granting him his stall in choir and place in chapter.

Esher, 1 June 1349

PROCESS OF THE ELECTION OF FR. JOHN DE MERLAWE AS PRIOR OF THE CATHEDRAL CHURCH OF WINCHESTER

556. LETTER REQUESTING FROM THE BISHOP LICENCE TO ELECT A PRIOR after the death of Alex' de Herierde, the late prior; the bearers of the letter are fr. Thomas de Berton' and fr. Robert de Popham.

Chapter House, Winchester, 5 March 1349

557. GRANT OF THE LICENCE TO ELECT, the bishop having considered the letter brought by the brothers. He indicates the spirit in which the convent should proceed to elect.

Esher, 7 March 1349

101   558. SUPPLICATORY LETTER from fr. William de Basynge subprior and the convent of the cathedral church. After the death of the late prior, having received licence to elect a successor, by unanimous consent fr. John de Merlawe, their confrater, a professed monk and in holy orders, was elected as their prior. Therefore they beg the bishop to accept this election, granting his assent and proceeding as is customary. They will transmit the decree and the process of the election to him as speedily as they can. Together they beg to be excused on account of the shortage of time.

The chapter-house Winchester, 21 March 1349

559. THE BISHOP also excuses himself, for he cannot grant their request to proclaim the election, as it would be contrary to canon law as hitherto observed. By their confrater fr. Robert de Popham he returns their letter.

560. SECOND SUPPLICATORY LETTER from fr. William de Basynge concerning the election. The convent constitutes fr. Edmund de Bolesdon' and Robert de Popham to be their proctors in this matter, begging the bishop to act favorably.

The chapter-house Winchester, 23 March 1349

561. GRANT OF A LETTER OF PROCLAMATION. Since the chapter has elected fr. John de Merlawe as prior, after receiving the consent of the bishop as patron, the bishop intends that the examination of the election shall take place on the second law-day after Passion Sunday, i.e. 31 March, after the announcement in the cathedral, citing objectors to appear in the parish church of Farnham on that day, so that there may be no delay in terminating the vacancy. The bishop wishes to be informed by letter of the date of the announcement, with the names of those wishing to be cited.

Farnham, 21 March 1349

562. COMMISSION TO EXAMINE THE ELECTION entrusted to M. John de Lech' professor of canon law and canon of Salisbury and John de Wolveleye chancellor of Winchester, with powers to confirm or annul.

Farnham, 31 March 1349

102   563. JUDICAL PROCESS OF THE ELECTION, when the proctors for the convent (as named in 560) appeared before the commissaries. M. Roger the official was ordered to produce those wishing to express opposition; when none appeared, the commissaries proceeded to draw up the decree. The witnesses were fr. Richard de Merwelle and fr. William de Sparsholte who presented the case; fr. Edmund de Bolesdon', Roland de Wykford', John de Merlawe priest and Walter de Merlawe, who had all been sworn and examined.

The parish church Farnham, 31 March 1349

564. PRONOUNCEMENT OF THE CONFIRMATION by M. John de Lech', followed by the *Te Deum*. The new prior took the oath of canonical

obedience to the bishop (full text) in the chapel of the castle and received the blessing.

565. LETTER FROM THE BISHOP TO THE NEW PRIOR confirming the election with his episcopal authority, praying that it may be fruitful.

Farnham, 31 March 1349

103 **566.** LETTER TO THE SUBPRIOR AND CONVENT, whom he has entrusted to their new prior, requesting them to show devotion, obedience and reverence in receiving his admonitions.

Date as above

567. MANDATE TO THE OFFICIAL OF WINCHESTER to entrust the care of souls and the administration of the priory to the new prior, to induct him according to law and custom, and to install him.

Date as above

568. ADMISSION of Thomas de Aulton priest to the vicarage of the church of Basingstoke, vacant, at the presentation of the prior and convent of Selborne, patrons of the vicarage. He will be perpetual vicar according to the constitutions for which he took the oath. Letter for the induction to the archdeacon of Winchester.

Esher, 3 June 1349

569. ADMISSION of William Goudman priest to the vicarage of Ockham, vacant, at the presentation of the abbot and convent of Chertsey patrons. He will be perpetual vicar according to the constitutions for which he took the oath. Letter for the induction to the archdeacon of Surrey.

Esher, 3 June 1349

570. ADMISSION of Richard de Elynge priest to the church of St Peter Chesil outside the East Gate of Winchester, vacant, at the presentation of the prior and convent of St Denys, Southampton, patrons. Letter for the induction to the archdeacon of Winchester.

Esher, 5 June 1349

571. ADMISSION of Thomas de Halghton priest to the vicarage of Leatherhead, vacant, at the presentation of the prior and convent of Leeds, patrons. To be perpetual vicar according to the constitutions for which he took the oath. Letter for the induction to the archdeacon of Surrey.

Esher, 4 June 1349

572. ADMISSION of William de Stowell' priest to the vicarage of the church of Godalming, vacant, at the presentation of M. William de Askeby canon of Salisbury, vicar-general for Arnald son of Usisi Usisus, dean of Salisbury, papal notary, patron of the said vicarage, holding full powers from the dean. He will be perpetual vicar according to the constitutions for which he took the oath. Letter for the induction to the archdeacon of Surrey.

Esher, 5 June 1349

573. ADMISSION of Walter Noght subdeacon as rector of the church of Dibden, vacant, at the presentation of Nicholas de Depedene, patron for this turn. Letter for the induction to the archdeacon of Winchester.

Esher, 6 June 1349

574. COMMISSION to M. John de Ware sequestrator-general of the archdeaconry of Winchester to enquire into the presentation of M. Roger de Fulford', professor of civil law, to the church of Abbots Ann, vacant, made by the abbot and convent of Hyde as patrons. then to admit M. Roger if the presentation is in order, to institute him as rector and to induct him.

Esher, 6 June 1349

575. ADMISSION of John Lumbard priest as rector of the church of Headley, vacant, at the presentation of [   ]. Letter for the induction to the archdeacon of Surrey.

Southwark, 9 May 1349

104   **576.** COMMENDATION by the bishop of the church of Abbots Ann, vacant, with the consent of the abbot and convent of Hyde, to M. Roger de Fulford' professor of civil law.

Southwark, 12 May 1349

577. LETTER OF PROCLAMATION citing objectors to appear in the matter of the election of Margaret de Molyneux, nun of the abbey of St Mary, Winchester, vacant, directed to the official of Winchester.

Esher, 7 June 1349

578. ADMISSION of John de Welewyk' priest to the vicarage of Herriard, vacant, at the presentation of the subprioress of Wintney, the priory being without a prioress. To be perpetual vicar residing according to the constitutions for which he took the oath. Letter to the archdeacon of Winchester for the induction.

Esher, 7 June 1349

579. ADMISSION of John called Ridere clerk as rector of the church of Laverstoke, vacant, at the presentation of the abbot and convent of Hyde patrons. Letter for the induction to the archdeacon of Winchester.

Esher, 11 June 1349

580. ADMISSION of John Bocke priest to the vicarage of the chapel of Shorwell, Isle of Wight, vacant, at the presentation of Reginald de Welyngton' rector of the said chapel, patron of the vicarage. To be perpetual vicar with obligation of residence according to the constitutions for which he took the oath. Letter for the induction to the archdeacon of Winchester.

Esher, 12 June 1349

581. ADMISSION of Robert de Snokeshull' clerk to the chantry of the manor chapel of la Vacherie in the parish of Cranleigh, vacant, at the presentation of William de Newenham clerk, attorney in England for Thomas de Dagworth, knight, patron of the chantry and chapel. Letter for the induction to the archdeacon of Surrey.

Esher, 13 June 1349

582. DISPENSATION for one year granted to Walter de Friland' rector of Ockham acolyte, for study, without obligation of residence or of proceeding to further orders beyond the subdiaconate, as he had promised Robert at first according to the constitutions of Boniface to do within a year.

Esher, 13 June 1349

583. COMMISSION OF ENQUIRY INTO THE ELECTION, following the death of fr. Robert de Welles, prior, of fr. John de Pecham canon of the conventual church of St Mary, Southwark, entrusted to John de Wolveleye canon of Salisbury by the bishop. The enquiry was held in the church of St Margaret Southwark the third law-day after Trinity Sunday, i.e. 10 June 1349. The subprior and convent were represented by their proctors and as no objectors to the election appeared, the witnesses were examined on oath and the election was declared canonical. Then the cure of souls and the administration was committed to the newly elect.

105

584. LETTER FROM THE BISHOP to the new prior of Southwark, confirming the election with his episcopal authority.

Southwark, 10 June 1349

585. LETTER TO THE SUBPRIOR AND CONVENT announcing the confirmation and recommending them to observe their prior's admonitions.

Same date

586. MEMORANDUM that M. John de Wolveleye, the bishop's commissary for the election, inducted the new prior to his stall in choir and place in chapter in the customary manner.

Same date

587. ADMISSION of Thomas Sely of Kempston priest to the vicarage of the church of Odiham, vacant, at the presentation of Elyas de Sancto Albano, chancellor of Salisbury cathedral and rector of Odiham, patron. He will be perpetual vicar with obligation of residence for which he took the oath. Letter for the induction to the archdeacon of Winchester.

Esher, 13 June 1349

588. CERTIFICATE OF THE CONFIRMATION OF THE ELECTION of Margaret de Molyneux as abbess of St Mary's Winchester, from the prior of the cathedral church and the official, by mandate from the bishop, who gave them full powers to confirm or annul.

Esher, 7 June 1349

They examined the election and found it canonically celebrated. Hence they confirmed to the new abbess the care and administration of the convent. They annex the process.

Winchester, under the seal of the official, 12 June 1349

106   **589.** LETTER TO THE NEW ABBESS from the bishop confirming her in her office after the death of Matilda de Spyne.

Esher, 14 June

590. LETTER TO THE PRIORESS AND CONVENT recommending them to act as members towards the head, showing her obedience and reverence.

Same date

591. COMMISSION to the archdeacon of Winchester to induct abbess Margaret to her stall in choir and place in chapter.

Same date

592. LETTER TO KING EDWARD requesting him to restore the temporalities.

Same date

593. MEMORANDUM that Sunday 14 June during the pontifical Mass in the manor chapel of Esher, abbess Margaret made her profession and was blessed (full text of the profession).

594. Repetition of 587, adding the dean of Basingstoke for the induction.

595. ADMISSION of Ralph de Hyde priest to the chantry chapel of Sherborne Coudray, vacant, at the presentation of Fulk de Coudray knight, patron. To be perpetual chantry priest. Letter to the archdeacon of Winchester for the induction.

Southwark, 17 June 1349

596. ADMISSION of Robert de Stanford to the church of Church Oakley, vacant, at the presentation of king Edward, the temporalities of [Monks] Sherborne being in his hands. Letter for the induction to the archdeacon of Winchester.

Southwark, 17 June 1349

107   **597.** ADMISSION of William Lever priest as rector of the church of Clatford, vacant, at the presentation of king Edward, the priory of Carisbrooke being in his hands. Letter for the induction to the archdeacon of Winchester.

Southwark, 17 June 1349

598. ADMISSION of Peter Travers priest to the vicarage of the church of Shalfleet, [Isle of Wight,] vacant, at the presentation of John Seys rector of Shalfleet, patron of the vicarage. Letter to the archdeacon of Winchester for the induction.

Southwark, 17 June 1349

599. ADMISSION of Michael Cormailles priest to the vicarage of the church of Itchen Stoke, vacant, at the presentation of the abbess and convent of Romsey. To be perpetual vicar according to the constitutions for which he took the oath. Letter for the induction to the archdeacon of Winchester.

Southwark, 17 June 1349

600. ADMISSION of Robert de la Moure priest as rector of the church of Colemore, vacant, at the presentation of Thomas de Commere, patron for this turn. Letters for the induction to the archdeacon of Winchester and to the dean of Basingstoke.

Southwark, 18 June 1349

601. ADMISSION of Robert Grenhull' priest to the vicarage of Whitsbury, vacant, at the presentation of the subprior of Breamore, the prior being lately deceased. To be perpetual vicar residing according to the constitutions for which he took the oath. Letter for the induction to the archdeacon of Winchester.

Southwark, 19 June 1349

602. ADMISSION of William Domnowe priest to the church of Wanborough, vacant, at the presentation of the abbot and convent of Waverley, patrons. To be perpetual vicar for which he took the oath. Letter for the induction to the archdeacon of Surrey.

Southwark, 20 June 1349

603. COLLATION by the bishop of the church of Crawley on M. John de Ware acolyte as rector. Letter for the induction to the archdeacon of Winchester and the *prepositus* of the chapel of St Elizabeth.

Southwark, 20 June 1349

604. ADMISSION of Walter Flemmyng' priest to the vicarage of the church of Barton Stacey, vacant, at the presentation of the prior and convent of Llanthony by Gloucester, patrons. To be perpetual vicar according to the constitutions for which he took the oath. Letter for the induction to the archdeacon of Winchester.

Southwark, 20 June 1349

605. ADMISSION of John de Sancta Ecclesia priest as rector of the church of Farleigh [Wallop,] vacant, at the presentation of Robert la Zousch', lord of the manor of Farleigh, patron. Letter for the induction to the archdeacon of Winchester.

Southwark, 21 June 1349

606. ADMISSION of William de Durbath' priest as rector of the church of St George, Winchester, vacant, at the presentation of the abbot and convent of Hyde, patrons. Letter for the induction to the archdeacon of Winchester.

Southwark, 22 June 1349

607. ADMISSION of John de Wichebury priest to the vicarage of the church of Kingsclere, vacant, at the presentation of the prior and convent of Bisham Montagu, patrons. To be perpetual vicar according to the constitutions for which he took the oath. Letter to the archdeacon of Winchester for the induction.

Esher, 23 June 1349

608. ADMISSION of John de Kenesworth' priest as rector of the church of Merrow, vacant, at the presentation of the prioress and convent of Ivinghoe, patrons. Letter for the induction to the archdeacon of Winchester.

Esher, 24 June 1349

108   **609.** COLLATION by the bishop of the sacerdotal office, vacant, in the chapel of Marwell on John Pirie of Trowbridge. He was instituted as perpetual chaplain. Letter for the induction to J' de Nubbeleye rector of Alresford and Thomas de Wolves'.

Esher, 25 June 1349

610. ADMISSION of Mark le Boor priest as rector of the church of Bighton, vacant, at the presentation of the abbot and convent of Hyde, patrons. Letter for the induction to the archdeacon of Winchester.

Southwark, 26 June 1349

611. ADMISSION of John de Nubbeleye clerk to the prebend called the portion of St Laurence which Richard de Lusteshull' held in the conventual church of Romsey, vacant by his death. It is at the presentation of the king, the temporalities of the abbey being in his hands during the vacancy. Letter for the induction to William de Farlee canon of Salisbury and rector of Hursley and to M. John de Ware rector of Crawley; they will assign him his stall in choir and the place in chapter for the prebendaries.

Southwark, 27 June 1349

612. ADMISSION of Philip de Gatacre priest as rector of the church of Hartley Westpall, vacant, at the presentation of John Waspail, patron. Letter to the archdeacon of Winchester for the induction.

Southwark, 2 July 1349

613. ADMISSION of Thomas Draper of Stortford priest to the vicarage of Caterham, vacant, at the presentation of the abbot and convent of Holy Cross Waltham, patrons. He will be perpetual vicar according to the constitutions for which he took the oath. Letter for the induction to the archdeacon of Surrey.

Southwark, 2 July 1349

614. COLLATION by the bishop of the church of Esher on John Mayheu of Stow on the Wold, vacant by the resignation of John de Lond' the last rector. Letters for the induction sent to the rector of Cobham and to the perpetual vicar of Kingston.

Southwark, 3 July 1349

615. ADMISSION of Alan de Oteryngham priest in the person of Walter de Appelton' his proctor as rector of the church of Streatham, vacant, at the presentation of the prior of Ogbourne, fr. Richard de Beausenall', and the abbot and convent of Bec Herlewin in the diocese of Rouen—in the hands of the king, but presenting by his commission. Letter for the induction to the archdeacon of Surrey.

Southwark, 3 July 1349

616. ADMISSION of M. Richard Wodelond' clerk as rector of Niton, [Isle of Wight,] vacant, at the presentation of king Edward for the priory of Carisbrooke in his hands on account of the war. Letter for the induction to the archdeacon of Winchester.

Southwark, 4 July 1349

617. ADMISSION of Nicholas le Barbour of Stafford priest as rector of Warlingham, vacant, at the presentation of Ralph earl of Stafford, patron. Letter for the induction to the archdeacon of Surrey.

Highclere, 12 July 1349

618. COMMISION to M. Roger de Fulford the official of Winchester to examine the election of fr. Edmund de Popham canon of the conventual church of Selborne as prior, vacant at the death of fr. Thomas de Wynt'. He will confirm or annul the election and act as required.

Southwark, 29 June 1349

109 **619.** ADMISSION of William de Bures priest as vicar of Romsey, vacant, at the presentation of M. Andrew de Offord' canon and prebend of the portion of St Laurence and of Timsbury with the chapel of Imber, annexed by reason of the canonicate and the prebend. To be perpetual vicar according to the constitutions. Letter for the induction to the archdeacon of Winchester.

Highclere, 13 July 1349

620. ADMISSION of Walter de Wanynden' priest to the vicarage of Malden, vacant, at the presentation of the warden and scholars of Merton in Oxford, patrons of the vicarage. To be perpetual vicar according to the constitutions for which he took the oath. Letter for the induction to the archdeacon of Surrey.

Highclere, 13 July 1349

621. ADMISSION of William de Oldhale priest to the vicarage of Odiham, vacant, at the presentation of Elyas de Sancto Albano, chancellor and canon of Salisbury and rector of Odiham, as annexed to the office of chancellor, patron. To be perpetual vicar with obligation of residence according to the constitutions for which he took the oath. Letter for the induction to the archdeacon of Winchester.

Highclere, 14 July 1349

622. ADMISSION of Richard de Hamme priest as rector of the church of Pittleworth, vacant, at the presentation of John de Kenne patron for this turn. Letter to the archdeacon of Winchester for the induction.

Highclere, 17 July 1349

623. ADMISSION of William de Radclive priest to the vicarage of the church of Shalford, vacant, at the presentation of the prior and convent of the new hospital of St Mary without Bishopsgate, London. To be perpetual vicar with obligation of residence according to the constitutions for which he took the oath. Letter for the induction to the archdeacon of Surrey.

Highclere, 17 July 1349

624. ADMISSION of John Smith of Risyndon priest as rector of the chapel of Freefolk in the parish of Whitchurch, vacant, at the presentation of Katherine Husee, widow of Henry Husee knight, deceased, patroness of the chapel. Letter to the archdeacon of Winchester for the induction and to the perpetual vicar of Whitchurch.

Highclere, 17 July 1349

625. ADMISSION of John Scherston' priest to the vicarage of the church of St Swithun, Nutley, vacant, at the presentation of the prior and convent of Southwick, patrons of the vicarage. To be perpetual vicar with obligation of residence for which he took the oath. Letter for the induction to the archdeacon of Winchester.

Highclere, 17 July 1349

626. LETTER OF INSTITUTION for M. John de Fulford' to the church of Froyle, vacant by the resignation of M. John de Beautre acting as proctor for M. Thomas de Enham the former rector, by way of exchange for the church of Abbots Ann. This is at the presentation of the abbess and convent of St Mary Winchester, Roger de Fulford' acting as proctor for M. John. Letter for induction to the archdeacon of Winchester.

Highclere, 17 July 1349

627. SIMILAR LETTER OF INSTITUTION for M. Thomas de Enham in the person of John de Beautre his proctor to the church of Abbots Ann, through Roger de Fulford' as proctor for John de Fulford', rector of Abbots Ann now resigned. Letter for the induction to the archdeacon of Winchester.

Highclere, 17 July 1349

628. COLLATION by the bishop of the church of Millbrook, vacant, on John de Somborne priest as rector. Letter for the induction to the archdeacon of Winchester.

Highclere, 20 July 1349

110   **629.** ADMISSION of Richard Hosclore priest to the vicarage of the church of Eling, vacant, at the presentation of the prior and convent of Mottisfont, patrons. To be perpetual vicar with obligation of residence for which he took the oath. Letter for the induction to the archdeacon of Winchester.

Highclere, 20 July 1349

630. COLLATION by the bishop of the church of North Waltham, vacant, on John de Sannford' acolyte as rector. Letter for the induction to the archdeacon of Winchester.

Highclere, 20 July 1349

631. ADMISSION of Richard de Bromleye Abbatis priest as rector of the church of Laverstoke, vacant, at the presentation of the abbot and convent of Hyde, patrons. Letter for the induction to the archdeacon of Winchester.

Highclere, 20 July 1349

632. CERTIFICATE OF THE PROCESS OF THE ELECTION at Wintney. John de Beautre rector of Burghclere has received the letter from the bishop: Mandate to examine the election of Emma de Winterburn', nun of Wintney of the Cistercian order as prioress, after the death of Couma Gervaise, last prioress; then to confirm or annul the election. If confirmed, he will put Emma into possession of the monastery with all its rights, inducting her to her stall in choir and customary place in chapter and do whatever else is required.

Highclere, 17 July 1349

He has examined the election and found it canonically correct, putting the prioress in possession 18 July, with the customary procedure. The seal of the dean of Basingstoke is added to his own.

Winchfield, 19 July 1349

Memorandum that prioress Emma received the customary letters for her election 18 July 1349.

633. ADMISSION of Thomas le Irmongere of Leighton Buzzard priest to the vicarage of Farley, vacant, at the presentation of the warden and scholars of Merton in Oxford, patrons. To be perpetual vicar with obligation of residence according to the constitutions, for which he took the oath. Letter for the induction to the archdeacon of Surrey.

Highclere, 21 July 1349

634. DISPENSATION granted for one year to Richard Bromleye rector of Laverstoke priest to be at the service of Hugh de Aston and to be absent from the parish.

Highclere, 22 July 1349

635. ADMISSION of John Corn priest to the perpetual chantry of the manor of Gatcombe [Isle of Wight,] vacant, at the presentation of Joan widow of John de Insula of Gatcombe, knight, lately deceased, by reason of the custody of the son and heir until his majority as granted by the king. Letter to the archdeacon of Winchester for the induction.

Highclere, 25 July 1349

636. ADMISSION of Adam de Lichefeld acolyte to be rector of the church of Hartley, vacant, at the presentation of Henry earl of Lancaster, Derby and Leicester, seneschal of England, patron. Letters for the induction to the archdeacon of Winchester and the dean of Alton.

Highclere, 26 July 1349

637. ADMISSION of Richard de Bradewell' priest to be rector of the parochial church of Crux Easton, vacant, at the presentation of Thomas de Drokenesford', knight, patron. Letter for the induction to the archdeacon of Winchester.

Highclere, 26 July 1349

111 **638.** ADMISSION of John de Upton' priest as rector of the church of All Saints, Southampton, at the presentation of the prior and convent of St Denys, patrons. Letter for the induction to the archdeacon of Winchester and the dean of Southampton.

Marwell, 29 July 1349

639. ADMISSION of Richard de Farham subdeacon as rector of the church of Abbotston, vacant, at the presentation of Gerard de Insula, patron. Letter to the archdeacon of Winchester for the induction.

Marwell, 29 July 1349

640. ADMISSION of Richard Habbegod' chaplain as rector of the church of Lainston, vacant, at the presentation of John de Wynton' patron. Letter for the induction to the archdeacon of Winchester.

Marwell, 29 July 1349

641. ADMISSION of Walter atte Nasscroft priest as rector of St Peter in Colebrook Street, Winchester, vacant, at the presentation of the abbess and convent of St Mary Winchester, patrons. Letter for the induction to the archdeacon of Winchester.

Marwell, 1 August 1349

642. ADMISSION of Adam de Houghton' priest to the perpetual chantry chapel of the Holy Trinity in the cemetery of St Mary Winchester, which John Goudman had first obtained, vacant by a resignation, at the presentation of John de Ingepenne patron of the chantry. Letter for the induction to the archdeacon of Winchester.

Marwell, 1 August 1349

643. ADMISSION of Milo de Wodeham priest to the vicarage of the parochial church of Cobham, vacant, at the presentation of the abbot and convent of Chertsey. To be perpetual vicar with obligation of residence for which he took the oath. Letter to the archdeacon of Surrey for the induction.

Marwell, 1 August 1349

644. NOMINATION OF THE PRIOR OF REIGATE BY DEVOLUTION. Letter from the bishop to fr. Robert de Scoteney canon of the priory of Tandridge, augustinian. Relying on the reports of his praiseworthy life, the bishop with the consent of the canons appoints Robert to be prior of Reigate, for which priory he had made profession. The nomination devolves on the bishop through lapse of time.

Marwell, 2 August 1349

Under same date letter for induction to the archdeacon of Surrey, who will install him in choir and chapter and remind the canons of their duty of reverence and obedience.

645. SIMILAR NOMINATION BY DEVOLUTION of the Master or Prior of St Thomas, Southwark. Letter from the bishop to fr. Walter de Merlawe, brother of the hospital, who has been dispensed from his illegitimacy, nominating him to be master of the hospital and relying on his sagacity in spiritual and temporal affairs.

Marwell, 28 July 1349

Letter under the same date for the induction to the prior of the conventual church of Southwark and to Robert de Pernicote, sequestor-general for Surrey, to install Walter, reminding the brethren and sisters of their duty of obedience.

646. ADMISSION of Geoffrey de Rannvile clerk as rector of the church of Ellisfield, vacant, at the presentation of Joan des Roches, patroness. Letters for the induction to the archdeacon of Winchester and to the dean of Basingstoke.

Hursley, 8 August 1349

112 **647.** ADMISSION of Henry Manncel priest to be rector of the church of Titsey, vacant, at the presentation of Thomas de Uvedale, knight, patron. Letter for induction to the archdeacon of Surrey.

Hursley, 8 August 1349

648. ADMISSION of William de Kirketon' priest to the vicarage of the church of Hartley Wintney, at the presentation of the prioress and convent of Wintney, patrons of the vicarage. To be perpetual vicar with obligation of residence for which he took the oath. Letter to the archdeacon of Winchester and to the dean of Basingstoke for the induction.

Hursley, 8 August 1349

649. COLLATION by the bishop of the priestly office in the manor chapel of Marwell on Thomas Wadenast priest, to be perpetual chaplain. Letters for the induction to John de Nubbelegh', treasurer of Wolvesey and John provost of the church of St Elizabeth.

Hursley, 8 August 1349

650. ADMISSION of William de Morton' priest as rector of the church of Winslade, vacant, at the presentation of M. Nicholas Hagheman, patron. Letter for induction to the archdeacon of Winchester.

Marwell, 6 August 1349

651. COMMISSION from the bishop to M. John de Ware rector of Crawley and John de Craneborne rector of Itchin Stoke to examine the presentation of M. Roger de Fulford' clerk to the church of South Waltham by the king, and his admission as rector there. They are then to act with the bishop's authority.

Hursley, 11 August 1349

652. COLLATION of the parochial church of Upham, vacant, on Thomas de Wolverton'. Letter for the induction to the provost of the chapel of St Elizabeth.

Hursley, 11 August 1349

653. ADMISSION of William de Ranby clerk as rector of the parish church of Newnham, vacant, at the presentation of the king, the priory of Sherborne being in his hands. Letter for the induction to the archdeacon of Winchester and the dean of Basingstoke.

Southwark, 18 August 1349

654. ADMISSION of William Elyot priest as rector of the church of Farleigh [Wallop], vacant, at the presentation of Robert la Zouch', patron. Letter for the induction to the archdeacon of Winchester.

Southwark, 19 August 1349

655. COLLATION by the bishop of the vicarage of the church of Twyford, vacant, on Geoffrey le Mason of Saling, priest. To be perpetual vicar with obligation of residence according to the constitutions. Letters for the induction to the official of Winchester and the perpetual chaplain of St Elizabeth.

Southwark, 20 August 1349

113   **656.** ADMISSION of John de Tudeworth' clerk as rector of [North] Stoneham, vacant, at the presentation of the abbot and convent of Hyde. Letter for the induction to the archdeacon of Winchester and the dean of Southampton.

Fareham, 3 September 1349

657. ADMISSION of William Chuert priest to be rector of the church of Worplesdon, vacant, at the presentation of John de Cobeham, knight, patron. Letter to the archdeacon of Surrey for the induction.

Bitterne, 3 September 1349

658. COLLATION by the bishop of the priestly office in the chapel of St Elizabeth, Winchester, vacant, on Walter Fynacourt of Hinton Ampner, priest. To be perpetual chaplain according to the ordinance of John de Pontissara, late bishop and founder of the chapel. Letter for the induction to the provost of the chapel to admit Walter to the office.

Bitterne, 4 September 1349

659. ADMISSION of Henry Payn priest to the perpetual vicarage of the church or chapel of St Mary, Southampton, at the presentation of John Payn rector or precentor of that church and patron of the vicarage. He will be perpetual vicar, residing according to the constitutions for which he took the oath. Letter to the said John Payn for the induction.

Bitterne, 4 September 1349

660. DISPENSATION granted to Roger de Stanford rector of Church Oakley clerk, to be at the service of Roger de Bellocampo, knight, for one year, without obligation of residence.

Downton, 7 September 1349

661. VISITATION OF THE PRIORY OF ST MARY, SOUTHWARK. Memorandum that this was carried out by M. Roger de Fulford official of Winchester and John Wolvel' chancellor, in the conventual church of St Mary, Southwark, 24 and 25 August 1349. Fr John de Pecham, prior, in the presence of the bishop in his manor chapel of Southwark and before John de Beautre public notary—with the said MM. Roger and John, Thomas de Durley rector of Faringdon and William Lovel the bishop's chaplain as witnesses—resigned his office into the hands of the bishop (formula recited). The bishop then accepted the resignation (formula recited) and provided fr Richard de Stakes, canon of the same church, to be prior, entrusting to him the cure of souls and the temporal administration.

114   **662.** INSTITUTIONS FOLLOWING AN EXCHANGE OF BENEFICES. Having heard and examined the reasons for the proposed exchange, under the authority of the commission set out below, M. Peter de Croyndon, formerly perpetual vicar of Croydon, has been admitted to the church of Sanderstead and John de Stanfeld, formerly rector of that church, to the perpetual vicarage, for which he took the oath for continuous residence according to the constitutions. Letter for the induction of Peter to the archdeacon of Surrey.

Waltham, 15 September 1349

Commission for the above from Robert prior of Christchurch, Canterbury, the see being vacant, to the bishop of Winchester. The vicarage of Croydon being under the immediate jurisdiction of Canterbury and the church of Sanderstead being under that of the bishop of Winchester, while John and Peter wish to effect exchange, the prior of Christchurch approves. The vicarage of Croydon is at the presentation of John de Toneford rector of the church of Croydon. Requesting that a certificate of the process of examination with the requisite resignations and the oath of residence be transmitted.

Canterbury, 10 September 1349

663. ADMISSION of John de Monstede priest to the vicarage of the church of Romsey, vacant, at the presentation of John de Nubbelegh' prebend of the portion of St Laurence, patron for this turn, to be perpetual vicar according to the constitutions for which he took the oath. Letter for the induction to the archdeacon of Winchester.

Wolvesey, 17 September 1349

664. INSTITUTION of Thomas le Halterwrighte priest to be rector of the church of Cliddesden, vacant, at the presentation of John de Valoyns, patron. Letters for the induction to the archdeacon of Winchester and the dean of Basingstoke.

Waltham, 18 September 1349

665. ADMISSION of John de Bampton' priest to the vicarage of the church of Ashstead, at the presentation of John de Broughton', the rector, to be perpetual vicar according to the constitutions for which he took the oath. Letter for the induction to the archdeacon of Surrey.

Waltham, 18 September 1349

666. COLLATION by the bishop of the church of Exton on Robert Stowyng' of Ludgarshall priest, vacant. He was instituted as rector, a letter being sent to the official of Winchester for the induction.

Waltham, 20 September 1349

667. ADMISSION of John de Upton' priest as rector of the church of St Cross, Southampton, at the presentation of the prior and convent of St Denys, patrons. Letters for the induction to the archdeacon of Winchester and to the dean of Southampton.

Waltham, 20 September 1349

668. PRESENTATION by the bishop of the church of Brightwell in the diocese of Salisbury, vacant by the death of Thomas de Brayles, to M. John de Wolveleye his chancellor.

Waltham, 19 September 1349

115   **669.** ADMISSION of Thomas Brommyng' priest to the vicarage of the chapel of St Nicholas in Carisbrooke Castle, vacant, at the presentation of the abbot and convent of Quarr, patrons. To be perpetual vicar according to the constitutions for which he took the oath. Letter for the induction to the archdeacon of Winchester and the dean of the Island.

Waltham, 20 September 1349

670. ADMISSION of Thomas de Aumbresbury priest and canon of Titchfield, premonstratensian, to the vicarage of the church of Titchfield, at the presentation of the abbot and convent of Titchfield in accordance with their privileges. He will be perpetual vicar for which he took the oath. Letter for the induction to the archdeacon of Winchester.

Waltham, 20 September 1349

671. ADMISSION of Peter de Banenwyk' priest as rector of the church of All Saints, Southampton, vacant by the resignation of John de Upton' the last rector, at the presentation of the prior and convent of St Denys, patrons. Letter for the induction to the archdeacon of Winchester.

Southwark, 25 September 1349

672. ADMISSION of John atte Lyste of Pershore priest as rector of the church of Bisley, vacant, at the presentation of Edward, prince of Wales, patron. Letter to the archdeacon of Surrey for the induction.

Southwark, 25 September 1349

673. COLLATION by the bishop of the church of Binstead, Isle of Wight, on John Duddelee priest, vacant, to be rector. Letter for the induction to the archdeacon of Winchester.

Waltham, 20 September 1349

674. ADMISSION of John le Horsman priest as rector of the church of Widley, vacant, at the presentation of the prior and convent of Southwick, patrons. Letter for the induction to the archdeacon of Winchester.

Southwark, 30 September 1349

675. PRESENTATION by the bishop of the church of Elyndon in the diocese of Salisbury, of his patronage, to Thomas de Beauford priest, vacant by the death of Richard de Ludeshull'.

Southwark, 4 October 1349

676. COMMISSION OF ENQUIRY INTO EXCHANGE OF BENEFICES. Letter from Hamo bishop of Rochester to the bishop. Since M. John de Cranborne rector of Itchen and John de Bradeweye rector of Trottiscliffe in the diocese of Rochester desire to exchange benefices, to expedite matters will the bishop hold the necessary enquiries, receive the resignation from Itchen and then proceed with the induction.

Halling, 9 October 1349

The enquiry was held and John de Bradeweye admitted to the church of Itchen. Letter for the induction sent to the archdeacon of Winchester.

Southwark, 9 October 1349

116   **677.** COLLATION of the church of Trottiscliffe to John de Craneburne by the bishop of Rochester took place later.

678. COLLATION by the bishop of the church of Hannington to Thomas de Whitecroft priest, vacant, to be rector. Letters for the induction to the rectors of Overton and Hannington (sic).

Southwark, 12 October 1349

679. ADMISSION of Robert de Aspale subdeacon to be rector of Sherborne St John, vacant by the death of the last rector Robert de Jarum, at the presentation of Thomas de Aspale and Walter de Haywode as attorneys for John de Sancto Philiberto knight, patron, deputising for him in his patronage of vacant benefices in the county of Southampton. Letter for the induction to the archdeacon of Winchester.

Southwark, 13 October 1349

680. DISPENSATION for study for one year granted to John de Tudeworth rector of North Stoneham, acolyte, in preparation for the subdiaconate, without obligation for more.

Southwark, 14 October 1349

681. ADMISSION of M. Thomas de Enham clerk, in the person of M. Walter de Brugge his proctor, to the church of Froyle as rector, vacant, at the resignation of John de Fulford, by reason of an exchange for the church of Abbots Ann, vacant, at the presentation of the abbess and convent of St Mary, Winchester. Letter to M. John de Wolvel' rector of Michelmersh and M. Thomas or his proctor for the induction.

Southwark, 9 October 1349

682. ADMISSION of the said John de Fulford to the church of Abbots Ann, vacant by the resignation of M. Walter de Brugge, through his proctor, at the presentation of the abbot and convent of Hyde, patrons. Letters for the induction to Roger de Fulford, official of Winchester.

Southwark, 9 October 1349

683. ADMISSION of Symon Thony priest to the vicarage of Horley, vacant, at the presentation of the abbot and convent of Chertsey, patrons of the vicarage. To be perpetual vicar with obligation of residence for which he took the oath. Letter for the induction to the archdeacon of Surrey.

Southwark, 15 October 1349

684. ADMISSION of Peter de Otryngham priest as rector of the church of Streatham, vacant, at the presentation of Peter de Sancto Stephano prior of Ogbourne, procurator of the abbey of Bec Heluin, by commission of the king. Letter for the induction to the archdeacon of Surrey.

Southwark, 16 October 1349

685. ADMISSION of Henry de Titynge priest to the vicarage of Shalford, vacant, at the presentation of the prior and convent of the hospital of St Mary without Bishopsgate, London, patrons. To be perpetual vicar residing according to the constitutions for which he took the oath. Letter for the induction to the archdeacon of Surrey.

Southwark, 16 October 1349

117   **686.** ADMISSION of Thomas de Chakyndon' priest as rector of the church of Hartley Wespall, vacant, at the presentation of John Waspayl, patron. Letter for the induction to the archdeacon of Winchester.

Southwark, 17 October 1349

687. ADMISSION of Walter Selot priest to the vicarage of the church of St Martha, vacant, at the presentation of the prior and convent of Newark. To be perpetual vicar residing according to the constitutions for which he took the oath. Letter for the induction to the archdeacon of Surrey.

Southwark, 21 October 1349

688. COLLATION by the bishop of the church of Bishopstoke on John Beneyt of Newton priest, to be rector. Letters for the induction to the archdeacon of Winchester and the provost of the chapel of St Elizabeth.

Southwark, 23 October 1349

689. ADMISSION of Richard Habbegod priest as rector of the church of Compton, vacant, at the presentation of John de Edyngdon patron for this turn. Letter for induction to the archdeacon of Winchester.

Southwark, 23 October 1349

690. PRESENTATION of John de Edyngdon by the bishop to the church of Brightwell in the diocese of Salisbury.

Southwark, 23 October 1349

691. ADMISSION of Adam Payn priest as rector of South Tidworth, vacant, at the presentation of Nicholas Sampson of Hampton, patron for this turn. Letter for the induction to the archdeacon of Winchester.

Southwark, 24 October 1349

692. ADMISSION of Robert le Whelere priest as rector of the church of Hatch, vacant, at the presentation of John de Valoynes patron. Letter for the induction to the archdeacon of Winchester.

Southwark, 27 October 1349

693. ADMISSION of Symon de Watele priest as rector of the church of Hambledon, vacant, at the presentation of Edward prince of Wales, patron. Letter to the archdeacon of Surrey for the induction.

Southwark, 27 October 1349

694. COLLATION by the bishop of the church of West Meon on John de Kenyngton', vacant, to be rector. Letters for induction to the archdeacon of Winchester and the provost of St Elizabeth.

Southwark, 28 October 1349

695. PROCESS OF THE EXAMINATION OF THE ELECTION of the prior of Sherborne St John. By commission of the bishop M. John de Wolveleye held th enquiry into the election of fr. Denis de Vanceye, monk of St Vigor of Cérisy, diocese of Bayeux, to its dependent priory of Sherborne St John, vacant by the death of fr. Robert Corbel, late prior. He found the election correct and confirmed it (formula given).
The new prior received his letters of confirmation; letters were sent for his induction and to the king for the restoration of the temporalities, as are found elsewhere in this register.

Southwark, 22 October 1349

118   **696.** ADMISSION of Robert le Gamene priest as rector of the church of King's Worthy, vacant, at the presentation of the abbot and convent of Hyde, patrons. Letter for the induction to the archdeacon of Winchester.

Southwark, 3 November 1349

697. MANDATE FOR INDUCTION AFTER EXCHANGE OF BENEFICES directed to the archdeacon of Winchester, on receipt of the certificate from Robert, bishop of Chichester, concerning the exchange of benefices between John de Risyngdon' lately rector of Freefolk in the diocese of Winchester and John de Tolyton' perpetual vicar of Harting in the diocese of Chichester. The archdeacon will induct the latter to the church of Freefolk.

Southwark, 5 November 1349

698. INSTITUTIONS FOLLOWING AN EXCHANGE OF BENEFICES. Robert de Pernycote priest was admitted to the church of Ash, vacant by the resignation of John Gogh' late rector of the same, at the presentation of the abbot and convent of Chertsey. John Gogh' was admitted to the church of Mickleham which Robert de Pernycote had vacated, at the presentation of the prior and convent of Reigate, patrons of Mickleham. Letter for the induction to the archdeacon of Surrey.

Southwark, 6 November 1349

699. ADMISSION of John de Lewedham priest as rector of the church of Gatton, vacant, at the presentation of the prior and convent of St Pancras, Lewes, patrons. Letter for the induction to the archdeacon of Surrey, or in his absence to the prior of Reigate.

Southwark, 12 November 1349

700. ADMISSION of John de Wonham priest to the vicarage of the church of Betchworth, vacant, at the presentation of the prior and convent of Southwark, patrons of the vicarage. To be perpetual vicar residing according to the constitutions for which he took the oath. Letter to the archdeacon of Surrey for the induction.

Southwark, 12 Novmeber 1349

701. COLLATION by the bishop of the church of Weston Corbet, vacant, to Thomas de Lanynton' priest, devolving to the bishop's collation by lapse. To be rector. Letter for the induction to M. John de Ware, sequestrator-general for the archdiaconate of Winchester.

Southwark, 14 November 1349

702. ADMISSION of Gilbert de Blakemere to be rector of the church of Tunworth, vacant, at the presentation of John de Grey of Codnor, knight, patron. Letter for the induction to the archdeacon of [Winchester] and to the dean of Basingstoke.

Southwark, 22 November 1349

703. ADMISSION of Richard Matheu priest to be rector of the church of Linkenholt, vacant, at the presentation of the abbot and convent of St

Peter, Gloucester, patrons. Letter to the archdeacon of Winchester and to the dean of Andover for the induction.

Southwark, 26 November 1349

704. ADMISSION of Henry atte Hethe priest as rector of the church of Little Bookham, vacant, at the presentation of Thomas de Breouse, knight, patron. Letter to the archdeacon of Surrey for the induction.

Southwark, 27 November 1349

705. COLLATION by the bishop of the parish church of Hinton Ampner on Richard de Papham priest as rector, vacant by the resignation of Walter Richon, last rector, into the hands of the bishop, with M. John de Wolveleye, chancellor, Thomas de Aspale, William de Fyfhide and John de Beautre, public notary, called to be witnesses, 29 November 1349, at Southwark. Letter for the induction to the archdeacon of Winchester.

Southwark, 30 November 1349

119   **706.** DISPENSATION for study granted for one year at some *studium generale* to Almaric de Pontiliaco rector of the church of Beddington, and to farm out his church to any suitable person, provided that divine service and the cure of souls are maintained by a suitable person, who will also care for the buildings.

Southwark, 27 November 1349

707. COLLATION by the bishop of the priestly office in the chapel of St Elizabeth on Thomas de Goldeston' priest, to be perpetual chaplain according to the constitutions laid down by John de Pontissara, late bishop and founder of the chapel. Letter to the provost for his admission.

Southwark, 3 December 1349

708. ADMISSION of Robert Taillour of Raunds priest as rector of the church of Bedhampton, vacant, at the presentation of John earl of Kent and lord of Wake, patron. Letter to the archdeacon of Winchester for the induction.

Southwark, 3 December 1349

709. ADMISSION of William Dorsete deacon as rector of the church of St Mary Magdalen at Widley, vacant, at the presentation of the prior and convent of Southwick, patrons. Letter for the induction to the archdeacon of Winchester.

Southwark, 10 December 1349

710. ADMISSION of John de Tiryngham' priest as rector of the church of Hartley, vacant, at the presentation of Henry de Walton' archdeacon of Richmond as attorney for Henry earl of Lancaster, patron. Letter for the induction to the archdeacon of Winchester.

Southwark, 10 December 1349

711. ADMISSION of Robert de Hynkele priest to the vicarage of the church of Kingston, vacant, at the presentation of the prior and convent of St Mary, Merton, patrons. To be perpetual vicar, residing according to the constitutions, for which he took the oath. Letter for the induction to the archdeacon of Surrey.

Southwark, 11 December 1349

712. DISPENSATION for study for one year granted to Thomas de Clopton' rector of Blendworth, according to the constitutions and to lease the church at farm, provided that the divine office be praiseworthily maintained.

Southwark, 16 December 1349

713. ADMISSION of John de Rympton priest as rector of the chapel of Yaverland, Isle of Wight, vacant, at the presentation of Eleanor widow of Theobald Russel, knight, patroness. Letter to the archdeacon of Winchester for the induction.

Southwark, 18 December 1349

714. ADMISSION of Richard Hugeman priest to the vicarage of the church of Addington, vacant, at the presentation of the prior and convent of St Mary, Southwark, patrons. To be perpetual vicar, residing according to the constitutions for which he took the oath. Letters for the induction to the archdeacon of Surrey and to the dean of Ewell.

Southwark, 20 December 1349

715. ADMISSION of John Clerc of Cumberton priest to the vicarage of the church of Tooting vacant, at the presentation of the prior and convent of Southwark, patrons of the vicarage. To be perpetual vicar continuously residing according to the constitutions for which he took the oath. Letter for the induction to the archdeacon of Surrey and the dean of Ewell.

Southwark, 20 December 1349

120 **716.** ADMISSION of William de Blaston' priest to the vicarage of Great Bookham, vacant, at the presentation of the abbot and convent of Chertsey, patrons. To be perpetual vicar with obligation of residence for which he took the oath. Letters for the induction to the archdeacon of Surrey and to the dean of Guildford.

Farnham, 28 December 1349

717. ADMISSION of Richard Humfray priest as rector of the church of Lainston, vacant, at the presentation of John de Wyncestre, knight, patron. Letter to the archdeacon of Winchester for the induction.

Farnham, 29 December 1349

718. ADMISSION of Geoffrey de Ludeford' priest as rector of the church of Fifehead, vacant, at the presentation of king Edward, the abbey of Delapré near Northampton being in his hands on account of a vacancy. Letter for the induction to the archdeacon of Winchester.

Farnham, 30 December 1349

719. ADMISSION of William Thomas priest as rector of Kingsgate, Winchester, vacant, at the presentation of M. Richard Vaghan archdeacon of Surrey, patron. Letter for the induction to the archdeacon of Winchester and to the dean of Winchester.

Farnham, 30 December 1349

720. ADMISSION of John Champayne of Dunham as rector of the church of Worting, vacant, by the resignation of M. Walter de Sevonhampton', last rector, at the presentation of the abbot and convent of Hyde, patrons. Letters for the induction to the archdeacon of Winchester and to the dean of Basingstoke.

Farnham, 5 January 1350

721. ADMISSION of Thomas le Fadir clerk as rector of the church of St Peter Whitebread, Winchester, vacant, at the presentation of the abbot and convent of Hyde, patrons. Letters for the induction to the archdeacon of Winchester and to the dean of Winchester.

Farnham, 4 January 1350

722. ADMISSION of M. Walter Punamit of Stratton clerk as rector of the church of Dunsfold, vacant by the resignation of Robert de Wapford, last rector, at the presentation of the prior and convent of the hospital of St Mary without Bishopsgate, London, patrons. Letter for the induction to the archdeacon of Surrey.

Southwark, 17 January 1350

723. DISPENSATION granted to M. John de Ashton' rector of Stratfield Saye to be for one year at the service of Edmund de Bereford, without obligation of residence.

Farnham, 6 January 1350

724. DISPENSATION granted to John Mayheu of Stow on the Wold, rector of Esher, to be at the service of Amand de Fitlynge, canon of London, without obligation of residence.

Southwark, 22 January 1350

725. PRESENTATION by the bishop of Thomas de Edyngton to the church of Orchard, diocese of Bath and Wells, vacant, at the presentation by reason of the custody of the lands and heirs of Thomas de Orchard, who held from him *in capite*.

Southwark, 21 January 1350

121 **726.** PROCESS OF THE ELECTION at Southwick. Commission from the bishop to Roger de Fulford', official of Winchester, and John de Wolveleye, canon of Salisbury, for the enquiry held in the parish church of Farnham the next law-day after the feast of the Circumcision 1350, into the election of Richard de Bromden', canon of Southwick as prior of that house, vacant by the death of John de Gloucestr', last prior. They are to confirm or annul the election.

Farnham, 1 January 1350

The proctors were John de Merwe, canon, and Roger Bryan, subprior of Southwick. The election was found to have been canonical and the document drawn up by fr. John de Merwe and fr. John Stake. The official Roger de Fulford. and John de Wolveleye confirmed the election and entrusted to the new prior the cure of souls and administration.

Under the same date were sent out letters to the new prior, to the king for the restoration of the temporalities, to the subprior and convent for their obedience and to the archdeacon of Winchester for the induction in the customary form.

727. ADMISSION of Thomas de Querle subdeacon as rector of the church of St George, Winchester, vacant, at the presentation of the abbot and convent of Hyde. Letters for the induction sent to the archdeacon of Winchester and to the dean of Winchester.

Southwark, 24 January 1350

728. ADMISSION of Thomas de Laynton' priest as rector of the church of Silchester, vacant, at the presentation of king Edward, by reason of the custody of the lands and heir of William de Cusancia, knight, deceased. Letters for the induction to the archdeacon of Winchester and to the dean of Basingstoke.

Southwark, 31 January 1350

122 **729.** ADMISSION of Richard son of John priest as rector of Farnborough, vacant, at the presentation of John de Schirburn' patron. Letter to the archdeacon of Winchester and to the dean of Basingstoke.

Southwark, 31 January 1350

730. PRESENTATION by the bishop of the church of Elingdon to James de Beauford'. It is of the bishop's patronage in the diocese of Salisbury.

Southwark, 7 February 1350

731. ADMISSION of Robert atte Mere priest as rector of the church of St Mary, Guildford, at the presentation of the prior and convent of Merton, patrons. Letter for the induction to the archdeacon of Surrey.

Southwark, 11 February 1350

732. ADMISSION of William de Sandyacre priest to the vicarage of the church of Banstead, vacant, at the presentation of the prior and convent of St Mary, Southwark, patrons. To be perpetual vicar with obligation of residence for which he took the oath. Letter for the induction to the archdeacon of Surrey.

Southwark, 13 February 1350

733. ADMISSION of Robert de Cougham clerk as rector of the church of Whippingham, Isle of Wight, vacant, at the presentation of king Edward, the priory of Carisbrooke being in his hands by reason of the war. Letters for the induction to the archdeacon of Winchester and to the dean of the Island.

Southwark, 17 Februry 1350

734. ADMISSION of Walter de Mortestrete priest to the church of Yarmouth, Isle of Wight, vacant, at the presentation of king Edward, patron. Letters to the archdeacon of Winchester and to the dean of the Island for the induction.

Southwark, 18 February 1350

735. ADMISSION of Laurence atte Welle of Thurnby priest to the vicarage of the church of Tooting, vacant, at the presentation of the prior and convent of St Mary, Southwark, patrons. To be perpetual vicar residing according to the constitutions for which he took the oath. Letter to the archdeacon of Surrey for the induction.

Southwark, 19 February 1350

736. ADMISSION of John son of Roger de Skeryngton' priest as perpetual chaplain to the chapel of Knighton, Isle of Wight, vacant, at the presentation of Theobald de Gorges, knight, patron. Letters for the induction to the archdeacon of Winchester and to the dean of the Island.

Southwark, 21 February 1350

737. COLLATION by the bishop of the church of St Anastasius in the suburb of Winchester, vacant, on John Wynhale of Wynt'. Letter to the archdeacon of Winchester for the induction.

Southwark, 4 March 1350

738. ADMISSION of John Persons of Upper Clatford priest to the vicarage of the prebendal church of Goodworth [Clatford], vacant by the resignation of Robert Ballok, last vicar, at the presentation of William de Osbereton', prebendary of that church. To be perpetual vicar according to the constitutions for which he took the oath. Letter for the induction to the archdeacon of Winchester.

Esher, 16 March 1350

123 **739.** PROCESS FOR AN EXCHANGE OF BENEFICES. Letter to the bishop of Salisbury saying he has received the letter concerning the desire of M. Nicholas de Andele rector of the church of Ovington and Alexander de Chelseye perpetual vicar of Aldermaston in the diocese of Salisbury to exchange benefices. The bishop approves the exchange and entrusts the matter to the bishop of Salisbury.

Southwark, 3 March 1350

The bishop of Salisbury has examined the matter, received the resignation of Nicholas and with the authority of the bishop of Winchester grants the church of Ovington to Alexander, reserving the induction and oath of obedience to the bishop of Winchester.

Woodford his manor, 12 March 1350

Letter received at Esher 17 March, letter to the official of Winchester on that date for the induction.

740. ADMISSION of Roger Edmund' priest to be rector of the church of Quarley, vacant by the resignation of Thomas de Lanyngton last rector, at the presentation of Peter de Falk', prior of Ogbourne, by commission of the king, the temporalities of the priory being in his hands. Letter for the induction to the archdeacon of Winchester.

Esher, 19 March 1350

741. ADMISSION of Richard son of William le Masonn of Somerton priest to the vicarage of the church of Hound, vacant by the resignation of William de Craneslegh', at the presentation of the king Edward, the priory of Hamble being in his hands on account of the war. To be perpetual vicar according to the constitutions for which he took the oath. Letter for the induction to the archdeacon of Winchester.

Esher, 22 March 1350

742. PRESENTATION by the bishop who is lord of the manor of Timsbury, to the bishop of Bath and Wells of John de Caldecote priest for the church of Timsbury in that diocese, vacant.

Esher, 28 March 1350

124 **743.** ADMISSION of John de Maydeneford' priest to the church of Preston Candover, vacant, at the presentation of the prior and convent of St Mary, Southwick. To be perpetual vicar, residing according to the constitutions for which he took the oath. Letter to the archdeacon of Winchester for the induction.

Southwark, 10 April 1350

744. (in French) NOMINATION OF A NUN. The abbess and convent of Romsey are to receive into their community Margaret, daughter, of Hugh Descote, by right of the cathedral church at the confirmation of an abbess.

Southwark, 12 April 1350

745. PRESENTATION to the bishop of Bath and Wells by the bishop, as lord of the manor of Timsbury in that diocese, of William Bey as priest for the church of Timsbury, vacant and at his presentation.

Southwark, 15 April 1350

746. FACULTY FOR THE SOLEMNIZATION OF MATRIMONY granted to his dear friend Richard Laser, citizen of London, by the bishop, contracted or to be contracted between Richard and Margaret Rondulf' of the parish of Leatherhead in the said Margaret's chapel within the said parish will be valid; it was preceded by banns but outside the jurisdiction of the parish.

Southwark, 15 April 1350

747. COLLATION by the bishop of the chantry of St Edmund the Confessor at Wootton, vacant and devolving on the bishop by lapse of time, on Thomas le Barber, chaplain. He was instituted as perpetual chaplain and letters for the induction were sent to the archdeacon of Winchester and to the dean of the Isle of Wight.

Southwark, 21 April 1350

748. ADMISSION of Henry de Kemeseye priest to the church of Wanstead, vacant, at the presentation of the prior and convent of Southwick, patrons. Letter for the induction to the archdeacon of Winchester.

Southwark, 24 April 1350

749. ADMISSION of John de Frowbury priest as rector of the church of Litchfield, vacant, at the presentation of Eva de Sancto Johanne, patroness. Letter to the archdeacon of Winchester for the induction.

Southwark, 25 April 1350

750. ADMISSION of John de Wythewelle priest as rector of the church of Eversley, vacant, at the presentation of M. Nicholas de Hagheman, patron. Letter for the induction to the archdeacon of Winchester.

Southwark, 26 April 1350

751. ADMISSION of Nicholas Whithors priest as perpetual chaplain of the chapel of East Standen, Isle of Wight, vacant, at the presentation of Thomas Haket, patron. Letter for the induction to the archdeacon of Winchester, and the dean of the Island.

Southwark, 22 April 1350

752. EXCHANGE OF BENEFICES. The bishop writes to M. John de Sarum priest that he has received letters from M. Robert de Askeby canon of Salisbury and vicar-general of Reginald de filiis Ursi dean of Salisbury, informing him that William de Wotton' canon of the collegiate church of Heytesbury in the diocese of Salisbury and prebendary of the prebendal church of Swallowcliff, of the collation of the said dean, wishes to exchange benefices with M. John de Sarum rector of the church of Warnford in the diocese of Winchester. The bishop consents to the exchange and commissions the enquiry, with authority to admit to the prebend of Swallowcliff, reserving the oath of obedience from M. John to the bishop.

125

London, 8 May 1350

Having examined the case, received the resignation of William from the canonry and prebend of Swallowcliff with all its rights, he confirmed them to M. John. A certificate of the process sent to M. Robert.

Southwark, 10 May 1350

753. INSTITUTION of William de Wotton' clerk as rector of the church of Warnford, vacant by the resignation of John de Sarum late rector, by reason of an exchange for the prebend of Swallowcliff in the collegiate church of Heytesbury, presented by Thomas de Aspale, patron. Letter for the induction to the archdeacon of Winchester.

Same date

754. ADMISSION of Richard de Aston' priest as rector of St Laurence at Wathe, Isle of Wight, vacant, at the presentation of Eleanor, widow of Theobald Russel, patroness. Letters for the induction to the archdeacon of Winchester and to the dean of the Island.

Southwark, 20 May 1350

755. COLLATION by the bishop of the church of Weston Corbett, vacant, of the bishop's collation by lapse of time, on William de Boys priest as rector. Letters for the induction to the archdeacon of Winchester and to the dean of Basingstoke.

Southwark, 22 May 1350

756. DISPENSATION granted for one year to Robert de Cougham rector of Whippingham, Isle of Wight, subdeacon, to be at the service of Isabella queen of England.

Southwark, 22 May 1350

757. ADMISSION of William Midewynter priest as rector of the church of St George Winchester, vacant, at the presentation of the abbot and convent of Hyde. Letter for the induction to the archdeacon of Winchester.

Southwark, 26 May 1350

758. ADMISSION of Bartholmew Sperven priest as rector of the chapel of Wootton, Isle of Wight, vacant, at the presentation of Elizabeth de Insula, patroness for this time. Letters for the induction to the archdeacon of Winchester and the dean of the Island.

Southwark, 30 May 1350

126 **759.** ADMISSION of Robert de Eversden' priest as rector of the chapel of Brook, Isle of Wight, vacant, at the presentation of king Edward, in his hands by reason of the lands and tenements of Nicholas de Clamorgan *ydiote.* Letter for the induction to the archdeacon of Winchester and to the dean of the Island.

Southwark, 3 June 1350

760. ADMISSION of Ralph Knyght de Sulthorn' priest as rector of Ewhurst, vacant, at the presentation of the prior and convent of Merton. Letter to the archdeacon of Surrey for the induction.

Southwark, 3 July 1350

761. ADMISSION of Richard Gladiere of Tytho priest as rector to the church of Headley, at the presentation of king Edward, entrusted to Nicholas de Plescy, knight, with a letter addressed to the bishop and entered into his registry, by reason of the lands of Westminster abbey being in the king's hands. Letter to the archdeacon of Surrey.

Southwark, 11 July 1350

762. ADMISSION of John Hoo of Upwell priest to the vicarage of Godstone, vacant, at the presentation of the abbot and convent of

Lesnes. To be perpetual vicar residing according to the constitution for which he took the oath. Letter for the induction to the archdeacon of Surrey.

Southwark, 22 July 1350

763. DISPENSATION granted to Peter de Den' rector of Mapledurham to be at the service of Ralph bishop of London for one year and to lease the church at farm.

Esher, 24 July 1350

764. ADMISSION of Geoffrey de Alrynton' priest to the chantry or guardianship of the house of St John at Andover, vacant, at the presentation of the burgesses (*hominum communitatis*) of the town of Andover. Letter for the induction to the archdeacon of Winchester.

Highclere, 13 August 1350

765. ADMISSION of John de Exon' clerk as rector of the church of Whippingham, Isle of Wight, vacant, at the presentation of the king, the priory of Carisbrooke being in his hands. Letters to the archdeacon of Winchester and to the dean of the Island for the induction.

South Waltham, 29 August 1350

766. COLLATION by the bishop of the church of St Mary-in-the-Vale, near Winchester, on John de Westbury priest, vacant. To be rector. Letter for the induction to the archdeacon and to John de Ware, sequestrator.

South Waltham, 4 September 1350

767. ADMISSION of John Warmer' acolyte as rector of the church of Newton, vacant, at the presentation of Thomas West, knight, patron. Letter for the induction to the archdeacon of Winchester.

Esher, 12 September 1350

768. COLLATION by the bishop of the priestly office in the chapel of Marwell, vacant, on John called Le Taillour of Hursley. To be perpetual chaplain. Letter for the induction to the provost of the chapel of St Elizabeth.

Sutton, 22 September 1350

769. PRESENTATION by the bishop to the bishop of Salisbury of Robert le Squyer of Fernham priest to the church of Buttermere in the diocese of Salisbury, of the bishop's patronage.

Highclere, 20 September 1350

127 **770.** COLLATION by the bishop of the church of Alverstoke on Thomas de Durleye priest, vacant by the death of M. Peter de Hope, last rector. Commission to John Payn precentor of St Mary, Southampton for the induction.

Sutton, 5 September 1350

771. COMMISSION by the bishop to M. Bernard Brocaz rector of St Nicholas, Guildford and official of the archdeaconry of Surrey to enquire into the presentation of Simon Tony Pakenham to the church of Little Bookham. If the enquiry shows the benefice to have been vacant, then to admit him.

South Waltham, 17 August 1350

772. ADMISSION of John Blondel clerk to the church of Laverstoke, vacant, at the presentation of the abbot and convent of Hyde, patrons. Letter for the induction to the archdeacon of Winchester.

Highclere, 19 September 1350

773. PRESENTATION by the bishop to the bishop of Bath and Wells of M. Walter de Sevenhampton' priest for the church of Rimpton in that diocese, vacant.

Wargrave, 26 September 1350

774. COLLATION by the bishop of the church of Calbourne, Isle of Wight, of his collation, vacant by the resignation of Nicholas de Kaerwent the former rector, who exchanges for the church of Michelmersh, also of the bishop's collation, which M. John de Wolvel' has resigned for Calbourne. The bishop institutes these into their benefices. Letters for the induction to the official of Winchester, M. John de Ware sequestrator-general of the archdeaconry of Winchester to induct them as rectors.

Esher, 26 September 1350

775. COLLATION by the bishop of the church of Alverstoke vacant by the resignation of Thomas de Durleye, rector, by exchange for the church of Calbourne, which had been held by M. John de Wolveleye and then resigned in favour of Thomas de Durleye. The bishop institutes M. John to Alverstoke and Thomas to Calbourne as rectors. Letters as in the preceding entry.

Esher, 27 September 1350

776. ADMISSION of John Bury of Netheraven priest to the vicarage of the prebendal church of Middleton near Wherwell and to be prebend of the prebendal church of Wherwell, vacant, at the presentation of Philip de Weston' and the canons, patrons of the vicarage and the prebend. To be perpetual vicar, residing according to the constitutions for which he took the oath. Letter to the archdeacon of Winchester for the induction.

Southwark, 4 October 1350

777. ADMISSION of Walter de Wanyndon' priest to the vicarage of the church of Horley, vacant, at the presentation of the abbot and convent of Chertsey, patrons of the vicarage. To be perpetual vicar according to the constitutions for which he took the oath. Letter to the archdeacon of Surrey for the induction.

Southwark, 4 October 1350

128   **778.** ADMISSION of William de Aldeluestre priest to the vicarage of the church of Epsom, vacant, at the presentation of the abbot and convent of Chertsey, patrons. To be perpetual vicar residing according to the constitutions, for which he took the oath. Letter for the induction to the archdeacon of Surrey.

Southwark, 4 October 1350

779. EXCHANGE OF BENEFICES between William de Bradelegh priest, rector of Holy Trinity, Guildford and Thomas [   ] perpetual vicar of West Farleigh, diocese of Rochester. The bishop has received letters from Hamo bishop of Rochester concerning the proposed exchange, who approves and sends to the bishop of Winchester a certificate of the resignation of Thomas, requesting the bishop to proceed with the matter and to forward a certificate, reserving the oath.

Trottiscliffe, 4 October 1350

As a result of the enquiry William will be admitted to West Farleigh at the presentation of the prior and convent of Leeds, patrons. To be perpetual vicar residing according to the constitutions for which he took the oath. A certificate was sent to the bishop of Rochester.

Southwark, 7 October 1350

780. ADMISSION of Thomas Mere priest to the church of Holy Trinity, Guildford, vacant by the resignation of William de Bradelee last rector, by exchange for the vicarage of West Farleigh, diocese of Rochester. It is at the presentation of the prior and convent of Merton, patrons. Letter to the archdeacon of Surrey for the induction.

Southwark, 7 October 1350

781. ADMISSION of Roger de Kerselawe as rector of Ewhurst, vacant, by exchange between Ralph Knyght of Sulthorn, its last rector, for the vicarage of Egham, both in the diocese of Winchester. It is at the presentation of the prior and convent of Merton. Letter for the induction to the archdeacon of Surrey.

Southwark, 9 October 1350

782. ADMISSION of Ralph Knyght of Sulthorne priest to the vicarage of the church of Egham, vacant by the resignation of Roger de Kerselawe by exchange for Ewhurst. At the presentation of the abbot and convent of Chertsey. To be perpetual vicar residing according to the constitutions for which he took the oath. Letter to the archdeacon of Surrey for the induction.

Southwark, 9 October 1350

783. COLLATION by the bishop of the church of Wroughton (Elendon), vacant, on William de Natton' priest by devolution through lapse of time. He will be rector. Letter to the archdeacon of Winchester for the induction.

Southwark, 9 October 1350

784. DISPENSATION granted for study for one year to John de Tudeworth' rector of North Stoneham, subdeacon, without obligation of receiving further orders.

Southwark, 4 October 1350

129   **785.** ADMISSION of James atte Nok' priest to be rector of the church of Whippingham [Isle of Wight], vacant, at the presentation of king Edward, the priory of Carisbrooke being in his hands. Letter for the induction to the archdeacon of Winchester.

Southwark, 9 October 1350

786. DISPENSATION granted to Bugo Mauduyt rector of Dean [Maudut] to be at the service of the king at Calais for one year.

Southwark 24 October 1350

787. COLLATION by the bishop of the priestly office in the chapel of St Elizabeth, vacant, on John Comyn priest. To be perpetual chaplain according to the ordinance of bishop John de Pontissara, founder. Letter for the induction to the provost of the chapel.

Southwark, 28 October 1350

788. EXCHANGE OF BENEFICES between Walter atte Hull' priest vicar of Wandsworth and Richard Bernard vicar of the church of Arundel, diocese of Chichester. Robert bishop of Chichester approves and having examined the case has received the resignation of Richard. He is prepared to admit Walter to Arundel and asks the bishop to deal with the question, reserving the oath and the induction, and requesting a certificate.

Chichester, 26 October 1350

The bishop has examined the matter, as commissioned by the bishop of Chichester and admits Walter atte Hulle, in the person of Peter rector of Clapham his proctor, to the vicarage of Arundel, at the presentation of king Edward, the priory of Arundel being in his hands, the prior being an alien. He will be perpetual vicar, residing according to the constitutions for which he took the oath.

Southwark, 28 October 1350

On the same date the certificate of the process was sent to Chichester.

789. ADMISSION of Richard Bernard to the vicarage of the church of Wandsworth, vacant by the resignation of Peter rector of Clapham, as proctor for Walter atte Hull', by exchange for Arundel. At the presentation of the abbot and convent of Westminster, patrons of the vicarage. He will be perpetual vicar, residing according to the constitutions. Letter for the induction to the archdeacon of Surrey.

Southwark, 28 October 1350

130   **790.** CERTIFICATE FOR THE EXCHANGE OF BENEFICES between Symon de Northwode rector of Colmworth, diocese of Lincoln and Nicholas de Wikewane rector of Overton, diocese of Winchester. The bishop writes to John bishop of Lincoln that he approves and will accept the resignation of Nicholas from Overton and admit Symon to that church. He authorizes the bishop of Lincoln to deal with the matter and to send his certificate.

Southwark, 18 October 1350

The bishop of Lincoln has examined the matter and approves the exchange. He has accepted the resignation of Nicholas from the church of Overton and conferred that church on Symon by the authority of the bishop of Winchester, reserving all that is to be reserved.

Buckden, 26 October 1350

Memorandum that the certificatory letters were received at Southwark 29 October and letters were sent to the official of Winchester and M. John de Ware for the induction of Symon or his proctor.

791. ADMISSION of Thomas le Halterwort' priest as rector of Farleigh [Wallop] near Basingstoke, vacant by the resignation of William Elyot the last rector, at the presentation of Robert la Zouche, lord of the manor of Farleigh and patron. Letter for the induction to the archdeacon of Winchester.

Southwark, 5 November 1350

792. ADMISSION of Michael Bacon of Donhead St Mary priest as vicar of the church of Ashley, vacant, at the presentation of the prior and convent of Holy Trinity Mottisfont, patrons. To be perpetual vicar residing according to the constitutions for which he took the oath. Letter to the archdeacon of Winchester for the induction.

Southwark, 5 November 1350

793. LICENCE granted for one year to Thomas de Heyford rector of Tatsfield to be at the service of [   ] de Say, without obligation of residence.

Southwark, 13 November 1350

794. ADMISSION of William de Bagworth' priest to the church of Chalton, vacant by the resignation of John Heynot last rector. William de Holmeswell' clerk acted as proctor. Letter to the archdeacon of Winchester for the induction.

Southwark, 16 November 1350

795. DISPENSATION granted for one year to William de Bagworth' to be absent from the church of Chalton, with licence to lease it at farm to a suitable person, maintaining the divine office.

Southwark, 21 November 1350

796. ADMISSION of John Smogg' priest as rector of Chidden, vacant, at the presentation of John de Valeys' patron. Letters for the induction to the archdeacon of Winchester and to the dean of Basingstoke.

Southwark, 25 November 1350

797. DISPENSATION granted for one year to Almaric de Ponterliaco rector of Beddington for study, without obligation of residence but to lease the church at farm to a suitable person.

Southwark, 1 October 1350

131	**798.** COLLATION by the bishop of the church of Swarraton on Robert de Colyngburn' of the city of Winchester, clerk. The church is vacant and devolves on the bishop through lapse of time. Letter to the archdeacon of Winchester for the induction.

Southwark, 27 November 1350

799. ADMISSION of John Basely priest as rector of the church of Woodmansterne, vacant, at the presentation of the prior and convent of St Mary, Southwark, patrons. Letter to the archdeacon of Surrey for the induction.

Southwark, 16 December 1350

800. ADMISSION of John Waleys priest to the vicarage of the church of Malden vacant, at the presentation of the warden and scholars of Merton college, Oxford. To be perpetual vicar residing according to the constitutions for which he took the oath. Letter for the induction to the archdeacon of Surrey.

Southwark, 16 December 1350

801. ADMISSION of John Clerc of Camerton priest as rector of the church of St Mary Magdalen, Bermondsey, vacant, at the presentation of the prior and convent of St Saviour, Bermondsey, patrons. Letters for the induction to the archdeacon of Surrey and to the dean of Southwark.

Southwark, 18 December 1350

802. ADMISSION of William de Hascombe priest as vicar of Shalfleet, Isle of Wight, vacant, at the presentation of John Seys, rector and patron of the vicarage. To be perpetual vicar, residing according to the constitutions for which he took the oath. Letters for the induction to the archdeacon of Winchester and to the dean of the Island.

Esher, 29 December 1350

803. ADMISSION of Peter Lucy priest to the vicarage of Arreton, Isle of Wight, vacant, at the presentation of John de Lech' rector and patron of the vicarage. To be perpetual vicar, residing according to the constitutions for which he took the oath. Letters for the induction to the archdeacon of Winchester and to the dean of the Island.

Esher, 30 December 1350

804. ADMISSION of John Bonere priest to the church of Kingsgate in the city of Winchester, vacant, at the presentation of M. Richard Vachan archdeacon of Surrey, patron. Letters for the induction to the archdeacon of Winchester and to the dean of Winchester.

Southwark, 27 January 1351

805. ADMISSION of John Hendema' of Basingstoke priest to the vicarage of Monk Sherborne, vacant, at the presentation of king Edward, the priory of Monk Sherborne being in his hands on account of the war. To be perpetual vicar, residing according to the constitutions for which he took the oath. Letters to the archdeacon of Winchester and to the dean of Basingstoke for the induction.

Southwark, 4 February 1351

806. ADMISSION of Stephen Wyot clerk as rector of the church of Hatch, vacant, at the presentation of John de Valence, patron. Letters for the induction to the archdeacon of Winchester and to the dean of Basingstoke.

Southwark, 6 February 1351

807. PRESENTATION of John de Blebury rector of Houghton to the church of Brightwell in the diocese of Salisbury, by exchange with John de Edyngdon, rector.

Southwark, 21 February 1351

132   **808.** ADMISSION of M. Walter Beneit clerk as rector of the church of Newchurch, Isle of Wight, vacant, at the presentation of king Edward, the temporalities of the abbot of Lyre, alien, being in his hands on account of the war. Letters to the archdeacon of Winchester and the dean of the Island to induct M. Walter in the person of John Synbon his proctor.

Southwark, 24 January 1351

809. INSTITUTION BY PAPAL DISPENSATION of M. John de Lech', doctor of canon law and rector of Harrow, diocese of London to the church of Newchurch, Isle of Wight.
The bishop has inspected the apostolic letter from Clement VI to M. John de Lech', canon of Salisbury. In view of his learning and merits the pope accedes to his request to hold two benefices. He is already rector of Harrow; he holds canonries in Salisbury, Hereford, Bosham in the diocese of Chichester and Abergwili, diocese of Menevia, with the expectation of one in St Paul's, London, as also the chapels of Bockingfield and Newstead, diocese of Canterbury. The pope expects that the divine office and the cure of souls will not be neglected in these benefices.

Avignon, 26 May 1349

Since M. John has sufficiently shown his dispensation to hold Arreton as well as Harrow, he can legitimately exchange Arreton for Newchurch, vacant by the resignation of Walter Beneyt and at the presentation of king Edward, by mode of exchange. Letters for the induction to the archdeacon of Winchester and the dean of the Island.

Southwark, 26 February 1351

810. ADMISSION of M. Walter Beneyt, in the person of John de Edyndon *domicellus* of the bishop as proctor, to the church of Arreton, vacant by the resignation of M. John de Lech' by exchange for Newchurch, at the presentation of the king, the priory of Carisbrooke being in his hands on account of the war. Letters for the induction to the archdeacon of Winchester and the dean of the Island.

Southwark, 21 February 1351

811. DISPENSATION granted to M. Walter Beneit, rector, acolyte, to study for seven years at some *studium generale*, in view of ordination to the subdiaconate, according to the constitutions.

Same date

133   **812.** CERTIFICATORY LETTER FOR EXCHANGE OF BENEFICES received from Robert bishop of Salisbury.
He has received the bishop's commission concerning the exchange proposed between John de Edyndon' of Brightwell and John de Blobury of Houghton, rectors. The bishop of Winchester will examine the matter, receive the resignation of John de Blobury from Houghton and will admit John de Edyndon'.

Southwark, 21 February 1351

The bishop of Salisbury has examined the question, received the resignation of John de Blebury from Houghton and admitted John de Edyndon' in the person of Nicholas de Kaerwent his proctor, reserving the oath and the induction.

Woodford, 25 February 1351

Letter to the official of Winchester and M. John de Ware for the induction to Houghton.

813. COMMISSION CONCERNING AN EXCHANGE OF BENEFICES received by the bishop from Simon archbishop of Canterbury. 1 March 1351
William Lovel rector of Bennington, diocese of Canterbury and Edward de Cherdestok' rector of Nursling seek an exchange. Fr. Philip de Thame, prior of the hospital of St John of Jerusalem in England presents Edward to the church of Bennington, vacant. The archbishop approves and commissions the bishop to examine the case, receive the resignation of William from Bennington and to admit Edward, reserving the oath of obedience and the induction to the archbishop. He will forward a certificate.

Lambeth, 27 February 1351

134   Acting on the authority of the archbishop, the bishop has accepted the resignation of William and admitted Edward as rector, at the presentation as above.
On same date the collation by the bishop of the church of Nursling, vacant by the resignation of Edward de Chirdestok', on William Lovel. Letters for the induction to M. John de Ware, sequestrator, and to the official of the archdeacon of Winchester.

Southwark, 1 March 1351

814. COLLATION by the bishop of the church of Houghton, vacant by the resignation of John de Edyndon' by exchange for the church of East Clandon, which Hugh Broun of Pebworth priest had first obtained, now vacant, upon the said Hugh as rector. Letters for the induction to the official of Winchester and M. John de Ware.

At the same time the bishop admitted John de Edyndon' as rector of the church of East Clandon, vacant by the resignation of Hugh by exchange for Houghton, at the presentation of the abbot and convent of Chertsey. Letter to the archdeacon of Surrey for the induction.

Southwark, 1 March 1351

815. COLLATION by the bishop of the church of Ringwood on *dilecto filio suo* M. John de Edyndon' clerk as rector. the church is vacant and devolves on the bishop by lapse of time. Letter to the archdeacon of Winchester and to the dean of Fordingbridge to induct M. John or M. Walter de Sevenhampton' his proctor.

Southwark, 2 March 1351

816. ADMISSION of Richard de Eccleshale clerk as rector of the church of Witley, vacant by the resignation of Thomas de Repplyngham' last rector, who exchanges for the church of Boothby, diocese of Lincoln, at the presentation of Philippa queen of England. Letters for the induction to the archdeacon of Surrey and the dean of Guildford.

Southwark, 2 March 1351

817. ADMISSION of John London' priest as rector of the church of East Clandon, vacant by the resignation of M. John de Edyndon' into the hands of the bishop, at the presentation of the abbot and convent of Chertsey. Letter for the induction to the archdeacon of Surrey and to the dean of Guildford.

Southwark, 5 March 1351

818. ADMISSION of M. Henry de Bagworth priest as rector of the church of Chalton, vacant, at the presentation of the prioress and convent of Nuneaton, order of Fontevrault. Letter to the archdeacon of Winchester and to the dean of Droxford.

Southwark, 8 March 1351

135 **819.** COLLATION by the bishop of the office of deacon in the chapel of St Elizabeth, Winchester, vacant, on Robert de Alresford' subdeacon. Letter for his institution to the provost of the chapel.

Southwark, 13 March 1351

820. ADMISSION of William Banel as rector of the church of Clapham, vacant, at the presentation of the prior and convent of Merton, patrons. Letter to the archdeacon of Surrey for the induction.

Southwark, 17 March 1351

821. ADMISSION of Richard Beche priest as rector of the church of Shalden vacant, at the presentation of the prior and convent of Southwick patrons. Letter for the induction to the archdeacon of Winchester.

Southwark, 23 March 1351

822. ADMISSION of William Becke acolyte as rector of the church of Colemore, vacant, at the presentation of Thomas de Westcote, patron. Letter for the induction to the archdeacon of Winchester.

Southwark, 23 March 1351

823. DISPENSATION granted for one year to William de Wotton' rector of Warnford subdeacon for study without obligation of proceeding to further orders or residing.

Southwark, 21 March 1351

824. ADMISSION of Gilbert Alwyne priest as rector of the church of Sherfield, vacant, at the presentation of the prior and convent of St Mary, Merton, patrons. Letter for the induction to the archdeacon of Winchester.

Southwark, 25 March 1351

825. LETTER CONCERNING AN EXCHANGE OF BENEFICES received from Ralph bishop of Bath and Wells. Since Henry de Trencham rector of Hatch Beauchamp, diocese of Bath and Wells, and Geoffrey de Ludeford' rector of Fifhead, diocese of Winchester, wish to exchange benefices, the bishop approves and the matter has been examined by the archdeacon of Taunton. If the bishop of Winchester will accept the resignation of Geoffrey, he will induct him to Hatch Beauchamp. He requests a certificate.

Wiveliscombe, 20 March 1351

Acting for the bishop of Bath and Wells, the bishop has examined the matter, accepted the resignation of Henry from Hatch Beauchamp and admits Geoffrey to Hatch Beauchamp, at the presentation of John de Beauchamp senior.

Esher, 29 March 1351

136 **826.** ADMISSION of Henry de Trencham priest as rector of the church of Fifhead, vacant by the resignation of Geoffrey de Ludeford, last rector, by exchange for the church of Hatch Beauchamp, at the presentation of the abbess and convent of Delapré near Northampton, patrons. Letter for the induction to the archdeacon of Winchester.

Esher, 29 March 1351

827. ADMISSION of John de Northon' priest to the vicarage of Farley, vacant, at the presentation of the warden and scholars of Merton College, Oxford. To be perpetual vicar according to the constitutions. Letter for the induction to the archdeacon of Surrey.

Esher, 30 March 1351

828. ADMISSION of William Belle priest as rector to the church of Tunworth, vacant, at the presentation of John de Grey of Codnor, knight, patron. Letter for the induction to the archdeacon of Winchester.

Esher, 14 April 1351

829. ADMISSION of John Chalkberd priest as rector of St Michael in Fleshmonger Street, Winchester, vacant, at the presentation of the prior and convent of St Denys, Southampton, patrons. Letter for the induction to the archdeacon of Winchester.

Esher, 16 April 1351

830. ADMISSION of William Cleygh of 'Trelowargh' priest as rector of the church of St Michael in Jewry street, Winchester, vacant, at the presentation of the abbot and convent of Hyde, patrons. Letter to the archdeacon of Winchester for the induction.

Esher, 16 April 1351

831. ADMISSION of Thomas de Sutton' clerk as rector of the church of Church Oakley, vacant, at the presentation of the king, the priory of Monk Sherborne being in his hands on account of the war. Letter for the induction to the archdeacon of Winchester.

Esher, 18 April 1351

832. ADMISSION of William de Twyford' priest in the person of Thomas de Durleye proctor, as rector of the church of Mottisfont, Isle of Wight, at the presentation of Edmund de Langeford, patron. Letters for the induction to the archdeacon of Winchester and the dean of the Island.

Esher, 24 April 1351

833. COLLATION by the bishop of the church of Avington on Robert de Wykford', vacant. Letter for the induction to the archdeacon of Winchester.

Esher, 8 May 1351

834. PRESENTATION by the bishop to Robert bishop of Salisbury for the canonry and prebend of Edington, of the diocese of Salisbury, in the conventual church of Romsey, vacant, the bishop presenting M. John de Edyndon' clerk. The bishop requests that the bishop of Salisbury institute him.

London, 28 May 1351

835. ADMISSION of William de Chetfeld' to the vicarage of Caterham, vacant, at the presentation of the abbot and convent of Holy Cross, Waltham. To be perpetual vicar, residing according to the constitutions, for which he took the oath. Letter for the induction to the archdeacon of Surrey.

Southwark, 3 May 1351

137   **836.** COMMISSION TO ENQUIRE INTO A PRESENTATION entrusted to M. John de Ware, sequestrator-general. John de Marmynton' priest, through his proctor Richard de Norwico has been presented as prebendary of the prebend of Leckford in the conventual church of Nunnaminster, Winchester to the vicarage of the said prebend, said to be vacant. To admit John to the vicarage according to the issue of the enquiry and to inform the bishop.

Southwark, 26 May 1351

837. LICENCE for study granted to John Warin' rector of Newton, priest, for one year, without obligation of residence.

Southwark, 31 May 1351

838. ADMISSION of Henry Ledwell' of Fritwell, priest, to the vicarage of Tooting, vacant, at the presentation of the prior and convent of St Mary Southwark, patrons. To be perpetual vicar residing according to the constitutions for which he took the oath. Letters for the induction to the archdeacon of Surrey and to the dean of Southwark.

Southwark, 1 June 1351

839. ADMISSION of John Chaumpaign' of Dunham, priest, to the free chapel with cure of souls of Eastrop near Basingstoke, vacant, at the presentation of Humphrey de Bohoun, earl of Hereford and Essex and earl of Brecon, as guardian of Joan, daughter and heiress of Hugh de Braybeof, during her minority. To be perpetual chaplain. Letter to the archdeacon of Winchester and to the dean of Basingstoke for the induction.

Southwark, 3 June 1351

840. ADMISSION of Bartholomew de Donnyngworth' priest to the chapel of Kingston, Isle of Wight, with a certain cure of souls (*aliquanter curata*), vacant, at the presentation of John de Kyngeston' knight. To be perpetual chaplain. Letter for the induction to the archdeacon of Winchester and to the dean of the Island.

Southwark, 30 June 1351

841. ADMISSION of William de Bienham' to the chapel of Frobury, vacant by the resignation of Thomas atte Berton', last rector, at the presentation of Henry de Loxle, patron. Letter for the induction to the archdeacon of Winchester and the dean of Basingstoke.

Southwark, 23 July 1351

842. LICENCE for one year to John Godard of 'Cantebrugg'', rector of St Mary Magdalen, Bermondsey, to be at the service of John Malwayn, citizen of and merchant of London.

Southwark, 28 July 1351

843. COLLATION by the bishop of the church of Thorley, Isle of Wight, vacant, on William de Mere, by devolution through lapse of time. To be perpetual vicar, residing according to the constitutions for which he took the oath. Letter for the induction to the archdeacon of Winchester.

Southwark, 18 July 1351

844. ADMISSION of John Capelanus of Basingstoke priest to be vicar of the parish church of Basingstoke, vacant, at the presentation of the prior and convent of Selborne. To be perpetual vicar, residing according to the constitutions for which he took the oath. Letters for the induction to the archdeacon of Winchester and the dean of Basingstoke.

Southwark, 3 September 1351

138 **845.** COLLATION by the bishop of the church of Morstead vacant on John Godwyne clerk. Letter to the rector of Kingsgate, Winchester for the induction.

Southwark, 2 September 1351

846. ADMISSION of Jocelyn de Brandeston' priest to the vicarage of Godstone, vacant by the resignation of John Hoo of Wells at the presentation of the prior and convent of Tandridge. To be perpetual vicar, residing according to the constitutions for which he took the oath. Letter for the induction to the archdeacon of Surrey.

Southwark, 17 September 1351

847. ADMISSION of Stephen de Cosgrave priest to the vicarage of Addington, vacant, at the presentation of the prior and convent of St Mary, Southwark. To be perpetual vicar residing according to the constitutions for which he took the oath. Letter for the induction to the archdeacon of Surrey.

Southwark, 14 October 1351

848. ADMISSION of John Beel priest as rector of the church of Chalton, vacant, at the presentation of Walter de Haywode and Henry Forest', rector of the church of Eton, proctors or attorneys of John de Sancto Philiberto, knight, patron. Letter to the archdeacon of Winchester for the induction.

Southwark, 15 October 1351

849. ADMISSION of Thomas de Olneye priest to the vicarage of Caterham, vacant, at the presentation of the abbot and convent of Holy Cross, Waltham. To be perpetual vicar, residing according to the constitutions for which he took the oath. Letter for the induction to the archdeacon of Surrey.

Southwark, 21 October 1351

850. ADMISSION of Richard de Wellesburn' priest as rector of the church of Warlingham, vacant, at the presentation of Ralph earl of Stafford, patron. Letter for the induction to the archdeacon of Surrey.

Southwark, 23 October 1351

851. ADMISSION of Thomas de Aulton' priest as rector of the church of Cliddesden, vacant, at the presentation of John de Valoynes, patron. Letter to the archdeacon of Winchester for the induction.

Southwark, 24 October 1351

852. ADMISSION of William de Banewell' priest to the vicarage of the church of Hartley Wintney, vacant, at the presentation of the prioress and convent of Wintney, patrons. To be perpetual vicar, residing according to the constitutions for which he took the oath. Letter for the induction to the archdeacon of Winchester and the dean of Basingstoke.

Southwark, 8 November 1351

853. COMMISSION FOR AN EXCHANGE OF BENEFICES from Simon archbishop of Canterbury to the bishop. Since Thomas Folk' rector of St Pancras of the deanery of the Arches, London, of the patronage of the dean and chapter of Canterbury, wishes to exchange with John Godwyne rector of Morstead, the archbishop approves and entrusts the matter to the

139   bishop, who will then accept the resignation from St Pancras and admit John to St Pancras by his authority.

Ford, 20 September 1351

On receipt of the commission from the archbishop the bishop examined the case, authorized the exchange, collated the church of Morstead upon Thomas Folk' and admitted John Godwyne to the church of St Pancras. They are to be rectors by way of exchange. Letters for the induction written to [   ], reserving to the archbishop what the commission had reserved.

Southwark, 26 September 1351

854. COLLATION by the bishop of the church of Cheriton, vacant by the resignation of M. John de Edyndon', lately rector, on Thomas Folk' by way of exchange for the church of Morstead.
On the same day, collation of the church of Morstead on M. John de Edyndon'. Letter written to [   ].

Farnham, 6 October 1351

855. COLLATION of the archdeaconry of Surrey, vacant by the resignation of M. Richard Vaghan on M. John de Edyndon', by exchange of benefices for the church of Morstead, at the collation of the bishop.
On the same day, collation of the church of Morstead on M. Richard Vaghan. Letter to the prior of the cathedral church of Winchester and to M. Thomas de Enham rector of Froyle for the induction and installation in the cathedral.

Esher, 9 October 1351

856. LICENCE granted to John de Wylye rector of Walton to be for one year at the service of Edward de Kendale, knight.

Southwark, 18 November 1351

857. COLLATION by the bishop of the vicarage of St Laurence of Empshot, vacant, by devolution through lapse of time. To be perpetual vicar residing according to the constitutions for which he took the oath. Letter to the archdeacon of Winchester for the induction.

Southwark, 27 November 1351

858. MEMORANDUM that on the last day of November the bishop received the certificatory letter from the bishop of Salisbury concerning the exchange of benefices between John Waker rector of Great Shefford, diocese of Salisbury, and John Beneyt lately rector of Bishopstoke, at the collation of the bishop. By commission from the bishop, the bishop of Salisbury admitted John Waker to the rectory of Bishopstoke. Letter to the official of Winchester to induct John Waker.

140   **859.** DISPENSATION for study granted to Robert de Wykford' rector of the church of Avington clerk for one year at some *studium generale*; he will be obliged only to advance to minor orders and the sub-diaconate.

Southwark, 2 October 1351

860. AUTHORIZATION FOR AN EXCHANGE from the bishop for M. John de Edyndon' lately warden of the hospital of St Nicholas in Portsmouth and Thomas de Edyndon' receiver of the tithes arising from the manor of Northanger, due to the mother church but separated from ancient times from the said hospital. After the customary resignations, the bishop conferred the tithes from Northanger on M. John through his proctor M. Walter de Sevenhampton and the wardenship of the hospital on Thomas through his proctor Thomas de Durleye. Letter to John Payn precentor of St Mary, Southampton for the induction of Thomas de Edyndon' to the wardenship and to Roger de Beautre rector of Highclere for the induction of M. John to the tithes—or their proctors.

Southwark, 12 November 1351

861. COLLATION by the bishop of the chapel of Brook in the parish of Freshwater, Isle of Wight, by devolution through lapse of time on John de Middleton' clerk as rector. Letter for the induction to the archdeacon of Winchester and to the dean of the Island.

Kimpton, 19 December 1351

862. COLLATION by the bishop of the chapel of Appleford, Isle of Wight, by devolution, on Richard de Elfeton' clerk. Letter for the induction to the archdeacon of Winchester and to the dean of the Island.

Overton, 20 December 1251

863. ADMISSION of Richard *natus Walterus Edith*' priest as rector of Compton near Guildford, vacant by the death of William de Testede late rector, at the presentation of the abbot and convent of Durford, patrons. Letter for the induction to the archdeacon of Surrey.

Esher, 24 December 1351

864. COLLATION by the bishop of the chapel of Knighton, Isle of Wight, vacant, by devolution through lapse of time on John Mongroye priest. Letter for the induction to the archdeacon of Winchester and to the dean of the Island.

Esher, 29 December 1351

865. COLLATION by the bishop of the church of Cheriton, vacant by the death of Thomas Folk' late rector, at the collation of the bishop himself, on M. John de Overton' priest as rector. Letter to the archdeacon of Winchester and to John de Nubbeleye rector of Alresford.

Esher, 29 December 1351

866. NOMINATION OF A PRIOR for the priory of Mottisfont by the bishop, by devolution through lapse of time, of fr. Richard de Caneford', of legitimate birth, a professed canon of the order of St Augustine, priest, to be prior, succeeding fr. Robert de Brommore, lately deceased. He **141** establishes him as prior with cure of souls and the administration.

Kimpton, 14 December 1351

Under the same date the customary letters to the subprior for the obedience; to the duke of Lancaster, patron, for the restoration of the temporalities; to the archdeacon for the installation in choir and chapter.

867. LICENCE granted to John Qeor rector of Botley to be absent for one year at the service of the citizens of Winchester.

Overton, 20 December 1351

868. ADMISSION of Robert de Surr' priest to the vicarage of Thorley, Isle of Wight, vacant, at the presentation of the prior and convent of Christchurch Twynham, patrons. To be perpetual vicar residing according to the constitutions. Letter to the archdeacon of Winchester for the induction.

Southwark, 11 January 1352

869. PRESENTATION AFTER AN EXCHANGE. The bishop has received letters from R' bishop of Chichester, replying to his request that he proceed with the business of the exchange between John Gogh' lately rector of Mickleham in the diocese of Winchester and Thomas de Barton' lately vicar of the prebendal church of Ferring in the diocese of Chichester. From the letter it is clear that this has been carried through by his authority. Letter to the archdeacon of Surrey for the induction.

Southwark, 23 January 1352

870. EXCHANGE OF BENEFICES effected by commission from the bishop to John bishop of Lincoln, between Richard de Eccleshale rector of Witley and Thomas de Eccleshale rector of the church of Potton, diocese of Lincoln. The said Thomas has been admitted to the church of Witley, as by the bishop of Lincoln as authorized by the bishop. Letter for the induction to the archdeacon of Surrey.

Southwark, 24 January 1352

871. LICENCE for study for one year granted to John de Tudeworth rector of [North] Stoneham, without obligation of residence.

Southwark, 26 January 1352

872. COMMENDATION by the bishop of the provostship of the chapel of St Elizabeth near Winchester, vacant, on John de Nubbeleye, priest, for the evident good of the chapel. Letter to the official of Winchester and to John Payn precentor of St Mary, Southampton for the induction.

Southwark, 27 January 1352

142   **873.** COLLATION by the bishop of the priestly office in the chapel of Marwell, vacant, on William de Westracton' priest. Letter to J' de Nubbelegh' treasurer of Wolvesey for the induction.

Southwark, 9 February 1352

874. LICENCE TO BE ABSENT FOR SEVEN YEARS for study granted to William de Farlee rector of Hursley priest and to his clerk at some *studium generale*.

Southwark, 18 February 1352

875. DISPENSATION granted to Robert de Wykford' rector of Avington acolyte to be absent for seven years at some *studium generale* without obligation of residence but of receiving minor orders within one year, according to the constitution of Boniface.

Southwark, 18 February 1352

876. LICENCE granted to Nicholas de Langeford' rector of the church of Chale, Isle of Wight, to be at the service of Edmund de la Beche archdeacon of Surrey and to farm out the church to some suitable person.

Southwark, 4 March 1352

877. ADMISSION of Ralph de Raveneston' priest as rector of Niton, Isle of Wight, vacant by the resignation of M. Richard Wodeland' late rector, at the presentation of the king, the priory of Carisbrooke being in his hands on account of the war. Letter for the induction to the archdeacon of Winchester.

Southwark, 9 March 1352

878. AUTHORIZATION OF AN EXCHANGE OF BENEFICES by the bishop between Almaric de Pontiliaco rector of Beddington and Richard de Hampton' rector of Baughurst, after their resignations. Letters for the induction of Richard to the archdeacon of Surrey and the parish chaplain of Beddington; to the official of Winchester and the parish chaplain of Baughurst for the induction of Almaric.

Esher, 24 March 1352

879. LICENCE to be absent from the parish and to lease the church at farm granted for one year to M. John de Florenc' rector of Chilbolton.

Southwark, 12 March 1352

880. LICENCE to be absent from his church granted by the bishop to Almaric de Pontiliaco rector of Baughurst by special permission and on the same day he was warned that immediately after the lapse of one year he must be back at his church or he will be penalized and from thenceforth he must be in residence.

[   ] 30 March 1352

881. COLLATION by the bishop of the church of Houghton, vacant by the death of Hugh Broun the last rector, on M. Walter de Sevenhampton priest. Letters for the induction to M. J' de Ware sequestrator-general in the archdiaconate of Winchester.

Southwark, 19 March 1352

882. COLLATION by the bishop of the church of Wolverton on Thomas de Edyndon' clerk, vacant by the death of the last rector Hugh de Burgh'. Letter to M. Thomas de Enham rector of Froyle for the induction.

Esher, 4 April 1352

143   **883.** COLLATION BY DISPENSATION OF THE APOSTOLIC SEE of the provostship of the chapel of St Elizabeth, Winchester, on John de Nubbelegh' rector of Alresford. Letter from Clement VI to John granting him at the request of the bishop, the provostship with its modest (*modica*) cure of souls. Because of its small revenue he may continue to be rector of Alresford or of some other benefice.

Villeneuve-les-Avignon, 21 May 1351

The bishop therefore institutes John de Nubbelegh' to the office of provost.

Southwark, 12 April 1352

884. MANDATE to the official and to M. John de Ware to induct the new provost, who has an apostolic rescript to hold two benefices.

Same date

885. DISPENSATION granted to John de Nubelaye from taking the oath to the bishop, despite the statutes of the founder of the chapel.

Southwark, 12 April 1352

886. ADMISSION of William Frylond priest as rector of the church of Wickham, vacant, at the presentation of John de Scures, knight, patron. Letter for the induction to the archdeacon of Winchester.

Southwark, 29 April 1352

887. INDUCTION, after receiving the certificatory letters from the bishop of Chichester concerning the exchange between Roger Knyght of Quarley and Thomas Ledebury of Chalvington in the diocese of Chichester. Letter to the archdeacon of Winchester to induct Thomas to Quarley.

Southwark, 7 May 1352

888. COLLATION by the bishop of the church of Ewhurst, by devolution through lapse of time on Thomas de Hemyngby priest as rector. Letter for the induction to the archdeacon of Winchester.

Southwark, 7 May 1352

144 **889.** COLLATION by devolution of the vicarage of Weybridge, vacant, on William Curteys of 'Sandm', priest. To be perpetual vicar residing according to the constitutions for which he took the oath. Letter for the induction to the archdeacon of Surrey.

Southwark, 10 May 1352

890. ADMISSION of Thomas Goldeston' priest to the perpetual chantry in the cemetery of Nunnaminster at the presentation of John de Ingepenn', patron. To be perpetual chaplain, carrying out the instructions of the founder, for which he took the oath. Letter for the induction to the official of Winchester and M. John de Ware sequestrator-general.

Southwark, 15 May 1352

891. EXCHANGE OF BENEFICES WITHIN THE DIOCESE. Admission of Richard de Popham' priest as rector of the church of Wickham, vacant by the resignation of William Frylond lately rector, by exchange for the church of Hinton [Ampner.] On the same date collation by the bishop of the church of Hinton, vacant by the resignation of Richard de Popham' through the exchange, on William Frylond as rector. Letter for the induction to the archdeacon of Winchester.

Farnham, 1 June 1352

892. DISPENSATION granted to John de Salynge rector of the church of Mottisfont to be absent for one year and to lease the fruits of the church to any suitable person.

Southwark, 16 May 1352

893. DISPENSATION to the prior and convent of Breamore to lease the church of Brading, Isle of Wight, which is appropriated to them, to the abbot and convent of Quarr. Valid for five years. They must repair the rectory buildings, care for the poor of the parish, grant alms and whatever else is incumbent upon them.

Southwark, 16 May 1352

894. COMMISSION addressed to the bishop by William archbishop of York and legate of the apostolic see. Since Peter Ingram of Ottringham rector of the church of Streatham, diocese of Winchester, and Peter de Daventree rector of the church of Sculcoates, archdiocese of York, wish to exchange benefices, the archbishop entrusts to the bishop the necessary procedure and if he approves of the enquiry held by the official of the archdeacon of the East Riding, to admit Peter Ingram to the church of Sculcoates as rector at the presentation of John de Grey of Rotherfield, knight, having first received the resignation of Peter de Daventree, **145** reserving the oath of obedience and the induction to the archbishop, requesting a certificatory letter.

at the manor of Cawood, 6 June 1352

Having examined the process and received the resignations, admission of Peter Ingram to the church of Sculcoates and of Peter de Davyntree to the church of Streatham, at the presentation of Peter de Falco prior of Ogbourne, procurator of the abbot of Tiron (*sic*) in England, the priory being in the hands of the king. Both priests were instituted as rectors. Letter to the archdeacon of Surrey for the induction of Peter de Davyntree to Streatham, reserving to the archbishop what was reserved in his commission.

Southwark, 16 June 1352

895. ADMISSION THROUGH EXCHANGE OF BENEFICES of Robert Aspal' in the person of William de Stedemersh' his proctor to the church of Warnford, vacant by the resignation of John de Wotton' as proctor for William de Wotton', by exchange for the church of Sherborne St John which Robert had previously held, now vacant by his resignation, at the presentation of Thomas Aspal', patron.
On the same day and hour, admission of William de Wotton, in the person of John his proctor to the church of Sherborne St John, vacant

by the resignation of Robert Aspal, through his proctor as above. Letter
for the induction to the archdeacon of Winchester.

                                        Southwark, 17 June 1352

896. ORDINATION OF THE VICARAGE OF KINGSTON. Notification by the
bishop that an agreement has been reached between Robert de Hynkele
perpetual vicar of Kingston on the one part, and the prior and convent
of Merton on the other, as patrons of Kingston with its dependent or
appropriated chapels of Ditton, Molesey and Sheen, thus ending a long
dispute over sharing the income. The bishop declares the vicar will have
all the offerings at the church and its chapels and at the chapel of St
Mary Magdalen, recently constructed; also the legacies and bequests and
the emoluments from confessions in Lent, on Good Friday, the sheep at
Easter and the late payments of offerings neglected through the year; the
tithes of cows and calves with cheese, milk, honey and the tithe of all
146 piglets in Kingston; the tithes of dovecotes and fisheries from the four
weirs along the Thames as far as West Sheen, orchards, curtilages and
everything which is dug with the foot, and flax and hemp; and the right
of warren at Kingston, Petersham, Ham, Norbiton, Surbiton, Coombe
[Warren], Hatch and Hook; and the tithes of all mills within the said
parish, except the mills mentioned below; the tithes of the merchants of
Kingston of their individual dealings; the tithes of all geese and the
mortuaries of all the dead of the parish of Kingston; all the offering and
gifts at Ditton, Molesey and Sheen, the tithes of corn grown outside the
said gardens; of hay and copse-wood, as also of the weir of the religious
near 'Draynford' and of their mills at Sheen and Molesey; all the greater
and lesser tithes of the manors and demesnes of the religious in the
parish of Kingston when not leased out, except for an estimated 10 qu.
of corn, viz. 4 qu. mixed corn, 2 qu. wheat, 2 qu. rye, 2 qu. barley,
which the religious receive annually at Michaelmas, Christmas, Easter
and Midsummer in equal portions, for whoever may be the vicar for the
future at Kingston, partly for the sustenance of the chaplain celebrating
and serving the chapel at Molesey; it is for the vicar himself to make up
the remainder, together with the quantity of this corn taken for the said
Robert for the time he is vicar. Further the bishop ordains that the
religious shall maintain a dwelling for the vicar on a plot next to the
brook and the main street to the east of the church, which stands between
the brook and the tenement with a close belonging to John de Kent, viz.
a hall (*aula*) with two upper rooms (*solariis*), one at each end of the
hall, with a priviy for each; also a decent kitchen with oven and hearth;
and a stable with a tiled roof for 6 horses to be built within a year in
the town of Kingston itself at their expense; the said plot to be built
upon for Robert the vicar and his successors for ever. Further the bishop
ordains that the religious are to repair the chancel and its roof whenever
necessary, solidly reconstructed. The vicar and his successors are to have
the cure of souls in the whole parish and all expenditure on books,
vestments and other ornaments for the church and its chapels, repairing
or renewing them, which by custom or law belonged to the religious, as
well as all ordinary burdens, they will bear in the future; they will
maintain the buildings of the vicarage, while extraordinary expenditure

will be met according to the assessment of the portions of the parties. The bishop declares that the vicar's portion will suffice for hospitality, episcopal dues. With this ordination, valid for all time, the vicar and the religious will be at peace; all earlier ordinations are now invalid.

Esher, 2 April 1352

897. PRESENTATION of Edward de Chirdestok' clerk to the church of Rimpton in the diocese of Bath and Wells, of the bishop's patronage.

Southwark, 8 July 1352

898. DISPENSATION granted to John de Nubbelaye, provost of the chapel of St Elizabeth, Winchester, for the first two years after his induction. In spite of the strictness of the founder's regulations and of his own oath, he will not be obliged to continuous residence, or the celebration of daily Mass, or to the financial statement of his administration; as for the simplicity of his dress and its colour, he may continue as before, for the aforesaid two years.

Southwark, 10 October 1352

147   **899.** COLLATION of the church of Harrow by exchange with the church of Crondall. The bishop informs M. Raymond Pelegrini clerk that he has received a letter from Simon archbishop of Canterbury informing him that M. John de Lech' rector of Harrow in the diocese of London but of the immediate jurisdiction of the archbishop and Raymond Pelegrini rector of Crondall wish to exchange benefices. The archbishop requests the bishop to proceed with the exchange which has his approval, to receive the resignation of John de Lech' and to institute Raymond to Harrow through the dean of Croydon. He asks for a certificate of the process.

Mayfield, 11 July 1352

With this authority the bishop has dealt with the matter, accepted the resignation of John from Harrow and collated the church on Raymond. By same date certificate sent to the archbishop of Canterbury.

Southwark, 17 July 1352

900. COLLATION of the church of Crondall by exchange. M. John de Lech' rector of Newchurch, Isle of Wight, has shown to the bishop the brief from Clement VI, dated Avignon, 26 May, granting him the dispensation to hold two benefices. Since he wishes to exchange Harrow **148**   for Crondall and M. Raymond Pelegrini has spontaneously resigned Crondall, the bishop institutes John as rector of Crondall.

Date as above

901. MANDATE to the archdeacon of Winchester and the dean of Alton to induct M. John de Lech' lately rector of Harrow to the church of Crondall, after an exchange with Raymond Pelegrini.

Date as above

902. INSTITUTION of Nicholas de Henton' priest to the church of Fetcham, vacant by the resignation of John de Kendale late rector, at the presentation of Adam de Swynburn', knight, patron. Letter for the induction to the archdeacon of Surrey.

Southwark, 25 July 1352

903. INSTITUTION of Nicholas de Houghem' priest to the chapel of East Standen in the parish of Arreton, Isle of Wight, vacant by the resignation of Nicholas de Whithors last chaplain, at the presentation of Thomas Haket patron. Letter for the induction to the archdeacon of Winchester.

Southwark, 29 July 1352

904. INSTITUTION of Richard in the Lane priest to the chapel of Freefolk, at the presentation of Andrew Peverel, knight, patron. Letters for the induction to the archdeacon of Winchester and to the vicar of Whitchurch.

Southwark, 29 July 1352

905. INSTITUTION of John Goudman to the church of St Martin in Parchment Street, Winchester, vacant, at the presentation of the abbess and convent of Wherwell, patrons. Letter for the induction to the archdeacon of Winchester.

Wolvesey, 18 September 1352

906. COLLATION by the bishop of the chapel of West Stratton in the parish of Micheldever, vacant, on Robert atte Clive, priest, by devolution through lapse of time. Letter for the induction to the archdeacon of Winchester.

Wolvesey, 18 September 1352

907. ADMISSION of Thomas David clerk as rector to the church of Shalfleet, Isle of Wight, vacant by the resignation of John Seys late rector, at the presentation of William de Monteacuto, earl of Salisbury. Letter for the induction to the archdeacon of Winchester.

Overton, 27 September 1352

908. DISPENSATION for study granted to William Richer rector of Stoke near Guildford, for one year at some *studium generale* in England, with permission to lease the church to any suitable person, at farm.

Southwark, 9 October 1352

149   **909.** PROVISION OF A PRIOR FOR MOTTISFONT. Letter from fr. Walter de Brouklond' subprior, John de Netherhavene sacrist, Richard de Caneford, Nicholas de Anne, John de Andevere, Thomas de Marlebergh', John de Wynton' and John de Stedeham', canons of Mottisfont, augustinians. Since by the resignation of fr. Richard de Caneford lately prior, the priory is vacant. Desiring to end a costly vacancy, the convent begs the bishop for this occasion to provide them a prior from their order. Under the conventual seal,

the chapter-house of Mottisfont, Tuesday, vigil of St Laurence (August 9) 1352

Accepting the resignation of fr. Richard de Canford, the bishop appoints Ralph de Thorleston, canon of Leicester, as prior [Formula of nomination]. The patron is the duke of Lancaster and the abbot of Leicester consents.

Southwark, 6 October 1352

910. LETTER TO THE NEW PRIOR confirming him in his position, with the cure of souls and the administration.

Date as above

150 **911.** LETTER TO THE SUBPRIOR AND CONVENT reminding them of the obedience and reverence due to the prior they have requested him to provide.

Date as above

912. MANDATE to the archdeacon of Winchester to induct the new prior, assigning him his stall in choir and his place in chapter.

Date as above

913. ADMISSION of John Corteys priest to the vicarage of Hartley Wintney, vacant by the resignation of William de Banewell', at the presentation of the prioress and convent of Wintney. To be perpetual vicar residing according to the constitutions, for which he took the oath. Letters for the induction to the archdeacon of Winchester and to the dean of Basingstoke.

Southwark, 10 October 1352

914. MEMORANDUM as to the appointment of fr. John de Ivingho as prior of the hospital of St Thomas, Southwark [formula in full], vacant by the death of Walter de Merlawe late master or prior. The bishop entrusts to him the care and administration of the hospital. M. John de Wolveleye, canon of Salisbury and chancellor, has been asked to induct and install the new prior.

Southwark, 18 October 1352

915. LICENCE to be absent for one year granted to John London' of Hinton and meantime to lease out his church at farm.

Southwark, 16 October 1352

151 **916.** ENQUIRY INTO THE ELECTION OF THE ABBESS OF ROMSEY entrusted to M. John de Lech', canon of Salisbury. Isabella Cammoys was elected abbess at the death of Joan Gerveise. The nuns were asked if they had objections to advance as to the conduct of the election. The prioress and convent spoke through Robert Hogham', their proctor, before M. R' de Fulford', the official of Winchester, by depositions from two nuns, Edith Eymer and Margaret Amiger', chosen by the convent to carry out the election. The process satisfactorily concluded, the election was confirmed formula in full.

The manor chapel of Southwark, next law-day after the feast of St Clement (23 Nov.) 1352

917. MANDATE to M. John de Lech' to enquire into the election and then to confirm.

Southwark, 24 November 1352

918. LETTER FROM THE BISHOP TO THE NEW ABBESS, Isabella Cammoys, confirming her election and entrusting the care and administration of the abbey.

Southwark, 25 November 1352

919. LETTER TO THE PRIORESS AND CONVENT for their obedience.

Date as before

920. LETTER TO THE ARCHDEACON of Winchester to induct the new abbess, assigning her stall in choire and place in chapter.

Date as above

921. LETTER TO KING EDWARD as advocate or patron for the restoration of the temporalities.

Date as above

922. MANDATE FOR AN EXCHANGE on the receipt of the certificatory letters from the dean and chapter of Salisbury. John de Somborne rector of the church of Millbrook of the bishop's collation wishes to exchange benefices with Robert de Mitford vicar of the church of Britford, of the patronage of the dean and chapter. The archdeacon of Winchester is asked to induct Robert de Mitford to the church of Millbrook.

Southwark, 26 November 1352

923. NOMINATION OF AN ARCHPRIEST for the house of the Holy Trinity, Barton, Isle of Wight. The bishop writes to Robert de Somborne perpetual chaplain of Barton that the office of archpriest being vacant by the resignation of Roger de Exon', he confirms him in the office by the powers granted to the bishop by the brethren, conferring the cure of souls and administration of the house.

Southwark, 26 November 1352

924. LETTER TO THE CHAPLAINS of Barton for their obedience to the new archpriest.

Date as above

925. MANDATE to the archdeacon of Winchester and to the dean of the Island to induct Robert de Somborne as perpetual chaplain of Barton, provided by the bishop at the request of the brethren.

Date as above

153

926. EXCHANGE OF BENEFICES. The bishop writes to M. John de Lech' that to the church of Ewell, now vacant by the resignation of William de Waverleye because of his exchange for Newchurch, Isle of Wight, which John had received in the first place, the abbot and convent of Chertsey present the same John and the bishop admits him,

Southwark, 27 November 1352

927. SIMILAR LETTER to William de Waverleye for his institution as rector of Newchurch, Isle of Wight, by exchange. Letters to the archdeacon of Winchester and the dean of the Island for the induction to Newchurch; to the official of the archdeaconry of Surrey and the perpetual vicar of Malden for the induction of M. John to Ewell.

Same date

928. ANOTHER LETTER for the institution to Ewell from the bishop addressed to M. John de Lech, rector of Crondall who has shown him the papal document from Clement VI for M. John de Lech', canon of Salisbury, granting him a dispensation to hold two benefices and to change one for another. At the resignation of William de Waverleye from the church of Ewell, on account of his exchange with Newchurch, the bishop institutes John de Lech' to Ewell, of which the patrons are the abbot and convent of Chertsey.

Southwark, 27 November 1352

929. MANDATE FOR THE INDUCTION AFTER AN EXCHANGE. The bishop has received certificatory letters from M. Adam Fitz o Weyn, archdeacon of Meath, Ireland, guardian of the spiritualities of Meath, the see being vacant. Thomas de Sudbur', lately vicar of Camberwell, is exchanging benefices with Edmund, lately rector of St Mary, Drogheda, diocese of Meath, to whom the prior and convent of Bermondsey present the vicarage of the church of Camberwell. Letter to the archdeacon of Surrey for the induction of Edmund.

Esher, 21 December 1352

930. DISPENSATION granted to Henry de Forde rector of Freshwater, Isle of Wight, to be absent for one year and to lease the church to the prior and convent of St Denys, Southampton.

Esher, 28 December 1352

154 **931.** ADMISSION of John Lent' of Exeter acolyte as rector of Whippingham, Isle of Wight, vacant by the resignation of James atte Ok' into the hands of the bishop in the presence of John de Wolveleye, Philip de Upton and John de Beautre. At the presentation of the king, the priory of Carisbrooke being in his hands by reason of the war. Letters for the induction to the archdeacon of Winchester and the dean of the Island.

Southwark, 8 December 1352

932. COMMISSION from Ralph bishop of London to the bishop concerning the exchange of benefices between Geoffrey fil' Theobaldi Kedyton' rector of Wolverton, diocese of Winchester, and Robert de Shutlyngton' rector of St Dunstan in the West *in suburbio* London. The bishop of London requests the bishop to deal with the matter, as he himself approves after the enquiry of his archdeacon, the process of which he sends to the bishop, who may admit him to St Dunstan, reserving the induction and the oath to the bishop of London. He requests a certificate.

Stepney, 15 December 1352

933. PROCESS OF THE EXCHANGE AFORESAID. Memorandum that the bishop discussed the proposed exchange, acknowledged the resignation from St Dunstan. The said Geoffrey was admitted to the church of St Dunstan by the authority of the bishop of London and Robert to the church of Wolverton, vacant by the resignation of Geoffrey, at the presentation of Matthew Fitzherbert patron. Letter for the induction to the archdeacon of Winchester.

Southwark, 17 December 1352

934. ADMISSION of Richard Elys clerk as rector of the church of Sherfield [English] at the presenttion of Alice widow of John Engleys, knight, deceased, with the consent of her second husband Robert Gerberd'. The church was vacant by the death of William Fromond' last rector. Letter for the induction to the archdeacon of Winchester.

Southwark, 17 July 1353

935. PROCESS FOR THE EXCHANGE OF BENEFICES between Geoffrey de Sallyng' lately perpetual vicar of the church of Twyford and John de Bochardeston' rector of Clanfield, both of the diocese and authorized by the bishop. Geoffrey was presented to Clanfield by the prioress and convent of Nuneaton and admitted; the perpetual vicarage of Twyford being of the bishop's own collation, after the resignation, was collated to John, who took the oath for residing according to the constitutions. Letters were sent to the official of Winchester for the induction of John to the vicarage and to the archdeacon of Winchester for Geoffrey.

Southwark, 24 January 1353

155 **936.** DISPENSATION for study at some *studium generale* granted for one year to Thomas David rector of Shalfleet, Isle of Wight, without obligation of residence or of receiving orders beyond the subdiaconate, according to the constitution of Boniface.

Southwark, 24 January 1353

937. DISPENSATION granted to Nicholas de Henton' rector of Fetcham to be for one year at the service of John de Bellocampo, knight.

Southwark, 21 February 1353

938. ADMISSION of Nicholas Poleyn priest as rector of the church of St Laurence, Southampton, vacant by the resignation of Ralph de Stapenhull', late rector, at the presentation of the prior and convent of St Denys, Southampton. Letter to the archdeacon of Winchester for the induction.

Southwark, 27 February 1353

939. ADMISSION of John de Wolveleye junior, clerk to the church of Itchen, vacant by the resignation of John de Bradeweye, late rector, by exchange for the church of Morestead of the same diocese, which the same John had first received. Letter for the induction to the archdeacon of Winchester. (*margin*) at the presentation of the abbess and convent of Nunnaminster.

Southwark, 16 March 1353

940. PROCESS FOR AN EXCHANGE OF BENEFICES at the commission of Ralph bishop of London. Since John de Keteryngham' rector of the church of St Alphege in the diocese of London and Walter de Mercham rector of the church of Limpsfield in the diocese of Winchester desire to exchange benefices, he requests the bishop to enquire into the matter relying on the enquiry made by the archdeacon of London; then he may proceed to admit Walter to the church of St Alphege as rector, after receiving the resignation of John de Keteryngham'—reserving the induction and the oath of obedience and requesting a certificate.

Wickham [Bishops], 7 March 1353

The bishop having examined the proposed exchange and received the resignations, admitted John as rector of Limpsfield at the presentation of the abbot and convent of Battle and Walter as rector of the church of St Alphege at the presentation of William de Cusancia, dean of the royal chapel of St Martin-le-Grand, London. Letters for the induction of John to the archdeacon of Surrey, the induction of Walter being reserved to the bishop of London in the commission.

Southwark, 20 March 1353

941. COLLATION by the bishop of the tithes of Northanger to Philip de Upton' clerk, being the tithes of the demesne of the manor of Northanger, due to the parish church but separated from ancient times and collated to the bishop.

Southwark, 9 April 1353

156   **942**. MANDATE from the bishop to M. John de Ware sequestrator-general to enquire into the vacancy of the church of Stratfield Saye to which has been presented John de Bleebury by Robert de Sancto Manifeo. If all is in order then to admit him and have him inducted and report to the bishop.

Esher, 30 March 1353

Nothing was found to impede the presentation. John was admitted in the person of M. John Broun his proctor, 3 April and inducted 5 April. Signed by the sequestrator-general.

Southwark, 8 April 1353

943. TESTIMONIAL LETTER announcing that the bishop has appointed fr. John de Bradewey', professed brother of the hospital of St Thomas the Martyr in Southwark, to be prior of the hospital, vacant by the death of John de Ivyngho. He has been given full powers of administration and been installed in choir and chapter.

Southwark, 9 April 1353

944. ADMISSION of Thomas Dissce priest to the vicarage of the church of Farley at the presentation of the warden and scholars of Merton College, Oxford. To be perpetual vicar residing according to the constitutions, for which he took the oath. Letter for the induction to the archdeacon of Surrey.

Southwark, 24 April 1353

945. DISPENSATION granted to Symon Daulyn of Gainsborough, rector of Winchfield to be absent for one year and to lease his church at farm to some suitable person.

Southwark, 1 May 1353

157   **946.** ADMISSION   of Richard de Amburle priest to the vicarage of the church of West Boarhunt, vacant, at the presentation of the prior and convent of Southwick, patrons. To be perpetual vicar residing according to the constitutions, for which he took the oath. Letter to the archdeacon of Winchester for the induction.

Southwark, 17 May 1353

947. ADMISSION of John Corteys priest to the vicarage of Heckfield, vacant, at the presentation of John, rector of the same church. To be perpetual vicar residing according to the constitutions, for which he took the oath. Letter for the induction to the archdeacon of Winchester.

Southwark, 18 May 1353

948. DISPENSATION granted to John de Nubbeleye provost of the chapel of St Elizabeth, Winchester, from continuous residence, the celebration of daily Mass and the presentation of the accounts for his administration, as demanded by the founder, John de Pontissara. He is dispensed from his oath, as also from wearing dress as demanded by his status.

Esher, 14 May 1353

949. COLLATION of the wardenship of the hospital of St Mary Magdalen, Sandon, vacant by the resignation of M. William de Caleton'. The numbers of the brethren are so reduced that the house is almost derelict. By devolution the bishop appoints Nicholas Chaun priest, reserving to himself the right to restore elections in the hospital.

Southwark, 13 June 1353

950. MANDATE to the archdeacon of Surrey and the dean of Ewell to induct Nicholas Chaun, whom by devolution the bishop nominates as warden and install him.

Date as above

951. ADMISSION of William de Hynkele priest to the chantry chapel of St Mary Magdalen, Kingston, vacant by the resignation of John Banfeld priest, at the presentation of John Lovekyn, citizen of London. Letter to induct William as perpetual chaplain sent to the archdeacon of Surrey and to M. John de Totteford' rector of Long Ditton.

Southwark, 13 June 1353

158 **952.** ADMISSION of William le Chamberlayn priest to the vicarage of the church of Hartley Wintney, vacant, at the presentation of the prioress and convent of Wintney. To be perpetual vicar residing according to the constitutions for which he took the oath. Letters for the induction to the archdeacon of Winchester and to the dean of Basingstoke.

Southwark, 21 June 1353

953. COLLATION by the bishop of the vicarage of Arreton, Isle of Wight, vacant, on Thomas de Clyve priest. Devolving on the bishop by lapse of time. To be perpetual vicar residing according to the constitutions for which he took the oath. Letters for the induction to the archdeacon of Winchester and to the dean of the Island.

Southwark, 5 July 1353

954. INSTITUTION of Thomas de Eccleshale priest to the vicarage of Godalming, vacant by the resignation of William de Stowell', late perpetual vicar, by exchange for the church of Witley, which he had first received and which had been vacant by the resignation of M. Hugh Pelegrini, canon of Salisbury, vicar-general of Reynald, cardinal-deacon of St Adrian, dean of Salisbury and patron of the vicarage, who authorized the exchange and holding of a second benefice of the dean's patronage. To be perpetual vicar residing according to the constitutions for which he took the oath. Letter for the induction to the official of the archdeacon of Surrey.

Southwark, 20 July 1353

955. INSTITUTION of William Stowell to the church of Witley, vacant by the resignation of Thomas de Eccleshale late rector, who has exchanged for the vicarage of Godalming which he had previously received at the presentation of Philippa queen of England, patroness. Letter for the induction to the archdeacon of Surrey.

Southwark, 20 July 1353

956. PROCESS FOR AN EXCHANGE OF BENEFICES. The church of Harrington, diocese of Lincoln, together with the prebend of Llansantffraid, diocese of St David's, both lately held by John Petyt, are being exchanged for the rectory of Mapledurham, diocese of Winchester, of which Peter de Dene is rector. By commissions from the bishops of Lincoln and St David's, the bishop admits Peter to the church of Harrington (reserving the induction and the oath to the bishop of Lincoln) and to the prebend of Llansanffraid (using a special formula). After the customary examination, he received the resignation of John Petyt and admitted Peter to the prebend, issuing a mandate for his installation.

Farnham, 31 July 1353

159 **957.** COLLATION by the bishop of the rectory of Mapledurham of John Petyt, vacant by the resignation of Peter de Dene. Letter for the induction to the archdeacon of Winchester.

Farnham, 31 July 1353

958. COMMISSION to the bishop from John bishop of Lincoln, concerning the proposed exchange of benefices between Peter de Dene, rector of Mapledurham, and John Petyt, rector of Harrington in the diocese of Lincoln. The bishop of Lincoln requests the bishop to deal with the matter, using the enquiry already held by the dean of Wycombe, then to admit Peter to Harrington as rector, having previously accepted the resignation of John (the induction and oath being reserved to the bishop of Lincoln), requesting a certificate of the process.

Stow Park, 28 June 1353

959. COMMISSION addressed to the bishop by Thomas bishop of Menevia. Since John Petyt, canon of the collegiate church of Abergwili and prebendary of Llansanffraid in that church, seeks an exchange with Peter de Dene rector of Mapledurham, the bishop of St David's requests the bishop to deal with the matter, to accept the resignation of John from the collegiate church and to confer the prebend on Peter. Reserving the oath to himself or his vicar-general and requesting a certificate.

Cliff, diocese of Rochester, 22 July 1353

960. CERTIFICATORY LETTER received from R' bishop of Salisbury, concerning the exchange of benefices entrusted to him by the bishop, as between John de Whitewell' late rector of Eversley in the diocese of Winchester and John Scryveyn of Dorchester, vicar of Aldermaston, in the diocese of Salisbury. The bishop of Salisbury authorizes the exchange. The presentation is by Thomas de Bradeston', knight, and the bishop of Salisbury had admitted John canonically, as authorized by the bishop.

Farnham, 2 August 1353

160   **961.** COMMISSION FOR THE PROCESS OF AN EXCHANGE OF BENEFICES from Ralph bishop of London. Since William de Ingulby rector of Wotton and Roger de Kyrkeby perpetual vicar of St Lawrence Jewry (*in veteri Judaismo*) London seek to exchange benefices, the bishop of London requests the bishop to deal with the matter and in the event to institute William to the perpetual vicarage with residence according to the constitutions and to institute him after receiving the resignation of John from the vicarage (reserving the induction and oath, and requesting a certificate).

Hadham, 31 July 1353

The bishop examined the case, accepted the resignation of Roger from the vicarage of St Lawrence, then instituted William de Ingulby to the vicarage. This was at the presentation of the master and scholars of Balliol college, Oxford, patrons.

Farnham, 3 August 1353

962. ADMISSION of Roger de Kyrkeby as rector of the church of Wotton, vacant by the resignation of William de Ingylby through an exchange, at the presentation of Thomas de Latimer, patron. Letter to the official of the archdeacon of Ssurrey for the induction.

Farnham, 3 August 1353

963. ADMISSION of James atte Ok' priest to the chapel of Wootton, Isle of Wight, vacant by the resignation of Bartholomew [Spervan] lately rector, at the presentation of Elizabeth, widow of Bartholomew de Insula, knight. Letter for the induction to the archdeacon of Winchester.

Southwark, 24 September 1353

964. DISPENSATION granted to M. Thomas David rector of Shalfleet, Isle of Wight to study at some *studium generale*, without obligation of receiving further orders.

Southwark, 28 September 1353

965. LICENCE granted by the bishop to William Richer, rector of Stoke near Guildford, priest, to be absent for one year.

Southwark, 10 October 1353

966. PROCESS OF THE EXCHANGE OF BENEFICES, by commission of the bishop of Lincoln, between Nicholas Poleyn lately rector of St Laurence, Southampton, and William Noble of Churchdown, lately rector of Bix Gibwyn, diocese of Lincoln. The resignations and approbations secured, Nicholas Poleyn was admitted as rector to the church of Bix, at the presentation of John de Stonore, knight, after the enquiry held by the archdeacon of Oxford, by mandate of the bishop of Lincoln (induction and oath of Nicholas reserved). Later William Noble was instituted to the church of St Laurence, vacant by the resignation of Nicholas, at the presentation of the prior and convent of St Denys, Southampton. Letter for the induction to the archdeacon of Winchester.

Southwark, 6 November 1353

161   **967.** CERTIFICATORY LETTERS received from John bishop of Rochester concerning the exchange of benefices between Robert de Monte of Lichfield, rector of Hartley in the diocese of Rochester and Richard de Tyshe rector of Headley in the diocese of Winchester. The letters show the exchange to be expedient, hence by the authority of the bishop of Rochester, Robert was instituted to Headley as rector at the presentation of the abbot and convent of Westminster, patrons. Letter to the archdeacon of Surrey for the induction.

Southwark, 15 November 1353

968. CERTIFICATORY LETTERS received from Ralph bishop of London, whom the bishop had requested to deal with the exchange between Edmund Barneby perpetual vicar of Camberwell, diocese of Winchester and Thomas de Mottynge rector of St Margaret Pattens' Lane, London. The letters show that the bishop of London had examined the matter and Thomas was admitted to the vicarage at the presentation of the prior and convent of St Saviour, Bermondsey, with obligation of residence according to the constitutions. Letters for the induction to the archdeacon of Surrey and the dean of Southwark.

Southwark, 4 December 1353

969. APPOINTMENT OF A PRIOR for St Thomas' Hospital, Southwark. The religious brothers fr. John de Bradeweye, John Bonenfaunt, John de

Asshewell' and Roger de [   ], brothers of the hospital of St Thomas the Martyr, professed in the order of St Augustine, assembled before the bishop of Winchester in the inner room of the hospital, submitted themselves to his will and decision in providing a superior for the hospital, vacant by the voluntary resignation of fr. John de Bradeweye: they gave him full powers to choose a suitable master in the presence of M. John de Wolveleye and Nicholas de Kerwent, with John de Beautre, public notary. With this authority, in the presence of John de Wolveleye the chancellor with M. Nicholas and John de Bebury, after a short interval on the same day, they examined the merits of the brethren in the chapter-house, finding fr. John Bonenfaunt the most suitable spiritually and temporally and chose him to be prior or master, conferring on him the care and administration of the hospital, conducting him to his stall in the church choir.

Southwark, 13 December 1353

162 **970.** COLLATION by the bishop of the priestly office in the chapel of st Elizabeth, Winchester, on John Carvor, priest, following the ordinance of John de Pontissara, founder. Letter to the provost of the chapel for the induction.

Farnham, 30 December 1353

971. COMMISSION from Robert bishop of Chichester to the bishop to examine the proposed exchange of benefices between Thomas de Gerlethorp' rector of Tortington and Thomas de Stanes rector of Coulsdon, requesting the bishop to accept the resignation from Tortington and to proceed, relying on the enquiry held by the archdeacon of Chichester and to admit to Tortington (reserving the induction and oath), requesting a certificate.

Aldingborne, 23 December 1353

The bishop received the resignation of Thomas de Gerlethorp' and admitted Thomas de Stanes as rector of Tortington and Thomas de Gerlethorp' to the church of Coulsdon, at the presentation of the abbot and convent of Chertsey. Letter to the archdeacon of Surrey for the induction.

Farnham, 31 December 1353

972. PRESENTATION, on receipt of certificatory letters from the bishop of Salisbury in the matter of the exchange between Thomas Duryval of Lavington, rector of the church of Silchester and John Stanton of Handborough, lately rector of the church of Fifehead Skydmore, in the diocese of Salisbury. From the letter it was clear that the bishop of Salisbury authorized the exchange, therefore the bishop admitted John de Stanton as rector of the church of Silchester, at the presentation of Peter de Cusancia, knight. Letter to the archdeacon of Winchester for the induction.

Southwark, 16 January 1354

973. CERTIFICATORY LETTERS received from John bishop of Lincoln on the matter of the exchange of benefices between Symon Daulyn rector of the church of Winchfield and John Harpour rector of Pilham, diocese of Lincoln, made it clear that the bishop of Lincoln authorized the exchange. John Harpour was instituted as rector of Winchfield, at the presentation of William de Clynton', earl of Huntingdon. Letter for the induction to the official of the archdeacon of Winchester and to the dean of Basingstoke.

Farnham, 22 December 1353

974. COLLATION by the bishop of M. Thomas de Enham as rector of the parochial church of Morestead of the bishop's patronage, vacant. A letter sent for the induction.

Farnham, 21 December 1353

163 **975.** AUTHORIZATION OF AN EXCHANGE granted by the bishop to Thomas de Edyndon' rectotr of Wonston and John de Nubbelaye rector of Alresford. They were instituted and letters were sent for the inductions to M. John de Ware sequestrator and John de Stok', rector of the church of St John on St Giles' Hill.

Farnham, January 1354

976. AUTHORIZATION OF AN EXCHANGE granted to Thomas de Edyndon' rector of Alresford and M. Thomas de Enham rector of Morestead. They were instituted in the person of their proctors. Letters sent for the inductions.

Southwark, 10 January 1354

977. ADMISSION of Laurence le Tonner priest to the vicarage of Porchester vacant by the resignation of Henry, late vicar, at the presentation of the prior and convent of Southwick, to be perpetual vicar, residing according to the constitutions. Letter for the induction to the archdeacon of Winchester.

Southwark, 23 January 1354

978. COMMISSION from John bishop of Lincoln to examine the exchange of benefices between Robert de Hynkele, vicar of Kingston on Thames and Nicholas de Irtlyngburgh' rector of half the church of East Kirkley near Bolingbroke in the diocese of Lincoln. The bishop carried out the examination and received the resignation of Nicholas from his half of the church and admitted to it Robert de Hynkele, at the presentation of the hospital of St John of Jerusalem, relying on the enquiry held by the archdeacon of Lincoln. The bishop instituted Robert with the induction and oath of obedience reserved. Subsequently Nicholas de Irtlyngburgh' was admitted to the vicarage of Kingston, at the presentation of the prior and convent of Merton, to be perpetual vicar residing according to the constitutions for which he took the oath. Letter for the induction to the archdeacon of Surrey and the dean of Ewell.

Southwark, 18 February 1354

979. LICENCE FOR STUDY granted for one year to Peter de Davyntre, rector of Streatham.

Southwark, 20 February 1354

980. ADMISSION by virtue of a commission from John bishop of Lincoln to the bishop, of M. John de Norwici clerk to the parochial church of Brampton, diocese of Lincoln, after an enquiry into the presentation had proved satisfactory. He was instituted as rector. A mandate for the induction was sent by the bishop to the archdeacon of Northampton.
Esher, 5 May 1353

164   981. ADMISSION of John de Stodeye clerk to the chapel of Whitefield, Isle of Wight, vacant by the resignation of John de Thorverton, at the presentation of Roger, patron of the chapel, in the person Richard de Saxlyngham' chaplain, his proctor. Subsequently on the same date a commission was set up to enquire into the exchange of benefices between Thomas de Brembre, canon and prebendary of the collegiate church of Chester le Street, diocese of Durham, and the said John de Stodeye.
Southwark, 19 March 1354

982. CERTIFICATORY LETTERS received from the bishop of Lincoln concerning the exchange between William Gervays, lately vicar of Woburn, diocese of Lincoln, and Thomas de Olneye, lately vicar of Caterham. The bishop of Lincoln authorizes the exchange and William was admitted to the vicarage of Caterham, with obligation of residence according to the constitutions. Letters for the induction of William to the archdeacon of Surrey and the dean of Ewell.
Farnham, 8 April 1354

983. ADMISSION of John Rontyng priest as rector of Quarley, vacant by the resignation of Thomas de Ledebury, last rector, at the presentation of John prior of Ogborne, procurator of the abbey of Bec Herluin, holding the temporalities at farm from the king. Letter for the induction to the archdeacon of Winchester.
Farnham, 16 April 1354

984. COLLATION by the bishop of the chapel of Briddlesford, Isle of Wight, vacant, by devolution through lapse of time, on Richard atte Greyne, chaplain. Letters for the induction to the archdeacon of Winchester and the dean of the Island.
Farnham, 17 April 1354

985. COMMISSION from John bishop of Lincoln to the bishop to admit M. John Norwici, clerk, to the church of Brampton, diocese of Lincoln, at the presentation of the king, relying on the enquiry held by the official of the archdeacon of Northampton (induction and oath reserved), requesting a certificate.
Holbeach, 2 May 1353

986. COMMISSION from the bishop of Exeter to act in the matter of the exchange between William de Middleton' lately vicar of Carshalton, diocese of Winchester and Roger de Dolby rector of the church of Michaelstow, diocese of Exeter, The bishop enquired into the exchange, then received the resignation of Roger from Michaelstow, at the

165 presentation of Edward prince of Wales. William was admitted to Michaelstow (oath and induction reserved). Subsequently Roger was admitted as perpetual vicar of Carshalton, vacant by the resignation of William; to be perpetual vicar with obligation of residence for which he took the oath. Letter for the induction to the archdeacon of Surrey.

Southwark, 6 May 1354

987. ADMISSION of John Saumon priest in the person of John de Bennebury his proctor as rector of the church of Stratfield Saye, vacant by the voluntary resignation of John de Bleobury lately rector, at the presentation of John de Haywode, patron. Letter for the induction to the archdeacon of Winchester for the induction of John or his proctor.

Southwark, 6 May 1354

988. COMMISSION from John bishop of Lincoln to enquire into the presentation by Philip Pellitoft, knight, lord of Watton, of John de Thorp' to the church of Watton-at-Stone, diocese of Lincoln, said to be vacant. An enquiry is being held by the dean of Hertford. On receipt of the certificate the bishop of Winchester will deal with the matter and admit John as rector and order his induction. He requests a certificate.

Kibblesworth, 11 June 1354

989. INSTITUTION of John de Thorp' as rector of Watton-at-Stone, as authorized by the bishop of Lincoln.

Southwark, 15 June 1354

990. MANDATE from the bishop, as commissioned by the bishop of Lincoln, to the official of the archdeacon of Hertford and the dean of Hertford for the induction of John de Thorp' to the church of Watton-at-Stone. A certificate of the whole process sent to Lincoln.

166 **991.** ADMISSION of Henry de Mershton' priest to the vicarage of the church of Horley, vacant, at the presentation of the abbot and convent of Chertsey, patrons. To be perpetual vicar residing according to the constitutions for which he took the oath. Letter for the induction to the official of the archdeacon of Surrey.

Southwark, 18 June 1354

992. ADMISSION of Gilbert Waryn priest to the church of Whippingham, Isle of Wight, vacant by the resignation of John de Exon', last rector, at the presentation of King Edward, patron for this turn. Letter for the induction to the archdeacon of Winchester and the dean of the Island.

Southwark, 19 June 1354

993. DISPENSATION granted to William Peyto rector of Buckland to be absent for one year.

Southwark, 19 June 1354

994. ADMISSION of Hugh *ad pontem* of Stanford Rivers to the church of Ockham, vacant by the resignation of Walter Friland, last rector, at the presentation of Ralph earl of Stafford, patron. Letter for the induction to the official of Surrey.

Downton, 1 August 1354

995. PROCESS OF AN EXCHANGE OF BENEFICES after letters received from John archbishop of Dublin and Robert bishop of Chichester concerning the exchange between Peter Grenet rector of Rye, diocese of Chichester and canon and prebendary of St Patrick, Dublin on the one part, and M. John de Kenyngton', rector of West Meon, diocese of Winchester. Executing the commission, the bishop examined the matter, authorized the exchange, accepted the resignation of Peter Grenet from the church with the canonry and prebend; then he admitted M. John de Kenyngton' to the church of Rye at the presentation of the king, as authorized by the bishop of Chichester, conferring on him the canonry and prebend, as authorized by the archbishop of Dublin (the induction to Rye and the canonry and prebend being reserved to the said bishop and archbishop). Subsequently the bishop conferred the church of West Meon, vacant by the resignation of the proctor for M. John, on Peter Crenet, writing to the official of Winchester for the induction.

Downton, 1 August 1354

996. CERTIFICATORY LETTERS received from M. John de Melburn', *locum tenens* for the dean and chapter of Lichfield, concerning the exchange between Robert de Lich' rector of the church of Headley and Symon de Bruynton' vicar of the stall of Richard Boule, canon of the said cathedral and prebendary there of the prebend of Bishop's Hull. From the letters the dean and chapter approved the exchange, hence Symon de Brynton was admitted to Headley. Letter for the induction to the official of the archdeacon of Surrey.

Downton, 2 August 1354

997. COLLATION by the bishop of the parish church of St Mary over Northgate, Winchester, vacant, on Roger de Aumbresbury priest, by devolution through lapse of time. Letter to induct him as rector sent to the archdeacon of Winchester.

South Waltham, 31 August 1354

998. COLLATION by the bishop of the priestly office, vacant, in the chapel of St Elizabeth, Winchester on Henry *dictus Cissor* of Winchester, priest. Letter to the provost of the chapel to admit the said Henry.

Sutton, 4 September 1354

167 **999**. CERTIFICATORY LETTERS received from M. John Barnet, canon of London, vicar-general of Michael, elect of London, to the bishop concerning the exchange of benefices between Richard de Orcheston', lately rector of St James, Winchester, and John Gosselyn rector of St Nicholas, Acton, diocese of London. It appears that by the authority of the commission the church of St James was conferred by M. John Barnet on John Gosselyn, who was canonically instituted as rector. Letter to the archdeacon of Winchester for induction.

Southwark, 2 October 1354

1000. DISPENSATION granted by the bishop to Thomas de Barton rector of Mickleham to be absent for one year at the service of John de Bellocampo, knight.

Southwark, 30 September 1354

1001. DISPENSATION granted by the bishop to Thomas de Whitecroft rector of Houghton to be absent for one year at the service of the king, with licence to lease at farm the fruits of that church.

Southwark, 24 september 1354

1002. CERTIFICATORY LETTERS received from Robert bishop of Chichester, concerning the exchange between John Lok' rector of Compton near Winchester and John de Kymberlee rector of Telscombe, diocese of Chichester, effected under the date, 30 July 1354. It appears from these letters that in this exchange the bishop of Chichester acted according to the commission from the bishop and admitted the new rector of Compton canonically. Letter for the induction to the official of Winchester and the sequestrator-general.

Southwark, 14 October 1354

1003. COLLATION by the bishop of the church of St Mary in the Forecourt, Winchester, vacant, by devolution through lapse of time, on Richard de Bolteford' priest to be rector. Letter for the induction to the provost of St Elizabeth.

Southwark, 7 October 1354

1004. DISPENSATION for study granted to John Scriveyn of Dorchester, rector of Eversley.

Southwark, 12 October 1354

1005. ADMISSION of Nicholas Swayn priest to the church of Wolverton, vacant by the death of the last rector, Robert, at the presentation of Matthew Fitzherbert, knight. Letters for the induction to the archdeacon of Winchester and the dean of Basingstoke.

Southwark, 14 October 1354

1006. CERTIFICATORY LETTERS received from M. John Barnet, canon of London and vicar-general of Michael, elect of London, confirmed, concerning the exchange between William Richer rector of Stoke next Guildford and John Whiteweye, rector of St Olave's next the Tower.

Southwark, 16 October 1354

The letters show that M. John has dealt with the matter and admitted John Whitewey as rector, by the authority of his commission. Letter to the archdeacon of Surrey for the induction.

Southwark, 18 October 1354

1007. LICENCE granted to John de Whiteweye, rector of Stoke next Guildford, to be for one year at the service of Hugh de Nevile, knight.

Southwark, 19 October 1354

168 **1008**. APPROPRIATION OF THE CHURCH OF FROYLE granted to the abbess and convent of St Mary Winchester (Nunnaminster). On account of the poverty of the nuns, due to the sterility of their lands and the destruction of their woods and their reduced income, they were gravely in debt, and Adam [de Orleton] granted them the patronage of the church of Froyle. They have appealed to the bishop that the church, where now is a perpetual vicar, be appropriated to them. The bishop, with the chapter of the cathedral and M. Thomas de Enham, rector of Froyle all consenting, has acceded to their request. The nuns will have full rights to the church, excepting the ordination of the vicar's portion of the revenue, and the institution of the vicar, after the resignation or death of the present rector. The nuns will pay an annual pension of 6s. 8d. to the bishop through the treasurer at Wolvesey at Ladyday; then to the

169 prior and chapter of Winchester 3s. 8d.; to the archdeacon 12d. Penalties for default.

Chapter-house, Winchester, 4 January 1354

1009. COLLATION by the bishop of the church of South Waltham on M. Walter de Sevenhampton priest, vacant by the resignation of M. Roger de Fulford', by an exchange for the church of Houghton. M. Walter was instituted and subsequently M. Roger was collated to Houghton, vacant by the resignation of M. Walter. Letter for both inductions to the archdeacon of Winchester.

Southwark, 3 October 1354

1010. EXCHANGE OF BENEFICES authorized between John de Merowe, lately rector of Peper Harrow and Thomas de Eccleshale, to become perpetual vicar of Godalming, vacant by the resignation of the said Thomas, at the presentation of Hugh Pelegrini treasurer of Lichfield, proctor and vicar-general in England for Reynald, cardinal-deacon of St Adrian and canon of Salisbury. To be perpetual vicar, residing according to the constitutions for which he took the oath. Subsequently the said Thomas was admitted to the church of Peper Harrow, vacant at the resignation of John, at the presentation of the king by reason of the custody of the lands of Andrew Braunche. Letters for the induction to the archdeacon of Surrey and the dean of Guildford.

Southwark, 4 November 1354

1011. DISPENSATION granted to Peter Grenet rector of West Meon to be for one year at the service of John archbishop of Dublin.

Southwark, 4 November 1354

1012. DISPENSATION granted to Symon de Brynton' rector of Headley to be for one year at the service of Ralph, earl of Stafford.

Southwark, 4 November 1354

1013. DISPENSATION granted to Richard de Barton' rector of Sutton near Carshalton, to be absent for one year.

Southwark, 4 November 1354

1014. ADMISSION of Richard de Snodenham priest to be rector of the church of Peper Harrow, vacant by the resignation of Richard le Cras, proctor for Thomas de Eccleshale, at the presentation of king Edward as custodian of Andrew Braunche. Letter to the induction to the archdeacon of Surrey.

Southwark, 7 December 1354

170 **1015.** ADMISSION of Thomas Cupping to the vicarage of the church of Empshott, at the presentation of the prior and convent of Southwick. To be perpetual vicar, residing according to the constitutions for which he took the oath. Letter for the induction to the archdeacon of Winchester.

South Waltham, 8 January, 1355

1016. ADMISSION of Symon le Straunge priest to the vicarage of the church of Portsea, vacant, at the presentation of the prior and convent of Southwick. To be perpetual vicar, residing according to the constitutions. Letter for the induction to the archdeacon of Winchester.

South Waltham, 7 January 1355

1017. ADMISSION of William Edenes' of Kirton in Lindsey priest to the vicarage of the church of East Worldham, vacant by the resignation o' John le Stertere, last vicar, in the presence of M. Thomas de Enham chancellor of the bishop and of Geoffrey de Salyng, rector of Clanfield, Robert Husee and of John de Beautre public notary, at Southwark, 6 October 1354. This is at the presentation of the prior and convent of Selborne. To be perpetual vicar residing according to the constitutions for which he took the oath. Letters for the induction to the archdeacon of Winchester and the dean of Alton.

Southwark, 4 February 1355

1018. CERTIFICATORY LETTERS received from M. Walter de Elvedon' precentor of the church of Hereford, vicar-general for W' bishop of Norwich, concerning the exchange of benefices between Adam de Ofham, vicar of the church of Amport, diocese of Winchester, and Elias le Blenuo, rector of Worlingworth, diocese of Norwich—received at Southwark, 17 January 1355. The bishop entrusted the matter to M. Walter, as his vicar in the process who admitted the said Elias to Amport at the presentation of M. William de Bergaveny, locum tenens for the dean and chapter as patrons, authorized by the bishop of Winchester. To be perpetual vicar residing according to the constitutions. Letter for the induction to the archdeacon of Winchester.

Southwark, 7 February 1355

1019. ADMISSION of John Salom priest to the vicarage of St Thomas martyr of Portsmouth, vacant by the demission of Symon le Straunge, late vicar at the presentation of the prior and convent of Southwick. To be perpetual vicar residing according to the constitutions, for which he took the oath. Letters for the induction to the archdeacon of Winchester.

Southwark, 13 February 1355

1020. ADMISSION of John Eorl priest to the church of Hambledon, vacant by the free resignation of [   ] last rector, in the presence of M. John de Wolvel', official, and Thomas de Enham, chancellor, Robert Husee and John de Beautre, public notary, at Southwark, 25 February. At the presentation of John de Bursebrugge, patron. Letter for the induction to the archdeacon of Surrey.

Southwark, 25 February 1355

1021. ADMISSION of Richard le Clerc of Shoreham to the vicarage of Weybridge, vacant, at the presentation of the prior and convent of Newark. To be perpetual vicar, residing according to the constitutions for which he took the oath. Letter for the induction to the official of the archdeacon of Surrey.

Southwark, 28 February 1355

171 **1022.** ADMISSION of John Say priest as rector of the church of Sutton, vacant by the death of Richard de Barton', at the presentation of the abbot and convent of Chertsey. Letter for the induction to the archdeacon of Surrey.

Southwark, 7 March 1355

1023. RATIFICATION granted to John Lombard, rector of Dogmersfield, at the request of R' bishop of Bath and Wells, to extend his stay with the said bishop, this being the first request for an extension.

Esher, 30 March 1355

1024. COLLATION by the bishop of the church of Headbourne Worthy on Nicholas Monuz priest, to be rector there. Letter for the induction to the archdeacon of Winchester.

Esher, 10 April 1355

1025. CERTIFICATORY LETTERS received from M. John Barnet, canon of London, vicar-general of Michael, bishop elect, concerning the exchange of benefices between John de Loudham, lately rector of Gatton, diocese of Winchester, and John de Keroolston, perpetual chaplain of the chantry or chapel of St Mary in the Guildhall, London—dated Southwark, 6 March 1355. As commissioned by the bishop, M. John has admitted John de Kercelston' as rector of Gatton, at the presentation of the prior and convent of St Pancras, Lewes. Letter for the induction to the archdeacon of Surrey.

Southwark, 14 April 1355

1026. CERTIFICATORY LETTERS from Robert bishop of Salisbury, commissioned by the bishop to proceed with the exchange between Richard Bekke lately rector of Chaldon and Thomas Aleyn lately rector of Manningford diocese of Salisbury, dated Esher, 28 March 1355. Thomas has been admitted as rector of Chalden, as authorized by the bishop. Letter to the archdeacon of Winchester for the induction.

Southwark, 16 April 1355

1027. LICENCE granted to Thomas de Barton' rector of Mickleham to be for one year at the service of John de Bello Campo, knight.

Southwark, 3 February 1355

1028. ADMISSION of John Whiteway priest as rector of the church of Stoke next Guildford, vacant, at the presentation of the prior and convent of Lewes. Letters for the induction to M. Thomas de Enham rector of Alresford and chancellor of Winchester.

Southwark, 18 April 1355

1029. LETTERS received from John bishop of Lincoln, stating that Geoffrey de Kyllum rector of Havant, diocese of Winchester, and John de Burton', rector of Market Overton, diocese of Lincoln, seek an exchange. The bishop of Lincoln requests the bishop to deal with the matter, on the basis of the enquiry held by the archdeacon of Northampton, and to admit Geoffrey to the church of Market Overton, at the presentation of John Veer, earl of Oxford. By letters dated Fingest, 6 March 1355. The bishop accepted the resignation from Havant and has instituted him to Market Overton.

172

1030. COLLATION by the bishop of the church of Havant on John de Burton' priest, vacant by the resignation of Geoffrey de Kyllum. To be rector; letters for the induction to the official of Winchester and the rector of Farlington.

Southwark, 19 May 1355

1031. LICENCE granted to fr. John de Fescamp' prior of St Helens, Isle of Wight, to have the care of souls of the parish church which is appropriated to the priory.

Southwark, 13 May 1355

1032. COMMISSION CONCERNING AN EXCHANGE OF BENEFICES received from R' bishop of Salisbury. Martin Bolt of Witchampton, diocese of Salisbury, and Gilbert Waryn rector of Whippingham seek an exchange. The bishop is to deal with the matter relying on the enquiry of the archdeacon of Dorset. He will receive the resignation of Martin from Witchampton and admit Gilbert.

Sherborne castle, 26 May 1355

Gilbert was admitted to Witchampton after the resignation of Martin Bolt, at the presentation of Wancilina Mautravers. Martin was admitted to Whippingham, at the presentation of king Edward, the priory of Carisbrooke being in his hands. Letter for his induction to the archdeacon of Winchester and to the dean of the Isle of Wight.

Southwark, 1 June, 1355

173 **1033.** LICENCE TO ELECT A PRIORESS granted to the subprioress of the convent of St Margaret, Ivinghoe, vacant by the death of Matildis de

Cheverdich'. The bishop underlines the spirit which should inspire the nuns.

Southwark, 9 June 1355

1034. LICENCE granted to John de Gerlethorp' rector of Coulsdon to be for one year at the service of Edward, prince of Wales, and to lease the church at farm.

Southwark, 1 June 1355

1035. CERTIFICATORY LETTERS received from M. John de Lech', professor of canon law and canon of Salisbury. He has received a letter from the bishop concerning the exchange desired between John de Clifton' rector of Winnall near Winchester and Robert de Bicton' rector of Heighton, diocese of Chichester. M. John has examined the request, received the resignation from the church of Winnall and admitted Robert de Bicton'.

London, 20 June 1355

Letters to the official of Winchester and to John, provost of the chapel of St Elizabeth for the induction.

Southwark, 21 June 1355

1036. ADMISSION of Thomas de Notyngham priest to the vicarage of the church of Banstead, vacant, at the presentation of fr. Nicholas de Raveneston', subprior of St Mary, Southwark, *locumtenens* for fr. John de Pekham, prior. To be perpetual vicar, residing according to the constitutions, for which he took the oath. Letter for the induction to the archdeacon of Surrey.

Southwark, 25 June 1355

174 **1037.** ADMISSION of John de Fakenhamdam' priest to the vicarage of St Thomas the Martyr, Portsmouth, vacant, at the presentation of the prior and convent of Southwick. To be perpetual vicar, residing according to the constitutions, for which he took the oath. Letter for the induction to the archdeacon of Winchester.

Southwark, 1 July 1355

1038. ADMISSION of William de Stodmarssh' acolyte to the church of Chiddingfold. vacant by the death of M. Robert de Chisenhale, last rector, at the presentation of Hugh Pelegrini, treasurer of Lichfield, procurator in England for Reynald, cardinal deacon of St Adrian and canon of Salisbury. Letter for the induction to the archdeacon of Surrey.

Southwark, 13 July 1355

1039. EXCHANGE OF PREBENDS. The bishop has received letters from the king and from R' bishop of Coventry and Lichfield, concerning the exchange of prebends between Thomas de Brembre, prebendary of the prebend of Alveley in the royal free chapel of Bridgenorth, diocese of Coventry and Lichfield, and Philip de Weston', prebendary of the prebend of Middleton in the conventual church of Wherwell, at the presentation of the abbess.

A commission to the bishop from the king, since the chapel at Bridgenorth is at his collation, to act in his name, but with the induction reserved to the king.

Westminster, 1 July 1355

A commission to the bishop from Roger, bishop of Coventry and Lichfield, authorizing the bishop to proceed in the exchange.

Haywood, 8 July 1355

The bishop has dealt with the matter and admitted Thomas to the prebend of Middleton at Wherwell.

Southwark, 18 July 1355

Mandate by the same date to the archdeacon of Winchester for the induction to his stall in choir and place in chapter.

1040. CERTIFICATORY LETTER sent to king Edward concerning the execution of his commission.

Date as above

175 **1041.** COLLATION by the bishop of the sacerdotal office in the chapel of St Elizabeth, Winchester, vacant, on Walter Thorald priest, as perpetual chaplain, according to the ordination of the founder, John de Pontissara. Letter for his admission to the provost of the chapel.

Farnham, 7 August 1355

1042. ADMISSION of Hugh FitzPeter of Alveston priest as rector of the church of Swarraton, vacant by the resignation of Robert de Colyngborne, at the presentation of fr. John Pavely, prior of the hospital of St John of Jerusalem in England. Letter for the induction to the archdeacon of Winchester.

Farnham, 17 August 1355

1043. COLLATION by the bishop of the sacerdotal office in the chapel of St Elizabeth, Winchester, on John Torald, priest.

Farnham, 23 August 1355

1044. COLLATION of the office of deacon in the chapel of St Elizabeth, at the instance of M. John de Nubbeleye, provost of the chapel, on William Cark' priest. Letters for admission to the said provost.

Highclere, 5 September 1355

1045. COLLATION OF A SECOND BENEFICE on M. John de Wolveleye, rector of Alverstoke, by apostolic concession, to be rector in the church of Shorwell, Isle of Wight, vacant, at the presentation of Thomas de Insula, clerk. Letter for the induction to the archdeacon of Winchester and to the dean of the Island.

Southwark, 11 October 1355

1046. INSTITUTION of John Edith' of Colthrop, priest to the perpetual chantry in the manor chapel founded formerly by Thomas de Coudray, knight, at Sherborne Coudray, in the parish of Sherborne St John. The chapel was endowed with certain rents and income and is at the presentation of William de Fyfhyde, lord of Sherborne Coudray. Letter for the induction to the archdeacon of Winchester.

Southwark, 16 October 1355

1047. ADMISSION of Thomas Goldston priest as rector of the chapel of Yaverland, vacant, at the presentation of Alianora widow of Theobald Russell, knight. Letter for the induction to the archdeacon of Winchester and to the dean of the Isle of Wight.

Southwark, 16 October 1355

1048. ADMISSION of Walter de Brouk' priest to the chantry chapel in the cemetery of Nunnaminster, vacant, at the presentation of John de Ingepenn'. To be perpetual chaplain, taking the oath to keep the ordinances of the founder. Letter for the induction to the official of Winchester and M. John de Ware, sequestrator-general.

Southwark, 5 November 1355

1049. ADMISSION of John de Cirencestr' priest to the vicarage of Whitsbury, vacant, at the presentation of the prior and convent of Breamore. To be perpetual vicar, residing according to the constitutions. Letter for the induction to the archdeacon of Winchester.

Southwark, 8 October 1355

176 **1050.** EXCHANGE OF BENEFICES. M. J' de Lech', rector of Crondall, has shown to the bishop letters from pope Clement VI allowing him to hold two benefices with cure of souls. The bishop by the authority of Robert bishop of Chichester, is commissioned to arrange the exchange for the church of Petworth, diocese of Chichester, at the patronage of Henry de Percy, knight. The church is vacant by the resignation of Thomas de Kaygnes priest and will be in exchange for the church of Ewell, which he had at first obtained. Letter from the bishop of Chichester, is recited. The bishop is given powers to admit M. John de Lech' to Petworth as rector.

Aldingbourne, 9 November 1355

Admitted and letter sent for the induction.

Southwark, 14 November 1355

1051. ADMISSION of Thomas de Kaynes as rector of the church of Ewell, vacant by the resignation of M. John de Lech' lately rector, by exchange for Petworth, which Thomas had first obtained, at the presentation of the abbot and convent of Chertsey. Letter for the induction to the archdeacon of Surrey and the dean of Ewell.

Southwark, 14 November 1355

1052. AUTHORIZATION OF AN EXCHANGE WITHIN THE DIOCESE by the bishop between Thomas de Chakynden' rector of Hartley Westpall and Alan de

Notyngham' vicar of the church of Crondall. Admission of Thomas to the vicarage, at the presentation of M. John de Lech' rector of Crondall, to be perpetual vicar residing according to the constitutions, for which he took the oath. Admission of Alan as rector of the church of Hartley Westpall, vacant by the resignation of the said Thomas, at the presentation of John Waspail. Letter for their induction to the archdeacon of Winchester.

Southwark, 3 December 1355

177   **1053.** COLLATION by the bishop of the church of Weston Corbet, vacant, by devolution through lapse of time, on Thomas Meleward' priest to be rector. Letter for the induction to the archdeacon of Winchester.

Southwark, 4 December 1355

1054. COLLATION of the church of Bonchurch and the chapel of St Edmund, Wootton, Isle of Wight, vacant, by devolution through lapse of time. The church to John born Roger de Skiryngton' and the chapel to Alan de Welleford' priests to be rectors. Letter to the archdeacon of Winchester for the induction.

Southwark, 4 December 1355

1055. LICENCE granted to John Whiteway rector of Stoke near Guildford to be at the service of Hugh de Nevill', knight, from this date until Michaelmas next.

Southwark, 8 December 1355

1056. CERTIFICATORY LETTERS received from R' bishop of Salisbury concerning an exchange sought between Thomas de Shifford rector of Church Knowle, diocese of Salisbury, and John de Pembrok' rector of Thruxton, diocese of Winchester. The letters showed clearly that the bishop of Salisbury authorized the exchange. Thomas was admitted to the church of Thruxton at the presentation of John de Bovedon, knight. Letter for the induction to the archdeacon of Winchester.

Esher, 16 December 1355

1057. ADMISSION of John de Warmynton' priest to the parochial church of Faccombe, vacant by the resignation of Oliver de Ponchardon, at the presentation of William de Fyfhyde. Letter for the induction to the archdeacon of Winchester.

Southwark, 29 January 1356

1058. ADMISSION of John Sclatter' of 'Hogenorton' priest as rector of St Peter in Colebrook Street, Winchester, vacant, at the presentation of the abbess and convent of Nunnaminster. Letter to the archdeacon of Winchester for the induction.

Southwark, 29 January 1356

1059. MEMORANDUM that fr. William abbot and the convent of Netley (*loci Sancti Edwardi*) presented to the bishop as rector of Shere John de

Sancto Neoto priest, by letters patent dated from the chapter-house at Netley.

1060. MEMORANDUM that subsequently the said abbot and convent by letters patent presented to the bishop Richard de Lyntesford' for the church of Shere, vacant by the death of the said Matthew.

Netley, octave of the Epiphany (Jan. 14) 1356

1061. ADMISSION of Richard de Lyntesford' to the church of Shere vacant by the death of Matthew Redeman, at the presentation of the abbey of Netley. Letter to the archdeacon of Surrey for the induction.

Southwark, 9 February 1356

1062. DISPUTATION between the bishop and M. John de Edyndon' rector of the church of Ringwood subdeacon, now studying for seven years that he should reside and proceed to major orders according to the constitutions of Boniface.

Southwark, 22 November 1355

178

1063. ADMISSION of Thomas de Helmenden' priest to the custody of the chapel of St Mary Magdalen in Kingston, vacant by the resignation of William de Hynkele, at the presentation of John Lovekyn of the city of London. To be in continuous residence according to the regulation of the founder. Letter for the induction to M. John de Chertseye rector of the church of Kingston.

Southwark, 3 March 1356

1064. ADMISSION of Elyas de Rodeston' priest to the chaplaincy of the chapel of St Mary Magdalen, Kingston, vacant, at the presentation of the aforesaid John Lovekyn. To be perpetual chaplain. Letter for the induction to M. John, rector of Long Ditton.

Same date

1065. ADMISSION of John de Birton' priest to the vicarage of the church of Leckford, vacant by the resignation of John de Warmynton, at the presentation of Richard de Norwico prebendary of the prebend of Leckford in the collegiate church of the nuns of Nunnaminster. To be perpetual vicar residing according to the constitutions, for which he took the oath. Letter for the induction to the official of Winchester.

Southwark, 5 March 1356

1066. CERTIFICATORY LETTERS received from John bishop of Lincoln concerning the exchange proposed between Nicholas de Irtlyngbur' vicar of Kingston, diocese of Winchester, and Thomas West, rector of Wadenhoe, diocese of Lincoln, by letters dated

Southwark, 6 March 1356

Since it is clear that the bishop of Lincoln has authorized the exchange, the bishop admits Thomas West to the vicarage of Kingston, at the presentation of the prior and convent of Merton. To be perpetual vicar residing according to the constitutions. Letter for the induction to the official of the archdeacon of Surrey.

Southwark, 17 March 1356

1067. ADMISSION of Ralph Tristram priest as rector of the church of East Tisted, vacant, at the presentation of John de Retherfeld. Letter for the induction to the archdeacon of Winchester.

Esher, 25 March 1356

1068. ADMISSION of Robert de Gaydone priest as rector of Stoke d'Abernon, vacant, at the presentation of William de Stokeauburnon, knight. Letter for the induction to the archdeacon of Surrey.

Esher, 6 April 1356

1069. ADMISSION of Roger de Havyndon' to the vicarage of the church of Arreton, Isle of Wight, vacant by the resignation of Thomas, last perpetual vicar, at the presentation of M. Walter Benet rector of the said church. To be perpetual vicar residing according to the constitutions. Letter for the induction to the official of the archdeacon of Winchester.

Esher, 10 April 1356

1070. ADMISSION of William Serl as rector of the church of Greatham, vacant, at the presentation of Thomas Devenish, patron. Letter to the archdeacon of Winchester for the induction.

Esher, 13 April 1356

1071. ADMISSION of Adam de Hilton clerk as rector of the church of Nether Wallop, vacant, at the presentation of John de Wynewyk' treasurer of York, patron. Letter for the induction to the official of the archdeacon of Winchester.

Esher, 26 April 1356

1072. COLLATION by the bishop of the office of subdeacon in the chapel of St Elizabeth, Winchester, vacant, upon Walter Clawe of Lockeridge priest, according to the regulations of John de Pontissara, founder. Letter to the provost of the chapel to admit Walter.

Esher, 2 April 1356

179 **1073.** CERTIFICATORY LETTERS received from Michael bishop of London concerning the exchange between Adam de Bridlynton' rector of Bletchingley and Nicholas Voirdire rector of Little Fobby' diocese of London, bearing the date

Southwark, 29 April 1356

From the letters the bishop of London authorizes the exchange and has admitted the said Nicholas to the church of Bletchingley, vacant by the resignation of Adam, at the presentation of Ralph earl of Stafford. Letter for the induction to the archdeacon of Surrey.

Southwark, 12 May 1356

1074. ADMISSION of William Whytberd' to the chapel of Brook, Isle of Wight, vacant by the resignation of John de Middleton' last rector, at the presentation of Geoffrey Rouklee, patron for this turn. Letter for the induction to the official of the archdeacon of Winchester.

Southwark, 13 May 1356

1075. COMMISSION received from the bishop of Lincoln to deal with the exchange of benefices between M. Adam de Hilton rector of Nether Wallop and Richard de Wynewyke rector of Glatton, diocese of Lincoln. Having examined the case and received the resignations from their benefices, the bishop admitted M. Adam to the church of Glatton, at the presentation of the abbot and convent of Missenden, relying on the enquiry made by the official of the archdeacon of Huntingdon, by mandate of the bishop of Lincoln.
The same day and hour M. Richard de Wynewyk' was admitted to the church of Nether Wallop, at the presentation of John de Wynewyk', treasurer of York, patron. Letters to the archdeacon of Winchester and the dean of Andover for the induction.

Southwark, 20 May 1356

1076. CERTIFICATORY LETTERS received from Michael bishop of London for the exchange proposed between Symon de Brynton' rector of Headley and John Morwy chaplain of the chantry chapel in the church of St Lawrence in Candlewick Street, London.

Southwark, 13 May 1356

From the letters it is clear that the bishop of London authorizes the exchange. John was admitted to Headley as rector, vacant by the resignation of Symon, at the presentation of the abbot and convent of Westminster. Letter for the induction to the archdeacon of Surrey.

Southwark, 24 May 1356

1077. CERTIFICATORY LETTERS from Robert bishop of Salisbury concerning the exchange between Richard de Lyntesford rector of Shere, diocese of Winchester, and John de Sancto Neoto rector of Oare, diocese of Salisbury.

Southwark, 21 May 1356

Since both the bishop and his commission authorized the exchange, the bishop admitted John de Sancto Neoto to the church of Shere, vacant by the resignation of the said Richard, at the presentation of the abbot and convent of Netley. Letter for the induction to the archdeacon of Surrey.

Southwark, 8 June 1356

1078. COMMENDATION by the bishop of John de Bleobury clerk to the parish church of Ewell, vacant, the church being in urgent need as the patron the abbot and convent [of Chertsey] declare. This is according to the Council of Lyons.

Southwark, 21 June 1356

180 **1079.** COMMISSION received from Symon archbishop of Canterbury to examine a proposed exchange between John Hanmull' rector of the church of St John the Evangelist in Friday Street, London, in the deanery of the Arches but of the immediate jurisdiction of the archbishop, and Henry de Tydynge vicar of St Mary, Shalford near Guildford. After examining the case and receiving the resignation, Henry was admitted to the church of St John at the presentation of the prior and chapter of Christ Church, Canterbury, relying on the enquiry of the dean of the church of St Mary Arches by mandate of the archbishop. John was admitted to the vicarage of Shalford at the presentation of the prior and convent of St Mary Bishopsgate. To be perpetual vicar, residing according to the constitutions for which he took the oath. Letter for the induction to the official of the archdeacon of Surrey.

Southwark, 14 July 1356

1080. CERTIFICATORY LETTERS received from Robert bishop of Chichester to whom the bishop had entrusted the proposed exchange between Giles de Fosses rector of Nutfield, diocese of Winchester, and William Chyntynge vicar of Cuckfield, diocese of Chichester, by mandate dated Southwark, 15 July.
The bishop of Chichester has duly examined the case and has admitted William as rector of the church of Nutfield, vacant by the resignation of Giles, at the presentation of John de Cokeham, knight. Letter for the induction to the official of the archdeacon of Surrey.

Southwark, 19 July 1356

1081. COMMISSION OF ENQUIRY AS TO THE VACANCY OF A BENEFICE. John bishop of Lincoln writes to the bishop that king Edward has presented John de Essex' deacon to the church of Brampton, diocese of Lincoln, vacant by the resignation of John de Noionn. To enquire as to the vacancy and if no impediment, to admit, reserving the oath and requesting a certificate.

Liddington, 19 July 1356

The bishop, after the resignation of M. John de Beautre, rector of Burghclere as proctor for M. John de Noionn, admitted John de Essex as rector of Brampton, at the presentation of the king, the priory of St Neots being in his hands.

Southwark, 25 July 1356

1082. MANDATE to induct John, sent by the archdeacon of Northampton; the bishop of Winchester has admitted John to the church of Brampton.

Same date

1083. CERTIFICATORY LETTER to John bishop of Lincoln in the terms of the two preceeding entries.

1084. APPOINTMENT OF A PRIOR OR MASTER for the hospital of St Thomas the Martyr, Southwark, vacant by the voluntary resignation of fr. John Boneufaunt, before MM. Thomas de Enham chancellor, Nicholas de

Kaerwent canon of Hereford, William Chevere, John Essex and John Beautre apostolic notary, in the bishop's chamber of the manor chapel, 25 July 1356. The appointment was requested by the said fr. John with ffr. John de Bradweye, John de Ashewelle and Robert de Draghten', brethren of the hospital. The process was heard 27 July before M. John de Beautre and the others named, when the bishop provided to the hospital as master fr. John de Bradeweye. M. Thomas was directed to install the new master.

Southwark, Wednesday, 27 July 1356

182

1085. TESTIMONIAL LETTER for the nomination and installation of the new master of the hospital, fr. John de Bradweye, at the spontaneous request of his brethren to the bishop, made the 27 July 1356.

Southwark, 29 July 1356

1086. COLLATION by the bishop of the vicarage of Twyford on John de Wolveleye, vacant by the resignation of John de Bocardeston', who exchanges vicarages for the church of Itchen, which John de Wolvesley had first held. To be perpetual vicar residing according to the constitutions. Letter for the induction to the official of Winchester.
At the same time admission of John de Bochardeston' as rector of the church of Itchen, vacant by the resignation of the said John de Wolvesey, at the presentation of the abbess and convent of Nunnaminster. Letter for the induction to the archdeacon of Winchester.

Esher, 29 September 1356

1087. INSTITUTION of Edmund de Eston' clerk to be rector of Ewell, vacant, at the presentation of the abbot and convent of Chertsey. Letter for the induction to the archdeacon of Surrey.

Southwark, 16 August 1356

1088. ADMISSION of John de Bennebury subdeacon to the church of Wotton, vacant by the resignation of Roger Wysman lately rector, by exchange for the church of Laverstoke, which John had first held, at the presentation of William Latimer, knight, patron of the church of Wotton. Subsequently the said Roger was admitted to the church of Laverstoke, by exchange, at the presentation of the abbot and convent of Hyde. Letter for the induction to the archdeacon of Surrey for both inductions.

Southwark, 4 October 1356

1089. LICENCE granted to John de Whiteweye rector of Stoke next Guildford to be absent for one year at the service of Hugh de Neville.

Southwark, 13 October 1356

1090. ADMISSION of John Roughbern' priest as rector of the church of Little Bookham, vacant by the resignation of William de Wantynge clerk as proctor for Symon Thoni, at the presentation of Thomas de Breousa, knight. Letter for the induction to the archdeacon of Surrey.

Southwark, 14 October 1356

1091. COLLATION by the bishop of the church of Havant, vacant, on M. John No 'm', clerk as rector. Letter for the induction to the offical of Winchester.

Southwark, 24 October 1356

Folio 91 has been cut out, i.e. pages 183 and 184. There are signs of writing on the stump.

185 **1092.** ADMISSION of John Geardyn clerk as rector of the church of Ashe near Winchester, vacant by the resignation of Henry atte Wyle of Farnham, at the presentation of John de Stonore, knight. Letter for the induction to the archdeacon of Winchester.

Southwark, 19 January 1357

1093. LICENCE granted to Geoffrey de Salynge rector of Clanfield to be for one year at the service of Symon abbot of Westminster and to lease his church at farm.

Southwark, 10 February 1357

1094. ADMISSION of John Migreyn to be rector of the church of Ewhurst, vacant by the resignation of John Hugheyn, at the presentation of Edward de Sancto Johanne, knight. Letter for the induction to the archdeacon of Winchester.

Southwark, 9 February 1357

1095. ADMISSION of John Hugheyn priest as rector of the chapel of [Cole] Henley, near Whitchurch, vacant by resignation of John Migreyn last rector, at the presentation of Peter de Watesford. Letter for the induction to the archdeacon of Winchester.

Southwark, 9 February 1357

1096. LICENCE granted to M. John de Bulkynton' rector of Nether Wallop to be absent for one year without obligation of residence.

Southwark, 10 February 1357

1097. LICENCE granted to Thomas de Clapton rector of Blendworth to be at absent for one year beginning at Easter at the service of Ralph, knight, and to lease his church at farm to a suitable person.

Southwark, 15 February 1357

1098. ADMISSION of M. Adam Hoton', priest and professor of canon law, to the portion of the church of Beddington, vacant by the death of M. William de Carrou', last portioner, at the presentation of Nicholas de Carrou', lord of the manor of Beddington and patron of the portion. Letter to the archdeacon of Surrey for the induction.

Southwark, 27 February 1357

1099. ADMISSION of Richard Uphull' of Hamine priest to the vicarage of the church of Combe, vacant, at the presentation of fr. Peter de Falco, prior of Ogborne, procurator for the abbot of Bec Helwyn, of which all the temporalities are at farm from the king. To be perpetual vicar with obligation of residing according to the constitutions for which he took the oath. Letter for the induction to the archdeacon of Winchester.

Southwark, 29 March 1357

1100. COLLATION by the bishop of the church of Morestead on William de Wolsche priest, vacant, at the presentation of the prior aforesaid, to be rector. Letter to the official of Winchester for the induction.

Southwark, 11 April 1357

1101. PRESENTATION by the bishop to the bishop of Salisbury of John de Wichford' priest, for the church of Patney, diocese of Salisbury, vacant.

Southwark, 13 April 1357

1102. LICENCE granted to Nicholas de Kyngeston' rector of Saint Faith near Winchester to lease his church at farm for one year.

Southwark, 11 April 1357

1103. ADMISSION of Richard almere priest as rector of the church of West Horley, vacant by the resignation of John Palmere of Bishopstone last rector, at the presentation of the attorneys of John de Berners, knight. Letter to the archdeacon of Surrey for the induction.

Southwark, 25 April 1357

1104. CERTIFICATORY LETTERS received from Michael bishop of London concerning the exchange between John Farendon' vicar of Warlingham with the chapel of Chelsham and Thomas Olney vicar of Isleworth, diocese of London, dated 25 April 1357. Since the bishop of London approved, Thomas was admitted to the vicarage with the chapel, with obligation of residence according to the constitutions. Letter for the induction to the archdeacon of Surrey.

Southwark, 5 May 1357

1105. COLLATION by the bishop of the vicarage of the church of Fareham on Bartholomew Sperven priest. To be perpetual vicar according to the constitutions. Letter for the induction to the vicar of Hambledon.

Southwark, 19 May 1357

1106. CERTIFICATORY LETTERS received from Michael bishop of London concerning the exchange between Edmund de Barneby, rector of St Margaret atte patyns, London and Richard Elys rector of Ockley, dated Southwark 14 May 1357. Since the bishop of London authorized the exchange, Edmund was admitted to Ockley as rector. Letter for the induction to the archdeacon of Surrey.

Southwark, 26 May 1357

1107. COLLATION by the bishop, by devolution through lapse of time, of the chantry of the manor of Gatcombe in the church of Gatcombe, Isle of Wight, on Edward Tannere of Glouc' priest, as perpetual chaplain.

Letter for the induction to the archdeacon of Winchester and the dean of the Island.

Southwark, 1 June 1357

1108. CERTIFICATORY LETTERS received from Robert bishop of Salisbury concerning the exchange between William de Cornhampton rector of Chaddleworth, diocese of Salisbury, and Michael rector of Itchen Stoke, dated 5 April 1357. By the authority of the bishop of Salisbury, William was admitted to the church of Itchen Stoke. Letter for the induction to the archdeacon of Winchester.

Southwark, 11 June 1357

1109. ADMISSION of William in le Lane, priest, as rector of the chapel of Freefolk, vacant, at the presentation of Andrew Peverel, knight. Letter for the induction to the archdeacon of Winchester.

Southwark, 12 June 1357

1110. CERTIFICATORY LETTERS received from Robert bishop of Salisbury concerning the exchange between John de Bochardeston' of Itchen and John de Benklond', rector of St Martin, Wareham, diocese of Salisbury, dated Southwark 6 June 1357. As authorized by the bishop of Salisbury, John was admitted to the church of Itchen. Letter for the induction to the archdeacon of Winchester.

Southwark, 15 June 1357

1111. ADMISSION of Nicholas Marcaunt of 'Terneye' priest to the vicarage of Shalford, vacant by the resignation of William Spyng' before M. Thomas de Enham, the chancellor, 14 June, in the *hospicium* of the bishop at Southwark, in the presence of M. Walter Benet and John Beautre. At the presentation of the prior and convent of Bishopsgate, London. To be perpetual vicar residing according to the constitutions. Letter for the induction to the archdeacon of Surrey.

Southwark, 16 June 1357

1112. CERTIFICATORY LETTERS received from R' bishop of Salisbury, to whom the bishop had entrusted the exchange between Alexander de Chelseye rector of Ovington and John de Newenham, rector of Brightwalton, diocese of Salisbury, dated Southwark, 18 July 1357. John was admitted by the bishop of Salisbury to the church of Ovington, at the collation of the bishop of Winchester. Letter for the induction to the official of Winchester and M. John de Ware, sequestrator.

Southwark, 30 July 1357

1113. CERTIFICATORY LETTERS received from Michael bishop of London to whom the bishop had entrusted the exchange between Geoffrey de Salynge rector of Clanfield and Symon Clerc of Wrangle, rector of Warley Abbess, diocese of London, dated Southwark, 24 July 1357. Symon was admitted to Clanfield. Letter to the archdeacon of Winchester for the induction.

Southwark, 3 August 1357

1114. ADMISSION of Nicholas de Kaerwent as rector of Dibden, vacant by the resignation of Walter Noht priest, last rector, in view of the exchange for the church of Michelmersh, which Nicholas had first obtained. Letter for the induction to the archdeacon of Winchester.

Southwark, 17 July 1357

1115. COLLATION by the bishop of the church of Michelmersh, vacant by the resignation of Nicholas de Kaerwent by reason of the exchange, to Walter Noht as rector. Letter for the induction to the archdeacon of Winchester.

Same date

1116. COLLATION of the sacerdotal office in the chapel of Marwell, vacant, on John Welde priest. Letter to John de Nubbelegh, provost of the chapel of St Elizabeth to induct and confer on him the rights and profits of the office.

Southwark, 1 August 1357

1117. CERTIFICATORY LETTERS received from J' bishop of Lincoln concerning the exchange of benefices between William de Dukebrigg' lately rector of Farleigh and John Edrith' rector of Hardwick, diocese of Lincoln. After examining the matter and accepting the resignation of John and William in view of the exchange, William was admitted as rector of Hardwick and John as rector of Farleigh. A certificatory letter was sent to the bishop of Lincoln.

Southwark, 6 August 1357

1118. CERTIFICATORY LETTERS received from M. John Thursteyn, vicar for Thomas bishop of Ely, to whom the bishop had entrusted the exchange between M. Thomas de Eltesle senior, rector of Lambeth, diocese of Winchester, and M. Thomas de Elteslee junior, rector of Long Stanton, diocese of Ely, dated Southwark, 9 August 1357. M. Thomas junior was presented to Lambeth by S' archbishop of Canterbury, patron, through M. John the vicar as authorized by the bishop of Winchester and was admitted. Letter for the induction to the archdeacon of Surrey.

Southwark, 12 August 1357

1119. INSTITUTION of Nicholas de Kyngeston' priest as rector of Dibden, at the presentation of Nicholas de Dupeden', patron for this turn. Letter to the archdeacon of Winchester for the induction.

Southwark, 4 September 1357

188   **1120.** ADMISSION of Walter de Listolgh' priest to the vicarage of Mitcham, vacant, at the presentation of fr. Henry de Colyngborne, subprior of the conventual church of Southwark, as *locum tenens* for fr. John de Pekham prior in his absence. To be perpetual vicar with obligation of residing according to the constitutions, for which he took the oath. Letter for the induction to the archdeacon of Surrey.

Southwark, 18 September 1357

1121. INSTITUTION of William Barneby as rector of Eversley, vacant, at the presentation of Thomas de Bradestan, knight. Letter for the induction to the archdeacon of Winchester.

Southwark, 18 September 1357

1122. ADMISSION of William Edenef' of Kyrketon' priest to the vicarage of Hartley Wintney, vacant by the resignation of William Chumberleyn voluntarily into the hands of the bishop, at the presentation of the prioress and convent of Wintney. To be perpetual vicar, residing according to the constitutions for which he took the oath. Letter to the archdeacon of Winchester for the induction, and to the dean of Basingstoke.

Southwark, 9 October 1357

1123. LICENCE for study at some *studium generale* for one year granted to M. Thomas de Elteslee rector of Lambeth, with permission to lease the church at farm to some suitable person.

Southwark, 7 October 1357

1124. LICENCE for study for one year granted to John de Williamstate, rector of West Meon, clerk, to receive the subdiaconate within a year.

Southwark, 1 October 1357

1125. COLLATION by the bishop of the church of Bramdean, vacant, on Hamon de la Solere priest, to be rector. Letter for the induction to the archdeacon of Winchester.

Southwark, 18 October 1357

1126. COLLATION by the bishop of the church of St Faith near Winchester, vacant, on John Ragebas, priest, to be rector. Letter for the induction to the official of Winchester and to M. John de Ware, sequestrator-general.

Southwark, 23 October 1357

1127. ADMISSION of Thomas Weye priest to the vicarage of the church of East Worldham, vacant by the voluntary resignation of William Edenef', of Kirketon', perpetual vicar, this same day in the presence of M. Thomas de Enham chancellor with Richard Cohone and Peter Pekke and J' Beautre, notary apostolic. At the presentation of the prior and convent of Selborne. To be perpetual vicar residing according to the constitutions for which he took the oath. Letter for the induction to the official of the archdeacon and the dean of Winchester.

Southwark, 23 October 1357

1128. LICENCE for study granted for one year to John de Fulford' rector of Abbots Ann.

Southwark, 27 October 1357

1129. LICENCE for study granted for one year to John de Bennbury rector of Wootton, subdeacon, without obligation of residence or of proceeding to major orders.

Southwark, 16 May 1357

189   **1130.** COMMISSION received from the bishop of Norwich concerning Thomas de Herteshorne clerk and the church of Horstead, diocese of Norwich, which Richard de Cersterfeld held by a "a peaceful association" with the church of Flintham, diocese of York. Thomas should be admitted to Horstead whenever a suitable vacancy should occur, other than the death of Richard. Then Thomas should be admitted and the bishop of Norwich informed.

London, 8 June 1355

By this authority the bishop admits Thomas as rector of the church of Horstead, now vacant by the resignation of the said Richard de Cesterfeld, who peacefully held the church of Flintham, diocese of York. This is at the presentation of the king, since the churches and lands of the abbess of Caen are in his hands because of the war. Letter for the induction to the archdeacon of Norwich.

Southwark, 9 July 1355

1131. CERTIFICATORY LETTERS received from R' bishop of Chichester concerning the exchange between Richard rector of Compton and Hugh de Morton' rector of Tillington, diocese of Chichester, dated Southwark, 6 November. Acting on that commission the bishop admitted Hugh as rector to Compton at the presentation of the abbot and convent of Durford. Letter for the induction to the archdeacon of Surrey.

Southwark, 16 November 1357

1132. LICENCE granted for study to Thomas de Harthorp rector of the church of St Olave in Southwark for one year; he will receive the subdiaconate.

Southwark, 3 November 1357

1133. LICENCE for study granted to John Jardyn rector of Ashe near Overton, for two years.

Southwark, 15 November 1357

1134. ADMISSION of John Taylour priest to the vicarage of the church of St Swithun at Nutley, vacant, at the presentation of the prior and convent of Southwick. To be perpetual vicar residing according to the constitutions. Letter for the induction to the archdeacon of Winchester and the dean of Alresford.

Southwark, 5 December 1357

1135. ADMISSION of Walter Neuman priest to the vicarage of Farley, vacant by the resignation of Thomas Disce, late vicar. To be perpetual vicar residing according to the constitutions. Letter for the induction to the archdeacon of Surrey. Walter was presented by the warden and scholars of Merton College, Oxford.

Southwark, 20 December 1357

1136. DISPENSATION granted to John de Whiteweye rector of Stoke next Guildford, to be absent at the service of John de Bohum, knight, for one year.

Southwark, 26 January 1358

190   **1137.** PROCESS for the exchange of benefices between John Sannford' rector of North Waltham and Thomas Shyford' rector of Thruxton, both in the diocese, heard before M. Thomas de Enham, chancellor. Having received their resignations, John was admitted to Thruxton at the presentation of John de Boughdon', knight, and Elizabeth his wife. Letter sent to M. John de Ware, sequestrator-general, for the induction. Subsequently the church of North Waltham was collated to Thomas de Shyford', with a letter to the archdeacon of Winchester for the induction.

Southwark, 21 December 1357

1138. COMMISSION to examine the presentation of M. Robert de Lemyngton rector of the church of St Peter outside Southgate in Winchester to the vicarage of the church of Milford by exchange with John Abban perpetual vicar of Milford. Then to accept the resignation of M. Robert, inducting him to the vicarage as perpetual vicar, residing according to the constitutions, for which he will take the oath. Certificatory letters to be sent to the bishop. Dated Southwark, 27 September 1357. The commission was carried out. John Abban resigned the vicarage and M. Robert was admitted.

1139. ADMISSION of John Nevill' clerk to the church of Ashe vacant by the resignation of John Jardyn lately rector, at the presentation of John Stoner, knight, patron. Letter for the induction to the archdeacon of Winchester.

Southwark, 8 February 1358

1140. ADMISSION of John Jardyn subdeacon to the church of Ashe, vacant by the resignation of John Nevill' late rector, as the public instrument of M. William de Peveseye, notary, shows. Letter to the archdeacon of Winchester for the induction.

Southwark, 24 February 1358

1141. EXCHANGE OF BENEFICES between William de Preston' rector of Colechurch, diocese of London and John de Grymesby rector of Bentworth, by commission of John bishop of London. The bishop received the resignations and admitted William to the church of Bentworth and John to the church of Colechurch, through his proctor Thomas de Alston'. The presentation to Bentworth was by reason of the manor of Bentworth being in the hands of the bishop. Letter to the bishop of London and for the induction to the archdeacon of Winchester.

Southwark, 26 February 1358

1142. COMMISSION from Robert bishop of Salisbury concerning the collation of the church of Houghton, now vacant by the resignation of Walter de Sevenhampton, the last rector, by exchange for the perpetual chantry of Edington, which Walter Scarlet had first held and has resigned. The church was collated to Walter Scarlet. Letter for the induction to the official of Winchester.

Southwark, 3 March 1358

191   **1143.** ADMISSION of Thomas de Mere priest to the vicarage of the church of Effingham, vacant by the resignation of William Tysour, by exchange with the church of Holy Trinity, Guildford, which Thomas had first held, at the presentation of the prior and convent of St Mary, Merton. To be perpetual vicar, residing according to the constitutions, for which he took the oath. Subsequently William was admitted to the church of Holy Trinity, at the presentation of the said prior and convent, as rector. Letter to the archdeacon of Surrey for both inductions.

Esher, 24 March 1358

1144. ADMISSION of M. Robert de Lemyngton priest to the church of Farley, vacant by the voluntary resignation of John Edrith, late rector, at the presentation of Thomas de Mussynden. Letter to the archdeacon of Winchester for the induction.

Esher, 26 March 1358

1145. ADMISSION of Henry de Kemeseye, priest, to the vicarage of the church of West Boarhunt, vacant by the resignation of Richard Symond, last vicar, at the presentation of the prior and convent of Southwick. To be perpetual vicar, residing according to the constitutions. Letter for the induction to the archdeacon of Winchester.

Esher, 4 April 1358

1146. ADMISSION of John de Wycham, deacon, to the vicarage of the church of Milford, vacant by the resignation of Robert de Lemynton, last vicar, at the presentation of the prior and convent of Christchurch Twynham. To be perpetual vicar, residing according to the constitutions. Letter for the induction to the archdeacon of Winchester.

Esher, 6 April 1358

1147. LICENCE granted to John Ware rector of Newton to lease at farm the fruits of his church for one year to William de Gaterugg', vicar of Alton and Thomas Warner, a layman.

Esher, 6 April 1358

1148. CERTIFICATORY LETTERS received from R' bishop of Salisbury concerning the exchange between William Wolf rector of the church of Meonstoke, at the bishop's collation and John de Bleebury, late rector of Brightwell, diocese of Salisbury, at the patronage of the bishop. By the authority of the bishop of Salisbury, the church of Meonstoke was conferred on John de Bleebury by the bishop and he was canonically instituted. The induction was entrusted to M. John de Ware, rector of the church of Cranleigh and to Michael rector of Droxford.

Southwark, 12 May 1358

1149. COMMISSION sent to the official of Winchester to examine the proposed exchange between John Payn precentor of St Mary, Southampton and John Bleebury rector of Meonstoke and to admit them, if he approves, to their benefices, after receiving their resignations.

Southwark, 17 April 1358

1150. COLLATION by the bishop of the precentorship of St Mary, Southampton, vacant by the resignation of John de Bleebury, on Walter de Sevenhampton, priest. Letter for the induction to the official of Winchester and M. John de Ware, sequestrator-general.

Southwark, 30 April 1358

1151. ADMISSION of Richard Consonde priest as rector of the church of Bramshott, vacant, at the presentation of William de Brembeschete, patron. Letter for the induction to the archdeacon of Winchester.

Southwark, 7 May 1358

1152. PRESENTATION of John atte Putte of Codford, priest, to the church of Fonthill Bishop, by exchange for the vicarage of Thatcham, which John had first obtained, with Hamond de Chakwelle then rector of Fonthill.

Southwark, 12 May 1358

192 **1153.** CERTIFICATORY LETTERS received from J' bishop of Lincoln concerning an exchange between John de Haverbergh' rector of Silchester and John de Staverne rector of Higham Gobion, diocese of Lincoln. Since the bishop of Lincoln authorizes the exchange, John de Staverne was admitted to the church of Silchester, at the presentation of Edmund Baynard, patron for this turn. Letter for the induction to the archdeacon of Winchester.

Southwark, 17 May 1358

1154. LICENCE FOR A PRIVATE ORATORY granted to Henry Peverel, knight, for the celebration of masses for his household in the manors of Chilworth and Sopley and the hospital in the parish of St Michael, Southampton. For one year.

Southwark, 2 April 1358

1155. LICENCE FOR AN ORATORY granted to William Croyser for masses in his manor in the parish of Aldebury for his family. For one year.

Southwark, 16 May 1358

1156. LICENCE granted to John atte Wode rector of Chaldon to be at the service of Ralph, earl of Stafford for one year.

Southwark, 18 May 1358

1157. ADMISSION of Robert Wircestre of Collingbourne to the vicarage of the church of Reigate, vacant, at the presentation of the prior and convent of St Mary, Southwark. To be perpetual vicar, residing according to the constitutions for which he took the oath.

Southwark, 15 June 1358

1158. COLLATION by the bishop of the church of St Anastasius by Winchester, vacant, on Thomas de Dodenham priest, as rector. Letter for the induction to the archdeacon of Winchester.

Southwark, 14 June 1358

1159. ADMISSION of John de Stodeye, clerk, to the chapel of East Standen, Isle of Wight, vacant by the free resignation of Nicholas de Houghton', last rector, at the presentation of Thomas Haket. Letters for the induction to the archdeacon of Winchester and the dean of the Island.

Southwark, 15 June 1358

1160. LETTER to Thomas de Burgo, priest, informing him that the bishop has received letters from John bishop of Lincoln concerning the exchange desired between the said Thomas lately rector of Abbots Ann and John de Uppyngham' rector of Kings Cliff, diocese of Lincoln. Carrying out the commission, after examining the case and receiving the resignation of John de Uppyngham', the bishop admits Thomas to the church of Kings Cliff, at the presentation of the prior and convent of St Mary, Merton, relying on the enquiry held by the dean of Oundle.

Southwark, 14 July 1358

1161. LETTER to John de Uppyngham' priest admitting him to Abbots Ann, vacant by the resignation of Thomas de Burgo, at the presentation of the prior and convent of Hyde.

Southwark, 14 July 1358

193 **1162.** AUTHORIZATION of the exchange of benefices between Richard Snodeham of Peper Harrow and Thomas Cobbild rector of Bramber, diocese of Chichester, by commission from Robert, bishop of Chichester. Richard was admitted to Bramber, at the presentation of the prior and monks of Sele and Thomas to Peper Harrow at the presentation of the king, as custodian of the lands and heir of Andrew Braunche, deceased, who held from the king *in capite*. Letter to the official of the archdeacon of Surrey for the induction of Thomas to Peper Harrow. The induction of Richard was reserved to the bishop of Chichester.

Southwark, 19 July 1358

1163. COMMISSION from the bishop to his official to enquire into the presentation of Hugh de Cheyneston' priest to the church of Yarmouth [Isle of Wight] by Isabella the king's daughter. If the benefice was indeed vacant, then to admit Hugh and accept his oath. A certificate to be returned.

Southwark, 23 July 1358

1164. ADMISSION of Henry Longe priest to the vicarage of the church of Betchworth, vacant, at the presentation of the prior and convent of Southwark. To be perpetual vicar, residing according to the constitutions for which he took the oath. Letter for the induction to the archdeacon of Surrey.

Southwark, 1 August 1358

1165. PRESENTATION to R' bishop of Salisbury of John Felawe of Cleeve for the church of Buttermere, diocese of Salisbury, but at the presentation of the bishop.

Farnham, 28 September 1358

1166. ADMISSION of Thomas de Huggate priest to be rector of the church of St Laurence, Wanstead, vacant, at the presentation of the prior and convent of Southwick. Letter for the induction to the archdeacon of Winchester.

Farnham, 28 September 1358

1167. ADMISSION of Thomas Chapman of Orwell, priest, to the vicarage of Reigate, at the presentation of the prior and convent of Southwark. To be perpetual vicar, residing according to the constitution for which he took the oath. Letter for the induction to the archdeacon of Surrey.

Farnham, 25 August 1358

1168. LICENCE to be absent for study granted to John Say, rector of Sutton, for one year.

Esher, 30 September 1358

1169. CERTIFICATORY LETTERS received from Michael bishop of London to whom the bishop had entrusted the exchange between Nicholas Voirdire rector of Bletchingley and John Useflet rector of St Nicholas in the Shambles, London. Since the bishop of London authorized the exchange, the bishop admitted John Useflet to the church of Bletchingley, at the presentation of Ralph, earl of Stafford. Letter for the induction to the archdeacon of Surrey.

Southwark, 15 October 1358

1170. DISPENSATION from residence granted by the bishop to John de Wyhamescote rector of the church of West Meon, subdeacon, for study for one year, without obligation of further orders according to the constitutions.

Southwark, 21 October 1358

194 **1171.** ADMISSION of John Hobbes of Southrop, priest, as rector of the church of Weston Corbett, at the presentation of John de Bogeham, knight. Letter for the induction to the archdeacon of Winchester.

Southwark, 8 November 1358

1172. CERTIFICATORY LETTERS received from John bishop of Lincoln concerning the exchange between William de Lambeth', rector of Bletchley, diocese of Lincoln and M. Thomas de Elteslee junior rector of Lambeth, dated Southwark, 23 November 1358. Since the bishop of Lincoln authorizes the exchange, after receiving the resignation of M. Thomas from the church of Lambeth, the bishop admitted William, at the presentation of the archbishop of Canterbury, patron. Letter for the induction to the archdeacon of Surrey.

Southwark, 26 November 1358

1173. ADMISSION of William Wodeford' priest to the vicarage of the church of Milford, vacant by the voluntary resignation of John de Wykham, before M. Thomas de Enham, chancellor, in the *hospicium* of the bishop at Southwark, 27 November, 1358, in the presence of John de Beautre and William de Leverington, public notaries, and M. Thomas de Shipton, Richard Colput and Peter Pekke as witnesses. At the presentation of the prior and convent of Christchurch Twynham, to be perpetual vicar, residing according to the constitutions for which he took the oath. Letter to the archdeacon of Winchester for the induction.

Southwark, 28 November 1358

1174. LICENCE granted to John de Whitewey rector of Stoke next Guildford, to be at the service of Hegham, knight, for one year.

Southwark, 3 December 1358

1175. ADMISSION of William Franceys priest to the vicarage of Weybridge, vacant by the voluntary resignation of Richard le Clerc of Shoreham before M. John de Wolveleye, official, at the presentation of the prior and convent of Newark. To be perpetual vicar residing according to the constitutions for which he took the oath. Letter for the induction to the archdeacon of Surrey.

Southwark, 10 December 1358

1176. AUTHORIZATION of an exchange granted as between Richard Hybury rector of Norton, diocese of Canterbury, and William de Stodmersh' rector of Chiddingfold, by commission of Symon archbishop of Canterbury, at the presentation of John, bishop of Rochester and the prior and chapter of Rochester, patrons. Chiddingfold was at the presentation of M. Philip Bernard, rector of Chilbolton, procurator and vicar-general in England of Reynald, cardinal-deacon of St Adrian and dean of Salisbury. They were canonically instituted, with rights reserved for the archbishop. Letter to the archdeacon of Surrey for the induction.

Southwark, 9 January 1359

1177. AUTHORIZATION of an exchange between William de Wreford, rector of Woodmancote, diocese of Chichester, and Nicholas Markannt, vicar of Shalford, by commission of Robert bishop of Chichester. Nicholas was presented to Woodmancote by fr. John Pavely, prior of St John of Jerusalem in England; William was presented to Shalford by the prior and convent of the hospital of St Mary, Bishopstoke, London. To be vicar residing according to the constitutions. Letter to the archdeacon of Surrey for the induction of William.

Southwark, 24 January 1359

1178. ADMISSION of John de Hoo priest to the vicarage of Walkhampstead, vacant, at the presentation of the abbot and convent of Lesnes. To be perpetual vicar residing according to the constitutions. Letter for the induction to the archdeacon of Surrey.

Southwark, 17 January 1359

195 **1179.** INSTITUTION of Elias de Rodeston' priest as perpetual warden of the chapel of St Mary Magdalen, Norbiton, vacant, at the presentation of John Lovekyn, citizen of London, patron, according to the statutes of the chapel. Letter for the induction to the archdeacon of Surrey.

Southwark, 16 January 1359

1180. INSTITUTION of Richard de Warmynton' as perpetual chaplain of the chantry of St Mary Magdalen, as above. Letter to the warden of the chapel to admit him.

Date as above

1181. ADMISSION of John Brugg' priest to the church of la Woe, vacant by the death of William the last rector, at the presentation of Thomas de la Pole, knight. Letter for the induction to the archdeacon of Winchester.

Southwark, 2 March 1359

1182. LICENCE granted to John de Sygleschore rector of Headbourne Worthy to be absent for two years to study at the university of Cambridge.

Southwark, 6 March 1359

1183. COLLATION by the bishop of the church of Houghton, vacant by the death of Walter Scarlet the last rector, on Robert de Wychford' clerk. Letter for the induction to the official of Winchester and to M. John de la Ware, sequestrator-general.

Southwark, 14 March 1359

1184. ADMISSION of John Groseur priest to the vicarage of the church of Send, vacant by the death of John Messag', at the presentation of the prior and convent of Newark. To be perpetual vicar residing according to the constitutions for which he took the oath. Letter for the induction to the archdeacon of Surrey.

Southwark, 18 March 1359

1185. LICENCE granted to John Morwy rector of Headley to be absent for one year for study.

Southwark, 20 March 1359

1186. AUTHORIZATION of and exchange between Robert de Burton', canon of the collegiate church of Bishops Auckland and prebendary of Kirk Merrington, diocese of Durham, and John Brettevill', rector of the church of Kempshot, diocese of Winchester, by commission from the bishop of Durham. After their resignations the bishop collated Robert to the canonry and prebend, and admitted Robert to the church of Kempshot as rector. Letter for the induction to the archdeacon of Winchester.

Southwark, 3 June 1359

1187. ADMISSION of Edmund de Gnowshale priest to be rector of the church of Chipstead, vacant by the resignation of William de Walyngford at the presentation of Ralph, earl of Stafford, by right of his deceased wife, Margaret, daughter and heiress of Hugh de Audeleye.

Southwark, 4 June 1359

1188. COLLATION by the bishop of the vicarage of Bourne and Hurstbourne, vacant, on John de Mershton Botiller, priest. To be perpetual vicar residing according to the constitutions. Letter for the induction to the official of Winchester and M. John de Ware, sequestrator.

Southwark, 4 June 1359

1189. PRESENTATION by the bishop of M. Robert de Wykford clerk to the bishop of Lincoln, for the church of Witney, diocese of Lincoln, vacant by the death of Roger Folyot, last rector.

Southwark, 7 June 1359

1190. COLLATION by the bishop of the church or precentory of St Mary, Southampton, vacant by the death of John Payn, last rector or precentor. Letter for the induction to the official of Winchester and M. John de Ware, sequestrator-general.

Southwark, 17 June 1359

196   **1191.** ADMISSION of Lambert de Thrykingham' clerk as rector of the free chapel of Oakwood, vacant by the death of Ralph de Hangelton', at the presentation of William Latymer. Letter for the induction to the official of the archdeacon of Surrey.

Southwark, 27 June 1359

1192. COLLATION by the bishop of the church of Hannington on John de Grenehurst' priest as rector. It was vacant by the resignation of Thomas de Whitecroft, last rector, at Southwark, 29 June, in the presence of John de Beautre, notary, M. Thomas de Enham chancellor, Thomas de Pentelowe and Richard Colput as witnesses. Letter for the induction to the official of Winchester and Roger Beautre rector of Highclere.

Southwark, 30 June 1359

1193. COLLATION by the bishop of the church or preceptory of St Mary, Southampton, vacant by the resignation of M. Robert de Wychford lately rector, by exchange with M. John de Swyniton and the church of Houghton, which John had obtained. After a discussion of the case John was collated to St Mary, Southampton. Letter for the induction to the official of Winchester and M. John de Ware sequestrator-general.

Southwark, 2 July 1359

1194. COLLATION by the bishop of the church of Houghton, vacant by the resignation of M. John de Staunton' last rector, by reason of an exchange with M. Robert Wychford' of the preceptory of St Mary, Southampton. Letter for the induction to the official and sequestrator of Winchester.

Southwark, 2 July 1359

1195. CERTIFICATORY LETTERS received from Robert bishop of Chichester concerning an exchange between M. William de Chesterton' perpetual vicar of Icklesham, diocese of Chichester, and Walter de Stracton' rector of the church of Duntesfold, dated Southwark, 22 May 1359. Since the bishop of Chichester authorizes the exchange, the bishop approves and accepts the resignation of Walter. At the presentation of the prior and convent of St Mary, Bishopsgate, London.

Southwark, 2 July 1359

1196. INSTITUTION of John de Briggeslee priest to the church of Woldingham, vacant by the free resignation of Richard de Wellesburn' last rector, in the presence of John de Beautre public notary, John Tibetot *domicelli* and Richard Colput layman as witnesses in the chancellor's office at the bishop's *hospicium* at Southwark, 27 June 1359; at the presentation of Ralph earl of Stafford. Letter for the induction to the archdeacon of Surrey.

Southwark, 11 July 1359

1197. TESTIMONIAL LETTER FOR THE ORDINATION OF THE VICARAGE of Wandsworth. The church was appropriated to Westminster abbey and the ordination took place before a deputation on visitation. Richard de Sutton' clerk was appointed perpetual vicar: to hold it with all the altarage and all its offerings and annual revenue, and from tithes except from the meadow which lies to the east of the water of Wandlesworth and the tithes of sheaves on all the lands of Hayford and Dunesford. Also from the lands of William Faulkes and William son of Henry of Wandsworth and John de Berkyng' which they as parishioners at the time of the asssessment held, save to the abbot and convent all the remaining tithes on corn in the parish, with the tithe on hay from the meadow to the west of the water and the free land of the church, together with the tithe on salmon. The said vicar and his successors will pay all customary episcopal and archidiaconal dues and extraordinary dues proportionately. Witnesses William and Walter *Subir' et Surr' archd'* Philip and Fulcher notaries, Walter de Brich', Richard de Freton', John de Leominster' and Stephen de Croyndon' clerks. Sealed at Southwark the morrow of St Mark (26 April) 1359.

Southwark, 16 July 1359

197
1198. CERTIFICATORY LETTER received from John bishop of Rochester concerning the exchange of benefices between John de Bennely rector of Wotton and Robert de Mildenhale rector of Gravesend, diocese of Rochester, dated Southwark, 14 July 1359. Since the bishop of Rochester approves, the bishop admitted Robert to the church of Wotton. Letter for the induction to the archdeacon of Surrey and the dean of Guildford.

Southwark, 19 July 1359

1199. ADMISSION of John Handesone priest to the vicarage of St Laurence, Morden, vacant by the death of Baldwin last vicar, at the presentation of the abbot and convent of Westminster. To be perpetual vicar residing according to the constitutions for which he took the oath. Letter for the induction to the archdeacon of Surrey.

Southwark, 31 July 1359

1200. APPROPRIATION OF THE CHURCH of Witley. Letter to the prioress and sisters of the monastery of Dartford, order of preachers, diocese of

Rochester, now in distress. Edward II had founded the house of St Margaret and endowed it with rents etc., now insufficient. They request the appropriation of the church of Witley, which the bishop grants them after a canonical enquiry, with the approval of the chapter and also of M. John de Edyndon', archdeacon of Surrey. Saving the right of the bishop to ordain the vicar's portion in the fruits of the church. The nuns will present the perpetual vicar; in vacancy they will receive the fruits. They will pay pensions of 6s. 8d. to the bishop, 3s. 4d. to the chapter of Winchester, 3s. 8d. to the archdeacon of Surrey annually at Easter, with sequestration for non-payment.

198

The chapter-house, Winchester, 15 December 1358

Ratified by John, prior and the chapter; also by John de Edyndon' archdeacon of Surrey. Joan prioress added her seal.

1201. ADMISSION of Richard de Stokes clerk to be rector of the church of Farnborough, vacant, at the presentation of Walter de Spridlynton' patron. Letter to the archdeacon of Winchester for the induction.

Southwark, 4 September 1359

1202. COLLATION by the bishop of the church of Widley on M. Thomas de Shipton' deacon, vacant at the death of Hugh de Patryngton' last rector. Letter to the official of Winchester and to the rector of Highclere for the induction.

Southwark, 2 October 1359

1203. LICENCE granted to M. Thomas de Schipton' to be absent for one year for study without obligation of residence or of proceeding to major orders.

Southwark, 9 October 1359

1204. ADMISSION of Thomas de Appelby priest to the vicarage of the church of Wonersh, vacant by the death of John de Wodeforde, at the presentation of the new hospital of St Mary, Bishopsgate, London. To be perpetual vicar residing according to the constitutions. Letter for the induction to the archdeacon of Surrey.

Southwark, 22 January 1360

199 **1205.** CERTIFICATORY LETTERS received from Robert bishop of Chichester concerning the exchange between Thomas de Orewell' vicar of Reigate and Richard Gregory of Kislingbury, lately rector of the church of Parham, diocese of Chichester, dated Southwark, 11 January 1360. Since the bishop of Chichester approves, the bishop admitted Richard to Reigate, at the presentation of the prior and convent of St Mary, Southwark. To be perpetual vicar residing according to the constitutions. Letter to the archdeacon of Surrey for the induction.

Southwark, 22 January 1360

1206. CERTIFICATORY LETTERS received from Robert bishop of Chichester concerning the exchange between Thomas Cobbild rector of Peper Harow and Robert de Stepyng rector of Elstead, diocese of Chichester, dated 18 February 1360. Since the bishop of Chichester approves of the exchange, Robert was admitted to Peper Harow, vacant by the resignation of Thomas and at the presentation of the king by reason of the custody of the lands and heir of Andrew Braunche, knight. Letter for the induction to the archdeacon of Surrey.

Southwark, 25 February 1360

1207. ADMISSION of William de Hull' clerk as rector of the church of Gatcombe [Isle of Wight], vacant, at the presentation of the king by reason of the custody of the lands and heir of John de Insula of Gatcombe. Letter for the induction to the archdeacon of Winchester.

Southwark, 15 February 1360

1208. ADMISSION of Thomas Laurens priest to the church of Ockham vacant, at the presentation of William de Peyce, attorney for Ralph, earl of Stafford and lord of Tonbridge. Letter to the archdeacon of Surrey for the induction.

Southwark, 12 March 1360

1209. ADMISSION of John Sladdok' priest to the vicarage of Weybridge, vacant, at the presentation of the prior and convent of Newark. To be perpetual vicar residing according to the constitutions. Letter to the official of the archdeacon of Surrey for the induction.

Southwark, 10 February 1360

1210. LICENCE for absence granted to Richard rector of Linkenholt for one year to be at the service of John de Uppyngham' rector of Abbots Ann.

Southwark, 13 March 1360

1211. APPROVAL OF AN EXCHANGE WITHIN THE DIOCESE after examination, and discussion between Martin de Newynton' rector of Avington and Ralph Tristram rector of East Tisted. Ralph was collated by the bishop to Avington and Martin admitted to East Tisted, at the presentation of John de Rutherfield'. Letter for the inductions to the archdeacon of Winchester.

Southwark, 18 April 1360

1212. COLLATION by devolution of the church of Hatch on William de Penynton' priest, as rector. Letter to the official of Winchester.

Southwark, 18 April 1360

1213. PRESENTATION by the bishop of Walter Waleys priest to the bishop of Salisbury for the church of Ebbesborne Episcopi or Bishopstone, diocese of Salisbury, vacant by the death of Lambert de Paulesholte late rector at the bishop's presentation.

Southwark, 19 April 1360

[Margin] Later the presentee renounced the presentation before the bishop of Salisbury at Southwark.

1214. PRESENTATION of Thomas de Durlee priest by the bishop to the bishop of Salisbury for the same church of Bishopstone.

Windsor, 23 April 1360

200   **1215.** CERTIFICATORY LETTERS received from Michael bishop of London concerning the exchange between William Chyntyng' rector of Nutfield, diocese of Winchester and Robert de Wyssyndon', rector of St Michael's, Wood Street, London. Dated Southwark, 26 April 1360. Since the bishop of London approved, Robert was admitted to Nutfield as rector, at the presentation of Fulk de Horwode, citizen of London. Letter for the induction to the archdeacon of Surrey.

Southwark, 28 April 1360

1216. AUTHORIZATION OF EXCHANGE of benefices between John Wengrave rector of Fawley, diocese of Lincoln, and Roger de Kerselawe, rector of Ewhurst, diocese of Winchester, by commission of John bishop of Lincoln, after an enquiry by the dean of Wycombe. The bishop of Lincoln authorizes the bishop to admit Roger to the church of Fawley, at the presentation of Matilda Sankevill' and Martin Chaunceux and Geoffrey de Weston' clerk, reserving the oath of obedience to the bishop of Lincoln and requesting a copy of the process. Dated the Temple, London, 13 February 1360. Admission of John to the church of Ewhurst, at the presentation of the prior and convent of St Mary, Merton. Letter for the induction to the archdeacon of Surrey.

Southwark, 28 April 1360

1217. PRESENTATION of Thomas de Durlegh' priest by the bishop to the bishop of Salisbury for the church of Bishopstone, diocese of Salisbury, vacant by the death of Lambert de Paulesholte, last rector.

Windsor, 23 April 1360

1218. COLLATION by the bishop of the portion of the tithes of the manor of Northanger on William David clerk. Letter to Roger, rector of the church of Highclere to induct William or his proctor to the possession of these tithes and to the building to house them.

Southwark, 5 May 1360

1219. COLLATION by the bishop of the church of Calbourne, Isle of Wight, vacant on Richard de Lyncheford his chaplain, to be rector. Letter to the rector of Brighstone and the vicar of Carisbrooke for the induction.

Southwark, 13 May 1360

1220. ADMISSION of John Burgh' acolyte to the church of West Clandon, vacant by the resignation of John London' de Henton', last rector, on the last day of May into the hands of the bishop; at the presentation of the abbot and convent of Chertsey. Letter for the induction to the official of the archdeacon of Surrey.

Southwark, 1 June 1360

1221. ADMISSION of Robert Hobyn priest as rector of the church of Laverstoke, vacant by the death of the last rector, at the presentation of the abbot and convent of Hyde. Letter for the induction to the archdeacon of Winchester.

Southwark, 18 June 1360

201 **1222.** LETTER CONCERNING AN EXCHANGE addressed to Thomas David, clerk. The bishop has received a commission from Thomas, bishop of St David's, concerning the exchange between William de Osberston' canon prebendary of St Davids and M. Thomas David rector of Shalfleet, Isle of Wight. The bishop is to act according to the results of his enquiry on behalf of the bishop of St David's. From his manor of Lantefey, 11 June 1360. The bishop has examined the case and received the resignation of William from the canonry and the prebend of Caerfai. He authorizes the exchange and will admit William through his proctor John de Walton'.

Southwark, 26 June 1360

1223. ADMISSION of William de Osberston' to the church of Shalfleet, vacant by the resignation of John de Walton', proctor for M. Thomas David, late rector, at the presentation of William earl of Salisbury and lord of the Isle of Man, patron. Letter for the induction to the archdeacon of Winchester.

Same date

1224. COLLATION by the bishop of the priestly office in the chapel of Marwell on John Sadelere priest, vacant by the resignation of Robert atte Grene in the presence of John de Beautre public notary, John Bennebury and Thomas Mountpeller on this same day. To be perpetual chaplain. Letter to Walter Nhot treasurer of Wolvesley for the induction; to share with his fellow chaplains in the income.

Southwark, 28 July 1360

1225. LICENCE granted to John de Whiteweye rector of Stoke by Guildford to be absent for one year at the service of John de Bogham, knight.

Farnham, 10 August 1360

1226. ADMISSION of John Renald priest as rector of Worting, vacant by the resignation of John de Denham, now rector of Codford, diocese of Salisbury, at the presentation of the abbot and convent of Hyde. Letter for induction to the archdeacon of Winchester.

Southwark, 21 August 1360

1227. DEPARTURE OF THE BISHOP FOR CALAIS
Memorandum that 24 August on the feast of St Bartholomew William, bishop and chancellor of the king of England set out from Southwark at the command of the king and constituted as his vicars-general fr. John prior of the church of Winchester and M. Thomas de Enham chancellor.

1228. GRANT OF POWERS to the vicars-general.

Southwark, 22 August 1360

202   FOR THE PERIOD OF THE VICARIATE:

1229. ADMISSION by Thomas de Enham, rector of the church of Alresford, of Thomas de Ixnynge to the vicarage of the church of Walkhampstead, at the presentation of the prior and convent of Tandridge, by exchange with the perpetual vicar of Sunbury, diocese of London, after the resignation of John Hoo of Upwell, vicar of Walkhamstead, taking the oath for residence according to the formula of Otto and Ottobon.

Under the same date admission of John de Hoo to the vicarage of Sunbury as perpetual vicar according to the same constitutions. Letter for the induction to the archdeacon of Surrey.

Winchester, 12 October 1360

1230. ADMISSION by M. Thomas as vicar-general of John Lane priest to the vicarage of Froyle, vacant by the death of Walter, last vicar. To be perpetual vicar according to the constitutions for which he took the oath. Letter for the induction to the archdeacon of Winchester.

Merton, 24 October 1360

1231. ADMISSION by M. Thomas as vicar-general of William de Sprocford' priest to the vicarage of Wonersh, vacant by the resignation of Thomas de Appelby, at the presentation of the prior and convent of St Mary, Bishopsgate, London. To be perpetual vicar residing according to the constitutions for which he took the oath. Letter for the induction to the archdeacon of Surrey.

Alresford, 15 October 1360

1232. RETURN OF THE BISHOP

Memorandum that William, bishop of Winchester, returned from Calais to Southwark, 6 November 1360.

1233. ADMISSION of Richard atte Halle of Thorp', clerk, to the church of Byfleet as rector, vacant by the resignation of Richard de Kerselewe, at the presentation of prince Edward. Letter for the induction to the archdeacon of Surrey.

Southwark, 8 November 1360

203   **1234.** COLLATION by the bishop of the church of Michelmersh on M. John de Turk clerk, vacant by the resignation of Walter Nhot' last rector. Letter for the induction to M. Robert de Lemyngton' rector of Farley.

Southwark, 24 August 1360

1235. COLLATION by the bishop in the chapel of St Elizabeth, at the instance of John de Nubbelegh' provost, of three sacerdotal offices vacant, on William de Byshopeston', Robert Thursteyn and Edmund Lutespade, according to the constitutions of John de Pontissara, founder.

Wolveseye, 12 December 1360

1236. AUTHORIZATION OF AN EXCHANGE between Robert de Stepynge, rector of Piper Harow and Thomas Clamvile, rector of Woodland of the patronage and jurisdiction of the archbishop of Canterbury, by his commission to the bishop. He accepted the resignations and collated the church of Woodland and instituted Thomas to Piper Harow, at the presentation of Mary, widow of Thomas Braunche. Letter to the archdeacon of Surrey for the induction of Thomas.

Farnham, 31 December 1360

1237. CERTIFICATORY LETTERS received from Michael bishop of London concerning the exchange between John de Kerolston', rector of Gatton, and Gerald Ricarii, chaplain of the perpetual chantry in the church of St Andrew, Holborn, London. Dated Farnham 22 December 1360. Since the bishop of London has authorized the exchange, Gerald was admitted to Gatton, at the presentation of the prior and convent of St Pancras, Lewes. Letter for the induction to the archdeacon of Surrey.

Southwark, 15 January 1361

1238. ADMISSION of Richard Laweles priest as rector of the church of Hambledon, vacant by the voluntary resignation of John de Stenynge, last rector, before M. Thomas de Enham chancellor at the chancellery at Southwark, 16 January 1361, in the presence of John Beautre, notary, and M. John de Denham and Thomas Solde, clerk; at the presentation of Richard, earl of Arundel as guardian of a certain woman, the patroness and heiress of the manor of Hambledon. Letter for the induction to the archdeacon of Surrey.

Southwark, 17 January 1361

1239. DISPENSATION granted to M. John Turke, rector of the church of Michelmersh subdeacon, to be absent for study somewhere in England for one year, without obligation of residence or of proceeding to major orders according to the constitutions of Boniface.

Southwark, 17 January 1361

1240. INSTITUTION of the prior of Carisbrooke. Letter to fr. Nicholas Gaugire, professed monk of the monastery of St Mary Lyre, diocese of Evreux, that the procurator fr. Peter de Elemosina has presented fr. Nicholas as prior of Carisbrooke, Isle of Wight. The bishop has admitted him and instituted him as prior.
Under same date, letter to the archdeacon of Winchester for the induction according to their customs.

Southwark, 27 January 1361

1241. ADMISSION of William le Couk' priest to the church of St Lawrence, Winchester, vacant by the death of Robert last rector, at the presentation of the abbot and convent of Hyde. Letter for induction to the archdeacon of Winchester.

Southwark, 27 January 1361

204   **1242.** ADMISSION of William de Peyto junior, priest, to be rector of the church of Buckland, vacant by the resignation of William de Peyto senior, before M. Thomas de Enham, chancellor, at Southwark, 14 February, 1361, in the presence of John Beautre, M. John Essex' and Peter Pekke as witnesses, at the presentation of Richard, earl of Arundel. Letter for the induction to the archdeacon of Surrey.

Southwark, 20 February 1361

1243. COLLATION by the bishop of the church of Binstead, Isle of Wight, on Henry de Husseborne, priest. Letter for the induction to the official of Winchester and the rector of Brighstone.

Southwark, 18 March 1361

1244. ADMISSION of John de Staunton' priest as rector of Eldon, vacant by the resignation of William Natton, at the presentation of John Bakere, lord of Eldon. Letter for the induction to the archdeacon of Winchester.

Southwark, 24 March 1361

1245. RESIGNATION OF THE PRIOR OF SOUTHWARK. Memorandum that 16 March 1361 fr. John de Pekham, walking in the garden with the bishop in his manor of Southwark, after a few words about his incapacity for governing the priory and holding the office of prior, in the presence of M. Thomas de Enham, chancellor, of John de Sancto Neoto and Robert de Newenham, the bishop's domestic clerks, called as witnesses with John Beautre, John Essex of Herlawe, apostolic notaries, voluntarily and definitively resigned his office, as also any cause pending at the Romas court concerning the priory. [Formula of resignation].

1246. PETITION from the subprior for licence to elect a successor from among the brethren. The text names: Henry de Colyngborne, subprior, John de Pekham, Richard de Stokes, Nicholas de Raveneston', John de Malmesbury, John de Durnham, John de Sanndrestede and William de Brakkelegh', order of St Augustine, with absentees: Walter de Thorneye and Thomas de Fitelton'. They ask to elect by compromission.

The chapter-house, Southwark, 24 March 1361

205   They agree to nominate fr. Henry de Colyngbourne, in the presence of Philip de Codeford, Thomas de Enham, John Beautre and John Essex.

1247. ELECTION OR PROVISION. The bishop has enquired into the life and qualities of Henry de Colyngbourne. He grants the priory licence to elect by compromission. Anyone opposing should appear in the chapel of the manor of Southwark, the 27th next.

1248. THE CONSENT. Subsequently, 26 March, 1561, fr. Nicholas de Raveneston', professed canon and acting as procurator, received the consent in a garden of the *hospicium*, to the west of the church of St Margaret, where fr. Henry was staying. Before witnesses fr. Henry consented after some delay to become prior. [Formula of consent].

27 March 1361

The same day, in the manor chapel with fr. Henry the elect and fr. Nicholas de Raveneston' procurator, before David de Wollors, Thomas de Brayton, John de Codynton' clerks of the king's chancery, and Nicholas de Kaerwent, John Beautre and John Essex, public notaries, at the request of the procurator, the bishop confirmed the election of the subprior fr. Henry de Colyngborne to be prior. M. Thomas the chancellor **206** is to induct him to his stall in choir and his place in chapter. Witnesses: John Beautre, John Essex, Thomas Mountpell', Thomas Selde, Peter Pekke and others.

1249. DISPENSATION granted to M. Thomas de Shypton' rector of Widley to be absent for one year for study.

Southwark, 6 April 1361

1250. NOMINATION of the prior of St Mary, Southwark, provided by the bishop at the request of the community.

Southwark, 24 March 1361

1251. TESTIMONIAL LETTER of the confirmation of the election.

Southwark, 27 March 1361

1252. ADMISSION of Roger Herman priest as vicar of the church of Hurstbourne Tarrant, vacant, at the presentation of M. Thomas de Enham, rector of Alresford, proctor for Saladun de Falletis canon of Salisbury and prebendary of the prebend of Hurstbourne Tarrant and Burbage. To be perpetual vicar, residing according to the constitutions for which he took the oath. Letter for the induction to the archdeacon of Winchester.

Southwark, 11 May 1361

1253. CERTIFICATORY LETTERS received from Michael, bishop of London, concerning the exchange between Geoffrey de Wondeye, lately rector of St Margaret, Pattens' Lane, London and William Barneby rector of the church of Eversley, dated Southwark, 8 May 1361. Since the bishop of London authorizes the exchange, the bishop admitted Geoffrey as rector of Eversley, at the presentation of Robert Murdac, rector of Winterbourne near Bristol, Robert Coigny, rector of Somerford Maudyt and John Wynchester, warden of the perpetual chantry of Winterbourne, patrons for this turn of the church of Eversley. Letter for the induction to the archdeacon of Winchester.

Southwark, 27 May 1361

1254. COLLATION by the bishop of the church of St Mary in Vallibus, Winchester, vacant by the death of John de Westbury, late rector, on John Payn clerk. Letter for the induction to the archdeacon of Winchester.

Southwark, 26 May 1361

1255. ADMISSION of Robert Bover priest as rector of the church of Woldingham, vacant, at the presentation of Ralph earl of Stafford. Letter for the induction to the archdeacon of Surrey.

Southwark, 1 June 1361

1256. ADMISSION of William Arvel priest to the church of Rotherhithe, vacant, at the presentation of the prior and convent of St Saviour, Bermondsey. Letter for the induction to the archdeacon of Surrey.

Esher, 14 June 1361

207

1257. ADMISSION of Bartholomew de Wynnecote priest to the church of Stoke Charity, vacant by the death of the last rector, at the presentation of Thomas de Hampton. In the vacancy of the archdeaconry, letter to the official of Winchester and to M. John de Ware, sequestrator-general.

Farnham, 17 June 1361

1258. PRESENTATION by the bishop of M. Walter Benyt, rector of Arreton, Isle of Wight, to the bishop of Salisbury for the church of Brightwell, diocese of Salisbury, of the bishop's patronage, by exchange with M. Walter de Sevenhampton' rector of Brightwell.

Farnham, 18 June 1361

1259. ARCHDEACONRY OF WINCHESTER, vacant by the death of Robert de Burton' lately archdeacon, conferred upon M. John de Wolveleye, clerk. Letter to John de Nubbelegh, provost of the chapel of St Elizabeth, Winchester, and M. John de Ware, sequestrator-general for the archdeaconry of Winchester, for the induction and installation of the new archdeacon in his stall in choir and his place in chapter in the church of Winchester.

Farnham, 18 June 1361

1260. COLLATION by the bishop of the church of Alverstoke on M. Thomas Yonge, clerk, as rector. Letter for the induction to the vicar of Farnham and to the parish chaplain of Alverstoke.

Esher, 20 June 1361

1261. ADMISSION of Richard Porter, chaplain, to the vicarage of Mitcham, vacant, at the presentation of the prior and convent of St Mary, Southwark. To be perpetual vicar, residing according to the constitutions for which he took the oath. Letter for the induction to the archdeacon of Surrey.

Southwark, 26 June 1361

1262. ADMISSION of Richard de Maythland, priest, to the vicarage of the church of Hurstbourne Tarrant, vacant, at the presentation of M. John de Corf', clerk, procurator for Saladin de Falecis, canon of Salisbury, prebendary of Hurstbourne Tarrant and Burbage, patron, and instituted as vicar in the person of Thomas Mounpell', proctor for the said Richard. To be perpetual vicar with obligation of residence according to the constitutions for which he took the oath. Letter for the induction to the archdeacon of Winchester.

Southwark, 26 June 1361

1263. ADMISSION of Nicholas called le Monnle', clerk, as rector of Linkenholt, vacant by the resignation before the bishop of Thomas

Mounpell', clerk, as proctor for Richard de Maythland lately rector of the said church, at the presentation of the abbot and convent of St Peter, Gloucester. Letter for the induction to the archdeacon of Winchester.

Southwark, 26 June 1361

1264. COLLATION by the bishop of the church of Alresford on M. Walter de Sevenhampton' priest, vacant by the death of M. Thomas de Enham. Letter for the induction to M. John de Ware, sequestrator-general.

Southwark, 29 June 1361

1265. ADMISSION of John de Bereford', subdeacon, to the church of Chaldon, vacant by the death of M. Henry de Bagworth' last rector, at the presentation of the prioress and convent of Nuneaton. Letter for the induction to the archdeacon of Surrey.

Southwark, 30 June 1361

1266. ADMISSION of Robert de Newenham priest to the church of Arreton, Isle of Wight, vacant, at the presentation of fr. William, procurator for the abbot and convent of Lyre, diocese of Evreux, for presentations in the diocese of Winchester and Salisbury. Letters for the induction to the official of Winchester, the dean of the Island and the vicar of the church of Arreton, to induct Robet in the person of John Magote, chaplain, or Roger Fontel' his proctors.

Southwark, 30 June 1361

208 **1267.** ADMISSION of Roger Herman priest to the vicarage of Farnham, vacant by the death of John, at the presentation of M. John de Edyngdon', archdeacon of Surrey and rector of Farnham. To be perpetual vicar residing according to the constitutions. Letter for the induction to the official of the archdeacon of Surrey and John de Caste, chaplain of the castle of Farnham.

Southwark, 1 July 1361

1268. ADMISSION of Nicholas de Byssebury priest to the church of Oxted as rector, vacant, at the presentation of Reginald de Cobeham, knight, lord of the manor of Oxted and of the advowson, recently acquired from Robert de Stangrave, knight, lately lord of the manor. Letter for the induction to the official of the archdeacon of Surrey.

Southwark, 5 July 1361

1269. ADMISSION of Walter Lucas priest to the vicarage of Carshalton, vacant, at the presentation of the prior and convent of Merton. To be perpetual vicar, residing according to the constitutions. Letter to the archdeacon of Surrey for the induction.

Esher, 5 July 1361

1270. ADMISSION of John Carn priest to the vicarage of Wellow, vacant, at the presentation of the abbot and convent of Netley. To be perpetual vicar residing according to the constitutions. Letter for the induction to the archdeacon of Winchester.

Esher, 6 July 1361

1271. ADMISSION of John Golegh of Pembroke, priest, to the vicarage of Effingham, vacant, at the presentation of the prior and convent of Merton. To be perpetual vicar residing according to the constitutions. Letter to the official of the archdeacon of Surrey for the induction.

Esher, 7 July 1361

1272. ADMISSION of Thomas Restwold' acolyte as rector of Fifehead, vacant, at the presentation of the abbess and convent of St Mary *de Pratis*, Northampton. Letter for the induction to the archdeacon of Winchester.

Wargrave, 18 July 1361

1273. ADMISSION of John Preston' priest as rector of the church of Walton, vacant, at the presentation of Thomas de Legh. Letter for the induction to the archdeacon of Surrey and the dean of Guildford.

Brightwell, 21 July 1361

1274. ADMISSION of John Gary priest to the vicarage of Wherwell, vacant, at the presentation of William de Osberton, canon and prebendary of the prebend of Wherwell. To be perpetual vicar residing according to the constitutions. Letter for the induction to the archdeacon of Winchester.

Buckland, 22 July 1361

1275. ADMISSION of John Oweyn priest as rector of the church of Crux Easton, vacant, at the presentation of Edward Avenel, knight. Letter to John de Ware, holding jurisdiction of the archdeaconry of Winchester during its vacancy.

Edington, 24 July 1361

1276. ADMISSION of William Botiler of Sudbury priest to the vicarage of Odiham, vacant, at the presentation of Richard de Hemmesby, proctor for Simon de Sudbury, chancellor of Salisbury and rector of Odiham, annexed to the chancellorship. To be perpetual vicar residing according to the constitutions. Letter for the induction to M. John de Ware.

Edington, 24 July 1361

1277. ADMISSION of Richard de Elyng' priest as rector of the church of St John in the Hills (*super Montem*), Winchester, at the presentation of the prior and convent of St Denys, Southampton. Letter for the induction to M. John de Ware.

Edington, 24 July 1361

1278. ADMISSION of Laurence de Alwarthorp' clerk as rector of Holy Trinity, Guildford, at the presentation of the prior and convent of St Mary, Merton. Letter for the induction to the archdeacon of Surrey.

Southwark, 12 July 1361

209

1279. ADMISSION of Walter Fynamore priest as rector of the church of Silchester, vacant, at the presentation of Peter de Cusancia, knight. Letter to M. John de Ware for the induction.

Edington, 27 July 1361

1280. ADMISSION of William Payn as rector of the church of Grateley, vacant, at the presentation of John Mauduyt, knight. Letter for the induction to M. John de Ware.

Edington, 27 July 1361

1281. ADMISSION of Peter de Knyghtecote priest as rector to the church of St Peter Chesil (*super Chushulle*), Winchester, vacant, at the presentation of the prior and convent of St Denys, Southampton, Letter to M. John de Ware for the induction.

Highclere, 6 August 1361

1282. ADMISSION of John Brode priest as rector of the church of East Tisted, vacant by the resignation in the hands of the bishop of Richard Monch' clerk, as proctor for Martin de Neweton' last rector, at the presentation of John de Rutherfeld'. Letter for the induction to M. John de Ware.

Highclere, 10 August 1361

1283. ADMISSION of Thomas Englishe priest to the vicarage of the church of Banstead, vacant, at the presentation of the prior and convent of St Mary, Southwark. To be perpetual vicar residing according to the constitutions. Letter to the archdeacon of Surrey for the induction.

Highclere, 10 August 1351

1284. ADMISSION of Adam atte Fengate as rector of the church of Ockham, vacant, at the presentation of Ralph, earl of Stafford. Letter for the archdeacon of Surrey.

Highclere, 11 August 1361

1285. ADMISSION of John de Hokenorton priest as rector to the church of St Peter Chesil, Winchester, vacant by the death of Peter de Knyghtecote, at the presentation of the prior and convent of St Denys, Southampton. Letter to M. John de Ware for the induction.

Highclere, 12 August 1361

1286. ADMISSION of Geoffrey de Norton' priest to the vicarage of the church of Battersea, vacant, at the presentation of the abbot and convent of Westminster, immediately subject to the Roman see. To be perpetual vicar, residing according to the constitutions, for which he took the oath. Letter for the induction to the archdeacon of Surrey.

Highclere, 16 August 1361

1287. ADMISSION of Richard de Wantynge priest to the vicarage of the church of Shipton, vacant, at the presentation of the prior and convent of Novo Loco, near Ripley. To be perpetual vicar residing according to the constitutions, for which he took the oath. Letter for the induction of M. J' de Ware.

South, i.e. Bishop's Waltham, 18 August 1361

1288. ADMISSION of Robert Page priest to the vicarage of the church of Reigate, vacant, at the presentation of the prior and convent of St Mary, Southwark. To be perpetual vicar residing according to the constitutions, for which he took the oath. Letter for the induction to the archdeacon of Surrey.

Bishop's Waltham, 19 August 1361

1289. ADMISSION of Richard de Gretton' priest to the vicarage of the church of Carshalton, vacant, at the presentation of king Edward, the priory of Merton being vacant. To be perpetual vicar residing according to the constitutions, for which he took the oath. Letter for the induction to the archdeacon of Surrey.

Bishop's Waltham, 20 August 1361

1290. COLLATION by the bishop of the church of Crondall on Thomas de Sutton', priest, vacant by the death of Thomas de Chakynden'. To be perpetual vicar residing according to the constitutions, for which he took the oath. Letter to M. J' de Ware for the induction.

Bishop's Waltham, 18 August 1361

210

1291. ADMISSION of John de Everdon' priest as rector of the church of Compton near Guildford, vacant, at the presentation of the abbot and convent of Durford. Letter for the induction to the archdeacon of Surrey.

Bishop's Waltham, 21 August 1361

1292. ADMISSION of Peter Warner priest to the vicarage of the church of Hartley Wintney, vacant, at the presentation of the prioress and convent of Wintney. To be perpetual vicar residing according to the constitutions, for which he took the oath. Letter for the induction to M. J' de Ware.

Bishop's Waltham, 21 August 1361

1293. ADMISSION of John de Kettelby priest to the vicarage of Caterham, vacant, at the presentation of the abbot and convent of the exempt monastery of Holy Cross, Waltham. To be perpetual vicar residing according to the constitutions, for which he took the oath. Letter for the induction to the archdeacon of Surrey.

Bishop's Waltham, 22 August 1361

1294. ADMISSION of Robert Hardewyn priest to the vicarage of Catherington, vacant, at the presentation of the prioress and convent of Nuneaton. To be perpetual vicar residing according to the constitutions, for which he took the oath. Letter for the induction to M. John Ware.

Bishop's Waltham, 23 August 1361

1295. ADMISSION of John Suyng' priest as rector of the church of Nately Scures, vacant, at the presentation of John de Scures, knight. Letter for the induction to M. John Ware.

Bishop's Waltham, 23 August 1361

1296. EXCHANGE OF BENEFICES authorized by the bishop of Salisbury between M. John Corf, rector of Radipole, diocese of Salisbury, and John Payn, rector of St Mary in the Vale, Winchester. After receiving the resignations the bishop instituted John Payn to Radipole, at the presentation of the abbot and convent of Cerne. Subsequently he collated the church of St Mary in the Vale on M. J' Corf as rector. Letter for the induction to M. J' de Ware. And immediately John Corf resigned the church of St Mary.

Bishop's Waltham, 23 August 1361

1297. ADMISSION of John Wake priest to the canonry of the conventual church of Wherwell and to the prebend of Wherwell, both vacant by the death of William de Osberton, at the presentation of the abbess and convent. Letter to M. John Ware for induction and installation.

Bishop's Waltham, 23 August 1361

1298. ADMISSION of John de Remmesbury priest to the church of Minstead, vacant, at the presentation of Richard de Bysthorn'. Letter to M. John Ware for the induction.

Bishop's Waltham, 24 August 1361

1299. COLLATION by the bishop of the priestly offices in the chapel of St Elizabeth, Winchester, on John Persyval' and on William le Hore, priests, according to the ordination of the founder, John de Pontissara. On the same day the office of subdeacon was conferred on Walter Cutel.

Bishop's Waltham, 25 August 1361

1300. COLLATION of the church of St Mary in the Vale, Winchester, vacant by the resignation of John Corf, on Thomas Crook' of Grove, priest. Letter to J' Ware for the induction.

Bishop's Waltham, 25 August 1361

1301. ADMISSION of John Weston' priest to the vicarage of the church of Betchworth, vacant, at the presentation of the prior and convent of St Mary, Southwark. To be perpetual vicar residing according to the constitutions. Letter for the induction to the archdeacon of Surrey.

Bishop's Waltham, 27 August 1361

211 **1302.** ADMISSION of John de Wheston as rector of Niton, Isle of Wight, vacant, at the presentation of fr. William, procurator of the abbot and convent of Lyre. Letter to M. John Ware for the induction.

Bishop's Waltham, 30 August 1361

1303. ADMISSION of Robert Pesshon, priest, to the vicarage of Andover, vacant, at the presentation of Philip, prior and rector of Andover. To be perpetual vicar, residing and ministering according to the constitutions. Letter for the induction to M. J' Ware.

Bishop's Waltham, 30 August 1361

1304. ADMISSION of fr. William de Albigneye, monk of St Sauveur-le-Vicomte, diocese of Coutances, to the dependent priory of Ellingham, vacant, at the presentation of the abbot and convent. Letter to M. J' Ware for the induction.

Farnham, 1 September 1361

1305. ADMISSION of Richard Arnwode, priest, as rector of the church of Holy Cross, Southampton, vacant, at the presentation of the prior and convent of St Denys, Southampton. Letter for the induction to M. J' Ware.

Farnham, 1 September 1361

1306. ADMISSION of Robert Brightrich' priest as rector of Albury, vacant, at the presentation of William Crozier, knight. Letter for the induction to M. J' Ware.

Farnham, 1 September 1361

1307. ADMISSION of Adam de Hertyngdon' clerk as rector to the church of Heckfield, vacant, at the presentation of William de Wykeham, by the manor of Heckfield with the advowson being granted at farm to him by Thomas de Seynt Legier, knight, and Elizabeth his wife, who had recovered the said manor in the king's court from Robert de Sancto Manyfeo, lately lord of the manor. Letter for the induction to M. J' Ware.

Farnham, 3 September 1361

1308. COLLATION of the church of Crondall on Nicholas de Kaerwent, priest. It was vacant by the death of M. John Lech. To be rector. The bishop requested John Beautre, rector of Burghclere, to induct.

Farnham, 3 September 1361

1309. ADMISSION of Richard de Branketre, clerk, as rector of the church of Broughton, vacant, at the presentation of M. John de Branketre, treasurer of the church of York, in the person of Richard de Ravenesere, provost of the church of Beverley, his proctor. Letter to M. J' de Ware for the induction.

Farnham, 4 September 1361

1310. ADMISSION of John de Eyton priest as rector of the church of Chawton, vacant, at the presentation of Thomas de Aldyngbourne, by right of Margaret his wife, daughter and co-heir of Hugh de Sancto Johanne, deceased. Letter to the aforesaid M. John and the dean of Alton.

Farnham, 8 September 1361

1311. ADMISSION of Robert de Wadden' priest to the church of Over Wallop, vacant, at the presentation of Thomas de Wallop'. Letter for induction to M. J' de Ware.

Farnham, 9 September 1361

1312. ADMISSION as rector of Hamo de la Solere, priest, to the church of Whippingham, Isle of Wight, at the presentation of William de Monasterio, procurator for the abbey of Lyre. Letter to M. J' de Ware for the induction.

Farnham, 11 September 1361

1313. PRESENTATION of M. Thomas Yonge, clerk, for the church of Wroughton,, diocese of Salisbury, at the resignation of Nicholas de Kaerwent.

Farnham, 9 September 1361

1314. ADMISSION of fr. Walter Oxneford', canon of Titchfield, premonstratensian to the vicarage of Titchfield, vacant, at the presentation of the abbey. To be perpetual vicar residing according to the constitutions. Letter for the induction to J' Ware.

Farnham, 13 September 1361

212 1315. COLLATION by the bishop of the church of Bramdean, vacant, on John Lombard of Stoke Goldington, as rector. Letter for the induction to J' de Ware.

Farnham, 11 September 1361

1316. COLLATION by the bishop of the church of Chilbolton on John de Gaundevill' priest, vacant. Letter for the induction to J' de Ware general commissary.

Farnham, 11 September 1361

1317. COLLATION by the bishop of the church of Alverstoke, vacant, on Robert de Lincoln' as rector. Letter to J' de Ware and the vicar of Farnham for the induction.

Farnham, 11 September 1361

1318. COLLATION by the bishop of the vicarage of the church of Twyford on William de Falloe priest. To be perpetual vicar residing according to the constitutions. Letter to J' de Ware for the induction.

Farnham, 13 September 1361

1319. COLLATION by the bishop of the church of Millbrook, vacant, on Nicholas de Wyneford' priest. Letter for the induction to John de Ware.

Winchester, 14 September 1361

1320. COLLATION by the bishop of the church of St Faith, Winchester, on Richard Laurence, priest, as rector. Letter for the induction to M. John de Ware.

Winchester, 14 September 1361

1321. ADMISSION of Nicholas Hammush' to the church of West Tytherleigh, vacant, at the presentation of William de Overton', knight. To be rector. Letter for the induction to J' Ware.

Farnham, 10 September 1361

1322. PRESENTATION of John Beautre priest by the bishop to the church of Steeple Morden, diocese of Ely, vacant, the custody of the spiritualities being granted to the bishop during the vacancy at Ely.

Farnham, 11 September 1361

1323. COLLATION by the bishop of the church of Alverstoke, vacant, on Robert de Lyncoln' clerk, as rector. Letters for the induction to J' Ware and the vicar of Fareham.

Farnham, 10 September 1361

1324. ADMISSION of Thomas de Rasen priest as rector of the church of Ewell, vacant, at the presentation of the abbot and convent of Chertsey. Letter for the induction to the archdeacon of Surrey.

Wargrave, 16 September 1361

1325. ADMISSION of Richard Hervy priest as rector of the church of Worting, vacant, at the presentation of the abbot and convent of Hyde. Letter for the induction to J' Ware.

Wargrave, 17 September 1361

1326. ADMISSION of Robert le Wheelere priest as rector of the chapel of Eastrop (*capella curata*), vacant by the death of M. John de Donham, at the presentation of Joan, widow of John de Podenhale, knight, deceased. Letter to J' de Ware and to the dean of Basingstoke for the induction.

Wargrave, 18 September 1361

1327. COLLATION by the bishop of the church of Wonston vacant by the death of John de Nubbelegh' last rector. Letter to M. Walter de Sevenhampton, rector of Alresford and treasurer of Wolvesey for the induction.

Wargrave, 16 September 1361

1328. COLLATION by the bishop of the church of Houghton, vacant, on John de Wychford priest as rector. Letter for the induction to M. J' Ware.

Wargrave, 16 September 1361

1329. COLLATION by the bishop of the church of Crawley vacant, on Walter Skilling' priest, as rector. Letter for the induction to M. W' de Sevenhampton.

Wargrave, 19 September 1361

213   **1330.** PRESENTATION of Robert de Bysshepeston' clerk to the church of Patney, diocese of Salisbury, vacant.

Wargrave, 21 September 1361

1331. COLLATION by the bishop of the church of Whitchurch on William in the Lane, of Lodesworth, to be vicar residing according to the constitutions. Letter for the induction to J' Ware.

Wargrave, 20 September 1361

1332. ADMISSION of Thomas Lombard of 'Estoklegh', priest to the vicarage of the church of Barton Stacey, vacant, at the presentation of the prior and convent of Llanthony near Gloucester. To be perpetual vicar residing according to the constitutions. Letter for the induction to J' Ware.

Wargrave, 22 September 1361

1333. ADMISSION of Peter Bray priest as rector of Fetcham, vacant, at the presentation of William Croisszer, knight. Letter to the archdeacon of Surrey for the induction.

Wargrave, 22 September 1361

1334. ADMISSION of William Crouk' clerk as rector of the church of St Peter in Colebrook Street, Winchester, vacant, at the presentation of the abbess and convent of Nunnaminster. Letter for the induction to M. J' Ware.

Wargrave, 23 September 1361

1335. ADMISSION of Ralph Caperon as rector to the church of Titsey, vacant, at the presentation of Thomas de Uvedale, knight. Letter for the induction to the archdeacon of Surrey.

Wargrave, 24 September 1361

1336. ADMISSION of Richard Pante priest as rector of Farleigh Mortymere, vacant, at the presentation of Robert la Zousch'. Letter for the induction to J' Ware.

Wargrave, 24 September 1361

1337. ADMISSION of William de Rede priest as rector of Hartley Mauditt, vacant, at the presentation of Matilda, countess of Lancaster. Letter for the induction to John de Ware.

Wargrave, 25 September 1361

1338. ADMISSION of John de Codeford' clerk as rector of the church of Arreton, Isle of Wight, vacant, at the presentation of fr. William de Monasterio, procurator for the abbey of Lyre. Letter to J' Ware and the vicar of Arreton for the induction.

Wargrave, 26 September 1361

1339. COLLATION by the bishop of the church of Burghclere on Richard Lynchesford' priest as rector. Letter for the induction to John rector of Litchfield and to the vicar of Clere.

Wargrave, 26 September 1361

1340. COLLATION by the bishop of the priestly office in the chapel of Marwell, vacant, on Roger de Sloughtre priest. To be perpetual chaplain. Letter for the induction to M. Walter de Sevenhampton, treasurer of Wolvesey.

Wargrave, 27 September 1361

1341. ADMISSION of Stephen le Mason priest as rector of the church of Hambledon, at the presentation of John Kyonus. Letter to the archdeacon of Surrey for the induction.

Wargrave, 28 September 1361

1342. ADMISSION of John de Maydewell' as rector of the church of Merrow, vacant, at the presentation of the prioress and convent of Ivinghoe. Letter for the induction to the archdeacon of Surrey.

Wargrave, 28 September 1361

1343. ADMISSION of Richard Travers priest as rector to the church of Blendworth, vacant, at the presentation of the prioress and convent of Nuneaton. Letter for the induction to J' de Ware and the dean of Droxford.

Wargrave, 29 September 1361

214 **1344.** ADMISSION of Thomas Hert priest to the church of Wickham, vacant, at the presentation of John de Scures, knight. Letter for the induction to J' de Ware and the dean of Droxford.

Southwark, 3 October 1361

1345. ADMISSION of Stephen Wyot priest as rector of Hartley Wespall, at the presentation of John Waspail. Letter for the induction to J' Ware and the dean of Basingstoke.

Southwark, 4 October 1361

1346. PRESENTATION by the bishop of M. John Blanchard' doctor at law, to the bishop of Salisbury for the church of Elyndon' in that diocese, vacant by the resignation of M. Thomas Yonge, last rector.

Southwark, 3 October 1361

1347. LETTER CONCERNING AN EXCHANGE OF BENEFICES from the bishop to William de Wykham, clerk. Robert bishop of Salisbury has commissioned the bishop to consider the exchange between Simon of de Northwode, canon of the conventual church of Shaftesbury and prebendary there of the prebend of Iwerne Minster, and William de Wykham, deacon of the king's free chapel of St Martin-le-Grand, London. The bishop of Salisbury authorizes the bishop to act. The abbess and convent of Shaftesbury are the patrons; the induction of William is reserved to the bishop of Salisbury, who requests a certificate.

Sherborne castle, 24 September 1361

Having examined the case and received the resignation of Simon, the bishop admitted William to the canonry and prebend.

Southwark, 3 October 1361

Memorandum that the king collated Simon to the diaconate in the free chapel and ordered him to be installed.

1348. Duplicate of 1344.

1349. EXCHANGE OF BENEFICES by commission of John archbishop of York to the bishop, as between Richard de Ely, rector of Parva Sandal and Laurence Alwarthorp', rector of Holy Trinity, Guildford. Richard was admitted to Guildford at the presentation of the prior and convent of St Mary, Merton; Laurence to Parva Sandal at the presentation of the prior and convent of St Pancras, Lewes. Letter for the induction to the archdeacon of Surrey.

Southwark, 5 October 1361

215

1350. ADMISSION of Hugh de Welleford' as rector of the church of Mottistone, Isle of Wight, at the presentation of Dionisia, widow of Edmund de Langeford, knight. Letter to M. J' Ware and the dean of the Island for the induction.

Southwark, 13 October 1361

1351. ADMISSION of Richard Pruwec, priest as rector of the church of Rowner, vacant, at the presentation of William Bruyn, knight. Letter for the induction to J' de Ware.

Southwark, 13 October 1361

1352. ADMISSION of John Aysshton' priest as rector of the church of Silchester, vacant, at the presentation of Edmund Baynard'. Letter to J' de Ware for the induction.

Southwark, 14 October 1361

1353. COLLATION by the bishop of the church of Compton near Winchester, vacant, on M. John de Wormenhale, doctor at law. Letter for the induction to J' de Ware and the dean of Winchester.

Southwark, 8 October df1361

1354. COLLATION by the bishop of the church of Calbourne on M. William de Bermyngham, doctor of sacred theology. Letter to J' de Ware and the dean of the Island for the induction.

Southwark, 9 October 1361

1355. ADMISSION of Roger de Rasen clerk as rector of the church of Ewell, vacant by the free resignation of Thomas de Rasen before M. Walter Benet, chancellor, Thomas de Mounpell, and John Beautre. At the presentation of the abbot and convent of Chertsey. Letter for the induction to the archdeacon of Surrey.

Southwark, 16 October 1361

1356. COLLATION by the bishop of the vicarage of Hambledon on William de Clere priest. To be perpetual vicar residing according to the constitutions. Letter for the induction to J' de Ware.

Southwark, 16 October 1361

1357. COLLATION by the bishop of the church of Chilcombe, vacant, on Nicholas de Elyndon' priest as rector. Letter for the induction to J' de Ware.

Southwark, 16 October 1361

1358. ENQUIRY INTO AN ELECTION. Commission entrusted to M. Walter Beneyt and John de Ware as to the election of fr. John de Tyssebury, canon of the conventual church of Breamore, as prior. They may confirm or annul as they find.

Southwark, 16 October 1361

1359. ADMISSION of John de Middleton' priest as rector of the church of Stoke near Guildford, at the presentation of the prior and convent of St Pancras, Lewes. Letter for the induction to the archdeacon of Surrey.

Southwark, 17 October 1361

1360. ADMISSION of John Lane priest to the vicarage of the church of Alton, vacant, at the presentation of the abbot and convent of Hyde. Letter for the induction to the archdeacon of Winchester.

Southwark, 17 October 1361

1361. COLLATION OF THE ARCHDEACONRY OF WINCHESTER, vacant, on M. Robert de Wykford'. Letter to the official of Winchester to induct and assign his stall in choir and place in the cathedral chapter.

Southwark, 18 October 1361

1362. ADMISSION of William Carnek' clerk, as rector of the church of King's Worthy, at the presentation of the abbot and convent of Hyde. Letter for the induction to the archdeacon of Winchester.

Southwark, 18 October 1361

1363. ADMISSION of John Chynham priest to the vicarage of the church of Micheldever, vacant, at the presentation of the abbot and convent of Hyde. To be perpetual vicar residing according to the constitutions. Letter for the induction to the archdeacon of Winchester.

Southwark, 18 October 1361

216 **1364.** ADMISSION of Adam Eyland priest to the vicarage of Portsmouth, vacant, at the presentation of the prior and convent of Southwick. To be perpetual vicar residing according to the constitutions. Letter for the induction to the archdeacon of Winchester.

Southwark, 18 October 1361

1365. ADMISSION of Walter Freland' clerk as rector of the church of Bletchingley vacant, at the presentation of William de Peyto, attorney for Ralph, earl of Stafford. Letter to the archdeacon of Surrey for the induction.

Southwark, 18 October 1361

1366. ADMISSION of John de Courneys priest as rector to the church of St Peter in the Jewry, Winchester, vacant, at the presentation of the abbot and convent of Hyde. Letter for the induction to the archdeacon of Winchester.

Southwark, 18 October 1361

1367. COLLATION by the bishop of the church of Millbrook, vacant, on John Peuseys priest as rector. Letter for the induction to the archdeacon of Winchester.

Southwark, 19 October 1361

1368. ADMISSION of John de Northwode priest to the prebend of the church of Leckford in the monastic church of Nunnaminster, Winchester, at the presentation of king Edward, by reason of the temporalities during a vacancy. Letter to the archdeacon of Winchester to induct and install in choir and chapter.

Southwark, 19 October 1361

1369. ADMISSION of Robert Sprynget of Carshalton priest to the vicarage of Epsom, at the presentation of the abbot and convent of Chertsey. To be perpetual vicar residing according to the constitutions. Letter to the archdeacon of Surrey for the induction.

Southwark, 21 October 1361

1370. ADMISSION of Thomas Conrreour priest as rector of the church of Chiddingfold, vacant, at the presentation of Silvester Nichol, procurator general for Arnald, cardinal of St Adrian and dean of Salisbury. Letter to the archdeacon of Surrey for the induction.

Southwark, 21 October 1361

1371. ADMISSION of John de Queynton' to the vicarage of the church of Froyle, vacant, at the presentation of the king, the temporalities of Nunnaminster being in his hands during the vacancy. To be perpetual vicar residing according to the constitutions. Letter for the induction to the archdeacon of Winchester.

Southwark, 22 October 1361

1372. PRESENTATION by the bishop of Ralph de Baston' priest to the bishop of Salisbury for the church of Ham in that diocese, vacant.

Southwark, 22 October 1361

1373. ADMISSION of Walter Horman priest, as rector of the church of Bradley, vacant, at the presentation of Bernard Brocatz, by right of Mary his wife, daughter and heiress of John des Roches, lord of the manor of Bradley. Letter for the induction to the archdeacon of Winchester.

Southwark, 22 October 1361

1374. ADMISSION of John Fabyan priest as rector of the church of Oakley, vacant, at the presentation of the king by reason of the vacancy of the priory of Monk Sherborne. Letter for the induction to the archdeacon of Winchester.

Southwark, 22 October 1361

1375. ADMISSION of Nicholas Monk' clerk as rector of the church of Pennington, vacant, at the presentation of the king, the lands of the late

Joan de Wynter being in his hands. Letter for the induction to the archdeacon of Winchester.

Southwark, 22 October 1361

1376. ADMISSION of John Blake clerk to the church of Cranleigh, vacant, at the presentation of Thomas de Bello Campo, earl of Warwick, lord of Gower and marshal of England. Letter for the induction to the archdeacon of Surrey.

Southwark, 22 October 1361

1377. ADMISSION of Nicholas Prosenhurst priest as rector of the church of Farleigh Mortymer, vacant, at the presentation of Robert de la Zouche. Letter for the induction to the archdeacon of Winchester.

Southwark, 23 October 1361

1378. ADMISSION of John Ernesbury priest to the vicarage of the church of Itchenstoke, vacant, at the presentation of the abbess and convent of Romsey. To be perpetual vicar residing according to the constitutions. Letter for the induction to the archdeacon of Winchester.

Southwark, 23 October 1361

217 **1379.** ADMISSION of Thomas de Bourne priest to the vicarage of Basingstoke, vacant, at the presentation of the prior and convent of Selborne. To be perpetual vicar residing according to the constitutions. Letter to the archdeacon of Winchester for the induction.

Southwark, 25 October 1361

1380. ADMISSION of Henry Chaumpeneys priest to the vicarage of the church of Sutton, vacant, at the presentation of the prior and convent of Merton. To be perpetual vicar residing according to the constitutions. Letter to the archdeacon of Winchester for the induction.

Southwark, 25 October 1361

1381. ADMISSION of Robert de Neubolt clerk as rector of the church of South Tidworth, vacant, at the presentation of Thomas de Bello Campo, earl of Warwick, as guardian of Roger Normannd, son and heir of Roger Normannd, knight, deceased. Letter to the archdeacon of Winchester for the induction.

Southwark, 25 October 1361

1382. ADMISSION of Thomas West priest to the vicarage of the church of Odiham, vacant, at the presentation of Richard de Hemesby, proctor for Simon de Sudburye, chancellor of Salisbury. To be perpetual vicar residing according to the constitutions. Letter for the induction to the archdeacon of Winchester.

Southwark, 26 October 1361

1383. ADMISSION of Robert Frannk', priest, as rector to half of the church of Abinger, vacant, at the presentation of Thomas de Jarpenvile. Letter to the archdeacon of Surrey for the induction.

Southwark, 23 October 1361

1384. ADMISSION of Walter Zelot priest to the church of Holy Trinity, Guildford, at the presentation of the prior and convent of Merton. Letter to the archdeacon of Surrey for the induction.

Southwark, 29 October 1361

1385. ADMISSION of John Muleward of Bramley priest, to the vicarage of Bramley, vacant, at the presentation of the king, the priory of Monk Sherborne being vacant. To be perpetual vicar residing according to the constitutions. Letter to the archdeacon of Winchester for the induction.

Southwark, 30 October 1361

1386. ADMISSION of Thomas Aleyn priest as rector of the church of Brown Candover, vacant, at the presentation of the abbot and convent of Hyde. Letter for the induction to the archdeacon of Winchester.

Southwark, 31 October 1361

1387. ADMISSION of M. Walter Gourda as rector of the church of North Stoneham, vacant, at the presentation of the abbot and convent of Hyde. Letter to the archdeacon of Winchester for the induction.

Southwark, 31 October 1361

1388. ADMISSION of Richard Chaumberleyn priest as rector of the church of Itchen, at the presentation of the king during the vacancy of Nunnaminster. Letter for the induction to the archdeacon of Winchester.

Southwark, 2 November 1361

1389. ADMISSION of William Redenesse clerk as rector of the church of Niton, [Isle of Wight,] vacant, at the presentation of fr. William de Monasterio, procurator for the abbey of Lyre, diocese of Evreux. Letter to the archdeacon of Winchester for the induction.

Southwark, 4 November 1361

1390. ADMISSION of John Gilbert of Wyxenhale, priest, as rector of the church of South Warnborough, vacant, at the presentation of the abbot and convent of Crowland. Letter to the archdeacon of Winchester for the induction.

Southwark, 5 November 1361

1391. ADMISSION of fr. William de Claverle, premonstratensian canon of Titchfield to be vicar of the parish church of Titchfield, vacant, at the presentation of the abbot and canons. To be perpetual vicar residing according to the constitutions. Letter for the induction to the archdeacon of Winchester.

Southwark, 6 November 1361

1392. ADMISSION of Richard Wantyng' priest to the vicarage of the church of St Martha at the presentation of the prior and convent of Newark, near Ripley. To be perpetual vicar residing according to the constitutions. Letter for the induction to the archdeacon of Surrey.

Southwark, 10 November 1361

1393. ADMISSION of Roger Benam priest to the vicarage of the church of Shipton, vacant by the free resignation of Richard de Wantyng', at the presentation of the prior and convent of Newark, near Guildford. To be perpetual vicar residing according to the constitutions. Letter for the induction to the archdeacon of Winchester.

Southwark, 10 November 1361

218　**1394.** ADMISSION of Stephen de Bradepol, priest as rector of the church of Tatsfield, vacant, at the presentation of Thomas Retherok, knight. Letter for the induction to the archdeacon of Surrey.

Southwark, 10 November 1361

1395. COMMISSION to the official of Winchester to admit Laurence Pipard' priest, as rector of the church of Shorwell, Isle of Wight, vacant, at the presentation of John de Lysle, knight. He will send a certificate.

Southwark, 12 November 1361

1396. ADMISSION of Thomas Berton' priest to the vicarage of the church of Effingham, vacant, at the presentation of the prior and convent of Merton. To be perpetual vicar residing according to the constitutions. Letter to the archdeacon of Surrey for the induction.

Southwark, 13 November 1361

1397. ADMISSION of Maurice Brut of Sydenham, priest, as rector of the church of St John Baptist, Southampton, vacant, at the presentation of fr. William de Monasterio, procurator for the abbey of Lyre. Letter for the induction to the archdeacon of Winchester.

Southwark, 13 November 1361

1398. ADMISSION of John de Bondeby clerk as rector of the church of Farnborough, vacant, by the resignation of Richard de Stokes into the hands of the bishop, at the presentation of William and Richard Spridhanton. Letter to the archdeacon of Winchester for the induction.

Southwark, 13 November 1361

1399. ADMISSION of Robert Mayn priest to the vicarage of the church of Empshot, vacant, at the presentation of the prior and convent of Southwick. To be perpetual vicar residing according to the constitutions. Letter for the induction to the archdeacon of Winchester.

Southwark, 16 November 1361

1400. ADMISSION of Giles de Wyngreworth' clerk in the person of Henry de Bukyngham his proctor as rector of the church of Nether Wallop, vacant, at the presentation of M. John de Branketree, treasurer of the church of York. Letter to the archdeacon of Winchester for the induction.

Southwark, 16 November 1361

1401. ADMISSION of M. Richard de Wodelond' priest as rector of the church of Lambeth, vacant, at the presentation of Simon, archbishop of Canterbury. Letter for the induction to the archdeacon of Surrey.

Southwark, 17 November 1361

1402. ADMISSION of Richard de Schetelyngton' priest as rector of the church of Mickleham, vacant, at the presentation of the prior and convent of Reigate. Letter for the induction to the archdeacon of Surrey.

Southwark, 19 November 1361

1403. ADMISSION of Robert atte Wyche priest as rector of the church of Dogmersfield, vacant by the resignation of John Lombard, at the presentation of Ralph, bishop of Bath and Wells. Letter to the archdeacon of Winchester for the induction.

Southwark, 20 November 1361

1404. ADMISSION of Thomas Lambyn clerk as rector of Gatcombe, Isle of Wight, vacant, at the presentation of the king, by reason of the custody of the lands and heir of John de Lisle of Gatcombe, deceased. Letter for the induction to the archdeacon of Winchester and the dean of the Island.

Southwark, 23 November 1361

1405. COLLATION BY THE BISHOP of the church of Woodhay on William Cersy priest as rector. Letter for the induction to the official of Winchester.

Southwark, 28 October 1361

1406. PRESENTATION by the bishop of Richard de Tresham priest for the church of Hinton, diocese of Salisbury.

Southwark, 28 October 1361

1407. COLLATION by the bishop of the church of Highclere on John Laurence, clerk.

Southwark, 2 November 1361

1408. COLLATION by the bishop of the vicarage of the church of East Meon on Edmund of Ludespade priest. To be perpetual vicar residing according to the constitutions. Letter for the induction to the official of Winchester.

Southwark, 3 November 1361

1409. COLLATION by the bishop of the church of St James outside the city of Winchester, vacant, on William de Bysshopeston'. Letter for the induction to the archdeacon of Winchester.

Southwark, 5 November 1361

219 **1410.** COLLATION by the bishop of the church of Overton on William Savage priest as rector. Letter for the induction to the official of Winchester.

Southwark, 8 November 1361

1411. COLLATION by the bishop of the church of Mapledurham on William Sandford priest. Letter for the induction to the archdeacon of Winchester.

Southwark, 25 November 1361

1412. COLLATION by the bishop of the church of St Martin outside Westgate, Winchester, vacant by the resignation of Michael, last rector, on John de Wynhale priest. Letter for the induction to the official of Winchester.

Southwark, 18 November 1361

1413. ADMISSION of Richard de Uphavene chaplain as rector of the church of Minstead, vacant, at the presentation of the king as custodian of the lands and heir of Richard de Butesthorne, deceased. Letter to the archdeacon of Winchester for the induction.

Southwark, 25 November 1361

1414. COLLATION by the bishop of the church of Avington vacant on Henry de Derneford' clerk. Letter to the archdeacon of Winchester for the induction.

Southwark, 26 November 1361

1415. ADMISSION of Robert Lavenden' priest to the vicarage of Addington, vacant, at the presentation of the prior and convent of Southwark. To be perpetual vicar residing according to the constitutions. Letter for the induction to the archdeacon of Surrey.

Southwark, 26 November 1361

1416. ADMISSION of Thomas Dalston clerk to the church of Shalfleet, Isle of Wight, vacant, at the presentation of William de Monte Acuto, earl of Salisbury. Letter for the induction to the archdeacon of Winchester and to the dean of the Island.

Southwark, 21 November 1361

1417. COLLATION by the bishop of the church of Compton near Winchester on Michael Dunheved priest. Letter to the archdeacon of Winchester for the induction.

Southwark, 28 November 1361

1418. DISPENSATION granted to Hugh Craft rector of Bishop's Waltham, clerk, to study for one year at some university, not being bound to residence or to proceeding to major orders, according to the constitutions.

Southwark, 28 November 1361

1419. SIMILAR DISPENSATION granted to Jophn Bondeby, rector of Farnborough, clerk.

Southwark, 28 November 1361

1420. ADMISSION of Geoffrey son of Walter, priest, to be rector of the church of Bradley, vacant by the resignation of Walter Herman, last rector, in the presence of John Beautre, public notary, John Waker, prebendary of Wherwell, and Robert Woderoue as witnesses, Southwark 29 November. At the presentation of Bernard Brocatz, knight, by right of his wife, Mary, daughter and heiress of the lord des Roches. Letter for the induction to the archdeacon of Winchester.

Southwark, 30 November 1361

1421. INSTITUTION of John Aleyn priest as rector of the church of St Andrew, Shalden, vacant by the resignation of Thomas Aleyn at Southwark, 29 November, in the presence of M. John Beautre, Thomas Mounpell' and Robert Woderoue as witnesses, at the presentation of the prior and convent of Southwark. Letter for the induction to the archdeacon of Winchester.

Southwark, 7 December 1361

1422. ADMISSION of Robert Broun priest to the church of Ockley, vacant, at the presentation of Adam atte Plesshete as farmer of one third of the manor of Ockley with its appurtenances, granted by Beatrice, widow of Otho de Grandisson, knight, deceased. Letter for the induction to the archdeacon of Surrey.

Southwark, 7 December 1361

1423. ADMISSION of Thomas West priest to be rector of the church of Winchfield, vacant, at the presentation of Juliana, countess of Huntingdon. Letter for the induction to the archdeacon of Winchester.

Southwark, 7 December 1361

220 **1424.** COMMENDATION by the bishop of the vicarage of the church of Hayling, for its evident benefit, to Robert de Schirford', rector of Warblington, according to the constitutions of Gregory X at the council of Lyons. Letters to the archdeacon of Winchester and to the dean of Droxford.

Southwark, 17 October 1361

1425. ADMISSION of John de Waterfall' as vicar of the church of Morden, vacant, with obligation of residence according to the constitutions at the presentation of the abbot and convent of Westminster. Letter for the induction to the archdeacon of Surrey.

Southwark, 11 December 1361

1426. APPOINTMENT of a warden for St Thomas' Hospital, Southwark. Letter from the bishop to Henry de Yakeslee, that since with the death of fr. John de Bradeweye, the last prior, all the brethren are dead except one and the hospital is almost destitute, through lapse of time the benefice is vacant. By devolution he confers the office of prior or warden on the said Henry. Under the same date a letter to the official of Winchester for the induction and installation.

Southwark, 10 December 1361

1427. DISPENSATION granted to Richard de Branketree, clerk, rector of Broughton, to be absent for study at some university in England according to the constitutions.

Southwark, 13 December 1361

1428. COLLATION by the bishop of the church of Droxford, vacant, on Richard de Hampton, priest. Letter for the induction to the archdeacon of Winchester.

Southwark, 14 December 1361

1429. ADMISSION of Walter de Penyton' priest as rector of the church of Linkenholt, vacant, at the presentation of the abbot and convent of Gloucester. Letter for the induction to the archdeacon of Winchester.

Southwark, 15 December 1361

1430. INSTITUTION of Henry de Netilworth' priest to the church of Weyhill, vacant, at the presentation of the king, by reason of the lands and tenements of the manor of Ramridge being in his hands on the death of Thomas de la Pole, knight. The advowson of the church is attached to the manor. Letter for the induction to the archdeacon of Winchester.

Southwark, 19 December 1361

1431. ADMISSION of William Aubrey clerk to the church of Beddington, vacant, at the presentation of the prior and convent of St Saviour, Bermondsey. Letters for the induction to the archdeacon of Surrey and the dean of Ewell.

Southwark, 23 December 1361

1432. ADMISSION of John atte Lane clerk to the chapel of Freefolk, vacant, at the presentation of Andrew Peverel, knight and Catherine his wife. Letter for the induction to the archdeacon of Winchester.

Southwark, 4 January 1362

1433. ADMISSION of M. John de Tarren, clerk to the portion of the church of Beddington shared with M. Adam de Houton', vacant, at the presentation of Nicholas de Carrou, patron. Letter for the induction to the archdeacon of Surrey.

Southwark, 5 January 1362

1434. ADMISSION of Thomas de Rasen priest to the church of Ewell as rector, vacant by the resignation of Thomas de Mountpell' as rector for Roger de Rasen late rector, before John Beautre with Robert Woderout and William Abraham as witnesses, 6 January, at Southwark. At the presentation of the abbot and convent of Chertsey. Letter for the induction to the archdeacon of Surrey.

Southwark, 6 January 1362

221 **1435.** COLLATION by the bishop of the church of St Mary in the Vale, Winchester, vacant by the resignation of Thomas Crook' of Grove, on Walter Smyth priest. Letter to the archdeacon of Winchester for the induction.

Southwark, 7 January 1362

1436. ADMISSION of William le Hore priest to the church of Lainston, vacant, at the presentation of Richard de Wynton'. Letter for the induction to the archdeacon of Winchester.

Southwark, 14 January 1362

1437. ADMISSION of M. Robert de Lemyngton' priest to be rector of the church of Arreton, Isle of Wight, vacant, at the presentation of William de Monasterio, procurator for the abbey of Lyre. Letter for the induction to the archdeacon of Winchester.

Southwark, 17 January 1362

1438. ADMISSION of John atte Hethe priest to the vicarage of the church of Odiham, vacant, at the presentation of M. John Corf, procurator for Simon de Sudbury chancellor of Salisbury. To be perpetual vicar residing according to the constitutions. Letter to the archdeacon of Winchester for the induction.

Southwark, 19 January 1362

1439. ADMISSION of Gilbert Neel priest as rector of the church of Dunsfold, vacant, at the presentation of the prior and convent of St Mary, Bishopsgate, London. Letter for the induction to the archdeacon of Surrey.

Southwark, 24 January 1362

1440. ADMISSION of Thomas Person priest as rector of the church of Faccombe, vacant, at the presentation of the king as custodian of the lands of William de Fyfhide deceased. Letter for the induction to the archdeacon of Winchester.

Southwark, 1 February 1362

1441. ADMISSION of John Sacombe of Eston priest to the vicarage of Battersea, vacant, by the free resignation of Geoffrey the last vicar, at the presentation of the abbot and convent of Westminster. To be perpetual vicar, residing according to the constitutions. Letter for the induction to the archdeacon of Surrey.

Southwark, 1 February 1362

1442. ADMISSION of Thomas Barscot priest to be rector of the church of Fetcham, vacant, at the presentation of Alice widow of John Dabernon, knight. Letter for the induction to the archdeacon of Surrey.

Sutton, 18 February 1362

1443. ADMISSION of Walter Smyth' priest to the vicarage of the church of Brading, [Isle of Wight,] vacant, at the presentation of the prior and convent of Breamore. To be perpetual vicar residing according to the constitutions. Letter for the induction to the archdeacon of Winchester.

Sutton, 18 February 1362

1444. ADMISSION of Geoffrey de Rammule priest as rector of the church of Wellsworth, vacant, at the presentation of the prior and convent of Southwick. Letter for the induction to the archdeacon of Winchester.

Southwick, 20 February 1362

1445. ADMISSION of Giles de Caldecotte clerk as rector of the church of Farleigh [Chamberlain] vacant by the free resignation of M. Robert de

Lemyngton', at the presentation of Thomas de Missenden'. Letter for the induction to the archdeacon of Winchester.

Bishop's Waltham, 24 February 1362

1446. PRESENTATION by the bishop as lord of the manor of Timsbury, diocese of Bath and Wells, to the bishop of that diocese, of Nicholas de Crascombe priest for the church of Timsbury.

Bishop's Waltham, 24 February 1362

1447. COLLATION by the bishop of the priestly office in the chapel of Marwell, vacant, on Richard Aleyn.

Marwell, 25 February 1362

1448. COLLATION by the bishop of the church of North Waltham, vacant, on John Waryn clerk, as rector. Letter for the induction to the archdeacon of Winchester and John Ware, sequestrator.

Farnham, 1 February 1362

222   **1449.** CERTIFICATORY LETTER received from M. Thomas Yonge, acting for the bishop-elect of London, authorizing the bishop to act in the matter of the exchange of benefices between Thomas Restwold rector of Fifehead and John Togond' rector of Cowley, diocese of London. South Waltham, 21 February. After the examination the bishop instituted John Togond as rector of Fifehead, at the presentation of the abbess and convent of Delapre outside Northampton. Letter to the archdeacon of Winchester for his induction after the oath of obedience.

Southwark, 8 March 1362

1450. ADMISSION of John Wellys of Lynn priest as rector of the church of West Dean, vacant, at the presentation of Laurence de Sancto Martino. Letter for the induction to the archdeacon of Winchester.

Southwark, 17 March 1362

1451. ADMISSION of William Gervays clerk as rector of the church of Bentworth, vacant, at the presentation of the bishop by reason of the manor of Bentworth being in his hands. The archdeacon of Winchester has been requested to induct.

Southwark, 14 March 1362

1452. ADMISSION of M. Henry de Weston' deacon to the vicarage of Hayling, vacant, at the presentation of king Edward, the priory of Hayling being in his hands by reason of the death of the last prior. To be perpetual vicar residing according to the constitutions. Letter for the induction to the archdeacon of Winchester.

Southwark, 18 March 1362

1453. INSTITUTION of M. Henry to the aforesaid vicarage as perpetual vicar at the presentation of the abbot and convent of Jumièges, diocese of Rouen.

Same date

1454. CERTIFICATORY LETTERS received at Bishop's Waltham, 23 February from John, bishop of Lincoln authorizing the bishop to deal with the exchange of benefices between Henry de Nettelworth' rector of la Wee and John Grugg' rector of Wakerley, diocese of Lincoln. The bishop admitted John to the church of la Wee as rector, at the presentation of Michael de la Pole, knight. Letter for the induction to the archdeacon of Winchester.

Southwark, 19 March 1362

1455. ADMISSION of Robert Cranford' priest as rector of Knight's Enham, vacant, at the presentation of the warden and scholars of Queen's College Oxford. Letter for the induction to the archdeacon of Winchester.

Southwark, 19 March 1362

1456. ADMISSION OF THE PRIOR OF CARISBROOKE, Isle of Wight, fr. Robert de Gasturia, monk of Lyre, diocese of Evreux, at the presentation of the procurator fr. Gulielmus. Letter for the induction to the archdeacon of Winchester.

Southwark, 19 March 1361

1457. PRESENTATION by the bishop to M. Thomas Yonge, vicar-general for Simon bishop elect of London, of Robert Newborgh priest of the office of perpetual chaplain fo the second stall on the north side of the chapel of St Laurence in Candlewick Street, London, lately founded by John de Pulteneye, deceased, citizen of London, in honour of the feast of Corpus Christi, at the presentation of the bishops of Winchester.

Southwark, 15 February 1361

1458. PROCESS FOR THE ELECTION OF THE PRIOR OF MERTON, in the presence of M. Thomas Yonge, advocate of the court of Canterbury, and of the bishop concerning the election of fr. Geoffrey de Chadeslee, canon of St Mary, Merton, to the office of prior, vacant by the death of William de Freston', the last prior. The bishop was unanimously deputed by the convent to preside in the church of Farnham, 12 December 1361, in the presence of the subprior and with fr. Robert de Wyndesore and fr. John de Guldeford' as procurators, and the archdeacon of Surrey. After the formalities, objectors were summoned to appear in the chapel of the castle of Farnham.

1459. PRONOUNCEMENT OF THE ELECTION by the bishop, of fr. Geoffrey de Chadeslee; he was confirmed and granted the administration of the priory.

1460. TESTIMONIAL LETTER from the bishop to the newly elected prior.

Southwark, 4 September 1361

1461. LETTER TO THE SUBPRIOR requesting the obedience and reverence for the new prior.

1462. LETTER TO THE ARCHDEACON of Surrey for the induction and installation in choir and chapter.

224 **1463.** REQUEST TO THE KING for the restoration of the temporalities of Merton.

1464. PROCESS FOR THE ELECTION OF THE ABBESS OF WHERWELL before M. Thomas Yonge, advocate of the court of Canterbury, Walter Benyt, official of Winchester acting for the bishop. The election of Constance de Wyntreshull' for the office, vacant by the death of Amice Ladde, the last abbess, was examined in the chapel of the conventual church of Southwark, 23 October 1361, before a tribunal with William de Malmesbury, John Bradweye as procurators, before M. John de Ware, sequestrator-general, who called for the objectors in order to begin the formalities.

1465. CONFIRMATION OF THE ELECTION of Constance de Wyntreshull' as abbess by M. Thomas Yonge for the bishop.

1466. BLESSING OF THE ABBESS in the manor chapel of Southwark during pontifical mass.
                                                    Sunday, 24 October 1361

1467. TESTIMONIAL LETTER TO THE ABBESS on her election, granting her powers of administration.
                                          Sunday, Southwark, 24 October 1361

225 **1468.** MANDATE TO THE ARCHDEACON of Winchester to induct the new abbess, assigning to her her stall in choir and place in chapter.
                                                                 Same date

1469. LETTER TO THE PRIORESS and convent requesting their obedience to their new abbess.
                                                                 Same date

1470. REQUEST TO THE KING to restore the temporalities of the abbey.
                                                                 Same date

1471. PROCESS FOR THE ELECTION OF THE ABBESS OF NUNNAMINSTER, Winchester held in the conventual church of St Mary, Southwark, 13 November 1361, before M. Thomas Yonge clerk and the bishop of Winchester as commissaries, concerning the election of Christina la Wayte as abbess. The archdeacon had made the request for objectors to come forward. At the commission the procurator for the convent was Roger de Colreche, with two witnesses Katerina de Colyngborne and Alice de la Mare, nuns of the monastery.

1472. CONFIRMATION OF THE ELECTION. M. Thomas Yonge and the bishop having heard the examination as to the election of Christina Wayte, declare the election to have been canonical and they confirm it.

1473. BLESSING OF THE ABBESS by the bishop at pontifical mass in the manor chapel of Southwark.

14 November 1361

1474. TESTIMONIAL LETTER TO THE ABBESS from the bishop confirming her election. Also letters for the obedience of the convent; to the archdeacon for the induction and installation; also to the king for the restoration of the temporalities—as in the preceding election.

226

1475. LICENCE TO ELECT A PRIOR granted to the canons of Taunton, diocese of Bath and Wells. The priory is vacant by the death of fr. Thomas de Pedirton. To avoid delapidations through a vacancy, the bishop who holds the custody, grants permission to elect a suitable prior from their community.

Southwark, 23 November 1361

1476. PROCESS FOR THE ELECTION OF THE ABBOT OF CHERTSEY held before M. Thomas Yonge, advocate of the court of Canterbury, and Walter Benyt, official of Winchester, concerning fr. William Clyve, monk of Chertsey, elected to fill the vacancy on the death of fr. John Benham. The process was heard in the bishop's chapel at Southwark, 4 December 1361, with fr. John Usk' a confrater as procurator. The certificate of the archdeacon of Surrey was read out, showing that the proclamation had been made that objectors to the election should come forward. The matter was duly discussed and the election was found to be valid and canonical.

1477. CONFIRMATION OF THE ELECTION by M. Thomas Yonge, with M. Walter Benyt as commissary, acting for the bishop.

1478. BLESSING OF THE NEW ABBOT during mass at the manor chapel of Southwark.

Sunday, 4 December 1361

1479. LETTERS to the new abbot confirming the election; to the convent for their obedience; to the archdeacon of Surrey for the induction and installation; to the king for the restoration of the temporalities—as above for the priory of Merton.

Same date

1480. PROCESS FOR THE ELECTION OF THE ABBESS OF WHERWELL, held before M. Thomas Yonge and M. Walter Benyt as commissaries, on the election of Joan Cokerel, vacant by the death of Constance Wyntreshull', held in the chapel at Southwark, 24 December 1361. The customary procedure was carried out by fr. William de Malmesbury; it was shown that the king had given licence for the election. The election was declared correct.

227

1481. CONFIRMATION by M. Thomas Yonge with M. Walter Benyt of the election of Joan Cokerel.

Same date

1482. BLESSING of the newly elected abbess during pontifical mass in the manor chapel of Southwark.

25 December 1361

1483. CUSTOMARY LETTERS sent to the abbess in confirmation; to the convent for its obedience; to the archdeacon of Winchester for the induction and installation; to the king for the restoration of the temporalities, as above for abbess Constance de Wintreshull'.

Same date

1484. COMMISSION from the bishop to M. John de Ware rector of Wonston, to examine and confirm the election of fr. Nicholas de Wynton', sacrist of Selborne, as prior, the election having been held by the bishop's licence. Then he may induct and install the new prior.

Southwark, 31 December 1361

1485. TESTIMONIAL LETTER sent to fr. William Benart, lately claustral prior of the abbey of St Vigor, diocese of Bayeux, nominated by the abbot for the dependent priory of Monk Sherborne, vacant by the death of fr. Denis de Vauxeio, with the licence of Thomas de Aldyngborne, by right of Margaret his late wife, patroness. The nomination has been examined and confirmed on behalf of the bishop.

Highclere, 28 February 1362

1486. MANDATE to the archdeacon of Winchester to induct and install the prior.

Same date

1487. INSTITUTION of fr. William de Monasteriis, monk of Tiron, diocese of Chartres, as prior of the dependent priory of Hamble, vacant by the death of fr. James Pasquerii. He was nominated by fr. John, abbot of St Mary, Arcisses, vicar general of J' abbot of Tiron. Letter to the official of Winchester and M. J' de Ware sequestrator-general for the induction.

[No date]

228

1488. LETTER OF ASSENT from the bishop to R'bishop of Bath and Wells to the election of Walter Grately for the canons of Taunton, after the death of fr. Thomas de Pedyrton'. The election was held by licence from the bishop of Winchester.

Southwark, 17 January 1362

1489. ADMISSION of Roger Mohant priest as rector of the church of Sutton, vacant, at the presentation of the abbot and convent of Chertsey. Letter for the induction to the archdeacon of Surrey.

Southwark, 30 March 1362

1490. PROCESS CONCERNING THE ELECTION OF THE PRIOR OF WINCHESTER held in the presence of the bishop, in the manor chapel at Southwark, 9 December 1361. The priory was vacant by the death of fr. John de

Merlawe, in whose place was elected fr. William de Thudden'. The procurator for the convent was fr. John de Guldeford; the objectors were summoned to appear etc. In a petition certain witnesses had articles to present; the procurator could call upon them, viz. Henry de Harwedon' and Richard de Merewelle, monks, with John, vicar of Wotton, Walter de Merlawe, Peter de Wylton', Robert Wodelock', Richard Wolmongere and Thomas Barbour. They were admitted and took the oath, declaring the election to be unopposed. The witnesses were to appear before M.

229 Thomas Yonge and Walter Benyt, 10 December, since the procurator wished to produce other matters (*plura*). They were summoned to appear 11 December. The publication of the evidence of the witnesses was sought, but, since the details of the election were not sufficiently explicit, they wished to examine the monks' depositions. The prior-elect and the procurator were summoned to appear in the cathedral of Winchester, 10 January or else 17 January, or the nearest law-day, to examine the depositions and so to end the process. On 17 January the elect was present, when fr. Richard de Merewelle was replaced by fr. John de Guldeford as procurator. The next day, 18 January, the procurator asked for the depositions to be declared; they were neither denied nor admitted. As the commissaries wished to deliberate, the elect and the procurator were ordered to appear the next day, 19 January, to hear the decision, when the depositions and allegations of the fellow-monks were ordered to be examined. On 20 January the procurator was replaced by M. Richard de Drayton, who asked that the election be confirmed. This meeting, ordered for 20 January continued until after the mid-day meal,

230 only to be again postponed to 11 February, when the elect did not appear. The procurator, now fr. Ralph de Pampilou, requested that the elect be declared contumacious.

1491. NULLIFICATION OF THE ELECTION AT WINCHESTER
After certain members of the community had appeared before the tribunal commissioned by the bishop, with a petition supported by documents, by which the election appeared legitimate, certain witnesses were examined privately. Then after due deliberation in consideration of the defects and nullity alleged by the parties, the bishop ordered a judicial enquiry, led by M. Walter Beneit. Finding the allegation were not trifling and there was an element of deceit, he declared the election uncanonical and, moreover, contrary to the form of the constitutions laid down by the general council. The convent had knowingly ratified this election, hence M. Walter pronounced it to be null and void. Further, by their action, the monks were now deprived of the right to elect.

14 February 1362

M. John Blaunchard doctor-at-law, William le Phyl, Ralph Knyght, M. John Cerf, Thomas Mounpell' and M. John Beautre.

1492. THE COMMISSION entrusted to M. Thomas Yonge and M. Walter Benet, with mandate to examine the election, which had been authorized by the bishop. According to their findings, they were to confirm or annul the election.

Southwark, 9 December 1361

1493. PROVISION AND NOMINATION OF A PRIOR BY DEVOLUTION. Since the
election of fr. William Thudden has been annulled, as being contrary to
231 the general council, with the monks at fault, they cannot elect a prior
for this turn. The bishop therefore nominates fr. William Basynge, monk
of the priory, to be prior with the customary powers of administration
in spiritual and temporal affairs.

Southwark, 11 February 1362

Witnesses: John Gleobury, rector of Witney, diocese of Lincoln, and
Richard de Lyncheford, rector of Burghclere, diocese of Winchester,
with M. John Beautre.

1494. TESTIMONIAL LETTER ON THE NOMINATION. The bishop confirms his
nomination of fr. William Basynge by devolution.

Southwark, 11 February 1362

1495. LETTER TO THE THIRD PRIOR requesting the obedience of the convent
to the prior of his nomination.

Same date

1496. MANDATE to induct and install the new prior, addressed to the
official of Winchester, with powers to coerce any contradictors.

Same date

232 **1497.** ADMISSION of Ralph Knyght priest as rector of the church of
Byfleet, vacant, at the presentation of Edward prince of Wales, patron.
Letter for the induction to the archdeacon of Surrey.

11 April 1362

1498. ADMISSION of Richard Prior priest to the vicarage of the church of
Arreton, Isle of Wight, vacant, at the presentation of M. Robert de
Lemyngton, rector. To be perpetual vicar according to the constitutions.
Letter for the induction to the archdeacon of Winchester.

Farnham, 23 April 1362

1499. ADMISSION of William de Burton' priest as rector of the church of
Farnborough, vacant by the resignation of John Bondeby in the presence
of John de Beautre and Ralph Knyght, rector of Byfleet, and Thomas
Mounpell' at Farnham Castle, 11 April 1362. At the presentation of
William de Spridlynton' and his brother Richard. Letter for the induction
to the archdeacon of Winchester.

Southwark, 30 April 1362

1500. LICENCE to be absent for study granted to M. John Turk rector of
the church of Michelmersh for one year, without obligation of residence.

Southwark, 4 May 1362

1501. ADMISSION of Melchior Wodelok' clerk as rector of the church of
Worting, vacant by the resignation of John Renaud priest before the

official of Winchester; at the presentation of the abbot and convent of Hyde. Letter for the induction to the archdeacon of Winchester.

Southwark, 6 May 1362

1502. ADMISSION of William Goudman priest to the vicarage of the church of Egham, vacant by the resignation of Ralph Knyght before M. Walter Beneyt, in the presence of John Bleebury and John Beautre at Southwark, 3 May 1362; at the presentation of abbot and convent of Chertsey. Letter for the induction to the archdeacon of Surrey.

Southwark, 7 May 1362

1503. ADMISSION of Richard Ronz as rector of the chapel of Brook, Isle of Wight, vacant, at the presentation of Isabella Houston', patroness for this turn. Letter for the induction to the archdeacon of Winchester

Southwark, 18 May 1362

1504. ADMISSION of John Petyt priest to the vicarage of the church of Weybridge, vacant, at the presentation of the prior and convent of Newark. To be perpetual vicar with obligation of residing according to the constitutions. Letter for the induction to the archdeacon of Surrey.

Southwark, 4 June 1362

1505. INSTITUTION of Thomas de Ditton' priest as rector of the church of Ashe, near Overton, at the presentation of the king as custodian of the lands and heir of John de Stonore, knight, deceased. Letter for the induction to the archdeacon of Winchester.

Southwark, 11 June 1362

1506. INSTITUTION of Robert Pyk' chaplain, to the vicarage of Sherborne, with obligation of residing according to the constitutions, at the presentation of the prior and convent of Sherborne. Letter to the archdeacon of Winchester for the induction.

Southwark, 16 June 1362

1507. COLLATION by the bishop of the office of warden of the hospital of St John, Fordingbridge, on Robert Michel, priest, vacant by the death of William Chichestr' late warden. Letter for the induction to the official of Winchester and J' Ware, sequestrator-general.

Southwark, 20 June 1362

233   **1508.** INSTITUTION of Arnald Brocaz, clerk, to the church of Whippingham, [Isle of Wight,] vacant, at the presentation of fr. John Basyn, procurator of the abbey of Lyre, diocese of Evreux. Letter for the induction to the archdeacon of Winchester.

Southwark, 22 June 1362

1509. INSTITUTION of Thomas de Ocle priest as rector of the church of Newchurch, Isle of Wight, vacant, at the presentation of fr. John Basyn, procurator of Lyre. Letter to the archdeacon of Winchester and to the dean of the Island for the induction.

Southwark, 26 June 1362

1510. INSTITUTION of Richard Herin priest as rector of St Peter *de albo pane* in the city of Winchester, at the presentation of the abbot and convent of Hyde. Letter to the archdeacon of Winchester for the induction.

Southwark, 26 June 1362

1511. INSTITUTION of Peter Golde priest as rector of the church of Whipstrode, vacant, at the presentation of Bernard Brocaz, knight. Letter for the induction to the archdeacon of Winchester.

Southwark, 29 June 1362

1512. INSTITUTION of Richard de Remston' priest to the vicarage of the church of Tooting, at the presentation of the prior and convent of Southwark—according to the constitutions of Otto and Ottobon concerning continued residence, for which he took the oath. Letter for the induction to the archdeacon of Surrey and the dean of Southwark.

Southwark, 3 July 1362

1513. INSTITUTION of John de Ernesby priest as rector of the church of Abbotsworthy, vacant, at the presentation of the abbot and convent of Hyde. Letter for the induction to the archdeacon of Winchester.

Southwark, 5 July 1362

1514. COLLATION of the church of Nutley on John Crabbe, clerk. The vacancy followed the death of William Lovel. Letter for the induction to the official of Winchester.

Esher, 24 July 1362

1515. INSTITUTION of John Schog' priest to the church of Elden, vacant by the resignation of John de Staunton', at the presentation of Thurstan de Chisenhale. Letter for the induction to the archdeacon of Winchester.

Esher, 30 July 1362

1516. CERTIFICATORY LETTERS received from Simon bishop of London, concerning an exchange of benefices between Richard de Brokesburn' rector of St Mary, Staining Lane, London, and Ralph Capron. rector of Titsey, by letters dated, Witney, 20 August 1362. Since the bishop of London authorized the exchange, the bishop instituted Richard to the church of Titsey, at the presentation of Thomas de Uvedale, knight. Letter for the induction to the archdeacon of Surrey.

Edington, 28 August 1362

1517. LICENCE granted to Thomas Parson rector of the church of Faccombe to be for one year at the service of Walter Whithors.

Highclere, 10 September 1362

1518. ADMISSION of [   ] to the vicarage of Itchenstoke, vacant, at the presentation of the abbess and convent of Romsey. To be perpetual vicar residing according to the constitutions. Letter for the induction to the archdeacon of Winchester.

Highclere, 11 September 1362

1519. DISPENSATION granted to John Laurence rector of Highclere to be absent for study for one year, without obligation of residence or of proceding to orders higher than the subdiaconate within the year, according to the constitutions of Boniface.

Highclere, 11 September 1362

1520. DISPENSATION granted to Giles de Caldecote, subdeacon, rector of Farley near Romsey, to be absent for study somewhere in England.

Highclere, 12 September 1362

234 **1521.** COLLATION by the bishop of the church of Ellisfield on John Purye priest, vacant, by devolution through lapse of time. Letter to the archdeacon of Winchester.

Farnham, 18 September 1362

1522. INSTITUTION of Richard de Schoreham' priest to the vicarage of the church of St Laurence, Empshott, vacant by the resignation of Robert late vicar, now vicar of Eastbourne, diocese of Chichester; at the presentation of the prior and convent of Southwark. To be vicar according to the constitutions. Letter for the induction to the archdeacon of Winchester.

Farnham, 18 September 1362

1523. COMMISSION received from Simon bishop of London, to negotiate the exchange of benefices between John Skot, rector of St Brides, Fynk', London and Gilbert Neel, rector of Dunsfold. The examination took place the same day, 18 September. Relying on the enquiry held by the official of the archdeacon of London the bishop approved and Gilbert was admitted to St Brides at the presentation of Alesia de Nevill', with the oath reserved. Subsequently John Skot was admitted to the church of Dunsfold at the presentation of the prior and hospital of St Mary outside Bishopstoke, London. Letter sent to the archdeacon of Surrey for the induction.

Farnham, 18 September 1362

1524. COLLATION of the provostship of the chapel of St Elizabeth near Winchester on John Schipton priest. The chapel was founded by John de Pontissara with constitutions for which John took the oath. Letter for the induction to the official of Winchester.

Esher, 25 September 1362

1525. COLLATION of the priestly office in the aforesaid chapel on William Aylmer, deacon. Letter for the induction to M. Walter de Sevenhampton', treasurer of Wolvesey and custodian of the chapel.

Esher, 24 September 1362

1526. PROCESS FOR THE ELECTION OF THE ABBOT OF HYDE. mandate to M. Walter Beneyt to enquire into the election of fr. Thomas Peythy as abbot, after the death of fr Walter de Fyfhyde.

The enquiry was held 24 September 1362, in the parish church of Esher, before the subprior and fr. John Wodelok' representing the convent, with M. Walter Condam. The usual formalities were conducted by the official and the final meeting was ordered to be held in the manor chapel **235** of Esher, when all was found to be correct.

1527. CONFIRMATION of the election and grant of powers of administration.

1528. BLESSING OF THE ABBOT of Hyde by the bishop in the manor chapel of Esher at pontifical mass.

Sunday, 25 September 1362

Testimonial letters sent to the community for their obedience, to the archdeacon and the dean of Winchester for the induction and installation, to the king for the restitution of the temporalities—as were sent out for the prior of Merton.

1529. ADMISSION of Hugh de Marlebergh' priest as rector of the church of Ewell, vacant by the resignation of Thomas de Rasen, as in the instrument drawn up by William de Wolveston' public notary, at the presentation of the abbot and convent of Chertsey. Letter for the induction to the archdeacon of Surrey.

Southwark, 8 October 1362

1530. DISPENSATION granted to John le Blake rector of Cranleigh to be for one year at the service of Thomas, earl of Warwick and to lease his church at farm.

Southwark, 12 October 1362

1531. EXCHANGE OF BENEFICES examined and discussed as between William de Wodeford' perpetual vicar of the church of Shalford and Geoffrey Edith' rector of Bradley, both of the diocese. The resignations were received and William was admitted to the church of Bradley at the presentation of Bernard Brocaz, knight, and Geoffrey to the vicarage of Shalford at the presentation of the prior and hospital of St Mary, Bishopsgate, London. To be perpetual vicar, residing according to the constitutions. Letters for the induction of the vicar to the archdeacon of Surrey and for the rector to the archdeacon of Winchester.

Southwark, 13 October 1362

1532. ADMISSION of John Symond priest as rector of the chapel of Brook, Isle of Wight, vacant by the free resignation of Richard Ronz in the presence of John Beautre, public notary, with Thomas Mounpeller clerk and Robert Woderoue as witnesses, at the presentation of Geoffrey

Rouclee, patron for this turn. Letter for the induction to the archdeacon of Winchester and to the dean of the Island.

Southwark, 14 October 1362

1533. ADMISSION of Ralph Knyght priest to the vicarage of the church of Woking, vacant by the resignation of John de Shipton, now provost of St Elizabeth, near Winchester; canonically instituted in the presence of John Beautre, Thomas Mounpell' and Robert Woderoue as witnessess. To be perpetual vicar residing according to the constitutions; at the presentation of the prior and convent of Newark. Letter for the induction to the archdeacon of Surrey.

Southwark, 14 October 1362

1534. ADMISSION of M. Walter de Sevenhampton' clerk to the canonry in the conventual church of Romsey and the prebend of St Laurence, vacant by the death of William de Farlee, last canon-prebendary, at the presentation of the abbess and convent. Letter to the archdeacon of Winchester to assign to M. Walter his stall in choir and place in chapter.

Southwark, 18 October 1362

236 **1535.** CERTIFICATORY LETTERS received from John bishop of Worcester, to whom the bishop had entrusted the matter of the exchange of benefices between John de Dodeford rector of Barford, diocese of Worcester, and John de Wengrave, rector of Ewhurst, dated 18 October 1362. As authorized by the bishop of Worcester, John de Dodeford was admitted to the church of Ewhurst, at the presentation of the prior and convent of Merton. Letter for the induction to the archdeacon of Surrey.

Southwark, 21 October 1362

1536. ADMISSION by the bishop of M. Walter Beneit, doctor at law, to the canonry and prebend of All Cannings (diocese of Salisbury) in the conventual church of Nunnaminster.

Southwark, 21 October 1362

1537. LETTER to Robert bishop of Salisbury informing him of the above, requesting the bishop to induct M. Walter to the prebend which is in his diocese.

Same date

1538. MANDATE to the archdeacon of Winchester to induct and install M. Walter.

1539. INSTITUTION of John Petit priest to the church of Byfleet, vacant, at the presentation of prince Edward, patron. Letter to the archdeacon of Surrey for the induction.

Southwark, 21 October 1362

1540. EXAMINATION OF AN EXCHANGE by commission of the bishop, as between Thomas de Mottyng' perpetual vicar of Camberwell and Everard Volet rector of the church of St George, Southwark. The resignations were received and they were instituted, Thomas at the presentation of the prior and convent of Bermondsey and Everard also, who will be perpetual vicar according to the constitutions. Letter for the induction to the archdeacon of Surrey.

Southwark, 25 October 1362

1541. LICENCE granted to John de Bereford, rector of Chalton to be absent for one year at the service of Thomas, earl of Warwick and to lease his church at farm.

Southwark, 26 October 1362

1542. INSTITUTION of William Rode subdeacon as rector of the church of Shalfleet, [Isle of Wight,] vacant by the free resignation of Thomas de Alston late rector, before John Beautre, M. John Corf public notaries, with Thomas Mounpell' and William Canon as witnesses, 2 November in the royal palace of Westminster; at the presentation of William, earl of Salisbury. Letter for the induction to the archdeacon of Winchester and the dean of the Island.

Southwark, 4 November 1362

1543. DISPENSATION granted to Arnald Brocaz, rector of Whippingham clerk, to be absent for a year for study and to receive further orders during the year according to the constitutions.

Southwark, 4 November 1362

237 **1544.** ADMISSION of John Mays priest to the church of Botley, vacant by the death of John Queor last rector, at the presentation of the provost and chaplains of St Elizabeth. Letter for the induction to the archdeacon of Winchester.

Southwark, 8 November 1362

1545. CERTIFICATORY LETTERS received from Simon bishop of London, to whom the bishop had entrusted the matter of the exchange between Ralph, lately rector of St Mary in Staining Lane, London, and Richard Gerard vicar of Wandsworth, dated 25 November. By the authority of the commission, Ralph was admitted to the vicarage at the presentation of the king by reason of the temporalities of Westminster being in his hands. To be perpetual vicar according to the constitutions. Letter to the archdeacon for the induction.

Southwark, 27 November 1362

1546. INSTITUTION of Henry Marmyon priest to be rector of South Tidworth, vacant by the resignation of Robert de Neubolt, at the presentation of Richard de Cavendistz and Juliana his wife, John de Glemesford' and Beatrice his wife and William Chaumberlayn and Christina his wife, patrons collectively. Letter for the induction to the archdeacon of Winchester.

Southwark, 27 November 1362

1547. DISPENSATION granted to John Godard, rector of St Mary Magdalen, Bermondsey, to be absent for one year and to lease the profits of his church.

Southwark, 10 December 1362

1548. INSTITUTION of John de Clestorp' priest to the vicarage of the church of Sherborne St John, vacant, at the presentation of William de Wotton rector. Letter for the induction to the archdeacon of Winchester.

Southwark, 11 December 1362

1549. COLLATION of the chantry of Baddesley, established by Henry de Welles, late lord of the manor and endowed by him, on John de Sutton' by devolution through lapse of time. To be perpetual chaplain according to the ordination of the founder. Letter for the induction to the archdeacon of Winchester.

Farnham, 27 December 1362

1550. INSTITUTION of Thomas Solle of Witchford, priest, to the chantry chapel in the manor of Sherborne Coudray in the parish church of Sherborne St John, established and endowed by the late Thomas Coudray, knight, late lord of the manor; the custody is with the king by reason of the lands of William de Fyfhide, which had been held *in capite*. To be perpetual chaplain according to the ordination of the founder, for which he took the oath. Letter for the induction to the archdeacon of Winchester and to the perpetual vicar of Bramley.

Farnham, 5 January 1363

1551. INSTITUTION of John Tybotes of Watford, priest, to the vicarage of Weybridge, vacant by the resignation of John Petyt, now vicar of Byfleet; at the presentation of the prior and convent of Newark. To be perpetual vicar residing according to the constitutions. Letter for the induction to the archdeacon of Surrey.

Farnham, 4 January 1363

238   **1552.** ADMISSION of William Gervays clerk as rector of the church of Bentworth, at the presentation of William de Edynton, lord of the manor. Letter to the archdeacon of Winchester for the induction.

Farnham, 31 December 1362

1553. CANONICAL INSTITUTION of Walter de Sevenhampton to the canonry of the conventual church of Romsey, with the prebend of St Laurence, Timsbury, diocese of Winchester, to which is annexed the chapel of Imber, diocese of Salisbury; at the presentation of the abbess and convent of Romsey. Letter to the archdeacon of Winchester for the induction and installation.

Southwark, 18 October 1362

1554. LETTER to R' bishop of Salisbury informing him of the above institution, requesting him to put M. Walter in possession of the chapel.

Same date

1555. INSTITUTION of Richard atte Mulle of Henley priest, as vicar of the church of Camberwell, vacant by the resignation of Everard de Pratell' the last vicar, at the presentation of the prior and convent of Bermondsey. To be continuously in residence according to the constitutions, for which he took the oath. Letter for the induction to the archdeacon of Surrey.

Esher, 12 January 1363

1556. ADMISSION AS PRIOR OF ANDOVER of fr. Denis Cano, monk of St Florent near Saumur, diocese of Angers, presented by fr. William, the abbot. The bishop instituted him and granted the powers of administration. Letter to the archdeacon of Winchester for the induction.

Southwark, 16 January 1363

1557. MEMORANDUM that dispensation was granted to M. Hugh Craft, rector of Bishop's Waltham to be absent for study without obligation of residence or proceding to major orders.

Southwark, 29 November 1362

1558. INSTITUTION of Walter de Estbury priest to the church of Cranleigh, vacant by the resignation of John Blake, at the presentation of Roger de Clifford, lord of Westmorland, patron for this turn. Letter for the induction to the archdeacon of Surrey.

Southwark, 19 January 1363

1559. PRESENTATION by the bishop of John de Newenham priest to R' bishop of Salisbury for the church of Little Hinton, diocese of Salisbury, vacant by the death of Richard de Tresham.

Southwark, 16 January 1363

239 **1560.** MANDATE ON THE OBSERVANCE OF HOLY-DAYS. The bishop to his archdeacon: he has received from Simon, bishop of London, the mandate of Simon, archbishop of Canterbury. To the commandment of God that the Sabbath should by free from work, the Church has in course of time added other days, some only locally obliging. Now we see feasting, drinking and business contracted on these days, whereas the vigils of feasts should be days of abstinence. He gives a list of holy-days: Sundays from the vespers of the Saturday; the feasts of Our Lord, then the saints' days; the feasts of the dedication and the patron saint of the local church. The clergy are to admonish the people, indicating that they should attend mass and other services. The clergy will report what has been done to further the observance of holy-days.

Mayfield, 17 July 1362

240 The archdeacon will carry out the mandate.

Stepney, 31 July 1362

The clergy will certify what has been done as regards church attendance on feast-days before Christmas.

Southwark, 2 November 1362

1561. DISPENSATION granted to M. Richard de Branketree rector of Broughton, subdeacon, to be absent for one year at some university in England.

Southwark, 20 February 1363

1562. COLLATION by the bishop of the church of Hound by devolution through lapse of time, on John Mason of Botley, priest, to be perpetual vicar according to the constitutions. Letter for the induction to the archdeacon of Winchester.

Esher, 24 February 1363

1563. COLLATION by the bishop of the vicarage of the church of Farley, vacant, by devolution through lapse of time, on Robert Plain of Oundle, priest; to be perpetual vicar residing according to the constitutions. Letter to the archdeacon of Surrey for the induction.

Esher, 5 March 1363

1564. COLLATION of the church of Wisley, vacant, at the presentation of Edward, prince of Wales, at collation of the bishop through lapse of time, on John Virly, priest. Letter for the induction to the archdeacon of Surrey.

Esher, 10 March 1363

1565. LICENCE granted to Henry Marmyon, rector of South Tidworth, to study for one year at some university and to lease his church at farm.

Esher, 15 March

1566. COLLATION of the church of Ellingham, vacant, at the presentation of the bishop through lapse of time, on John Michael. To be perpetual vicar residing according to the constitutions for which he took the oath. Letter for the induction to the archdeacon of Winchester.

Esher, 18 March 1363

1567. INSTITUTION of Thomas son of William Herdeby of Denton, priest, as rector of Chaldon, at the presentation of Margaret de Conert. Letter for the induction to the archdeacon of Surrey, or William Ermynne his proctor.

Esher, 12 April 1363

1568. COLLATION by the bishop, by devolution through lapse of time, of the chapel of St Nicholas in Carisbrooke Castle, on Robert Grey, priest. To be perpetual vicar residing according to the constitutions for which he took the oath. Letter to the archdeacon of Winchester for the oath.

Esher, 16 April 1363

241 **1569**. LICENCE to be absent for study granted to M. John Turk, rector of Michelmersh, priest, for an additional year to the one granted.

Southwark, 17 April 1363

1570. INSTITUTION of John Madhurst chaplain as perpetual vicar of the church of Banstead, vacant by the resignation of Thomas Englisse; residing according to the constitutions at the presentation of the prior and convent of St Mary, Southwark. Letter to the archdeacon of Surrey for the induction.

Esher, 26 April 1363

1571. INSTITUTION of William de Wykeham, clerk, to the canonry of the conventual church of Wherwell and to the prebend of Wherwell, vacant by the dismissal of John Waker, who resigned after judicial proceedings; at the presentation of the king, the abbey being in his hands during a vacancy. Letter to the archdeacon of Winchester for the induction and installation.

Esher, 26 April 1363

1572. COMMISSION received by the bishop from M. Antony de Goldesburgh', precentor and official of Lincoln, *sede vacante*, to expedite the exchange of benefices between Philip de Nassyngton rector of Faringdon, diocese of Winchester, and William Potente, rector of Edmerthorp, diocese of Lincoln. After examination and receiving the resignations, William was admitted to Faringdon, at the presentation of John bishop of Exeter, and Phillip to Edmerthorp, at the presentation of John, the king's son, duke of Lancaster, Richmond, Derby, Lincoln and Leicester and seneschal of England. Letter to the archdeacon of Winchester to induct William. The induction and oath of Philip was reserved to the official of Lincoln.

Esher, 28 April 1363

1573. DISPENSATION granted by the bishop to Walter de Estham' rector of Cranleigh, to be for one year at the service of Thomas, earl of Warwick.

Esher, 2 May 1363

1574. COMMISSION received from R' bishop of Salisbury for the exchange between John de Northwode rector of Keevil, diocese of Salisbury, and Thomas de Oclee rector of Newchurch, Isle of Wight. After the discussion and the resignations, John was admitted to the church of Newchurch, at the presentation of fr. Guillaume Mignot, procurator for the abbey of Lyre, diocese of Evreux, and Thomas to the church of Keevil, at the presentation of the abbess and convent of Shaftesbury. Letter for the induction to the archdeacon of Winchester. The induction of Philip was reserved to the bishop of Salisbury.

Southwark, 6 May 1363

1575. COMMISSION received by the bishop from John, archbishop of York, concerning the exchange between Thomas de Hasthorp' rector of St Olave, Southwark, and John de Pevereth, vicar of the church of Burton Agnes, diocese of York. The examination was held and the resignation received and John was admitted to St Olave, Southwark, at the presentation of the abbot and convent of St Pancras, Lewes; Thomas to the church of Burton Agnes as perpetual vicar according to the constitutions, at the presentation of the abbot and convent of St Peter York. Letter to the archdeacon of Surrey for the induction of John.

Esher, 10 May 1363

242   **1576.** CERTIFICATORY LETTERS received from William, bishop of Rochester, who had been requested to negotiate the exchange between

John Sacombe, vicar of the church of Battersey, diocese of Winchester, and John de Tichemersh, vicar of Shorne, diocese of Rochester, dated 1 June, Highclere.

John Tichemershe was admitted to Battersey, at the presentation of the abbot and convent of Westminster. To be perpetual vicar residing according to the constitutions. Letter to the archdeacon of Surrey for the induction.

Highclere, 9 June 1363

1577. [*in margin*] COLLATION of the church of Calbourne, [Isle of Wight,] on John Gurnel, priest.

Highclere, 8 June 1363

1578. COLLATION by the bishop of the church of St Mary over Northgate, Winchester, on Geoffrey Frere, priest, by devolution through lapse of time. Letter for the induction to the archdeacon of Winchester.

Highclere, 8 June 1363

1579. ADMISSION of John Monk' priest to the church of Litchfield, vacant by the resignation of John de Frollebury, at the presentation of John de Sancto Johanne. Letter for the induction to the archdeacon of Winchester.

Highclere, 8 June 1363

1580. ADMISSION of John Bradeford' priest as rector of Grately, in the person of Alexander priest of the parish church of Grately his proctor, at the presentation of John Maudyt, knight. Letter for the induction to the archdeacon of Winchester.

Wargrave, 28 June 1363

1581. LICENCE to be absent for study at some university in England granted to John Brode, rector of East Tisted for one year.

Wargrave, 5 July 1363

1582. COMMISSION received from Simon, archbishop of Canterbury to negotiate the exchange between John Clere rector of St Mary Magdalen, Bermondsey, diocese of Winchester, and Simon Blake of Hayes in the deanery of Shoreham, of the archbishop's immediate jurisdiction. By the authority of the commission the bishop examined the case, received the resignations, admitted Simon to Bermondsey, at the presentation of the prior and convent of St Saviour, Bermondsey, and John to the church of Hayes, at the presentation of M. Nicholas de Istele, rector of the church of Orpington. Letter to the archdeacon of Surrey for the induction of Simon.

Wargrave, 7 July 1363

1583. ADMISSION of William de Saltemersh' priest to the vicarage of the church of Monk Sherborne, vacant by the resignation of Robert de Hogenorton', at the presentation of the prior and convent of Sherborne.

To be perpetual vicar residing according to the constitutions. Letter to the archdeacon of Winchester for the induction.

Wargrave, 9 July 1363

1584. LICENCE to lease his church at farm for one year granted to John de Burghton', rector of Highclere.

Wargrave, 19 July 1363

1585. INSTITUTION of Robert Cadeham priest as rector of the church of Worting, vacant by the free resignation of Melchior Wodelok', at the presentation of the abbot and convent of Hyde. Letter for the induction to the archdeacon of Winchester.

Farnham, 29 July 1363

1586. INSTITUTION of John de Brewode priest as rector of the church of Wolverton, vacant, at the presentation of Edward de Sancto Johanne, knight. Letter for the induction to the archdeacon of Winchester.

Farnham, 29 July 1363

243   **1587.** LICENCE to be absent for one year for study at some university in England granted to William Gervays, clerk, rector of Bentworth, to receive minor orders and the subdiaconate; meantime divine service is to be maintained by others.

Southwark, 20 February 1363

243   **1588.** COLLATION by the bishop of the church of Tunworth, by devolution through lapse of time, on Thomas de Monte priest as rector. Letter for the induction to the archdeacon of Winchester.

Farnham, 8 August 1363

1589. INSTITUTION of Andrew Mareschal priest to the vicarage of the church of Morden, vacant, at the presentation of the abbot and convent of Westminster, immediately subject to the Roman see. To be perpetual vicar residing according to the constitutions of Otto and Ottobon. Letter for the induction to the archdeacon of Surrey.

Wolvesey, 16 August 1363

1590. CERTIFICATORY LETTERS received at Marwell from John bishop of Lincoln to whom the bishop had entrusted the exchange between John Penrech', lately rector of St Olave, Southwark, and John Aleyn lately perpetual vicar of the church of Clee, diocese of Lincoln, dated from Wolvesey, 14 August. As authorized by the letters, after the resignations John Penrech' was instituted, at the presentation of the prior and convent of St Pancras, Lewes. Letter for the induction to the archdeacon of Surrey.

Marwell, 29 August 1363

1591. COLLATION of the priestly office in the chapel of Marwell on William de Tuderlee. Induction the same day by the official of Winchester.

Marwell, 1 September 1363

1592. INSTITUTION of John de Sandford as rector of the church of Over Wallop, vacant, at the presentation of John Mareschal and Margaret his wife, by reason of the lands and advowson which had belonged to Thomas de Overwallop, now belonging to Margaret for her lifetime, by fine in the king's court. Letter to the archdeacon of Winchester for the induction.

Compton, 15 September 1363

1593. DISPENSATION granted to M. Richard de Branketree subdeacon rector of Broughton to study for one year in any university in England, without obligation of residence or of proceeding to further orders and with permission to lease at farm the profits of the church.

Esher, 28 September 1363

1594. DISPENSATION granted to Giles de Caldecote subdeacon, rector of Farley Chamberlayne, to be absent for one year for study in some English university, according to the constitutions.

Esher, 28 September 1363

1595. EXCHANGE OF BENEFICES authorized by Simon, bishop of London, between Robert atte Welle, lately rector of Cobham, diocese of Winchester, and Nicholas Waleys, rector of St Mary Abchurch, London; Robert was admitted on the resignation of Nicholas, at the presentation of St Mary, Southwark. Subsequently Nicholas was admitted in the person of John atte Welle, his proctor, at the presentation of the abbey and convent of Chertsey. Letter for the induction to the archdeacon of Surrey.

Southwark, 8 October 1363

244 **1596.** CERTIFICATORY LETTERS received from Simon bishop of London concerning the exchange between Ralph Caperon, perpetual vicar of the church of Wandsworth, diocese of Winchester, and Henry de Iddebury rector of the church of Woodford, diocese of London. Authorized by the bishop of London, Henry was admitted to the vicarage of Wandsworth, at the presentation of the abbot and convent of Westminster, to be perpetual vicar residing according to the constitutions. Letter for the induction to the archdeacon of Surrey.

Southwark, 12 October 1363

1597. INSTITUTION of John de Bridecombe priest as rector of the church of Thruxton, vacant by the resignation of John de Sandford', at the presentation of John de Buttesthorn' by right of Goda his wife, who holds the manor and the advowson. Letter for the induction to the archdeacon of Winchester.

Southwark, 13 October 1363

1598. COLLATION by the bishop of the vicarage of Hursley on William de Middelton' priest, with the fair share of the revenue of the church which is appropriated to the chapel of St Elizabeth—the vicar's portion recently ordained by the bishop. To be perpetual vicar residing according to the constitutions. Letter to the official of Winchester for the induction.

Southwark, 19 October 1363

1599. LICENCE to be absent for one year granted to Thomas de Denton', rector of Chaldon, to be at the service of John de Ronceby, clerk to the king, with permission to lease his church at farm.

Southwark, 24 October 1363

1600. LICENCE granted to Robert Frannk rector of Abinger to spend on year at a university in England.

Southwark, 24 October 1363

1601. LICENCE granted to Thomas Lambyn rector of Gatcombe, Isle of Wight to be absent for one year, leasing his church at farm.

Southwark, 24 October 1363

1602. LICENCE granted to Robert de Wykford, archdeacon of Winchester, to be absent for three years for study in a university in England, on condition he arranges a suitable official and staff for the archdeaconry to carry out the canonical obligations of his office and pays the annual dues.

Esher, 9 November 1363

1603. LICENCE granted to John de Lewes rector of Dunsfold acolyte to be absent for one year for study, without obligation of proceeding to further orders, according to the constitutions of Boniface.

Esher, 4 November 1363

245   **1604**. CERTIFICATORY LETTERS received from John, bishop of Lincoln, to whom the bishop had entrusted the exchange between John de Tichemersh', vicar of the church of Battersea, diocese of Winchester, and William Bay, then rector of Stockerston, diocese of Lincoln, showing that the exchange was authorized and that the resignation had been received. William was admitted as perpetual vicar with obligation of residence according to the constitutions, at the presentation of the abbot and convent of Westminster. Letter to the archdeacon of Surrey for the induction.

Southwark, 22 November 1363

1605. DISPENSATION granted to M. Hugh Craft, rector of Bishops Waltham, subdeacon, to be absent for one year for study, without obligation of residence or reception of orders.

Highclere, 12 December 1363

1606. PRESENTATION by the bishop of Roger Gold priest to the bishop of Bath and Wells for the church of Bleadon, in that diocese but of the collation of the bishop of Winchester. It was vacant by the death of

Reginald de Gugwell'ab and presented to the custodian of the see of Bath and Wells, *sede vacante.*

Highclere, 22 December 1363.

1607. INSTITUION of Thomas Faukes priest to the church of West Tytherley, vacant by the voluntary resignation of Nicholas Hemmisch' before the bishop, in the presence of M. Nicholas Kaerwent, John Corf and John Beautre as witnesses, in the chapel of Farnham Castle, shortly before the institution of Thomas, at the presentation of King Edward, the priory of Ivychurch being in his hands. Letter for the induction to the archdeacon of Winchester.

Highclere, 29 December 1363

1608. INSTITUTION of Peter de Falwell' clerk in the person of John de Bennebury clerk as proctor. To be rector of Newton Valence near Alton, vacant by the death John Warner, at the presentation of William de Edydon, clerk, patron. Letter for the induction to the archdeacon of Winchester and the dean of Alton.

Highclere, 2 January 1364

1609. LICENCE to be absent for study granted to William Savage, rector of Overton, priest, for one year at some university.

Overton, 21 December 1363

1610. LICENCE granted to John de Berghton' rector of Highclere, deacon, to be absent for study without obligation of residence or of proceeding to the priesthood.

Highclere, 6 January 1364

1611. COLLATION by the bishop of the church of Calbourne, Isle of Wight, on Henry Hennte, priest, vacant by the resignation of John Gurnel. Letter for the induction to the archdeacon of Winchester and the dean of the Island.

Esher, 12 January 1364

246   1612. APPROPRIATION of the church of Newton Valence to the rector and brethren of the Augustinian house of Edington, diocese of Salisbury, to increase the endowment of the house and to maintain scholars at a university. A vicar's portion to be ordained and pensions to be paid: 5s. to the bishop and to the priory of Winchester, with 12d. for the archdeacon. Date.
Ratification by the prior and chapter of Winchester.
247   Consent of the archdeaon. Date.

Winchester, 9 January 1364

1613. LICENCE granted to William Rode, rector of Shalfleet, Isle of Wight, to be at the service of William earl of Salisbury for one year and to be absent from his church.

Southwark, 23 January 1364

1614. INSTITUTION of John Parsones priest to the church of Monxton, vacant , at the presentation of fr. Peter, prior of Ogbourne. Letter for the induction to the archdeacon of Winchester.

Southwark, 28 January 1364

1615. DISPENSATION granted to M. Hugh Craft, deacon, rector of Bishops Waltham to be absent for study for one year in view of his advancement to the priesthood according to the constitutions.

Southwark, 2 February 1364

1616. INSTITUTION of John de Tanerton chaplain as rector of the church of Heckfield, vacant by the resignation of Adam de Hertyngdon, at the presentation of William de Wykham' patron for this turn. Letter to the archdeacon of Winchester for the induction.

Southwark, 6 February 1364

1617. COLLATION by the bishop of the church of Baughurst, vacant, on Robert atte More, priest. Letter for the induction to the official of Winchester, the rector of Burghclere, the vicar of Kingsclere and William David.

Southwark, 7 February 1364

1618. COLLATION by the bishop of the office of deacon, vacant, in the chapel of St Elizabeth, on John Cole of Stockbridge, deacon. He took the oath to observe the conditions of the constitutions of John de Pontissara, founder of the chapel. Letter to M. W' de Sevenhampton, treasurer of Wolvesey for the induction.

Bishops Waltham, 9 March 1364

1619. INSTITUTION of fr. Peter de Ultra Aquam, monk of the abbey of Lyre, diocese of Evreux, as prior of Carisbrooke, at the presentation of John Basyn, procurator for abbot William. Letter for the inducion to the archdeacon of Winchester.

Bishops Waltham, 15 March 1364

1620. INSTITUTION of Henry de Boteston' acolyte as rector of Mottistone, Isle of Wight, vacant, at the presentation of Edward Chike. Letter to the archdeacon of Winchester and the dean of the Island for the induction.

Bishops Waltham, 19 March 1364

1621. LICENCE granted to M. John Turk' rector of Michelmersh to be absent for study at some university in England.

Bishops Waltham, 23 March 1364

1622. DISPENSATION granted to Arnald Brocaz, subdeacon, rector of Whippingham, Isle of Wight to be absent for study at some university in England, without obligation of residence or proceeding to further orders, according to the constitutions of Boniface.

Bishops Waltham, 30 March 1364

248   **1623.** INSTITUTION of John Gyles, deacon, to the chantry of St Edmund in the parish church of Wootton, Isle of Wight, vacant, at the presentation of Elizabeth, widow of Bartholomew de Insula, knight, deceased. He took the oath to be perpetual chaplain according to the ordinances of the founder. Letter for the induction to the archdeacon of Winchester and to the dean of the Island.

Bishops Waltham, 2 April 1364

1624. COLLATION of half the church of Abinger, vacant, on Robert de Snokeshull', priest, by devolution through lapse of time. Letter for the induction to the archdeacon of Surrey.

Farnham, 8 April 1364

1625. INSTITUTION of William Fogor' to the vicarage of Goodworth Clatford, vacant by the resignation of John Parsones, last vicar of the church now instituted to the church of Monkston, at the presentation of Thomas Girchet, prebendary of the prebendal church of Goodsworth, patron of the vicarage. With obligation of residence for which he took the oath. Letter for the induction to the archdeacon of Winchester.

Southwark, 27 April 1364

1626. INSTITUTION of William Valevan priest to the church of Byfleet, vacant by the resignation of John Petit last rector before M. Thomas Yonge, official of the court of Canterbury, at his lodging in London; at the presentation of Edward prince of Wales. Letter to the archdeacon of Surrey for the induction.

Southwark, 30 July 1364

1627. LICENCE for absence granted to Henry Marmyon, restor of South Tidworth, priest, for one year.

Southwark, 17 April 1364

1628. COLLATION of the sacerdotal office in the chapel of St Elizabeth, Winchester, on Henry Coule deacon. He took the oath to observe the ordinances of the founder.

Wolvesey, 6 May 1364

1629. COLLATION of the church of Ewhurst near Kingsclere, by devolution through lapse of time, on William Redynge priest, presented by Edward de Sancto Johanne. Letter to the archdeacon of Winchester for the induction.

Wargrave, 17 May 1364

1630. CONFIRMATORY LETTER for the institution of the rector of Shorwell, Isle of Wight, addressed to Laurence Pipard, whom John de Lysle of Wootton, knight, had presented to the church of Shorwell. Since the vacancy and the merits of the presentee were not known to the bishop, he ordered the official to make an enquiry and if all was in order to admit him.

Southwark, 12 November 1361

249   The official found no obstacle and admitted Laurence as rector

Winchester, 22 November of that year

The bishop granted his approbation.

Wargrave, 24 May 1364

1631. INSTITUTION of Robert Piers priest to the church of St Peter Chesil vacant by the resignation of John Hoghenorton' last rector voluntarily before M. John Rennebury, apostolic notary; at the presentation of the prior and convent of St Denys, Southampton. Letter for the induction to the archdeacon of Winchester.

Wargrave, 28 June 1364

1632. COMMISSION received from Simon archbishop of Canterbury to negociate the exchange of benefices between Thomas Spencer rector of Preston, deanery of Croydon under the immediate jurisdiction of the archbishop, and Peter Hattere rector of Sanderstead. On that authority the bishop examined and approved the exchange, receiving the resignations. He admitted Thomas to Sanderstead at the presentation of the abbot and convent of Hyde and Peter to the church of Preston, at the presentation of Richard Wodenvyle. Letters to the archdeacon of Surrey to induct Thomas and a certificatory letter for Peter.

Wargrave, 15 June 1364

1633. CERTIFICATORY LETTERS from William bishop of Rochester to whom the bishop had entrusted the exchange between Geoffrey Wendye rector of Eversley, diocese of Winchester, and Stephen Randal, rector of Cowden, diocese of Rochester, by letter dated Wargrave 12 June. The bishop of Rochester approved the exchange, received the resignations and instituted Geoffrey to the church of Cowden and Stephen to the church of Eversley; at the presentation of Robert Mordak, rector of Winterbourne near Bristol, of Robert Coygny rector of Somerford and John Wyncestre warden of the perpetual chantry of Winterbourne, lords of the manor of Eversley, by grant and feoffment of Thomas de Bradeston', to which manor the advowson of Eversley is annexed. They were admitted as rectors. Letter to the archdeacon of Winchester for the induction of Stephen.

Southwark, 5 July 1364

1634. INSTITUTION of John de Staunton' priest to the church of Stoke Charity, vacant, at the presentation of Thomas de Hampton. Letter for the induction to the archdeacon of Winchester.

Southwark, 17 July 1364

1635. MANDATE to M. John Corf, canon of Wells, archdeacon of Surrey. Through John de Kyngesfold and Thomas de Jarpenville, parishioners of the one and of the other halves of the church of Abinger, the bishop has been informed that the said halves are so small that neither is sufficient to maintain a curate (*curatus*) or rector, and to pay the dues during his incumbency in these times, and if they were united they would be sufficient. They beg that these two moieties, hitherto shared by two rectors, should be united to provide a living and sustenance. The bishop orders that the revenue of the parish be assessed, the patronage and right of presentation be declared and other circumstances be made known. The archdeacon is to go in person, convoking the rectors and vicars of the deanery, and also the parishioners of the church to carry out the enquiry.

250

Wargrave, 1 July 1364

1636. ENQUIRY INTO THE MATTER OF UNITING THE TWO HALVES OR PORTIONS OF THE CHURCH OF ABINGER. John Corf reports that through the rectors and vicars as set out below, from the deanery of Guildford and the parishioners of Abinger, convoked and appearing, viz.

Rectors: Robert Pernicote of Ash, William Cherwere of Worplesdon, Robert of Albury, John of Ewhurst, Robert of Ockley, Robert of West Clandon.

Vicars: John of Send, Walter of Dorking.

Parishioners: John Scamayle, Thomas atte Dene, Walter atte Mede, John Lorens, Walter Hakker', Thomas Upfeld, William Muleward, John Upton', John Greyneweye, William le Clerk, John Suthbrok', Robert Wylons.

Examined under oath in the said church they declare that the lord of Padingden presented to one half of the church, to which John Kyngesfold had presented Robert Snokeshull', because the said John had acquired the manor of Padyngdon, with the advowson of half of the church; and the predecessors of Thomas Jarponville, lord of the manor of Abinger, in their time presented to the other half and has done so many times. They say that the two halves are not assessed separately, but that the church is assessed at 10 marks; that the rectors paid a tenth jointly when a tenth was imposed.

The portion to which the lord of Padyngdon presents consists of: fruits of corn, valued annually at 20s. and no more these days; tithe of wool and lambs at 5s.; tithe of pigs and geese 20d.; of flax and hemp 20s.; honey and wax 5d.; eggs 6d.; offerings 6s. 8d.; tithe of dairy and calves 20d.; mortuaries are casual and cannot be estimated.

The portion of the other half to which Thomas Jarponville presents: tithe of corn 10s. and no more; wool and lambs 5s.; pigs, geese, flax and hemp 3s. 4d.; honey and wax 5d.; eggs 6d.; dairy and calves 20d.; mortuaries as above; offerings 6s. 8d.

Dues payable by the church: synodals and martinales 2s. 1d.; procurations of the archdeacon 6s. 8d.; admission to office etc. 10s.

While the church is divided, no worthy parson will hold it.

Abinger, 8 June 1364

1637. PRONOUNCEMENT OF THE UNION OF THE TWO HALVES of the parish of Abinger. With the consent of the two patrons and for the reasons

advanced, the bishop unites the two portions into one rectory, since from the enquiry the profits of the whole church are sufficient for an incumbent.
251 The bishop declares the union binding, through M. John de Wormenhale doctor at law, chancellor, in the chapel at Esher, 11 July 1364, in the presence of the bishop with M. Nicholas de Kaerwent, John Corf and John Beautre, public notary.

1638. PRESENTATION to the church of Abinger by Thomas Jarponville to whom the presentation belongs, to the bishop for the united parish Robert de Snokeshull' priest.

Abinger, 12 July 1364

1639. INSTITUTION of Robert de Snokeshull' priest as rector. Letter for the induction to the archdeacon of Surrey.

Esher, 12 July 1364

1640. INSTITUTION of John de Staunton priest to the church of Stoke Charity (*Duplicate of 1634*).

1641. INSTITUTION of John Symond of Stretton priest as rector of the church of Mottistone, Isle of Wight, vacant by the resignation of Henry de Boteston clerk before M. John de Wormenhale the chancellor at the manor of Highclere, 5 August with John de Mottesfonte, Thomas de Mucheldevere *domicellus* of the bishop and John Beautre as witnesses; at the presentation of Edward Chike. Letter for the induction to the archdeacon of Winchester and the dean of the Island.

Highclere, 5 August 1364

1642. INSTITUTION after receiving the mandate concerning the presentation, and the exchange of benefices between John Gukke lately perpetual vicar of the church of Shorwell, Isle of Wight, and Bartholomew de Dennyngworth, lately rector of the chapel (*capelle curate*) of Kingston, Isle of Wight. After the examination by mandate of the bishop and the resignations, John was instituted to Kingston, at the presentation of John de Kyngeston and Bartholomew to Shorwell, with obligation of residence according to the constitutions and at the presentation of Laurence Pipard, rector of Shorwell. Letter for the induction to the archdeacon of Winchester and to the dean of the Island.

Highclere, 9 August 1364

1643. COLLATION by the bishop of the vicarage of Ashley, vacant by the free resignation of Michael de Dunheved, 27 December 1361, of the bishop's collation by lapse of time, on Robert atte Weye, priest. To be perpetual vicar according to the constitutions. Letter for the induction to the archdeacon of Winchester.

Bishop's Waltham, 16 August 1364

1644. COLLATION by the bishop of the church of Binstead, Isle of Wight, on Richard atte Grene priest, vacant by the resignation of Henry de Husseborn' last rector, in the presence of John Giles, apostolic notary.

Letter for the induction to the archdeacon of Winchester and to the rector of Brighstone.

Bishop's Waltham, 24 August 1364

1645. COMMISSION from John, bishop of Lincoln, to negociate the exchange of benefices between William Bay perpetual vicar of Battersea, diocese of Winchester, and William de Hanleye, rector of St Peter, Roughton, diocese of Lincoln. The bishop approved the exchange, accepted the resignations and instituted William de Hanleye to the vicarage of Battersea, at the presentation of the abbot and convent of Westminster; to be perpetual vicar with obligation of residence, and subsequently William Bay to the church of Roughton. Letter to the archdeacon of Surrey for the induction of William de Hanleye.

East Meon, 29 August 1364

1646. INSTITUTION of William de Alne priest as perpetual vicar of Itchenstoke, vacant, with obligation of residence, at the presentation of the abbess and convent of Romsey, without an enquiry. Letter for the induction to the archdeacon of Winchester.

Downton, 10 September 1364

1647. COLLATION by the bishop of the vicarage of the church of Ellingham, vacant by the resignation of John the last vicar, 18 October 1363, on Henry Gode priest, by devolution through lapse of time. To be perpetual vicar residing according to the constitutions. Letter to the archdeacon of Winchester for the induction.

Downton, 17 September 1364

1648. DISPENSATION granted to John de Lewes rector of Dunsfold, deacon, to study at a university for one year without obligation of residence or of proceeding to the priesthood.

Southwark, 20 September 1364

1649. COLLATION BY APOSTOLIC AUTHORITY of the church of Clapham on James Fehw, poor priest of the diocese of Dublin. The church of Clapham is vacant and at the presentation of the prior and convent of Merton. Letter to the rector of the church of St Mary Magdalen, Bermondsey, to induct James by authority of the Holy See.

Southwark, 24 September 1364

1650. CERTIFICATORY LETTERS received at Dummer from R' bishop of Salisbury, to whom the bishop had entrusted the matter of the exchange between Richard Elyot vicar of the church of Nether Wallop and William Knot rector of Tidpit, diocese of Salisbury, by letters dated Downton, 17 September. Since the bishop approved, William Knot was instituted to the vicarage of Nether Wallop, at the presentation of Roger Holm, rector of Wallop. To be perpetual vicar residing according to the constitutions. Letter for the induction to the archdeacon of Winchester.

Dummer, 20 October 1364

1651. INSTITUTION of Roger de Wymondham priest to the church of Farnborough, vacant, at the presentation of William de Spridlynton and Richard, his brother, patrons. Letter for the induction to the archdeacon of Winchester.

Southwark, 24 October 1364

1652. LICENCE granted to Robert Aspale, rector of Warnford, to be absent for one year without obligation of residing.

Southwark, 24 October 1364

1653. INSTITUTION of Richard de Hamme priest as rector of the church of Greatham, vacant, at the presentation of Thomas de Devenissh'. Letter to the official of the archdeacon of Winchester for the induction.

Farnham, 21 November 1364

1654. DISPENSATION granted to Giles de Caldecote rector of Farley Chamberlayne near Romsey, subdeacon, to be absent for study, without obligation of residence or proceeding to further orders.

Southwark, 30 September 1364

253 **1655.** COMMISSION addressed to M. John Blaunchard, doctor at law and John de Totteford', rector of Ditton, on information from king Edward, to examine the presentation of William Othyn clerk to the church of Bighton. Then to induct the rightful presentee.

Southwark, 24 September 1364

1656. LICENCE granted to John de Everdon rector of the church of Compton near Guildford to farm out the fruits of his church for one year, provided that divine service be maintained.

Southwark, 27 October 1364

1657. COMMISSION received from R' bishop of Salisbury to negotiate the exchange between John Curtoys, vicar of the church of Heckfield and John Hendeman, rector of the church of Stanford, diocese of Salisbury. After the enquiry made by the archdeacon of Berkshire and the resignation the bishop instituted John Hendeman to Heckfield, at the presentation of John de Tamerton, rector of Heckfield, with obligation of residing according to the constitutions. Letter for the induction to the official of the archdeacon of Winchester for John Hendeman to Heckfield. The induction of John Curtoys reserved to the bishop of Salisbury.

Southwark, 10 December 1364

1658. LICENCE granted to Roger de Wymondham, rector of Farnborough, to be at the service of William de Spridlynton' clerk, for one year and to lease the church to some suitable person.

Farnham, 4 November 1364

1659. LICENCE granted to the abbot of Lesnes to lease the greater tithes of the church of Godstone for one year to Stephen de Hepworth rector of Isfield and Richard atte Nasshe.

Southwark, 8 November 1364

1660. INSTITUTION of Roger de Slonghore priest to the vicarage of the prebendal church of Godsworth, vacant by the resignation of William Foger, at the presentation of Thomas Birchet, prebendary of the prebendal church. Letter for the induction to the archdeacon of Winchester. Obligation of residence.

Farnham, 20 December 1364

1661. DISPENSATION granted to M. Hugh Craft, rector of the church of Bishops Waltham, to be absent for study for one year, without obligation of residence or of proceeding to further orders.

Farnham, 21 December 1364

254 **1662.** LICENCE granted to Thomas Quarreor, rector of the church of Chiddingfold, to be for one year at the service of Edward de Sancto Johanne, knight.

Farnham, 4 January 1365

1663. LICENCE for non-residence granted to John Brode, rector of the church of East Tisted.

Farnham, 4 January 1365

1664. INSTITUTION of Simon Bacon priest to the chapel of Knighton, Isle of Wight, vacant, at the presentation of Theobald de Gorges, knight. Letter for the induction to the archdeacon of Winchester.

Farnham, 4 January 1365

1665. COLLATION by the bishop of the church of St Martin in Parchment Street, Winchester, vacant, by devolution through lapse of time, on John Godman. Letter for the induction to the official of the archdeacon.

Wolvesey, 13 January 1365

1666. ADMISSION of M. Thomas Yonge, clerk, to be canon of the conventual church of Nunnaminster, vacant by the death of M. Walter Beneit, at the presentation of the abbess and convent, with all the rights of the canonry. Letter to M. Walter de Sevenhampton, treasurer of Wolvesey, and Walter Gourda, commissary of the bishop, to induct the canon, assigning him or his proctor, his stall in choir and place in chapter.

Southwark, 20 January 1365

1667. COLLATION by the bishop on Peter Muchelmor and Richard Aylwyn two sacerdotal offices in the chapel of St Elizabeth, Winchester, vacant. To live according to the constitutions of the founder, John de Pontissara.

Wolvesey, 13 January 1365

1668. LICENCE granted to William, rector of the church of Overton to be absent for one year to study at Cambridge.

Farnham, 16 January 1365

1669. CERTIFICATORY LETTERS received from John bishop of Lincoln, to whom the bishop had entrusted the exchange of benefices between Roger Helm rector of the church of Cottered, diocese of Lincoln, canon of Chichester, prebendary of the prebend of Fittleworth in the same canonry, prebendary of the collegiate church of Abergwyli, diocese of Menevia and prebendary of the prebend of Landeilo in the same church and Giles Wyngreworth' rector of the church of Nether Wallop; by letters dated Wargrave, 14 May, 1364. As the bishop of Lincoln approved, after the resignation of Giles, Roger was admitted to the church of Nether Wallop, at the presentation of M. John de Branketre, treasurer of York. Letter for the induction to the archdeacon of Winchester.

Southwark, 4 June 1365

1670. LICENCE granted to Walter de Estham rector of Cranleigh to be absent for one year at the service of Thomas de Bello Campo, earl of Warwick.

Southwark, 14 June 1364

1671. DISPENSATION granted to M. Hugh Craft, deacon, rector of Bishops Waltham, to be absent for study for one year: with obligation of residing or of proceeding to the priesthood, according to the constitutions.

Southwark, 8 January 1365

1672. DISPENSATION granted to John Laurence of Broughton, rector of the church of Highclere, deacon, to be absent for one year for study at some university according to the constitutions of Boniface.

Highclere, 9 January 1365

255 **1673.** COMMISSION received from Simon, archbishop of Canterbury, to deal with the exchange of benefices between John Lorkyn, vicar of East Malling, under the immediate jurisdiction of the archbishop, and Simon Blake, rector of St Mary Magdalen, Bermondsey. The bishop approved and by the authority of the archbishop, after receiving the resignation, admitted John to St Mary Magdalen, at the presentation of the prior and convent of Bermondsey, and Simon to East Malling, at the presentation of the abbess and convent of Malling, with obligation of residing according to the constitutions of Otto and Ottobon. Letter to the archdeacon of Surrey for the induction of John; the induction of Simon was reserved to the archbishop.

Southwark, 13 February 1365

1674. INSTITUTION of William Tyrwyt, priest to the church of Farlington, vacant, at the presentation of the prior and convent of Southwick. Letter for the induction to the archdeacon of Winchester.

Southwark, 20 February 1365

1675. PRESENTATION of Adam Kente of Stoke by Nayland, priest, by the bishop to the church of Hinton, diocese of Salisbury, vacant at his presentation by reason of the manor of Hinton being in his hands.

Southwark, 20 February 1365

1676. INSTITUTION of Thomas de Cuntasthorp' as chaplain to the chapel of St Nicholas in the manor of Whitefield, Isle of Wight, vacant by the resignation of John de Stodeye, clerk, at the presentation of Isabella the king's daughter. Letter for the induction to the archdeacon of Winchester.

Highclere, 4 March 1365

1677. INSTITUTION of John Aleyn of Huntingdon, priest, to the church of Walton, vacant by the resignation of William Tirwyt, last rector, at the presentation of king Edward by reason of the fee and advowson of John de Brewes *ydiote* being in the king's hands. Letter for the induction to the archdeacon of Surrey.

Highclere, 5 March 1365

1678. COMMISSION received from Louis bishop of Hereford to negotiate the exchange between Robert de Bokenhull' vicar of Lydney, diocese of Hereford, and John vicar of Kingston-on-Thames. The bishop examined the case and after the resignations instituted Robert to the vicarage of Kingston, at the presentation of the prior and convent of St Mary, Merton, and John Wyli to the vicarage of Lydney, at the presentation of the dean and chapter of Hereford, both with obligation of residing according to the constitutions of Otto and Ottobon. Letter for the induction of Robert sent to the archdeacon of Surrey.

Highclere, 6 March 1365

1679. ADMISSION of William de Walton' priest to the vicarage of the church of Warlingham, vacant by the voluntary resignation of Thomas de Olneye at Highclere before M. John de Wormenhale chancellor, John Corf', Thomas de Cherdeslee, apostolic notary, and John Aleyn as witnesses, 5 March; at the presentation of the prior and convent of St Saviour, Bermondsey. To be perpetual vicar residing according to the constitutions of Otto and Ottobon. Letter for the induction to the archdeacon of Surrey.

Highclere, 9 March 1365

1680. DISPENSATION for study granted to Richard de Branktree, rector of the church of Broughton, subdeacon, for one year at some university in England, without obligation of residence or of proceeding to further orders.

Farnham, 26 April 1365

256 **1681.** DISPENSATION granted to Arnald Brocaz, rector of the church of Whippingham, Isle of Wight, subdeacon, to study at a university in England for one year.

Farnham, 2 May 1365

1682. DISPENSATION granted to M. John Turk, rector of the church of Michelmersh, to be absent for study at some university in England, without obligation of residence.

Farnham, 9 May 1365

1683. PRESENTATION by the bishop of John de Fedryngeye, rector of the church of Borley, diocese of London, to the church of Portland, diocese of Salisbury, at the presentation of the bishop, by way of exchange with Edward Chaumberlayn, rector of that church.

Farnham, 15 May 1365

1684. INSTITUTION of Stephen de Botlesham priest as rector of the church of St Laurence, Southampton, vacant, at the presentation of the prior and convent of St Denys, Southampton. Letter for the induction to the archdeacon of Winchester.

Wargrave, 27 May 1365

1685. INSTITUTION of John Fairford, acolyte, as rector of the church of Dibden, vacant by the resignation of Nicholas de Kyngeston', at the presentation of Richard de Hangre. Letter for the induction to the archdeacon of Winchester.

Wargrave, 8 June 1365

1686. PRESENTATION by the bishop of Robert Wiche, rector of the church of Dogmersfield, to the church of Hinton, diocese of Salisbury, of the bishop's own patronage, by way of exchange with John de Newenham, rector of Hinton. Commission sent to the bishop of Salisbury to negotiate the exchange. The induction and obedience of John reserved to the bishop of Winchester.

Southwark, 21 June 1365

1687. CERTIFICATORY LETTERS received from Robert bishop of Salisbury for the exchange between Robert Wyche, rector of Dogmersfield and John de Newenham, rector of Hinton, according to the commission entrusted to him. The bishop admits John to Dogmersfield, at the presentation of John, bishop of Bath and Wells. Letter for the induction to the archdeacon of Winchester.

Wargrave, 30 June 1365

1688. INSTITUTION of Richard atte Mulle priest to the vicarage of the church of Great Bookham, vacant, at the presentation of the abbot and convent of Chertsey, with obligation of residing according to the constitutions of Otto and Ottobon. Letter to the archdeacon of Surrey for the induction.

Wargrave, 4 July 1365

1689. CERTIFICATORY LETTERS received from Simon bishop of London, to whom the bishop had entrusted the exchange between Robert Hood, rector of the church of Nutfield, and Nicholas Stoke, rector of the church of St Andrew, Cornhill in the city of London and chaplain of the free chantry for the soul of Godfrey de Wesenham in St Paul's. By letter dated Wargrave, 2 July. Since the bishop of London has approved, the bishop inducted Nicholas Stoke to the church of Nutfield, at the presentation of Nicholas Lonaigne, knight. Letter to the archdeacon of Surrey to induct Nicholas or John Roo his proctor.

Witney, 8 July 1365

1690. COLLATION by the bishop of the church of Wotton, of the patronage of William Latymer, knight, vacant by the voluntary resignation of Robert de Mildenhale, last rector, 1 August 1364. Collation by devolution through lapse of time, on Robert Dalton' *capellanus.* Letter to the archdeacon of Surrey.

Witney, 19 July 1365

257   **1691.** CONFIRMATION OF THE APPROPRIATION OF THE CHURCH OF HURSLEY AND ORDINATION OF THE VICARAGE. The bishop has looked very attentively into the letters of his predecessor, John de Pontissara, concerning the appropriation of the church of Hursley to the provost and chaplains of St Elizabeth, Winchester. Considering, moreover, the misfortunes of the chapel and the epidemics in the kingdom, with the consent of the chapter, the bishop ratifies the appropriation and ordains the vicar's portion:— all the greater and lesser tithes, all the offerings and emoluments of the chapel of Otterbourne within the parish; all the offerings at the church of Hursley and the lesser tithes within the parish, viz. tithes on cheese, milk, honey, wax, piglets, lambs, calves, eggs, colts, geese, doves, flax, hemp, apples, pears and other titheable fruit from gardens and orchards; also all tithes of mills in the parish; all personal tithes of tradesmen, servants and craftsmen due to the church; all mortuary fees, even in kind; the herbage of the cemetery and all tithes of bakehouses belong to the vicar. He will have for his dwelling the house newly erected on the space to the south of the cemetery and rectory ($27 \times 16\frac{1}{2}$ perches), with the buildings upon it. The remaining tithes not mentioned above:—tithes of all grain, hay and wool; all profits from the jurisdiction of the archdeacon due to the rector, all trees in the cemetery belong to the provost and chaplains of St Elizabeth. And to avoid any disputes the bishop ordains that all the dues payable by the church and its chapel will be paid by the provost and the chaplains. The provost will rebuild and re-roof the chancel. He will pay to the bishop a pension of 13s. 4d. in compensation for the revenue which the bishop used to receive from the church when it was vacant; he will pay the 7s. 5d. in procurations at visitations by the official of Winchester and any unforeseen expense; the annual value of the church is £10. The vicar will repair books, vestments and provide lights, for which the rectors were formerly responsible. The vicars will provide a secondary chaplain for Hursley and one at the chapel at Otterbourne at their expense. The vicars will make announcements and denunciations at their expense. The vicars will make announcements and

258   denunciations as directed by the provost. The right to change this ordination is reserved to the bishop.

Southwark, 29 October 1362

1692. AUGMENTATION OF STIPENDS AT ST ELIZABETH. The provost and chaplains will wear surplices and black capes, simple clothes of black burnet or russet. For this clothing and food and drink, the provost will receive 6 marks, each chaplain 40s., each clerk 20s. Considering the high cost of goods and the reduction of the income of the chapel, the provost will receive in addition to what was laid down in the preceeding ordination 26s. 8d., each chaplain 20s., each clerk 13s. 4d., the sacristan 6s. 8d., each of the 6 choristers 20s. to be divided equally among them. Also the provost and chaplains, annually on 3 September, will celebrate the anniversary of John de Nubbelaye, the late provost; 13s. 4d. will be distributed: for masses in Winchester 5s., for candles at his tomb 3s. 4d., for a pittance for the chaplains and clerks 3s. 4d., for distribution among the choristers 20d. If any chaplain or clerk be absent, his share is to be distributed among the poor and prisoners on the anniversary.

On the vigil of St James the apostle (24 July) the provost and chaplains will sing an office for the bishop's parents and all the faithful departed; and on the morrow a solemn requiem mass. After the bishop's own death, a full office and mass will be sung on the anniversary in perpetuity, with a distribution of 13s. 4d., i.e. 2s. for the provost, 12d. each to the 6 chaplains, 6d. to each clerk, 2d. to each of the 6 choristers, 4d. to the sacristan, in addition to the 12d. just mentioned. Also, the 12d. remaining is to be expended on the purchase of wax for 3 candles to stand in the middle of the choir on the anniversary in perpetuity.

Southwark, 29 October 1362

The confirmation by the prior and chapter of the ordination of the vicarage, augmentation of stipends and anniversaries will be found on the second folio to come.

1693. DISPENSATION granted to William Othyn rector of Bighton, subdeacon, for study for one year at some university in England, without obligation of residence or proceeding to higher orders according to the constitutions of Boniface.

Southwark, 29 August *anno prescripto*

1694. ENQUIRY INTO THE ELECTION OF THE ABBESS OF NUNNAMINSTER.
Commission to the official of Winchester to examine the election of Alice de la Mare as abbess of St Mary's abbey, Winchester, vacant by the death of Christina la Wayte. Any objector to the election was ordered to appear, so that it could be confirmed and induction etc could follow.

Wargrave, 28 July 1365

After the proclamation, the matter was examined and the election was found to be canonically correct and the election was confirmed.

Alresford, [11 August] 1365

1695. LETTER OF CONFIRMATION to the abbess from the bishop granting her powers of jurisdiction and administration.

Hursley, 19 August 1365

260   **1696.** MANDATE TO INDUCT AND INSTALL the new abbess addressed to the archdeacon, official or dean of Winchester.

Date as above

1697. MANDATE TO THE PRIORESS AND CONVENT to show towards the new abbess all due obedience and reverence.

Date as above

1698. LETTER TO THE KING acknowledging the receipt of his brief requesting the fealty of the new abbess.

Hursley, 18 August 1365

1699. BRIEF OF EDWARD III to the bishop to receive the fealty of abbess Alice.

Westminster, 28 July 1365

1700. FORM OF THE OATH OF FEALTY (in French)

1701. BLESSING OF THE ABBESS at pontifical mass in the parish church of Hursley.

17 August 1365

1702. INSTITUTION of Hugh de Worston' clerk as rector of the church of Wolverton, vacant by the resignation of John de Breewode in the church of Staunton near Highworth, diocese of Salisbury, at the presentation of Edward de Sancto Johanne. Letter for the induction to the archdeacon of Winchester and the vicar of Kingsclere.

Hartley Wintney, 20 July 1365

261   **1703.** CERTIFICATORY LETTERS received from M. John de Gotes, priest of the church of Lancing, official of the diocese of Chichester and vicar-general of W' bishop in his absence concerning the exchange between Thomas Quarreor rector of Chiddingfold, diocese of Winchester, and Ralph de Dodelesfold, rector of Chilington, diocese of Chichester, by request from the bishop, dated Farnham, 3 November 1365. Since the vicar-general authorizes the exchange, Thomas having resigned the rectory of Chiddingfold, the bishop institutes Ralph to Chiddenfold, at the presentation of Laurence de Nigris canon *fulginatis* acting for Raynald cardinal deacon of St Adrian, dean of Salisbury, patron of the church by reason of the deanery. Letter for the induction to the archdeacon of Surrey.

Farnham, 10 November 1365

1704. CONFIRMATION OF THE ORDINATION OF THE VICARAGE OF HURSLEY. Prior Hugh and the convent of Winchester register their approval.

Chapter-house, 29 November 1362

1705. CONFIRMATION OF THE AUGMENTATION OF THE STIPENDS AT HURSLEY by prior Hugh and the convent.

Chapter-house, 29 November 1362

1706. LICENCE granted to James son of Hugh, rector of the church of Clapham to farm out the revenue of his church to fr. Henry, prior of St Mary's Southwark, until the feast of the Purification and then for a full year.

Southwark, 4 October 1365

.

1707. DISPENSATION granted to Giles de Caldecote rector of the church of Farley near Romsey to be absent for study for one year without obligation of residence or of taking further orders.

Southwark, 4 October 1365

262 **1708.** COMMISSION received from John bishop of Lincoln, to negotiate the exchange of benefices between Robert Page, perpetual vicar of the church of Reigate and Richard de Aumberden' chaplain of the perpetual chantry in Allhallows, Barking, London, founded for the soul of Thomas Pylkes and all the faithful departed. The bishop examined the matter, accepted the resignation of Robert and instituted Richard to the vicarage of Reigate, at the presentation of the prior and convent of St Mary, Southwark. To be perpetual vicar residing according to the constitutions of Otto and Ottobon. Subsequently, receiving the resignation of Richard from the chantry, the bishop collated Robert to the chantry by the authority of [Simon,] bishop of London. Letters the same day to the archdeacon of Surrey for the induction to Reigate.

Southwark, 6 December 1365

1709. MEMORANDUM that the aforesaid Richard de Aumberden' of his own free will swore that he would, before the feast of the Purification next, provide at his own expense a second priest for the church of Reigate, and from that feast henceforward would continue to provide for him as long as he was vicar. Or else he would pay to the parishioners 100s. in two annual payments from the fruits of the vicarage towards the support of the chaplain, unless the parishioners find a more favourable solution. Were present at the oath John Beautre public notary, Henry de Northavene, Robert Page priest and John de Twyford clerk.

Date as above

1710. COMMISSION received from John bishop of Lincoln, to examine the exchange proposed between John de Bereford' rector of the church of Chawton and Andrew de Wolde vicar of Claybrooke, diocese of Lincoln, according to the enquiry of the official of the archdeacon of Leicester. Then to admit John to the said vicarage, at the presentation of the prioress and convent of Nuneaton; to be perpetual vicar residing according to the constitutions, with induction and obedience reserved to the bishop of Lincoln. Subsequently Andrew was admitted to Chalton in the person of Richard de Haselbech', his proctor. Letter for the induction to the archdeacon of Winchester and the dean of Droxford.

Farnham, 18 December 1365

1711. INSTITUTION of Arnald Brocaz subdeacon as rector of the church of Ash, vacant, at the presentation of M. Bernard Brocaz clerk, farmer of the manor of Ash, annexed to the abbey of Chertsey, with the advowson. Letter for the induction to the archdeacon of Surrey.

Farnham, 19 December 1365

1712. PRESENTATION by the bishop of John Hering of Gytyng' rector of Halton, diocese of Bath and Wells, to the church of Buttermere, diocese of Salisbury, of the patronage of the bishops of Winchester. This is by exchange with John and William atte Rode of Corsham, rector of the church of Buttermere.

Highclere, 3 January 1366

1713. ADMISSION of John Kyng' priest to the church of Freshwater, Isle of Wight, vacant by the death of John Mot, last rector, at the presentation of the abbot and convent of Lyre. Letter for the induction to the archdeacon of Winchester and the dean of the Island.

Highclere, 4 January 1366

1714. DISPENSATION granted to John Laurence, deacon rector of the church of Highclere, to be absent for study for one year, without obligation of residence or of taking further orders.

Highclere, 5 January 1366

263 **1715.** COMMISSION to the official of Winchester to examine the patronage of the chapel of East Standen, Isle of Wight and to act accordingly. Claiming to be patrons, Thomas Haket and Isabella Houston presented Thomas de Constasthorp' to the chapel, vacant.

Highclere, 4 January 1366

1716. INSTITUTION of Thomas de Stafford', bachelor of civil law, to the church of Fordingbridge, at the presentation of Ralph, earl of Stafford. Letter to the archdeacon of Winchester to induct Thomas or his proctor William Gardyner.

Southwark, 18 January 1366

1717. INSTITUTION of Thomas de Cantasthorp' priest to the chapel of East Standen, Isle of Wight, vacant by the voluntary resignation of John Stodeye, last warden and possessor of the chapel, at the presentation of Isabella de Houston', patron for this turn. Letter for the induction to the archdeacon of Winchester and the dean of the Island.
Memorandum that by the enquiry ordered by the bishop, the warden is bound to find a chaplain to celebrate three days a week.

Southwark, 18 January 1366

1718. DISPENSATION to Arnald Brocaz, rector of the church of Ash, subdeacon, to study for one year at a university in England, without obligation of residence or of proceeding to further orders, according to the constitutions of Boniface.

Southwark, 12 January 1366

1718a. DISPENSATION granted to Andrew de Wold' rector of Chalton to be absent for study at the university of Oxford until Michaelmas.

Highclere, 25 January 1366

1718b. INSTITUTION of Robert Pydefer' priest to the church of Whippingham, Isle of Wight, vacant by the resignation of Arnald Brocaz, late rector, now rector of Ash near Farnham, at the presentation of

Ralph Maylok', procurator for the abbot of Lyre. Letters for the induction to the archdeacon of Winchester and the dean of the Island.

Highclere, 3 February 1366

1719. COLLATION of the chantry in the chapel of Sherborne Coudray, in the parish of Sherborne St John, founded by Thomas de Coudray, knight, by devolution by lapse of time, on John Solle, priest. To be perpetual chaplain. Letter to the archdeacon of Winchester for the induction.

Wolvesey, 21 February 1366

264

1720. INSTITUTION of William de Hulle, priest to the church of Newchurch, Isle of Wight, at the presentation of the abbot and convent of Lyre, diocese of Evreux. Letter for the induction to the archdeacon of Winchester and the dean of the Island.

Wolvesey, 25 February 1366

1721. COLLATION by the bishop of the church of Yarmouth, Isle of Wight, by devolution through lapse of time, vacant by the voluntary resignation of the last rector, on Robert Wager, priest, to serve the church fittingly himself or by another. Letter for the induction to the archdeacon of Winchester and the dean of the Island.

Wolvesey, 27 February 1366

1722. DISPENSATION granted to Thomas de Stafforde, rector of Fordingbridge, acolyte, to study at some English university, without obligation of residing or of receiving orders beyond the subdiaconate within the year, according to the constitutions *Cum ex eo.* He may farm out the revenue from the church to a suitable person.

Wolvesey, 28 February 1366

1723. INSTITUTION of John Sweyn priest, in the person of John Sandford, rector of Over Wallop his proctor, as rector of the church of Ellisfield, vacant by the resignation of John Pyrie, carmelite; at the presentation of Bernard Brocaz, knight, by right of his wife, Mary. Letter for the induction to the archdeacon of Winchester.

Wolvesey, 28 March 1366

1724. EXCHANGE OF BENEFICES WITHIN THE DIOCESE between John Symond', rector of the church of Mottistone, Isle of Wight, and Edmund de Ludespade vicar of East Meon. The bishop examined the case, received the resignations and instituted Edmund to Mottistone, at the presentation of Edward Chike, patron by right of his wife; subsequently the bishop collated the vicarage of East Meon on John Symond', to be perpetual vicar, residing according to the constitutions of Otto and Ottobon, for which he took the oath. Letter for the induction to the archdeacon of Winchester and the rector of Alresford.

Wolvesey, 28 March 1366

1725. DISPENSATION granted to Hugh de Worston', rector of Wolverton, acolyte, to be absent for study at an English university, without obligation of residence or of advancing to orders beyond the subdiaconate in the one year, according to the constitution *Cum ex eo.*

Wolvesey, 29 March 1366

1726. PROCESS OF THE ELECTION OF A PRIOR FOR MOTTISFONT, order of St Augustine, before M. John Wormenhale, official of Winchester, John Beautre and J' Corf, concerning the election of John Netherhavene, canon of the priory, to be prior after the death of Ralph de Thorleston' held 26 March 1366, for which date the objectors were summoned. The proctor for the convent was M. William Lamport, who asked for prorogation until the 27th and then until 1 April, to meet in the parish church of Hursley. The matter was solemnly proposed by M. Robert de Lemynton' and the consent of John, duke of Lancaster was read out with other formalities. Finally the commissary pronounced the election to be valid.

1727. PROCLAMATION of the election by the commissaries (as named above), confirming it as being fully canonical.

1728. COMMISSION to enquire into the election, addressed to the official, to John Beautre and John Corf, canons of Exeter and Wells, for Thursday 26 March 1366, with prorogation to the cathedral the following days—with power to affirm or annul.

Wolvesey, 25 March 1366

1729. LETTER OF CONFIRMATION from the bishop, granting cure of souls and administration.

Date as above

1730. MANDATE from the bishop to the archdeacon to induct the new prior, installing him in choir and chapter.

Date as above

1731. MANDATE to the 'president' and convent of Mottisfont for their obedience to the new prior.

Hursley, 1 April 1366

1732. LETTER FOR THE RESTITUTION OF THE TEMPORALITIES to John duke of Lancaster, Richmond, Derby, Lincoln and Leicester, seneschal of England.

No date

1733. RESIGNATION of Robert Wager from the church of Yarmouth, Isle of Wight, before the bishop in the parish church of Hursley, in the presence of N' Karewente, M. John Corf and J' Beautre as witnesses.

9 April 1366

1734. ADMISSION of the same Robert Wager to the vicarage of Ellingham, at the presentation of fr. William Daubeneye, prior of Ellingham, patron of the vicarage. To be perpetual vicar, residing according to the constitutions. Letter for the induction to the archdeacon of Winchester.

Same date

1735. CERTIFICATORY LETTERS received from Robert bishop of Coventry and Lichfield, with commission to the bishop to negotiate the exchange between William Mountayne rector of the church of Wappenbury, diocese of Coventry and Lichfield, and Walter Freland' rector of the church of Bletchingley. Then if all is in order, to institute Walter to Wappenbury, at the presentation of Ralph, earl of Stafford as proctor for the prior and convent of Monks Kirby, after the resignation of William. The enquiry of the archdeacon of Coventry was sent; induction and obedience reserved.

'Heywode', 29 February 1366

By this authority, after the resignation of John de Weycombe, substitute for the proctor John de Herinthorp', chief proctor for William Mountayne, Walter Frelond' in the person of Peter atte Wode his proctor was admitted to the church of Wappenbury, at the presentation of Ralph, earl of Stafford.

267

1736. INSTITUTION of William Mountayne acolyte to the church of Bletchingley as rector, vacant by the resignation of Peter atte Wode proctor for Walter Frylond, by exchange for the church of Wappenbury, at the presentation of Ralph, earl of Stafford, patron. William was admitted in the person of John de Herinthorp' his proctor. Letter for the induction to the archdeacon of Surrey.

Southwark, 6 May 1366

1737. INSTITUTION of John de Netherhavene clerk as rector of the church of Wolverton, vacant by the resignation of Hugh de Worston, voluntarily into the bishop's hands, as is clear by the testimonial letter from the official of the bishop of Salisbury; at the presentation of Edward de Sancto Johanne, knight. Letter for the induction to the archdeacon of Winchester.

Southwark, 11 May 1366

1738. INSTITUTION of John Gernoun priest to the vicarage of the church of Tooting, vacant by the resignation of Richard de Rempston', in the presence of John Beautre, apostolic notary, John de Twyford' and Thomas de Corston as witnesses, at the same date and place. To be perpetual vicar residing according to the constitutions of Otto and Ottobon, at the presentation of the prior and convent of St Mary, Southwark. Letter for the induction to the archdeacon of Surrey.

Esher, 5 June 1366

1739. DISPENSATION granted to William Mountayn, rector of Bletchingley acolyte to be absent for study at some university, without obligation of residence or of proceeding beyond the subdiaconate, according to the constitution *Cum ex eo*.

Esher, 20 May 1366

1740. INSTITUTION of Thomas Parye *capellanus* to the church of Hartley Westpall, vacant by the resignation of Stephen Wyot, last rector, according to a public instrument drawn up by William Petir, notary of the diocese of Bath; at the presentation of William Waspail, patron. Letter for the induction to the archdeacon of Winchester.

Memorandum that, in the event of the return of Stephen to the church, and occupying it by virtue of his earlier institution, the said Thomas swore to the bishop that he would respect the first institution.

Wargrave, 2 July 1366

1741. LICENCE granted to Roger de Shetlyndon', rector of Mickleham, to lease at farm the profits of his church to the prior and convent of Reigate for one year.

Wargrave, 3 July 1366

1742. COMMISSION to the bishop from R' bishop of Salisbury to negotiate the exchange between Thomas Clannvule rector of Peper Harow and Richard de Wycombe, rector of Broadway, diocese of Salisbury. After the discussions and resignations from their benefices, Thomas was admitted to Broadway, with induction and obedience reserved; subsequently Richard was admitted to Peper Harow, at the presentation of John Giffard', by right of his wife, Mary, the advowson being part of her dowry. Letter for the induction to the archdeacon of Surrey.

Wargrave, 18 May 1366

268 **1743.** MANDATE from the bishop to the archdeacon, received by him 12 July. To Robert de Wykford, archdeacon to enquire into the vacancy and the patronage of the church of Winchfield, to which William Withened' was presented by Robert de Kymberlee, claiming to be patron. If all is in order, to admit him to the rectory. Ivinghoe, 8 July 1366.

The inquisition found Robert de Kymberlee the true patron. William was inducted.

Winchester, 31 July 1366

1744. CERTIFICATORY LETTERS received from Simon, bishop of London to whom the bishop had entrusted the exchange of benefices between Stephen Mason, rector of the church of Hambledon, and Thomas Joskin vicar of the church of Chigwell, diocese of London, by mandate, dated Highclere, 7 August 1366. Since the bishop of London authorized the exchange, after the resignation of Stephen from Hambledon, Thomas was admitted, at the presentation of Robert de Loxele, by right of his wife, heiress of the manor of Hambledon. Letter for the induction to the archdeacon of Surrey.

Bishop's Waltham, 20 August 1366

1745. COLLATION by the bishop of the church of St James near Winchester, vacant by the death of the last rector, on Thomas Jurdan priest. Letter for the induction to the archdeacon of Winchester and the dean of Winchester.

Bishop's Waltham, 25 August 1366

1746. INSTITUTION of Arnald Brocaz to the church or chapel of Whipstrode, vacant by the voluntary resignation of Peter Golde, last rector. Letter for the induction to the archdeacon of Winchester.

Bishop's Waltham, 29 August 1366

1747. DISPENSATION granted to Giles de Caldecote, rector of Farley Chamberlayne, deacon, to study at some university in England, without obligation of residence or of receiving the priesthood.

Bishop's Waltham, 29 August 1366

1748. ORDINATION OF THE VICARAGE OF NEWTON VALENCE. Since the rector and brethren of Edington, order of St Augustine, having suffered from epidemics and other calamities, have been granted by the bishop the appropriation of the church of Newton, diocese of Winchester, a fitting

269 portion for the vicar has been reserved. The vicars will retain the area, buildings and garden which the rectors used to occupy, with the wood and 52 acres of arable land, i.e. 40 acres in 3 crofts near the rectory and 12 acres in common with pasture for 4 oxen, 2 horses, 50 ewes with 1 ram in the manor of Newton belonging to the church. The vicars will receive all the emoluments and the profits from the grass in the churchyard; all the greater and lesser tithes from the lands of the hamlets or manors of Newton, of Westwood, 'Klakkes' and 'Marroie', as commonly known; also from the gardens cultivated in the whole parish. They will receive all the offerings and gifts, with the tithe of hay, timber, apples, pears and other titheable fruit, hemp, honey, wax, cheese, milk; the tithe of all mills now standing, or to be constructed; the tithe of lambs, calves, colts, piglets, eggs, geese and doves. Also all mortuaries and customary fees; the tithes from workmen and craftsmen. But the greater profits, rents with the tithe of wool belong to the religious. All the charges on the church and the chapel of Hawkley will be settled thus: the religious will maintain the chancel in repair, provide books, ornaments, vestments (for the repair of these the vicars will be responsible in future), also all taxes levied by the king or the church will be paid by the religious. Papal taxation will be shared equally. Other charges not here listed to be covered by the vicars, as previously by the rectors—repairs to buildings of the vicarage etc. The bishop reserves the right to change this ordination.

Bishop's Waltham, 18 August 1366

270 **1749.** INSTITUTION of John Combare priest as vicar of Newton Valence, now appropriated to the rector and convent of Edington, as apportioned by the bishop, at the presentation of the said religious. To be perpetual vicar residing according the constitutions of Otto and Ottobon. Letter for the induction to the archdeacon of Winchester.

Bishop's Waltham, 8 September 1366

1750. INSTITUTION of Robert Hardwayne priest to the church of Clanfield, vacant, at the presentation of the prioress and convent of Nuneaton. Letter for the induction to the archdeacon of Winchester.

Bishop's Waltham, 20 September 1366

1751. COLLATION by the bishop of the wardenship of the hospital of St Nicholas, Portsmouth, vacant by the voluntary resignation of M. Thomas de Edyngdon' at Bishop's Waltham in the presence of M. Walter de Sevenhampton', M. John Corf, John Beautre and Robert de Lincoln as witnesses, on M. John de Wormenhale, doctor-at-law. Letter for the induction to M. Walter de Sevenhampton', treasurer of Wolvesey and Robert de Lincoln, rector of Alverstoke.

Bishop's Waltham, 2 October 1366

1752. INSTITUTION of Henry de Putlye as perpetual vicar of Catherington, vacant by the voluntary resignation of Robert Hardwyne, lately vicar, in the presence of M. John Corf, J' Beautre, Adam vicar of Selborne and J' Twyforde, at the manor of Bishop's Waltham, at the presentation of the prioress and convent of Nuneaton. To be vicar residing according to the constitutions of Otto and Ottobon. Letter for the induction to the archdeacon of Winchester.

Bishop's Waltham, 2 October 1366

END OF VOLUME I

1. Pages 1–30, i.e. items 1–85, form the register of the bishop-elect. For the circumstances of the provision, as well as a monastic election for a successor to Adam de Orleton, see Introd. and *Reg.Com.Seal*, 5n.2.
3. Clement VI, 7 May 1342–6 December, 1352. of. *CPL*,iii,23,26.
4. John Stratford, archbishop, 1333–48.
12. Adam de Wamberghe had served with Edyndon under Adam de Orleton. See Introd.
18. Sir William Trussell of Cubblesdon, Staffs: father and son have the same name and their careers overlap. This is probably the son, who had been admiral of the fleet west and north of the Thames in 1339 and 1343 (*DNB*), taking part in the battle of Sluys. Trussell was keeper of the lands of Hugh de Sancto Johanne of Basing, when Edmund was aged 4 (*C.Inquis.*,viii,53).
20. *Pargamenorum*. The church of St Martin stood between St Peter Street and Parchment Street.
32. Tandridge: small house of Augustinian canons, Surrey.
36. Prorogation for 3 months of his consecration after lapse of the canonical time and dispensation to retain his benefices for the period, 2 Jan. 1345 (*CPL*,iii,214).
39. For the urgent business, i.e. about papal provisions and anti-papal legislation by Edward III, see *Adam Murimuth Continuatio* (*RS*), 161–2; the text here corroborates that the archbishop paid the money and then wrote to the bishops to order the collection. *Lunt*, 621,639–40.
41. Nicholas Haghman, Haghema or Hagheman. The family were lords of Eversley. Nicholas was rector of Eversley and in 1336 granted away the manor (*VCH. Hants.* iv,33,41)
42. Ralph Kelly, carmelite friar, had been bishop of Leighlin and was transferred to Cashel at this time, which perhaps explains why he was passing through London, cf. *CPR 1345–48*,53.
43. Ivychurch, *Ederosi. ad ecclesiam romanam nullo medio pertinente* an unusual formula; it must mean that his benefice was reserved to the Holy See (late Prof. W. Ullmann).
46. In 1336 Edward III sold for 500 marks the advowson of Kingsclere to William de Montagu, earl of Salisbury, towards the endowment of his augustinian foundation at Bisham Montagu (Berks). This he granted to the priory in 1337, which is the date of the appropriation, see Reg. Orleton, i, fos. 71v–72 and also Introd.
47. Edward III had sent a force to Brittany in March 1342 and himself landed in October. Some towns were beseiged but not captured, while the countryside around Vannes was ravished. Then, because

the English troops were finding their supplies cut off, they were obliged to arrange a truce through the intervention of pope Clement VII at Ste Madeleine, near Vannes. Edward wrote to the pope, 26 May 1345, that Philip had broken the truce and hence he was obliged to declare war. cf. *CCl.R,1346–49*, 559. Request for prayers, 25 Oct.1348; *DNB*, Edward III.

49. R. Sadington, deputy treasurer of the exchequer, 1339–40, chief baron of the exchequer, 1339, and chancellor, 1343–5. *lay fee*, estate of land held in consideration of secular services, as distinct from an ecclesiastical fee.

50. Church of Chalton granted to Nuneaton at its foundation by Robert, earl of Leicester; from it the nuns received 9 marks a year (*VCH.Hants*.iii,109).

57. Ralph Stratford, bishop of London, 1340–55.

61. Robert Wyville, bishop of Salisbury, 1330–75.

63. John Beautre served as notary to Adam de Orleton when bishop of Worcester and also as *scriba* or registrar. He followed the bishop to Winchester in 1333 to hold the same position. Not a university graduate, he was instituted to Freshwater, I.Wight, and later Orleton secured for him a canonry at Exeter. M. John de Usk, a canon lawyer from the diocese of Llandaff, archdeacon of Gloucester, also followed Orleton to Winchester, where he became official. For him Orleton secured a canonry at Lincoln.

67. litigious: a benefice disputable at law.

68. cf. 67.

69. i.e. the Black Prince.

70. Benedict 'Cardicensis' (Sardis or Sardica), prior of the Austin Friars of Norwich, suffragan of Norwich and Winchester.

81. Gilbert de Bruera, dean of St Paul's, 1335–54; cf. *Lunt*, 640.

84. The dispute between the bishops and the archdeacon of Surrey has a long history, cf. *Reg.Pont*.,i,1–2; various references to William Inge in Reg. Adam de Orleton, ii. There were two archdeacons, Winchester and Surrey: the latter had 3 rural deaneries, Southwark, Ewell and Guildford; each archdeacon had his own sequestrator-general. Surrey paid the bishop 20 marks, while the archdeacon of Winchester paid £20. For an analysis of this problem of jurisdiction, see Roy M.Haines 'Adam de Orleton and the Diocese of Winchester', *Journal of Eccles.Hist*.,xxiii (Jan. 1972),1–30. Since the archbishop of Canterbury had been bishop of Winchester, 1323–33, he was a most suitable arbitrator.

This composition, written up by John de Beautre, the notary, is out of place chronologically, but is conveniently inserted between two quires. It is now all very faint and difficult to decipher.

86. John Stratford was the elder brother of Robert: Ralph was probably a son of a sister. All came from Stratford-on-Avon (*DNB*).

92. *evidenti utilitate eiusdem ecclesie*, Council of Lyons,1274–5.

93. cf. 18.

95. Thomas Beck, bishop of Lincoln,1342–47.

96. The reference to the constitutions of the legates Otto and Ottobon which accompanies the oath for residence for vicarages, has been omitted from this point. The constitutions of Otto, legate at London in 1237, and of Ottobon at Lambeth in 1268, enforced residence on those being instituted to vicarages.

97. i.e. university. Boniface VIII by his constitution *Cum ex eo*, 1298, permitted short absence from a benefice for study at a university for a maximum of seven years. See Introd. and reference there to L. E. Boyle, *Pastoral Care*.

98. litigious, see 67.

100. in virtue of obedience, cf. 84.

103. Edward de Kendale, knight, lord of Shalden, near Alton; keeper of the peace in Hertfordshire (*CPR,1345–48*, 111).

104. Thomas de Lisle, bishop of Ely, 1345–62.

105. Thomas Beauchamp, earl of Warwick, 1329–69, marshal of England, took part in military expeditions in company of the Black Prince.

106. formula: probably refers to insistence on obedience on the part of the archdeacon of Surrey.

109. Wigtor or Weighton (Yorks).

110. Matthew Fitz Herbert, lord of Wolverton, near Basingstoke (*VCH*).

111. Pagham (Sussex), an archiepiscopal peculiar, with a dean. Raymond Pelegrini, papal tax collector from 1343, with his brother, natives of Gascony, then under the English king. He held various benefices in England, see *Lunt, Acc.*, xxxi.

Gaucelin de Eauze, one of two cardinals sent to England on a peace mission (McKisack, *Fourteenth Century*, 40)

112. Ogbourne St George, priory of Bec. Richard de Beusevalle, or Beauseville, prior from 1322 (*VCH*).

113. John de Pontissera founded this chapel or hospital or college, near Wolvesey, dedicated to St Elizabeth of Hungary—for a provost with 3 deacons and 3 subdeacons, also 6 boys for singing (*Reg.Pont.*,i,xxxviii).

117. in Norman French. Maud de Spine was abbess of Nunnaminster from 1337–49 (*VCH*). Henceforward Nunnaminster will be generally used for the sake of simplicity, instead of 'abbey of St Mary, Winchester'.

119. Ashstead must be a mistake; see 118.

122. Hurstbourne Tarrant. The advowson of Hurstbourne was attached to the prebend of Burbage. Since the prebendary had to reside in Salisbury, he had a perpetual vicar (*VCH,Hants.*,iv,323–4).

123. Inkpenne: this family, originally from Berkshire, is heavily indexed in *VCH*; they held much land from Wherwell abbey (*VCH,Hants*,iv,406n.).

Middleton, now called Longparish, belonged to Wherwell. the parish church, in which there was a prebend of Middleton, was in the gift of the nuns (*VCH,Hants.*,iv,409).

126. The lord of Yaverland was in charge of the defence of the I.Wight and was killed there in 1340 (Murimuth, *Continuatio Chronicarum*,

RS, 109n., where his name is incorrectly given as Peter). There is mention of his death in Reg. Orleton,i, fo.168.

127. William de Clinton, created earl of Huntingdon in 1337, was admiral of the ships of the Cinque Ports and in this capacity took part in the battle of Sluys. In July of this year he sailed from Portsmouth with the king to invade France; the earl was wounded and returned to England by mid-summer, bringing with him the French plan for an invasion of England (*Murimuth, Contin. Chron.*, 205, 363). This was published at Paul's Cross, 14 August 1346. This is precisely the date of the dispensation.

134. The church of Chaldon was always in the gift of the Covert family, as lords of the manor from the time of Henry II (*VCH,Surrey*,iv,189).

139. Edmund, earl of Kent: Edmund of Woodstock, youngest son of Edward I and so uncle of Edward III. He married Margaret, sister of Thomas, lord Wake of Liddell (cf.143); she died in 1349. Edmund had been arrested, charged with complicity in a plot against the king, and executed at Winchester, 1330 (*DNB*).

142. FitzHugh: a family connected with Odiham, where there is a Down Farm and a Down House (*VCH,Hants.*,iv,98).

143. cf. 139n.

148. de la Mare: a family associated with Crawley (*VCH,Hants.*,iii,410).

149. There is a big cross in the margin, probably to call attention rather than to delete. The bishop's absence ends by 152.

150. cf. 137.

152. Cevere—difficult initial. Marston, prob. N. Marston, Bucks.

153. The church of Odiham was granted for the use of the chancellor of Salisbury by Henry I, c.1115 (*VCH,Hants.*,iv,97).
    Elias de Sancto Albano, chancellor from 1340.

157. The abbey of St Peter, St Paul and St Erkenwald, Chertsey. Abbot John de Rutherwyk, 1307–46. Leave to elect granted, 19 Jan. 1347 (*CPR,1345–8*,223). Abbot John de Benham, 1347–61. Royal assent, 28 January 1347; restoration of temporalities, 15 February.

158. *Chertsey Cartulary* (Surrey Rec. Soc.,1958), xxxiii, xlviii. Called *de Novo Loco*, because rebuilt on a new site (*VCH,Surrey*,iii,365) Newark, near Pyrford, Surrey. Roger de Enham had resigned, 1 July 1344; John de Barton elected, 2 July 1344 (*Dugdale*,vi,383).

162. Royal assent to the election, 28 Jan. 1347 (*CPR,1345–48*,243); mandate to deliver the temporalities (*ibid.*,250), 15 Feb. 1347.

163. Sir John de Handlo held the manor of Knight's Enham by right of his wife, Maud Burnell. He died in 1346, having granted the advowson of the church to Queen Philippa's foundation of Queen's College, Oxford, in 1345. The heir was his wife's son, John, the 3rd lord Lovel, who himself died in 1347. (*VCH,Hants.*,iv,377–8; *Inquis.p.m.*, 20 Edw.III)

164. The name is rather *Roulge* here, *Boulge* earlier in the Register.

165. At All Saints there was a *precentoria*, a small group of clerks under a precentor or chanter. Later often referred to as a chantry (*VCH,Hants.*,iii,525). For the grant by the king, 6 June 1346, the

see of Winchester being vacant, see *CPR,1345–48*,95; then revoked, 3 December, as the king had no right to present.

166. For Raymond Pelegrini, see 111n.

      Gillingham, Dorset. The church was appropriated to a prebendal stall in Shaftesbury abbey; the prebendary employed a vicar, see *Reg.Roger Martival* (Cant. and York Soc.)ii,247, where in 1319 Richard de Lusteshal was the prebendary.

      Hospital of St Cross: William de Edyndon had himself been Master from 1345–6, while High Treasurer of England (*VCH,Hants.*,ii,195). Pelegrini was provided to the mastership (*C.Pap.*iii,185), but of this there is no question here. For papal reservation to him on its voidance by Edyndon, also *C.Pap.R*,i,51,90.

169. Probably North Waltham, as the archdeacon of Surrey is to induct. The priory of Eye (Norfolk) depended on Bernay and became independent in 1385, hence it survived until the Dissolution.

170. John, earl of Warenne, Surrey and Strathern, lord of Bromfield and Yale, 1286–1347 (d.30 June). For Bromfield and Yale, see *Cymmrodorion Record Society*,ii (1924), extent of Bromfield and Yale, Flintshire.

171. Mapledurwell, 3m. from Basingstoke. The foundress, Ela widow of Philip Basset, granted the bishop the right to present to the chapel, which is still dependent on Newnham (*VCH,Hants.*,iv,152).

      E' de Chakynden: the Christian name is tucked into the margin: ?Ehe.

172. Burgh (Surrey)?. The name is in the margin: Berugh'.

      Henry, earl of Lancaster, 1299?–1361, had been lieutenant and captain of Aquitaine, 1345–1 February 1347 and in June set sail for Gascony (*DNB*).

174. Boys or Roys.

178. Walter Reynolds, archbishop of Canterbury, 1308–28.

      Clapham (Surrey) now within Battersea. Thomas Romayn founded other chantries, K.L.Wood-Legh *Perpetual Chantries in Britain* (1965),24n.,112.

181. Drungewick, manor of the bishops of Chichester, in parish of Wisborough Green (Sussex).

      Robert Stratford, bishop of Chichester, 1337–62.

183. Laurence Hastings, earl of Pembroke (1318?–1348), his military career included the expedition to Aquitaine and Gascony.

186. cf.103, which shows this to be Walton-on-Thames.

189. For the straits of this foundation, see Introd.

190. 'Isham', probably Itchen Abbas (Hants).

192. For Dunton Waylett, Essex, church and manor of Bec, see M. Morgan *The English lands of the Abbey of Bec* (1946).

194. William de Monte Acuto, earl of Salisbury, d.1344, took a prominent part in the downfall of Mortimer; earl of Salisbury, 1337. Founded Bisham, where he was buried. Edward III granted him the church of Shalfleet, I.Wight, which the earl gave to Bisham.

195. South Malling, just north of Lewes, a college of canons in a vast possession of the archbishopric in the diocese of Chichester. The church of Stanmer was the centre of the deanery and annexed to the penitentiary (I. J. Churchill *Canterbury Administration*,i,76–7).
    Walkingstead, the old name of Godstone, Surrey (*Oxf. Place-Names*).

196. For Tandridge, see 32n.

199. St Nicholas of Coldabbey. *Stow* places this church near Old Fish Street and towards the west end of Knightriders Street, with the meaning of 'standing in a cold place, as cold harbour' (p.18,316).

202. Richard Vaughan, see 84 and Introd.

209. Isabella of Lancaster, of royal blood. She was the fourth daughter of Henry earl of Lancaster and grand-daughter of Edmund Crouchback, son of Henry III.

212. Ogbourne, see 192n.

215. The Winchester church is now said to be dedicated to St Anastasius, but the readings vary in the medieval registers, perhaps favouring St Anastasia. The Hereford church of St Andrew was destroyed in the Civil War in 1645. The gateway of St Andrews, or St Owens, was destroyed in 1786. St Owen's church stood just outside the city wall, near St Owen's Street.

216. William de Cusance, lord of Silchester, keeper of the Wardrobe (*VCH,Hants,* iv,53).

218–221. Chapel of St Elizabeth, see 113n.

217. Nicholas Devenish, d.1351, had interests in the wool trade. As mayor of Winchester he repaired the city fortifications after the attack on Southampton. He held various lands: Westbury in E. Meon, Greatham and Emsworth and Sutton in Wonston (*VCH,Hants.*,v,4;ii,137,456).

223. Blaise Doublel, presented as prior, 1336 (Reg. Orleton,2a,fo,53v). resigned 1348 (cf.262).
    For Hugh Gernon, the founder of the church of Chale, I.Wight, in 1114 and the endowment with half the tithes, see *Cartulary of Carisbrooke*, ed. S.F.Hockey (1981),15.

224. Ralph de Stafford, first earl (1299–1372) had a distinguished military career: 1345 appointed seneschal of Aquitaine, took part in the Gascony campaign, fought at Crecy, present at the surrender of Calais (*DNB*).

225. Bersted, part of the great archiepiscopal lands in West Sussex, cf. 195n.

227. William de Monte Acuto, see 194n.
    For the presentation by the king as custodian, see *CPR,1345–48*,438. By papal provision, Seys was canon of St Davids, being dispensed from illegitimacy (*CPL,*iii,316), dated 18 Oct.1349.

228. Isabella de Lancaster, mentioned for the first time with her illustrous name.

229. Abbey of St Vigor, Cérisy-le Forêt (Manche), The register names the priory, the largest alien house in Hampshire, Sherborne or Sherborne St John. Normally the prior of an alien house was

nominated by the mother-house, cf. *Cal.Fine R*,vi,83, referring back to *C.Fine R.*,v,262.

239. i.e. Farleigh Wallop. In 1328 the manor was settled on William de la Zouche of Ashby de la Zouche; Robert was his son. The manor was alienated early in the XVc. (*VCH,Hants*,iii,364,366).

240. The Old Temple (*Vetus Templum*) stood "beyond the bars"; it fell into ruin by 1184, but was not demolished until the XVIc. The inn of the bishops of Lincoln adjoined this Old Temple (*Stow*,390). Not to be confused with Lincoln's Inn, which was the house of the earl of Lincoln.

Missenden (Bucks), house of Augustinian canons.

242. For Ellingham priory, see *VCH,Hants*,ii,229–33.

243. Alverstone in Brading, I.Wight. *VCH,Hants*,v does not seem to know this free-chapel, yet as late as 1520 William Champeneis was admitted (Reg.Fox,iv,fo.ll). For the Umfraville family, which took its name from the Norman place of that name, see *VCH,Hants*,v,160n.

244. The church of St Peter *de Albo Pane*, St Peter Whitbread, in the High Street. Lord Darcy of Knaith (Lincs), d.1347, steward of the King's household, with a son, also John. He brought back the new of the victory at Crecy (*Chron.Murimuth*, 217).

246. Eleanor, widow of Guy Ferre, retained $\frac{1}{3}$ of the manor of Buckland and she presented to the church after 1346. The family had owned the manor and the advowson since 1293 (*VCH,Surrey*,iii,173).

249. Papal dispensation to hold a benefice and the wardenship, aged 18, dated 19 Nov. 1348 (*C.Pap.*,i,144).

253. Ratification of the estate of M.John de Usk, king's clerk, as parson of Cheriton by collation of the bishop (*CPR,1348–1350*,198).

255. cf. *C.Pap.R.*,i,170.

256. Richard Fitz Alan II (1307–76) held the custody of Rochester castle in 1341 (*VCH,Hants*,iii,158); served in the Crecy campaign with Edward III. In 1348 and 1350 was on a commission to treat with the pope at Avignon (*DNB*).

259. John de Grey, lord of Codnor in Derbyshire. His great-grandfather had been granted the manor of Tunworth on his marriage.

260. The Valence family held land at Wield, often in dispute (*VCH*).

261. Hospital for local poor and wayfarers (*Med. Rel.Houses*,359).

262. Carisbrooke priory depended on Lyre abbey, in diocese of Evreux, which nominated the priors. Fr Blaise Doublel had been prior since 1336 (cf.223).

264. Hospital of St Mary Magdalen, Kingston-on-Thames, for the poor, founded in 1304 by Edward Lovekin, a citizen of London originating from Kingston. The chapel is now the gymnasium of the grammar-school (*VCH,Surrey*,ii,125;iv,511).

267. For Henry, earl of Lancaster, see 172.

269. Raymond Pelegrini was to be provided to the prebend of Bishopstone, 1 Feb. 1350 by pope Clement VI, on the death of Peter Raymund (*Lunt,Acc.*,95) Ropistagno, i.e. St Rabastens (Tarn)

269B. Chardstock, manor of the bishops of Salisbury.

271. Premonstratensian canons. Peter de Wynton was the eighth abbot.
273. The Cormailles family held the manor of Thruxton. In 1346 Isabella, widow of John de Cormailles, held there two parts of a fee. She was granted a private oratory at Tallemache in Wherwell (ii,54).
   A marginal heading in French here.
276. Goldhill, seven miles south of Shaftesbury, Dorset, added by bishop John Trillek; see J. W. Tonkin 'The Palaces of the bishop of Hereford', *Woolhope Naturalists Field Club*,xlii(1976),53–64.
279. Marginal note: *ad Instanciam W' de Hurle*, at the request of W' de Hurle.
284. *Cum ex eo*, for this see Introd.
289. Roger Gervais was holding land in Bighton (Hants) in 1346; his son granted all his land to William Wykeham and so it passed to Winchester College (*VCH,Hants*,iii,39).
291. *Stanham Episcopi*, i.e. North Stoneham was Stoneham Abbatis (of Hyde); South Stoneham was Episcopi.
293. Stratfield Turgis was held by the Turgis family since c.1270. John Turgys held one fifth of a knight's fee in 1349 (*VCH,Hants*,iv,63). The name is Norman but of Scandinavian origin (*Oxf.Place Names*).
294. Dene or Deane Maudut.
297. Little Yarmouth, on the southern bank of the Yare, today known as Southtown. Most of Little Yarmouth has sunk and lies under Breydon Water.
298. The custody of the lands of William Latimer had been granted to Queen Philippa, who thus presented Wotton (*VCH,Surrey*,iii,163).
300. For Isabella of Lancaster, see 209.
301. For the church and Lord Darcy, see 244.
302. Knighton Gorges in the parish of Newchurch. The Gorges family came from the Cotentin peninsula. Theobald was prominent in the defence of the I.Wight against the French.
303. Elizabeth de Burgh, the lady of Clare, grand-daughter of the foundress of Clare College, Cambridge, also Elizabeth.
305. Nutfield, near Reigate.
306. Orton: several places have this name, here probably Hunts.
307. For the patron, see 41n. John de Valoyne or Valoignes, lord of Cliddesden, which after him passed to the Wallop family (*VCH,Hants.*,iv,146–7). John called the Marshall is John de Frollebury in 247.
308. The free chapel of St. Thomas at Frobury in Kingsclere.
309. Langton: at least three places bear this name in Leics.
   For Ralph, sixth earl of Stafford, see 224n.
314. John de Wynton held land in Penton Mewsey.
315. Laurence de Bremshett or Bramshott, held $\frac{1}{4}$ knight's fee in Elden (*VCH,Hants*,iv,477).
316. i.e. chapel of St Nicholas within the Castle. The d'Evercy family were lords of Standen, I.Wight.

317. The church of St Pancras stood where St Pancras land joined Wongar Street. It survived the great decline of the XIVc.; the parish was united with St Maurice in 1526.

316. The Brune family have been at Rowner since 1277, by grant of Edward I (*VCH*).

323. cf.113n.

325. The des Roches family were lords of Steventon.

327. In 1343 Sir Andrew Braunche had purchased the rights of Henry Stoughton to the manor of Peper Harow for £100. The advowson went with the manor (*VCH,Surrey*,iii,50–1).

332. First mention in Edyndon Reg. i of the Black Death.

334. Thomas de Bradwardine, the distinguished ecclesiastic, philosopher and mathematician, chancellor of St Pauls, 1337; elected archbishop of Canterbury. 1348, but election quashed by the king; consecrated at Avignon, 10 July 1349, but died of the plague on his return to England. These dates explain why he could not carry out Orleton's commission (*Emden*).

344. For the disputed advowson, see *VCH,Hants,*iv,524.

347. For this free chapel in the parish of Bossington and for the manor, see *VCH,Hants*,iv,492–3.

357. Tyngehurst, now Fingest, Bucks, a manor of the bishops of Lincoln.

362. There was in early times a chapel at Wellsworth, pensionary to the priory of Southwick (*VCH,Hants*,iii,110).

363. Church of St George *juxta barram*: next to the bar, the gate, cf. Temple Bar and the Bar, Southampton.

364. For Edmund, earl of Kent, see 139n.

366. A chapel dependent on Whitchurch. The Sifrewast family were still in Freefolk early in the XIVc., though Henry Husee had acquired the manor and advowson in 1269 (*VCH,Hants*,iv,282,284). In 1346 Henry Husee held $\frac{1}{2}$ a fee in Freefolk.

371. For Nicholas Devenish, see 217n.

374. Roger Normand held the advowson of South Tidworth, d.1349.

377. For Sir John Grey, see 259n.

383. St Mary without Bishopsgate, or St Mary Spital, was a hospital, yet a conventual house of Austin canons (*Med.Rel.Houses*); it was refounded in 1235 and called the New Hospital: *prioratus Novi Hospitalis* (*Dugdale*,vi,623).

384. Mary de Langressch held land in Farley Chamberlayne. Her first marriage was to John de la Barton; this was a second marriage (*VCH,Hants*,iv,443)

389. *prior et conventus Novi Loci* without Bishopsgate, see 383n. William de Bergeveny, chancellor, 1341–5.

392. See 178,179. The chantry was to have been established at Clapham.

398. *Novi Loci*, i.e. Newark, Surrey.
     Clandon Regis, i.e. West Clandon; the advowson had always descended with the manor and so with the Weston family in XIVc. (*VCH,Surrey*,iii,347,349).

399. Bishop Richard le Poor in 1209 acquired the church of Amport from Adam de Port, in whose gift it had been and appropriated it to the dean and chapter of Chichester (*VCH,Hants*,iv,344).

400. College of Marwell in Owslebury, Hants, founded by bishop Henry de Blois for 4 priests, to pray for the king and the bishops of Winchester. One of the four was elected prior and ordered a conventual life (*VCH,Hants*,ii,211).

402. For the Valoyne family, see 307n.

404. John de Offord, archbishop of Canterbury by papal provision, 24 Sept. 1348, after failing to secure election by the conventual chapter of Canterbury. He had shared the responsibilities of government with Edyndon during Edward III's long absences from the country; he died of the plague, 20 May 1349 (*Emden*).

405. For Ralph earl of Stafford, see 224n.

410. Hartley Waspail, where there is a brass in the chancel of John Waspail, patron, d.1448 (*VCH.Hants*,iv,44).

413. The manor of Faringdon was part of the honour of Bosham, Sussex, and so belonged to the bishops of Exeter.

417. For Nicholas de Hagheman, see 41n.
     Abinger (Abingeworth) had two rectories, sharing equal halves (*Wyk.Reg.*ii,380).

425. *VCH,Hants*,ii is in error for the date of the election and for the spelling of the name of the new prior.

428. Catherine, daughter of William de Grandison, married William de Monteacuto. She died in 1349 or 1354 and was buried at Bisham (*DNB*).

431. cf. Mandate to deliver the temporalities to Richard de Staunton, 10 March 1349 (*CPR,1348-50*,265).

436. The Cistercian abbey of Netley was founded in the parish of Hound, but it never held the advowson of the church, which remained with the Tironian priory of Hamble until all the possessions of the little priory were acquired by William de Wykeham for the college at Winchester (*VCH,Hants*,iii,478).

441. The free chapel of Briddlesford in Arreton parish. Elizabeth was the widow of Bartholomew de Insula, d.1345 (*VCH,Hants*,v,172).

442. The manor chapel of the Kingston family became a small parish church, and still survives.

443. Whipstrode St James, in Fareham, a free chapel of the lords of the manor, for the des Roches family. It was demolished in XVIc. (*VCH,Hants*,iii,215).

451. For the transfer of the greater tithes of the church of St Katherine to the nuns of Nuneaton, see *VCH,Hants*,iii,101.

455. The rectory of Wanborough, Surrey, at the presentation of the Cistercians of Waverley, see *Dugdale*,v,240.

456. The free chapel of St Mary Magdalen, East Parley (*Reg.Wyk.*i,93; *VCH,Hants*,v,108).

457. Elingdon, a lost place in Wroughton, Wilts, where the prior of St Swithuns had a pension (*Reg.Roger Martinval*,iii,158,795).

464. Collation given papal confirmation on its voidance by the death of Richard de Lustehulle, dated 14 June 1349 (*CPap.R*,i,165; *CPL*,iii,350).
468. Roger de Tichborne was the founder of the chantry within the manorial chapel of St Andrew. For the rents of £4, see *VCH,Hants*,ii,22;iii,338; cf. *CCIR.,1354–60*,329.
471. St Peter *supra Cheshull*: St Peter Chesil in the Strand or Chesil Street. MS reads 'archdeacon of Surrey', perhaps in error.
473. The advowson had a complicated history, see *VCH,Hants*,iv,82–3.
483. For John de Grey, see 259n.
485. Nothing was known of this church until the abbot presented to it, t. John de Stratford, bishop, 1323–33 (*VCH,Hants*,iv,325).
487. The advowson of Oxted belonged to the lords of the manor. As early as the XIIIc. the Stangrave family held land in Blechingley, called the manor of Stangrave and also the advowson of the church (*VCH,Hants*,iv,275).
489. For William de la Zouch, see 239n.
490. The advowson was in the d'Abernon family as lords of the manor since before the XIIIc. (*VCH,Surrey*,iii,73,77).
491. In 1317 Roger de Ingepenne received papal permission to found a chantry in the cemetery of Nunnaminster. It was to be served by 2 priests, a chaplain (491) and a guardian (492), the patronage remaining with the family (*VCH,Hants*,ii,123; *Cal.Pap.Pet.*, ii,160).
495. In 1306 the manor of Little Bookham passed from Mary de Braose to Ralph de Camoys, and the advowson followed the manor (*VCH,Surrey*,iii,338).
498. This church had been appropriated to the nuns of the priory; insufficient data to give a date.
501. The free chapel in Cole Henley, in Whitchurch, was a manor chapel originally. The manor had been conveyed to Peter de Whatteford in 1330. His son and heir, Peter, presented to the chapel (*VCH,Hants*,iv,302,304).
502. For Newark, see 158.
507. For Theobald Russel, see 126n.
509. The advowson of Headley belonged to Westminster abbey from the beginning of the XIVc., but Nicholas de Plesey is here presenting (*VCH,Surrey*,iii,292–3).
514. Joan Gervays, not included among the abbesses in *VCH*.
517. The family held West Deane, in Tytherley from the XIIIc. Sybil, as widow of Laurence, married John de Scures (cf.526). When she died in 1349, the estate passed to a posthumous son, Laurence (*VCH,Hants*,iv,521).
519. For the precentory, see 165n.
525. church of Kingsgate: either St Swithun above Kingsgate, or St Nicholas outside Kingsgate.
526. The Scures held the manor from early times. Scures, from Escures in Normandy.
531. Barton oratory in Whippingham.
536. see 134.

538. Southfleet, in Kent. The advowson is not mentioned until it was leased to Sir John Cobeham in 1291, since when it continued in his family (*VCH,Surrey*,iii,395).

542. St James, the most important church outside Westgate. Only the cemetery survives, now the Catholic cemetery.
St Martin outside Westgate, or in Wodestreet, or *de fossato*, in the ditch.

544. Royal assent to the election, 7 May 1349 (*CPR,1348–50*,285).

547. Sir John Pultenoy, city merchant, four times mayor of London. In 1332 he founded the chapel of Corpus Christi in the church of St Laurence, Candlewick Street (i.e. Cannon Street), hence its name: St Laurence Pountney. This was enlarged to form a college for a master, 13 priests and 4 choristers. There was a Poultney House and Lane. Sir John acquired the manor of Poplar in 1347, dying that same year the Monday after Trinity Sunday (*DNB;Stow*,212–3).

549. cf. *CPR,1348–50*,293, dated 28 May 1349.

550. Most probably the church of St Swithun.

551. Cuddington: the church was granted to Merton priory early in XIIc (*VCH, Surrey*,iii,270.) The family name was Cuddington, alias de Malden.

553. Jewry Street, *in vico judeorum*.

554. The chapel of the H. Spirit or of St M. Magdalen at Sandown or Sandon, had t. Henry II 6–8 chaplains. In 1338 only the warden survived (*Med. Rel.Houses* 389;*VCH,Surrey*,ii,118–9;iii,449).

556. *Le Neve* spells Heriad, prior since 1328.

558. *prout arctati temporis brevitate*, perhaps because of the approach of Holy Week (see 561), or on account of mortality and distress.

572. The advowson of Godalming was granted to Salisbury cathedral before 1158 (*Reg.St Osmund, RS*,i,203).
Arnald appears as cardinal and dean of Salisbury *infra* 954 and *CClR. 1346–68*,2. *Le Neve, Salisbury* (1962) gives the dean as Raynald Ursinus, who is followed by James Ursinus and Thomas Ursinus. cf. *C.Pap.L*,iii,236.

573. The manor of Dibden was in three parts, the lords taking turn to present. The Dibden family was one of these (*VCH,Hants*,iv,658).

575. In 509 *supra*, Headley was at the presentation of Nicholas Placy, knt.

581. The chapel was in the manor of Shiere Vachery or Shiere cum Vacchery and Canleigh, now Shere. The chapel of Vachery in which chaplains were appointed from 1302, was the north transept of the parish church of St Nicholas and dedicated to the H.Trinity. (*VCH,Surrey*,iii,91).

582. The second portion with 'Robert' suggests the conflation of two entries.

592. Royal assent, 4 June 1349; restoration of temporalities, 14 June (*CPR, 1348–50*,302,304).

600. The family name is usually 'de Colemere'.

608. Merrow, Surrey.

611. For the portion of St Laurence in Romsey, see 619n., cf. *CPR,1348–50*,328, for 18 June 1349.
613. The priory in Essex, founded by King Knut, which later became augustinian.
614. *Stowe Sancti Edwardi*, today Stow-on-the-Wold *(Oxf. Place Names)*.
617. For Ralph earl of Stafford, see 224n.
619. The church of Timsbury was a prebend of the conventual church of Romsey, which with the tithes of Imber in Wiltshire and $\frac{1}{3}$ of the tithes of Romsey made up the portion of St Laurence. The prebendary normally nominated a vicar for Timsbury.
622. John de Kenne held a messuage in Stanbridge Earls from 1329 *(VCH,Hants*,iv,458); also the manor of Pittleworth, with the advowson of the church by grant from Agnes Danvers *(Ibid.*iv,492).
624. Katherine, widow of Henry Husee,d.1349; she held the manor of Freefolk for life *(VCH,Hants*,iv,282).
    Bisyndon, ?Bishampton.
626. Froyle had been appropriated to Nunnaminster by bishop Adam de Orleton. It received papal confirmation to the abbey, 6 Dec.1346 *(C.Pap.L*,iii,225). For opposition from the bishop and the archbishop of Canterbury, see *C.Pap.Pet.*i,122.
631. Abbots Bromley, Staffs, i.e. abbey of Burton.
632. Couma Gervaise: the reference in the *VCH,Hants*,ii, should be to Reg. Orleton, i,fo.46b, where her name is Co . . . a de Mareys. The name Couma, Covina or Conina is unusual, but in any case the initial *Co* is quite clear.
636. Hartley Mauditt, which had passed by marriage in 1298 to Henry, earl of Lancaster.
637. Thomas de Drokenford, i.e. Droxford, Hants, would have been a nephew of the bishop of Bath and Wells, d.1329.
639. The Reg. reads clearly Gerard; *VCH,Hants*,iv,145 gives Gerald. Gerard had married Elizabeth de St John and so became lord of Bramley.
640. Lainston was not a primitive parish. John de Wynton had held the manor since 1342, and so presents. The parish probably owed its origin to the jealousy of the de Caritate and Sparsholt families *(VCH,Hants*,iii,444,447).
645. For the papal dispensation, 14 June 1349, see *C.Pap.L*,iii,330.
646. The church of Ellisfield had been in the patronage of the des Roches family since the end of the XIIIc. There had been two churches there, of St Martin and of All Saints *(VCH,Hants*,iii,363).
647. John de Uvedale had acquired $\frac{2}{3}$ of the manor of Titsey and the advowson of the church in 1305. There had been a dispute about the advowson, which in 1322 the king confirmed to John de Uvedale *(VCH,Surrey*,iv,331,334).
650. Nicholas de Hagheman: his ancestor, Alan, held Winslade in 1275; Nicholas in 1346 was said to be holding 1 hide in Winslade and so presented to the church *(VCH,Hants*,iv,179).

651. South Waltham, i.e. Bishops Waltham. The king recovered his presentation against the bishop, 15 Oct. 1349 and presented Roger, king's clerk (*CPR,1348–50*,449). But the dispute continued (*ibid.,1350–54*,29).

662. See of Canterbury vacant. John de Stratford had died, 23 Aug. 1348. John de Offord, d.20 May, 1349 before his consecration. Thomas de Bradwardine was provided to Canterbury, 19 June and consecrated the same day, but died 25/26 Aug. The successor Simon Islip was provided 7 Oct. and consecrated 20 Dec.

676. Hamo de Hethe, Ben. bishop of Rochester, 1317–52. Itchen will be Itchen Stoke, cf.651.

679. John de Sancto Philiberto had married the co-heiress of Edward de St John, lord of Sherborne St John, d.1348. His heirs were his two sisters and John de Sancto Philiberto married Margaret, the elder. The lords of the manor were the patrons.

702. For John de Grey, see 259.

704. Thomas de Breoso (Braose) was lord of Bramber. He sold the overlordship of Little Bookham in 1324 to Ralph de Camoys and the advowson went with it (*VCH,Surrey*,iv,335,338).

708. John of Woodstock, earl of Kent, and brother of the Fair Maid of Kent.

710. Hartley Wintney, cf.498.

718. The Cluniac nuns of St Mary de la Pré (*de Pratis*), Northants, had a church at Fyfhyde (given in *Dugdale* as in Bucks), in what was known as Wallop Fifehead, in Middle Wallop, Hants. The nuns had been endowed with Nether Wallop (*VCH,Hants*, iv,525,527).

719. i.e. St Nicholas outside Kingsgate.

729. John de Schirburn', a London vintner, had only recently acquired the manor. When he fell rapidly in debt, the manor was assigned to his creditors.

742. The bishop received a pardon, 2 Dec. 1347, for acquiring the manor of Tymbresbury and the advowson of the church without licence (*CPR,1345–48*,435).

746. The Randulfs held Parva Pakenham, or Randalls in Leatherhead.

749. Eva, widow of Edward St John. They had bought the manor of Litchfield in 1315. She died in 1354 (*VCH,Hants*,iv,268).

750. For Nicholas de Hagheman, see 650.

751. The presentation came to Thomas Haket by his marriage to one of the Clamorgan heiresses; the idiot heir appears in 759.

752. For Reginald or Raynald de filiis Ursini (Orsini), see 572.

761. Thytho, ?Tysoe, Warw.

Nicholas de Plessy (Placy), knt., was lord of Headley. During a vacancy Nicholas tried to claim the patronage against Westminster abbey, and here actually presents (*VCH,Surrey*,iii,281,293).

Received at the registry, i.e. not necessarily entered up.

762. 'Wolkestede', now Godstone, Surrey. Lesnes or Westwood, Kent, augustinian canons.

764. Hospital of St John Baptist, Andover, f.1247.

767. Of the long series of Thomas West in (*VCH,Hants*,ii,640 must refer to the one who died before 1343, of Hempston Cantilupe, Devon, to whom Queen Philippa gave the manor of Lyndhurst (*CPR,1330-4*, 408; *VCH,Hants*,iv,631). Then presumably a son Thomas West granted the advowson of Newenton to the bishop, 28 Oct. 1363 cf. *CClR,1360-4*,552.

780. Or Mare, More.

788. Arundel, alien priory of the Norman abbey of Séez.

808. M. Walter Beneit, Benet, of dioc. of Salisbury. He will be granted licence to study for 7 years (811). Doctor of canon law by 1453. For his career and pluralism, see *Emden*.

809. M. John de Lech, from North Leach, Glos. Chancellor of Oxford University, 1338. For his extraordinary career and library, see *Emden*. In this register he becomes rector of Arreton (444-5). The papal dispensation to hold two incompatible benefices, shows him to be also rector of Harrow, canon of Salisbury, Hereford, Bosham, Abergwili and St Pauls in London, with the free chapels of Bockingfield and Newstead, Kent.

813. Simon Islip, archbishop, 1349-1366.

   For Edward de Chardestoke, see *C.Pap.Pet.*,i,327.

822. Thomas de Westcote. Lord of the manor only since about 1339 (*VCH,Hants*,iv,423).

825. Hatch Beauchamp: Robert de Bello Campo was holding Hatch before 1215 (*Oxf. Place Names*).

828. For John de Grey, see 259n.

834. Licence was granted, 12 March 1351, to convey the prebend of Edington, in the conventual church of Romsey, to the bishop in view of his foundation Edington (*CPR,1350-54*, 64).

839. There was a chapel called Eastrop chapel, reckoned as in the parish of Basingstoke, but disendowed in 1536. Humphrey de Bohun was the overlord of the manor, which was held by the Brayboeuf family as lords of Eastrop (*VCH,Hants*,iv,148-9).

841. For the chapel at Frobury, see 308n.

842. Marginal index in error: *Licencia studii*.

   John Malwayn is to be connected with More Malwyn in Romsey, which Thomas de Aspale was to grant to Malwyn in 1353. He died in 1361, seized of the manor of Osborne, I. Wight. Evidently he was a city man investing capital in Hampshire property (*VCH,Hants*,iv,453;v,200)

848. For John de Sancto Philiberto, see 679.

   Walter de Haywode of the family which held land in Stratfield Saye for 300 years, which Walter was to sell. Now represented by Heywoods Farm (*VCH,Hants*,iv,60).

850. There is no mention of the earl of Stafford as patron in *VCH,Surrey*,iv,338, but of the priory of Bermondsey.

853. Ford: archiepiscopal manor in Heath, Kent.

857. The vicar's name is missing.

   Today the church of Empshott is dedicated to the Holy Rood; in *Reg.Wyk.* it is St Laurence.

860. Northangre, i.e. Nuthanger, a tithing in Kingsclere.

863. Premonstratensian abbey, Sussex.
866. At the end of the XIIIc. the Crown conferred the patronage of the priory on the earls of Lancaster. Severely hit by the Black Death (*VCH,Hants*,ii,173).
874, 875. Dispensation for 7 years appears for the first time.
883. *C.Pap.Pet.*,i,208.
894. William Zouche, archbishop, 1342–1352.
    John de Grey, baron Grey of Rotherfield, 1300–1359, of Rotherfield Greys (Oxon), constantly employed by Edward III in his wars, held property in Rotherfield and Sculcoates.
    Tiron in error for Le Bec Heluin, cf.740.
896. Chapel of St M. Magdalen, see 264
    ?Drainford.
    This arrangement was revised after another dispute with the vicar (*VCH,Surrey*,iv,513.).
899. For Raymond Pelegrini, see 111.
    Mayfield, Sussex, archiepiscopal manor.
904. Andrew Peverel, knt., to be associated with Barton Peverel, in South Stoneham. He married Katherine, widow of Henry de Hungtingfield of Freefolk (*VCH,Hants*,iii,486;iv,282-3).
906. There were chapels at both East and West Stratton. The chantry chapel of St John Baptist was at the presentation of the Wayte family (*VCH,Hants*,iii,394)
909. There were therefore only eight canons surviving.
916. Royal assent to the election, 10 Nov. 1352 (*CPR,1350-54*, 360).
921. Royal assent and mandate to deliver the temporalities (*CPR,1350-54*,360-1), 10 Nov. and 26 Nov. 1352.
928. This letter is repeated in different form in 1050.
928. cf. 900 and 926. Ratification of the estate of king's clerk, M. John Leech as parson of Crondall (*CPR,1350-54*, 417), 15 March 1353.
929. i.e. Edmund de Derby (*CPR,1350-54*, 322).
931. John Lent', probably the same person as John de Exon' in 765.
931. James atte Oki held various livings in the I.Wight, see *Insula Vecta*.
933. For Matthew Fitzherbert, see 110; for the family, see *VCH,Hants*,iv,270.
934. The Engleys family were here as early as 1254, hence the place name. For Robert Gerberd', see *VCH,Hants*,iv,510.
935. MS in error repeats John for Geoffrey at the conclusion.
940. St Alphege in Cripplegate.
    Wickham Bishops, an Essex manor of the bishops of London.
    For the college of secular canons at St Martin-le-Grand, see J. H. Denton *English Royal Free Chapels* (1970), 28–40, 276.
941. For these portioned tithes, see also 860.
942. Robert de Manefeo, lord of the manors of Heckfield, Newnham and Church Oakley (*VCH,Hants*,iv,45,60,150,227).
948. cf.898 which was valid for one year.
949. For this hospital, which was in a bad way long before the Black Death, see *Med.Rel.Houses*.

954. For Raynold, now styled cardinal-deacon of St Adrian, see 572n. Hugh was prebendary of Netherbury-Ecclesia (*Le Neve*, 73).
956. Items 956 to 959 are better taken in reverse order
    Harrington, Lincs or Northants.
    Llansantffraid: three places bear this name.
    Abergwili, where the bishops of St Davids had a palace. The prebends were often given to royal clerks, cf. here 809.
958. Wycombe, i.e. High Wycombe, Bucks.
959. Cliff, north of Rochester, Kent.
    Thomas, bishop of St Davids, 1352–62.
961. Hadham, Much or Little, Herts.
963. Spervan supplied from 758.
966. *Cerchiden'*, ?Churchdown, Glos.
968. Text reads *St Mary Patyns*, the marginal index correctly *St Margaret* in Pattens Lane.
970. Carvor, badly written, beginning with Q, probably pronounced Carvor.
971. *Tratynton*, ?Tortington.
972. *Fifhide Skydmore*, ?Fyfield, Wilts, in Overton, already a chapel in 1284 (*VCH,Wilts*,xi,199).
980. 1353, *sic* and in 985.
981. Whitefield was at that time Crown property.
985. 1353, *sic* and in 980.
988. For Philip de Peletot, holding the manor and advowson, see *VCH, Herts*,iii,164. Kibbleworth, Kibworth, Leics.
994. Reg. reads Stafford Rivers, in confusion with Stafford, below.
995. John de Saint Paul, archbishop of Dublin, 1349–62.
996. Bishops Hull, Som; originally each canon of a cathedral had a *prebenda* or share in the funds of the church; later each was assigned a particular estate for his support, hence he came to be known as the prebendary of . . .
999. Michael, elect of London. Elected 21 April 1354; received the spiritualities 3 July; consecrated 12 July (*Le Neve*).
1003. St Mary *in atrio cathedralis*.
1006. Michael Northborough, see 999.
    St Olaves in Hart Street, Tower Street Ward (*Stow*, 120, 434).
1008. cf. *CClR., 1354–1360*, 107.
1010. cf.572,954.
    For Andrew Braunche, see 327.
1011. cf.995.
1014. Andrew Braunche, cf.327,1010.
1016. Reg. *Portsea*; marginal index *Portchester* and cf.1019.
1017. *et mei Johannis de Beautre* shows him to be the writer, as also in 1020.
1019. cf.1016.
1020. i.e. Busbridge, Godalming. Hambledon had many changes of patron (*VCH,Surrey*,iii,43).
1021. Shoreham, Kent or Sussex.
1024. *Worthy comitis*, one among several variants for Headbourne Worthy.

1025. Chapel of St Mary, should read of St Mary Magdalen in the Guildhall (*Stow*,244).

1029. No date given. John Vere, de Veer, earl of Oxford, d.1360 seized of the manor of Market Overton, by right of his wife, Maude de Badlesmere (*VCH,Rutland*,ii,142).

1031. Cluniac priory. The licence shows that it was exceptional for the monks to have care of the parish church.

1032. *DNB* gives her name as Wensliana. Her husband, John baron Maltravers (cf.Lychett Maltravers, Dorset) was governor of the Channel Islands in 1351, so was presumably still abroad.

1035. i.e. Heighton Street or South Heighton, Sussex.

1038. See 954 for Pelegrini and 572 for the cardinal.

1039. For Bridgenorth, royal free chapel of St M. Magdalen, see J. H. Denton *English Royal Free Chapels, 1100–1300*. The king collates here, not the dean (*ibid*. 24n). It was a castle chapel with dependent parishes, cf.*CClR,1354–60*,145). Haywood, prob. Staffs.

1041. See 1043 for another Thorold to the same chapel.

1046. The notice ends with "and to the dean of the Isle of Wight" by confusion with 1045 and 1047.

1050. Henry de Percy, earl of Northumberland.

1054. *Johanni nato Rogero*.

1058. Hoggeston, Hoghton, Hognaston?

1059. Date absent.

1060. For the name of the said Matthew, see 1061.

1067. The Rotherfeld family was associated with East Tisted.

1070. For the father of John Devenish, see 217.

1071. From XIIIc. the treasurer of York cathedral, by arrangement with the dean and chapter, presented to the church of Nether Wallop.

1073. *Parva Fobby(our)*, ? Fobbing, Essex. For Stafford, see 224.

1074. For Geoffrey Roukley, see *Insula Vecta*.

1075. For the treasurer of York, see 1071.

1076. Candlewick Street, now Cannon Street.

1078. 2nd. Council of Lyons, 1274, demanded that all rectors of parishes must proceed to the priesthood.

1081. St Neots, alien priory of Bec, Hunts.

1086. i.e. Itchen Abbas.

1090. Thoni, cf.683.

1091. Surname at end of the line: ? Newman.

1093. Simon Langham, abbot, 1349–62.

1095. Cole Henley, tithing and manor in Whitchurch, where there was a free chapel (*VCH,Hants*,iv,299–304).

1098. Beddington, seat of the Carew family. Nicholas de Carew held the manor by lease in 1352 from Richard de Kenele (*VCH,Surrey*,iv,170). There is no mention of portions of the church in *VCH*.
   Hoton' or *Hocon*'.

1103. The names of the attorneys are illegible, except for Nicholas Devenish of Hengham and Sibyl. John de Berners was to be imprisoned in 1347 for trespass against the executors of M. John de Aumbury, late archdeacon of Surrey (*CPR,1345–48*,423).

1106. St Margaret, Pattens Lane.
1109. cf.904.
1111. Tneye or Tueke. Ink badly faded here.
1113. Warley Abbess, i.e. Great Warley, Essex, held by the abbess of Barking. Wrangle, Lincs.
1117. John Gynwell, bishop, 1347-62. Farleigh, prob. Farleigh Wallop. Hardwick, Leics or Lincs.
1118. Thomas de Lisle (de Insula), bishop, 1345-61; Simon Islip, archbishop, 1349-66.
1121. Thomas de Bradestan, knt., had been granted the reversion of the manor of Eversley by Nicholas de Hagheman (*VCH,Hants*,iv,33).
1129. Wootton St Laurence, Surrey.
1130. For the churches of the abbess, see *Charters and Custumals of the abbey of Holy Trinity, Caen*, ed. M. Chibnall (1982).
1141. In 1348 with the king's permission the manor was granted to the bishop by William de Melton, but it was not long held by him (*VCH,Hants*,iv,69). Colechurch: the middle of the name is not clear, but in both cases the capital C and the ending are certain. Could be Colecherche, as in *Taxatio*, 19, among the spiritualities of the archdiaconry of London; cf. also St Mary Colechurch in the City.
1144. i.e. Farley Chamberlayne. Thomas de Missenden presented (*VCH,Hants*,iv,443).
1153. Higham Gobion: recovered from *Reg.Sutton* (Cant. and York Soc.),i,index,ed. Rosalind Hill.
1154. Henry Peverel was lord of the manors of Chilworth and of Northavon in Sopley, d.1363 (*VCH,Hants*,iii,468;v,129)
       Leper hospital of St M. Magdalen.
1160. Kings Cliff, Kings Cleve, Northants (cf. *Reg.Repington*,ii,253).
1166. Wanstead in Southwick.
1169. St Nicholas *in Macell'* or of the Flesh Shambles (*Stow*,202).
1174. Hegham *sic* in the Register; nothing in *VCH*.
1175. Newark (*Novo Loco*) in Send, Surrey.
1176. For Reynald, cardinal-deacon, see 572.
1178. Walkingstead or Walkamstead, the old name for Godstone, Surrey.
1181. La Woe, now Weyhill or Penton Grafton. Grafton refers to the abbey of Grestein in Normandy. The abbey assigned the manor to Sir Thomas de la Pole in 1354 (*VCH,Hants*,iv,395).
1182. The first *studium generale* to be named.
1186. Kempshott in Winslade, Hants.
1187. Ralph second earl of Stafford married Margaret, daughter and heiress of Hugh de Audeleye. She was sister and heiress of Gilbert de Clare. Hugh was created earl of Gloucester in 1337 (*VCH,Hants*,iv,361).
1197. Wandsworth, now within the S.W. London area. The water, the *aqua* twice mentioned, will be the river Wandle, which there enters the Thames.
       Subir' et Surr'archd': a difficult piece of writing. With 'notaries' and 'clerks' following, this should read 'archdeacons', but in 1359 the archdeacon of Surrey was John de Edybdon.

1200. The priory of Dominican nuns was planned by Edward II; the buildings were not completed until 1356, cf.*C.Pap.Pet., 1342–1419*,244; *Med.Rel.Houses*,285. John Merlawe, prior 1349–1361.

1206. For Andrew Braunche, see 327.

1208. The earl of Stafford had a castle at Tonbridge, where he died (*DNB*).

1211. The presentation is added in the margin. Rotherfield in East Tisted (*VCH,Hants*,iii,32).

1215. John de Cobeham alientated the manor of Nutfield for life to Fulcon Horwode in 1359 (*VCH,Surrey*,iii,223).

1216. The lords of Fawley were the Sackville family; the lord at this time was Thomas, probably absent (*VCH,Bucks*,iii,39).

1222. Lantefey, i.e. the manor of Lamphey (Pembs, now Dyfed), principal manor of the bishops of St Davids (Conway Davis *Episcopal Acts . . . relating to Wales*,i,362).

　　　Thomas Fastolf, bishop of St Davids, 1352–61.

　　　William de Osberton had been provided to the canonry with reservation of the prebend of Caerfai.

1223. Edward III made over his rights to the Isle of Man to the first earl of Salisbury in 1333. The second earl, having no heir, sold the lordship and the crown of Man in 1393 (*DNB*).

1226. Either Codford St Mary or St Peter, Wilts.

1227. The peace of Brétigny was ratified by the two kings at Calais later in the same year.

1232. cf.1227.

1234. i.e. Farley Chamberlayne, cf.1144.

1236. Sir Andrew Braunche had purchased his rights in Peper Harow. Thomas died in 1360, leaving (though only aged 11) a widow, Mary, to whom the dower was assigned (*VCH,Surrey*,iii,50).

1238. Richard earl of Arundel held the lordship of Hambledon as guardian of the heir. The lady was Maud, wife of Thomas at Hull (*VCH,Surrey*,iii,43).

1244. The manor of Upper Eldon in King's Somborne had two churches. It was conveyed to John Baker of Horsebridge in King's Somborne in 1358 (*VCH,Hants*,iv,477).

1245. Walking in his garden: the first sign of any intimacy with the clergy. The next item indicates a community of ten canons.

1247. MS reads Thomas for Henry.

1252. For Saladin de Fallecis, see *Le Neve*, Salisbury diocese, 63. Prebend of Hurstborne (Hants) and Burbage (Wilts). *Lunt,Acc*,146 enters this receipt by Saladin de Fallet for the prebend, vacant by the death of John de Wythcherch', assessed at £53 6s. 8d.

1253. Somerford Mauduit, i.e. Little Somerford or Somerford Mauduit, Wilts.

1257. The manor of Stoke Charity was sold by Thomas de Alneto to Sir John de Hampton in 1344; Thomas was his son and heir, also knight of the shire of Southampton (*VCH,Hants*,iii,448).

1262. For Saladin de Fallecis, see 1252.

1268. For the acquisition, see *VCH,Surrey*, iv,313.

1273. i.e. Walton-on-Thames, see *VCH,Surrey*,iii,474.
1275. Crux Easton, near Burghclere. For the descent of the manor and advowson from the Croch to the Avenel family, see *VCH,Hants*,iv,312.
1276. Simon of Sudbury became bishop of London the same year and was translated to Canterbury, 1375, to be executed on Tower Hill during the Peasants' Revolt.
1282. For the advowson, see 1211.
1296. Last sentence inserted later.
1302. William de Monasterio, cf.1312.
1303. Andover priory, the church granted by the Conqueror to St Florent of Saumur, Philip Maghe, prior.
1304. i.e. institution as prior.
1307. For this recovery and lease, see *VCH,Hants*,iv,45. The St Manifeo family later recovered the manor. As bishop, Wykeham was to grant the advowson to his college. Wykeham was already in royal service, not yet in minor orders, but see 1347.
1309. The advowson of Boughton was attached to the dignity of the treasurer of York.
1310. For this descent, see *VCH,Hants*,v,100.
1311. The family held the manor for over five centuries.
1313. 'Elyndon', i.e. Wroughton, Wilts.
1326. The Brayboeuf family were the lords of Eastrop. Joan, daughter of Hugh de Brayboeuf, married as first husband John de Podenhale (*VCH,Hants*,iv,148).
1332. Presumably one of the many Stockleighs.
1336. The advowson of Farley Wallop was granted by Henry de Farley to Robert de Mortimer in 1279. In 1328 Roger de Mortimer settled the manor on William de la Zouche (*VCH,Hants*,iii,364–5).
1337. Maud, daughter of Henry first duke of Lancaster, had married William, count of Holland, son of the emperor Louis of Bavaria. She died in 1362 (*DNB*).
1349. Parva Sandal: known to *Dugdale*, but no longer to be found in the gazetteers. It must have been near Sandal Magna, West Riding, Yorks.
1358. A small entry for this election as compared with others.
1370. For this papal notary, see 572.
1371. cf. *CPR,1361–64*,87, for 18 Oct. 1361.
1373. Bernard de Brocas was the second husband of Mary, daughter of John des Roches, descendant of a nephew of bishop Peter des Roches (*VCH,Hants*,iv,202).
1377. i.e. Farleigh Wallop, see 1336.
1381. For the complicated descent of this manor, see *VCH,Hants*, iv, 342.
1382. For Simon of Sudbury, see 1276n.
1383. The Jarpenville family were at Abinger since the XIIIc. The church served two manors (*VCH.Surrey*,iii,134).
1386. Candover Abbatis.
1390. Wyxenhale, ?Wixhall, Shropshire.

1394. The manor had been held by Retherick son of Griffin in 1309; he was succeeded by his son Thomas before 1324, taking the name Thomas son of Retherick (*VCH.Surrey*,iv,330).

1406. Most probably Hinton Martell, Dorset.

1409. i.e. St James outside Westgate.

1413. The Bettesthorne family had been holding the moiety of Minstead since 1272 (*VCH,Hants*,iv,638).

1420. For Bernard Brocaz, knt., see 1373.

1422. Nicholas de Malemayne, knt., left three daughters. Beatrice married Otho de Grandisson, when the manor was divided between the three. Sir Otho died in 1359, seized of $\frac{1}{3}$ of the manor. His second son became bishop of Exeter (*VCH,Surrey*,iii,152).

1423. Juliana, daughter of Thomas de Leyburn, married as third husband William de Clinton, created earl of Huntingdon in 1336/7, d.1354 (*VCH,Hants*,iv,110).

1424. Council of Lyons, 1274-5.

1426. For situation after the Black Death, cf.*C.Pap.Pet.*,i,165; *C.Pap.Reg.*,iii,330. Henry Yakesley, d.1377 (*VCH,Surrey*,ii,124).

1430. Woe, today Weyhill. Thomas de la Pole, d.1361, holding the manor of Ramridge in Weyhill.

1432. Andrew Peverel married Katherine, widow of Henry Husee (*VCH,Hants*,iv,284).

1433. Nicholas Carew had married Lucy, daughter of Richard de Wylughby, who in 1352 had leased the manor to Nicholas (*VCH,Surrey*,iv,170).

1438. Simon de Sudbury would be bishop of London this same year, 20 March.

1445. Farley Chamberlayne, near Romsey.
   Thomas de Missenden presented by right of Mary, widow of James de Berton, Mary's first husband (*VCH,Hants*,iv,445).

1449. The see was vacant until the consecration of Simon de Sudbury, 20 March. M. Thomas Yonge was to be chancellor of the diocese in 1363.

1454. i.e. Weyhill. Michael de la Pole succeeded his father in 1361.

1456. Presumably Guillaume de Monasteriis, as elsewhere.

1457. For this chapel in Candlewick Street, now Canon Street, see *Stow*, 200. John Poultney, mayor of London, founded a college of Jesus and Corpus Christi, 1346.

1460. This date must be incorrect, see 1458.

1463. Royal assent to Geoffrey de Chaddesle, prior of Merton, 31 Aug. 1361, dated from Beaulieu (*CPR,1361-64*,56).

1464. This abbess was dead before the year was out, see 1480.

1470. Assent of the king to the election at Wherwell (*CPR,1361-64*,87, 4 Oct. 1361; restoration of the temporalities (*ibid*.91), 25 Oct. 1361

1471. This witness must be Alice de la Mare, abbess 1365-85. The predecessor of Christina Wayte was Margaret Molins. For the licence to elect for Nunnaminister, *CPR,1361-64*, 83, dated 16 Oct. 1361; for the restoration of temporalities *ibid*.91 and 106; assent to the election *ibid*. 100, 3 Nov. 1361.

1479. Mandate to restore temporalities, 5 Dec. 1361 (*CPR,1361–64*, 124).
1480. See 1464.
1483. Royal assent to the election, 22 Dec. 1361 (*CPR,1361–64*, 134); restoration of the temporalities, 27 Dec. (*ibid.*,136).
1485. St Vigor was the founder of Cérisy-la-Foret (Manche), which is its usual name.
    For Thomas de Aldyngborne, cf.695, 1310.
1487. Tiron, abbey in dioc. of Chartres. John III, abbot.
    Arcisses, in the same dioc., founded from Tiron.
1490. The process of this election occupies 3½ folios of close writing, punctuated by postponements and changes of personnel. The depositions are not given and it is not clear why the election was not made according to the constitutions of bishop John. The word *frustratum* can mean deceit and it seems that contumacy decided the case.
1491. The reference is to the Council of the Lateran, 1215, decree *Quia propter* (c.24), which is in the decretals of Gregory IX as book 1, title 6c. 42. The bishop's official and commissary says he found the election uncanonical, not being carried out according to the regulations established by that council. The monks were deprived of the election for this turn, saving the composition on free election made in the past between John de Pontissara and the prior and convent (see *Reg. J. de Pont.* 71–8, where the editor gives an incorrect reference to the Council). Nothing indicates why the commissary adjudged the election to be irregular. The form was irregular, not the man—but the bishop did not appoint the man, which he sometimes did if the objections were only formal. He does not *say* that the man was unsatisfactory (communicated by Prof. C. R. Cheney).
1493. The Register clearly reads William Basynge and also in the next item. This must be in error for Hugh, who is named below in 1704–5, yet all the lists of *Le Neve* and *VCH* refer to this entry.
1497. No place accompanies this date.
1503. Isabella, widow of Geoffrey de Hustane. She was the eldest daughter of John de Clamorgan, lord of Brook (*Insula Vecta*, 200).
1506. Sherborne: prob. Monk Sherborne, since the priory presented.
1511. Whipstrode in Fareham. The lords of N. Fareham presented to the chapel of St James at Whipstrode (*VCH,Hants,*iii,212,215).
1515. The lords of Upper Eldon presented to Eldon in King's Somborne (*VCH,Hants,*iv,480).
1516. St Mary Staining, near Haberdashers' Hall, at north end of Staining Lane (*Stow*, 272). For Thomas de Uvedale, see 647.
1518. This is an omission, no gap in the register.
1520. i.e. Farley Chamberlayne.
1522. The new vicar of Eastbourne was Robert Mayn (see 1399).
1523. St Brides, Finkes Lane.
1528. Royal assent, 17 September 1362 (*CPR,1361–64,*246).
1532. For Geoffrey Rouclee, see *Insula Vecta*, 200.
1535. *Bereford* in margin: *Berefeld* in text.

1536. For this prebend, see *Reg. R. Martival*,i,138,141n.

1540. *Everard Volet* is *Everard de Pratell'* in 1555.

1545. St Mary in 'Stanynglan'.

1546. Juliana, Beatrice and Christina were sisters and heiresses of Agnes Norton (*VCH,Hants*,iv,392).

1549. Henry de Welles d.1333 founded his chantry in a free chapel of South Baddesley, in the parish of Boldre (*VCH,Hants*,iv,616); for its endowment (*ibid.*622).

1550. Sherborne Coudray or the Vyne. The chantry was really a re-foundation (1337/8) (*VCH,Hants*,iv,170). William de Fifhyde had been granted the reversion of the manor but died in 1361; his son, also William, obtained his lands on coming of age in 1365 (*ibid.*,160). cf.*CPR,1361–64*,274, as Thomas Solle.

1552. The manor was granted to the bishop in 1348, but is not found in his possession at the inquest of 1362/3(*VCH,Hants*,iv,69).

1553. The portion of St Laurence consisted of the church of Timsbury, the tithes of Imber, Wilts. and $\frac{1}{3}$ of the tithes of Romsey. The church of Timsbury is dedicated to St Andrew. For Walter de Sevenhampton and the canonry and prebend, see *C.Pap.Pet.*i, 131,444.

1555. Everard de Pratell is called Volet in 1540.

1556. The name is here clearly *Cano*; in *VCH Canoun*.
     The abbot is William IV de Chanac, abbot from 1354.

1557. Botley, very faint entry: Botheby or Gotheby.

1567. The Covert family had held the manor since the XIIIc., the advowson was with the manor (*VCH,Surrey*,iv,194).
     Of the many places called Denton, that in Sussex is the nearest.

1569. For the first licence, see 1500.

1572. Lincoln was vacant from 1362 to 1363.
     Edmondthorp or Edmerthorp, Leics; the register uses the second form.
     The bishops of Exeter had a manor at Faringdon, Berks.
     John, the king's son, i.e. John of Gaunt.

1575. Abbey of St Peter, York, in error for St Mary.

1576. William Writtlesey, bishop 1362–4.

1582. Deanery of Shoreham in N. W. Kent, dioc. of Rochester, of the archbishop's immediate jurisdiction.

1592. Thomas de Overwallop had died in 1361, seized of the advowson (*VCH,Hants*,iv,532).

1597. Goda had first been married to John de Cormeilles; this was a second marriage (*VCH,Hants*,iv,388).

1598. Edendon took from the chapel the rectory house, which William de Wykenham restored to them (*Wyk.Reg.*ii,175). The church had been appropriated to the chapel at its foundation by John de Pontissara.

1606. The see was vacant from 14 Aug. 1363, on the death of Ralph de Salopia.

1607. Ivychurch, Wilts, augustinian.

1612. The bishop received royal licence to obtain the church of Newton Valence from Thomas West, and to appropriate it to his foundation (*VCH,Hants*,iii,29).

1613. i.e. William de Monte Acuto.

1614. The manor of Anne had been given to Bec by Hugh de Grandmesnil (M. Morgan *Lands of Bec*, 149).

1616. John de Tanerton or Timerton.

1620. As husband of Ann de Clamorgan, see *Insula Vecta*, 199–200.

1630. The dating of this item in the Register seems faulty.

1632. Preston, near Wingham, Kent.

1634. (Margin): institution without enquiry, by special favour..

1635. John de Jarpenville had committed the manor to trustees. The church of Abinger, or Abinger Clatford, served the two manors. After the union the advowson was in the hands of the lords of Abinger (*VCH,Surrey*,iii,134).

1641. For Edward Cheke, see 1620.

1651. In margin: *absque inquisitione*.

1657. Stanford in the Vale, Berks.

1659. Lesnes or Westwood, Kent: Augustinian abbey, which owned a portion of the tithe. The manor of Walkhamstead is in Godstone; king John granted ½ of the church to Lesnes. The abbey and the priory of Tandridge probably presented alternatively (*VCH,Surrey*, iv,290).

1660. Godsworth, i.e. Goodworth Clatford. The prebend was in the abbey of Wherwell.

1668. i.e. William Savage, cf.1609.

1669. Landegle, presumably Llandeilo Fawr, Carmarthen.
    From the XIIIc. the treasurer presented to Nether Wallop and received a pension. The church was later to be appropriated to the dean and chapter (*VCH,Hants*,iv,530).

1673. The archbishop's manor was at South Malling, Sussex; East Malling and the abbey were in Kent.

1676. Isabella, daughter of Edward III, who granted the lordship of the Isle of Wight to her in 1356. Whitefield, in Brading, was one of the manors of the lordship. Isabella continued to hold the lordship until her husband, Ingelram de Coucy, defected to the French in 1379 (*Insula Vecta*,137–8).

1677. i.e. Walton-on-the-Hill. John de Braose, minor and ward of John de Warenne, earl of Surrey, was heir to the manor at the death of the earl in 1347. After this, Mary, countess marshal, occupied the manor, followed by Sir Thomas de Braose, as guardian for John (*VCH,Surrey*,iii,316).

1678. Louis de Charlton, bishop of Hereford, 1361–69. The surname of John appears below: John Wyli.

1685. The manor of Dibden Hanger in Dibden (*VCH,Hants*,iv,656,658).

1690. Surrey omitted in the Register.

1691. Otterbourne did not become a separate parish until the XIXc.

1692. Last line: i.e. p.261, no. 1704.

1693. *anno prescripto* would be 1362; should almost certainly be 1365.

1694. Month omitted.

1699. Royal licence to elect, 21 July 1365 (*CPR,1364–67*,160); royal assent to the election (*ibid.*), 28 July; mandate to deliver the temporalities (*ibid.*) 28 July.

1703. Laurence de Nigris, a papal subcollector; a citizen of Rome, acting for Reynald Ursinus, cardinal of St Hadrian in his absence (*Lunt,Acc.*). Laurence was a canon of Lincoln by the seventies, perhaps before, and prebendary of West Beckhall in that diocese.
William de Lynne, bishop of Chichester, 1362–68.
fulginatis a place-name?
For the cardinal-deacon, cf.572.

1704. i.e. prior High Basyng since 1362.

1706. Or Fitzhugh.

1707. i.e. Farley Chamberlayne.

1708. *John bishop of Lincoln* in error for *Simon of London*, see below.
All Saints Barkyngchirch, i.e. All Hallows, Barking by the Tower.

1709. In margin: 100s. The conclusion seems to give the sense of a difficult entry.

1712. ?Gytyng, prob. Corsham, Wilts.

1715. The advowson had been in the Clamorgan family. For the division of the inheritance among eight daughters, see *Insula Vecta*, 199. The eldest, Isabella, married Geoffrey de Hustane. See 1717.

1717. See 1715.

1718. a and b. Omitted accidentally during transcription.

1724. The advowson had been in the Clamorgan family. Edward Cheke was the first husband of the youngest daughter, Ann (*Insula Vecta*,199–291).

1726. When the patronage devolved on the Crown (c.1300), it was conferred on the house of Lancaster. The date of Netherhavene is given as 1356 (*VCH,Hants*,ii,173).

1728. John Corf was canon of Wells and prebend of Combe Prima, dioc. Bath and Wells; John Beautre, canon in the dioc. of Exeter (*Le Neve*).

1733. No place is given; prob. Hursley.

1735. Robert Stretton, bishop 1360–85,
Haywood, Shropshire or Staffs. No final date.

1740. The advowson of Bletchingley changed hands in 1320 the patron was Maud de Clare; later the manor and church belonged to Margaret, sister of Gilbert and wife of Hugh de Audley the younger (*VCH,Surrey*,iv,264–5).

1742. John Giffard presented to Peper Harow by right of his wife, Mary. The advowson was part of her dowry, but:
(margin) Broadway "at presentation of prioress and convent of Clerkenwell".

1744. Andrew Braboeuf died seized of a quarter of Arlington in 1361/2, leaving as heir a daughter who married (1)Robert Danhurst, (2)Robert Loxley (*VCH,Surrey*,iii,43).

1746. Whipstrode in Fareham.

1748. Hawkley became a parish early. 'Marroie'?, there is Mary Land Copse in Newton Valence (*VCH,Hants*,iii,23).

1752. The bishop died 7/8 October (*Le Neve*,46). See last note of Part ii.

INDEX

The medieval spelling of place-names is given in brackets when this differs from the modern.

Suspensions remain, though the register in the latter part is careless about them.

For the religious orders: ben. for Benedictines and cist. for Cistercians; for the friars, dom. for the Dominicans, fm. for the Minors and carm. for the Carmelites.

References to the counties are to the historic counties, not to the modern administrative counties.

Abban, John, 412, 1138
Abbots Ann (Anne Abbatis), Hants, 351, 449, 476, 574, 576, 626, 627, 681, 682, 1128, 1161, 1210
Abbots Bromley (Bromleye Abbatis), Staffs, 631
Abbotstone (Aboteston), Hants, 18, 19, 93, 639
Abbotsworthy (Worthy Abbatis), Hants, 80, 1513
Abergwili (Aberghwyll), Caernav, ix, 809, 959, 1669
Abinger (Abyngeworth'), Surrey, 417, 418, 1383, 1600, 1624, 1635–9
Abraham, William, 1434
Acton, St Nicholas, 999
Addington (Adyngton'), Surrey, 407, 714, 847, 1415
Ad Pontem, Hugh, 994
Alba Marlea, Philip de, 243
Albigneye, William de, ben., 1304
Albury (Aldebury), Surrey, 490, 535, 1155, 1306, 1636
Aldeluestre, William de, 778
Aldermaston (Aldermanston), Berks, 739, 960
Aldingborne (Aldyngborne), Sussex, 971, 1050
Aldyngbourne, Thomas de, 1310, 1485
All Cannings (Canynges), Wilts, 1536
Alne, William de, 1646
Alneto, Thomas de, 1257n.
Alresford, Hants, 250, 251, 337, 463, 523, 609, 865, 883, 975, 976, 1028, 1134, 1229, 1231, 1264, 1327, 1694, 1724
, Robert de, 819
Alrynton', Geoffrey de, 764
Alston', Thomas de, 1141, 1542
Alton (Aulton), Hants, 337, 542, 1360
, dean of, 337, 413, 473, 516, 636, 901, 1017, 1147, 1310, 1608
Alveley (Alvithelee), Salop, 1039
Alverstoke (Alwarstok), Hants, 133, 770, 775, 1044, 1260, 1317, 1323, 1751
Alverstone (Alfredeston'), I. Wight, 243
Alveston, Warwk, 1042
Alwarthorp', Laurence de, 1278, 1349
Alwyne, Gilbert, 824
Amburle, Richard de, 946
Amesbury (Aumbresbury), Wilts, prioress, 131, 209, 228, 300
Amiger', Margaret, ben., 916
Amport (Annedeport), Hants, 399, 1018
Andele, Nicholas de, 739
Andevere, John de, 909
Andover (Andevere), Hants, 184, 395, 438, 488, 703, 1303, 1556
, dean of, 1075,
, hosp. of St John, 764
Angers, France, dioc., 1556
Annibaldus, bp., xiv
Appelby, Thomas de, 1204, 1231
Appleton, Walter de, 615
Appleford (Apelderford'), I. Wight, 862
Archer, John le, 145

Arcisses, abbey, Eure et Loir, France, 1487
Arlich, John, 138
Arlington (Erlington), Sussex, 181
Arnald filius Usisi, papal notary, 572, 1370
Arnwode, Richard, 1305
Arreton (Atherton), I. Wight, ix, 34, 84, 157, 197, 263, 302, 444, 445, 803, 809, 810, 903, 953, 1069, 1258, 1266, 1338, 1437, 1498
Arundel, ch. and priory, 788
, Richard earl of, 256, 1238, 1242
Arvel, William, 1256
Ash (Ashe), Surrey, 493, 698, 1636, 1711, 1718, 1718b
Ashbury (Asshebury), Berks, 12, 13, 17, 70
Ashby de la Zouche, Staffs, 239n.
Ashe, Hants., 1092, 1505, 1133, 1139, 1140
Ashley (Asschelegh), Hants, 497, 792, 1643
Ashtead (Asshstede), Surrey, xi, 98, 119, 422, 665
Ashton, John de, 723
Askam, John de, 554
Askeby, Robert de, 752
, William de, 572
Aspale, Robert de, 465, 504, 679, 895, 1652
, Thomas de, 679, 705, 753, 842n., 895
Asshe, Henry de 171
Asshewell', John de, 969, 1084
Asshton, John de, 285, 1352
Aston', Hugh de, 634
, Richard de, ben., 754
, Walter de, 98
At Hull, Maud, wife of Thomas, 1238n.
Aubrey, William, 1431
Audeleye, Hugh and d. Margaret, 1187, 1736n.
Aulton, Thomas de, 568, 851
Aumberden', Richard de, 1708, 1709
Aumbresbury, John de, viii, 63, 100, 108
, Roger de, 997
, Thomas de, 670
Aumbrey, John de, 1103n.
Avenel, Edward, knt, 1275
Avignon, 3–10, 39, 78, 256n., 810, 883, 900

Avington (Avyngton'), Hants, 833, 859, 875, 1211, 1414
Aylmer, William, 1525
Alwyn, Richard, 1667

Bachiler, William, 180
Bacon, Michael, 792
, Simon, 1664
Baddeby, John de, 346
Baddesley Clinton (Baddeslie Clynton), Warw, 84
Baddesley (Baddeslee), Hants, 1549
Baddington, xi
Badlesmere, Maud de, 1029n.
Bagworth, Henry de, 818, 1265
, William de, 794, 795
Bakere, John, 1244
Ballok, Robert, 375, 738
Bampton, Oxon, 191
Banel, William, 820
Banewell', William de, 852, 913
Banenwyk', Peter de, 671
Banfeld, John, 951
Banstead (Banstede), Surrey, 68, 98, 358, 732, 1036, 1283, 1570
Banylon, John, 451
Barbour, Nicholas le, 617
, Thomas le, 747, 1490
Barford (Berefeld), Warw, 1535
Barnabas, Maurice, 54, 190, 201,
Barneby, Edmund, 968, 1106
, William de, 1121, 1253
Barnet, John, x, 999, 1006, 1025, 1687 (bp.)
Baron, John, 365
Barscot, Thomas, 1442
Barton (Burton), I. Wight, 531, 923–5,
, Camb, 138
Barton Stacy (Berton Sacy), Hants, 604, 1332
Barton, Richard de, 1013, 1022
, Thomas de, 869, 1000, 1027
Baseley, John, 799
Basing, Basingstoke (Basystok', Baysyngstok), Hants, 238, 391, 414, 437, 489, 568, 791, 805, 839, 844, 1379
, dean of, 171, 594, 600, 632, 646, 648, 653, 664, 702, 720, 728, 729, 755, 796, 805, 806, 839, 841, 844, 852, 913, 952, 973, 1005, 1122, 1326, 1345
Baston, Ralph de, 1372
Basyn, John, ben., 1508, 1509, 1619
Basynge, Hugh de, ben., viii, 1704, 1705
, William de, ben., 558, 560, 1493, 1494

Bath and Wells, dioc., xv, 52, 72, 73, 92, 379, 725, 742, 825, 897, 1446, 1475, 1488, 1606, 1712, 1740
, bishops, *see* Barnet, Shrewsbury.
Bathe, William de, 311
Battersea (Batricheseye), 178n., 1286, 1441, 1576, 1604, 1645
Battle (Bello), abbey, Sussex, 940
Baughurst (Bagehurst), Hants, xi, 328, 329, 330, 513, 878, 880, 1617
Bavaria, Louis of, 1337n.
Bay, William, 1645
Bayeux, dioc. 229, 695, 1485
Baynard, Edmund, 1153, 1352
Beauford', James de, 730
, Thomas de, 675
Beaulieu (Bello Loco), Hants, 1465n.
Beausenall, Richard de, 352, 403, 476, 615
Beautre, John de, ix, 63, 78, 79, 84, 85, 135, 145, 171, 203, 204, 261, 262, 268, 393, 394, 406, 409, 626, 627, 632, 661, 705, 931, 969, 1017, 1020, 1081, 1084, 1111, 1127, 1173, 1192, 1196, 1224, 1238, 1242, 1245, 1246, 1248, 1308, 1322, 1355, 1420, 1421, 1434, 1491, 1493, 1499, 1502, 1532, 1533, 1542, 1607, 1641, 1709, 1726, 1728, 1733, 1738, 1751, 1752
, Roger de, 192, 530, 860, 1192
, Thomas de, 171, 204
Bebury, John de, 969
Beche, Edmund de la, 876
, Richard, 821
Bec-Herluin, Herlewin, Normandy, abbey, 112, 212, 403, 615, 684, 983, 1081n., 1099, 1100
Becke, William, 822
Beddington (Bedyngton'), Surrey, 216, 706, 797, 878, 1098, 1431, 1433
Bedfield (Bedefeld), Suff, 169, 170
Bedhampton, Hants, 25, 97, 185, 266, 364, 708
Bedwyn, Wilts, 52
Bee, William atte, 455
Beel, John, 848
Bekenesfeld, Andrew de, 529
Bekke, Richard, 1026
Belle, William, 828
Bello Campo, John de, 1000, 1028
, Roger de, 660, 937
, Thomas de, 1381, 1670; *and see* Warwick.
Benacre, William de, 228

Benart, William, ben., 1485
Benedict, bp. of Cahors, 71
, bp. of Cardicensis (Sardis), x
Beneit, Beneyt, Benet, Bennet, John, 688, 858, 1258
, Walter, ix, 808–811, 1069, 1111, 1355, 1358, 1464, 1476, 1477, 1480, 1481, 1490–2, 1502, 1526, 1536–8, 1666
Benham, John de, ben., 157–162, 1476
Benklond', John de, 1110
Bennebury, John de, 987, 1088, 1129, 1224, 1608
Bennely, John de, 1198
Bennington (Benynton'), Herts, 813
Bentworth (Bynteworth), Hants, 1141, 1451, 1552, 1587
Benyt, *see* Beneit.
Bereford, Edmund de, 285, 723
, John de, 1265, 1541, 1710
Bergeveney, William de, 389, 1018
Berghton, John de, 1610
Berkhamsted, John de, carm., 43
Berkshire, archd. 1657
Berkyng', John de, 1197
Bermondsey, priory, 43, 91, 331, 334, 354, 363, 500, 801, 850n., 929, 968, 1256, 1431, 1540, 1555, 1673, 1679
, ch. of St. M. Magdalen, 331, 801, 842, 1547, 1582, 1649, 1673
Bermyngham, William de, 1354
Bernab', Roger de, fm., 43
Bernard, Philip, 1176
, Richard, 788, 789
Bernay, abbey, France, 169n.
Berners, John de, knt., 1103
Berneye, Walter de, 192, 212, 213
Bersted, South (Berghestede), Sussex, 111, 225
Berton, Thomas de, ben., 21, 60, 556, 1396
, Thomas atte, 308, 841
, Thomas and John de la, 511; *and cf.* Barton
Berugh, ? Baughurst, Hants, 172
Betchworth (Bechesworth), Surrey, 700, 1164, 1301
Bette, Andrew son of John, 488
Beusevall', Richard de, 112
Beverley (Beverlacum), Yorks, 1309
Bicerle, Stephen de, 49
Bey, William, 745
Bicton, Robert de, 1035
Bienham', William de, 841
Bighton (Biketon), Hants, 289n., 494, 610, 1655, 1693

Binstead (Benstede), I. Wight, 268, 281, 282, 318, 673, 1243, 1644
Birchet, Thomas, 1660
Biret, Roger, 470
Birton, John de, 1065
Bisham (Bustlesham Montagu), Berks, xv, 46, 189, 220, 391, 428n., 607
Bishops Auckland (Aukland), Durham, 1186
Bishops Hull (Bishopeshull'), Som, 996
Bishops Lavington (Lavyngton Episcopi), Wilts, 112
Bishopstoke (Stok' episcopi), Hants, 249, 275, 465, 504, 688, 858
Bishops Stortford (Storteford), Herts, 199
Bishopstone (Bysshopeston'), Wilts, 136, 269, 270, 312, 1103, 1213, 1214
, ? also Ebbesborne Episcopi, 1213
Bishops Sutton, *see* Sutton.
Bishops Waltham, *see* Waltham.
Bisley (Busheleigh), Surrey, 672
Bitterne (Biterne), Hants, x, 291, 292, 657–9
Bix Gibwyn (Bixe Gybewyne), Oxon, 966
Blaby, Hugh de, ben., 24
Blake, John le, 1376, 1530, 1558
, Simon, 1582, 1673
Blakelond', William de, 532
Blakemere, Gilbert de, 702
Blanchard, John, 1346, 1491, 1655
Blasius, prior, 223
Blaston', William de, 716
Bleadon (Bleodon), Som, 379, 430, 1606
Blebury, Bleobury, John de, viii, 481, 807, 812, 942, 987, 1078, 1148–1150, 1493, 1502
Blendworth (Blendeworth'), Hants, 130, 210, 274, 286, 540, 712, 1097, 1343
Blenuo, Elias le, 1018
Bletchingley (Blecthynglech, Blecthynglegh), Surrey, 487n., 1073, 1169, 1365, 1735, 1736, 1739
Bletchley (Blecchele), Bucks, 1172
Blois, Henry de, bp., 400n.
Blondel, John, 772
Blount, Thomas le, 156, 248, 299
Blytheworth', William de, 392
Bochardeston', John de, 510, 935, 1086, 1110
Bocke, John, 580
Bockingfield (Bokenfeld), Kent, 809

Bogeham, John de, 1171
Boger, Mielus son of John, 335
Bogham, John de, knt., 1225, 1136
Bohoun, Humphrey de, earl of Hereford, 839
Bokenhull', Robert de, 1678
, Thomas de, 238, 239, 379, 430
Boketon, Philip de, 121, 122
Bokkebrugg', William de, 384
Bokyngham, John de, 191
Boldre (Bolre), Hants, 1549n.
Bolesdon', Edmund de, ben., 560, 563
Bolingbroke (Bolyngbrok'), Lincs, 978
Bolt, Martin, 1032
Bolteford', Richard de, 1003
Bonchurch (Bonechirch'), I. Wight, 1054
Bondeby, John de, 1398, 1419, 1499
Bonenfaunt, John, 969, 1084
Bonere, John, 804
Boniface VIII, pope, x, 97, 283, 875, 936, 1062, 1239, 1603, 1622, 1672, 1693, 1718
Bonterwyk, John de, fm., 43
Bookham, Great (Magna Bokham), 439, 716, 1688
, Little (Bocham minor), Surrey, 495, 704, 771, 1090
Boor, Mark le, 610
Borley (Berle), Essex, 1683
Bosco, *see* Boys.
Bosewyne, Robert de, 306
Bosham (Boseham), Sussex, 413n., 809
Bossington, Hants, 347n.
Boteston, Henry de, 1620, 1641
Botiler, Botillier, William, 1276
Botlesham, Stephen de, 1648
Botley (Bottelegh'), Hants, 361, 867, 1544, 1562
Bottisham (Batykesham), Cambs, 54, 190
Boughdon, John de, 1137
Boule, Richard, 996
Boulge, William, xi, 53, 94, 164
Boun, David, 319, 320
, William, 126
Bourne, Thomas de, 1397
, (Burn'), Hants, *see* St Mary Bourne.
Boughden, John de, knt., Elizabeth, 1137
Bovedon, John de, knt., 1056
Bover, Robert, 1255

Boxgrove, Bosegrove, John de, *cf.*
John Longwyne de Boxgrave, 63, 79, 219, 220, 221, 247, 355, 395
Boys, John de, ix, 174
    , William de, 755
Bradeford', John, 1580
Bradelegh, Bradele, Bradeley, Bartholomew, 111, 338, 339
    , William de, 79, 779, 780
Bradepol, Stephen de, 1394
Bradestan', Thomas de, knt., 960, 1121, 1633
Bradewell', Richard de, 637
Bradeweye, John de, 676, 939, 942, 969, 1084, 1085, 1426, 1464
Brading (Brerdynge), I. Wight, 211, 291, 893, 1443
Bradley (Bradele), Hants, 1373, 1420, 1531
Bradwardyn, Thomas de, bp., 334, 662n.
Brailles, Brayles, Thomas de, 104, 105, 198, 668
Brakkelegh, William de, 1246
Bramber (Brembre), Sussex, 704n., 1162
Bramdean (Bromden), Hants, 191, 279, 1125, 1315
Bramley (Bromleye), Hants, 1385
Brampton, Northants, 980, 985, 1081, 1082
Bramshot (Brembeschete), Hants, 1151
Brandeston', Goselin de, 846
Branketree, John de, 1309, 1400, 1669
    , Richard de, 1309, 1427, 1561, 1593, 1680
Braunche, Andrew, knt., 327, 1010, 1014, 1162, 1206
    , Mary widow of Thomas, 1236
Bray, Brey, John, 195, 196, 197
    , Peter, 1333
Braybeof, Andrew de, 1744n.
    , Hugh and Joan de, 839, 1326n.
Brayton, Thomas de, 1248
Breamore (Bromore), Hants, priory, xi, 211, 291, 381, 601, 893, 1049, 1358, 1443
Brembelschete, Laurence de, 77, 180, 315
Brembeschete, William de, 1151
Brembre, Thomas de, 981, 1039
Bret, Bernard de la, xv
Bretevill', William, 186

Brétigny, France, xiii, 1227n.
Brewode, John de, 1586, 1702
Brewes, Breouso, Thomas de, knt., 495, 704, 1090, 1677n.
    , John de, 1677
Breydon, Norf, 297n.
Breynton, Roger de, 328
Brian, Guy, knt., 245
Brich', Walter de, 1197
Briddlesford (Bridelesford), I. Wight, 441, 984
Bridecombe, John de, 1597
Bridgenorth (Bruggenorth), Salop, 1039
Bridlynton', Adam de, 1073
Briggeslee, John de, 1196
Brighstone (Brighteston'), I. Wight, ix, 41, 174, 192, 212, 213, 282, 1219, 1243, 1644
Brightrich', Robert, 1306
Brightwalton (Brightwelton), Berks, 1112
Brightwell, Berks, x, 198, 668, 690, 807, 812, 1148, 1258, 1273
Bristol, 1253
Britford (Brutford), Wilts, 922
Brittany, 47
Broad Hinton (Hyneton'), Wilts, 61
Broadway (Brodeweye), Dorset, 1742
Brocaz, Arnold, 1508, 1543, 1622, 1681, 1711, 1718, 1718b, 1746
    , Bernard, 771, 1373, 1420, 1511, 1531, 1711, 1723
Brode, John, 1282, 1581, 1663
Brokesburn', Richard de, 1516
Brokhampton, Geoffrey de, 325
Bromden', John de, 472
    , Richard de, 726
Bromfield (Bromfeld), 170
Bromleye Abbatis, Richard de, 631, 634
Brommyng', Thomas, 669
Bromore, Robert de, 43, 459 fm., 543, 866 aug.
Brook (Brok', la Broke), I. Wight, 759, 861, 1074, 1503, 1532
Broughton (Burghton, Bergton), Hants, 1309, 1427, 1561, 1593, 1672, 1680
    , John de, 118, 119, 422, 665
Brouk', Walter de, 1048
Brouklond', Walter de, 909
Broun, Hugh, 281, 401, 814, 881
    , John, 942
    , Robert, 1422
Brown Candover (Candevere Abbatis), Hants, 1386
Brugg', John 1181

, Walter de/atte, 503, 516, 681, 682

Brustowe, *see* Bristol.

Brut, Maurice, 1397

Breon, Bruyn, i.e. Brune, Maurice de, 319, 408, 456

, William, 1351

Bruynton, Henry de, ben., 24

, Simon de, 996, 1012, 1076

Bryan, Roger, 726

Buckden (Buckeden), Hunts, archd., 95

Buckhorn Weston (Boukares Weston), Dorset 235

Buckland (Bokelonde), Berks, 1274

, Surrey, 246, 993, 1242

Buketon, Phililp de, 297

Bukyngham, Henry de, 1400

, Robert de, 389

Bulkynton', John de, 1096

Burbage (Burbache), Wilts, 122, 1252, 1262

Bureford, John and Rosyia de, 178

Bures, William de, 619

Burgate, Robert de, ben., 29

Burgh (Bergh), Surrey, 98, 172, 390, 478

Burgh', Hugh de, 882

, John de, 1220

Burghclere (Bourgclere), Hants, 63, 230, 251, 252, 409, 632, 1081, 1308, 1339, 1493, 1617

Burghton, John de 1584

Burgo, Elizabeth de, lady of Clare, 303

, Thomas de, 1160, 1161

Burnell, Maud 163n.

Bursebrugge, John de, 1020

Burstall', William de, 201, 303, 304

Burton, dioc. Worcs, 194

Burton Agnes (Burton Anneys), Yorks, 1575,

Burton, John de, 1029, 1030

, Robert de, 1186, 1259

, William de, 1499

Bury, John 776

, Robert de, knt., 294

Busbridge, Hants, 1020n.

Butesthorne, Richard de, 1413, 1597

Buttermere (Butermere), Wilts, 466, 505, 769, 1165, 1712

Byfleet (Byflete), Surrey, 1233, 1497, 1499, 1539, 1551, 1626

Byketon, William de, 513

Byrlyngham, Richard de, 497

Byshopeston, William de, 1409

Byssebury, Nicholas de, 1268

Bysshop', John, 343

Bysshopeston', Robert de, 1330

, William, 1235, 1409

Bysthorn, Richard de, 1298

Cadeham, Robert, 1585

Caen, abbey of H. Trinity, 1130

Caerfai (Keer'), 1222

Calais (Calesia, Caleys), xiii, xiv, 224n., 786, 1227, 1232

Calbourne (Caubourne), I. Wight, 174, 282, 774, 775, 1219, 1354, 1577, 1611

Calcott (Caldecote), Berks, 139, 140

Caldecote, Giles de, 1445, 1520, 1594, 1654, 1707, 1747

, John de, 742

Caleton', William de, 949

Calverton, William de, 483

Camberwell (Camerewelle), Surrey, 353, 354, 929, 968, 1540, 1555

Cambridge (Cantebrigg'), x, 1182, 1668

, Clare College, 303n.

Camera, John de, 104

Camerton, ?Som, 801

Cameros, John, 525, 541

Cammoys, Isabel, ben., 916–921

, Ralph de, 473, 495n., 704n.

Caneford, Richard de, 866, 909

Canmell, William de, 111

Cano, Denis de, ben. 1556

Canon, William, 1542

Cantebrugg', ? 842

Canterbury, archbps., *see* Stratford, Islip, Reynolds; 404, 444, 813, 1172

, curia, 230, 1626

, dioc., 809, 1176, 1236, 1582, 1673

, Christchurch, ix, 85, 662, 853, 1079

, St Augustine, 89

Cantuar, Thomas de, carm., 43

Capelanus, John, 844

Caperon, Capron, Ralph, 1335, 1516, 1596

Capocci, Nicholas, xiv, xv

Cardicensis, *see* Benedict.

Carisbrooke (Karesbrok'), I. Wight, 214, 223, 262, 263, 444, 484, 597, 616, 733, 765, 785, 810, 877, 931, 1032, 1219, 1240, 1619

, castle chapel, 316, 669, 1568

Cark, William, 1044

Carn, John, 1270

Carnek, William, 1362

Carpenter, Simon le, 535

Carrou', Nicholas de, 1098, 1433
    , William de (Carew), 1098
Carshalton (Kersaulton, Creshelton),
    Surrey, 68, 474, 986, 1269, 1289, 1369
Cartere, Henry le, 26
Carvor, John, 970
Cary, Thomas, 38
Cashel (Casselen), archbp., 42; see
Kelly.
Caste, John de, 1267
Caterham (Katerham), Surrey, 613,
    835, 849, 982, 1293
Catherington (Keterington), Hants,
    451, 1294, 1752
Cauleston', John de, fm., 43
Cavendish, Richard and Juliana, 1546
Cawood, Yorks, 894
Cerf, see Corf.
Cerisy, abbey (de Ceraseio), France,
    229, 695, 1485n.
Cerne, (Cernelium), Dorset, xi, 1296
Cersy, William, 1405
Cestrefeld, Richard de, 1130
Cevere, William de, called Waverleye,
    78
Chaddleworth (Chadelesworth), Berks,
    1108
Chadeslee, Geoffrey de, 1458–1463
Chakynden, Chakendon, E' de, 171
    , Thomas de, 686, 1052,
    1290
Chakewelle, Hamond de, 1152
Chalbury (Chalbergh), Dorset, 217, 218
Chaldon (Chalvedon', Chaldon,
    Schalden), Surrey, 134, 144, 222, 536,
    1026, 1156, 1567
Chale, I. Wight, 76, 132, 223, 876
Chalfont St Peter (Chelfunte S. P.),
    Berks, 240, 241
Chalkeberd, John, 553, 829
Chalton (Cha;ughhton'), Hants, 50, 51,
    74, 254, 284, 794, 795, 818, 848, 1541,
    1599, 1718a
Chalvington (Chaldrynton), Sussex, 887
Chamberlayn, Chaumberlayn, Edward
le, 147, 1683
    , Nicholas le, 79
    , Richard, 1388
    , William and Christina,
    1546
Champenais, William, 243n.
Chanac, William, 1556n.
Chaumpayne, John, 720, 839
Chaumpeneys, Henry, 1380
Chapman, Thomas, 1167

Chardstock (Chardstok'), Som, 269
Charford, North, (Chardeford), Hants,
    539
Charlton, Louis de, bp., 1678n.
Chartres, France, dioc., 1487
Chaun, Nicholas, 949, 950
Chaunceux, Martin, 1216
Chawton (Chauton), Hants, 118, 337,
    1310, 1710
Cheddarne, Madoc de, 318, 462
Cheke, Chike, Edward, 1620, 1641,
    1724
Chelseye, Alexander de, 739, 1112
Chelsham (Chelesham), Surrey, 1104
Cherdeslee, Thomas de, 1679
Cherdestok', Edward de, 813
Cheriton (Cheryton, Chiriton), Hants,
    vii, 123, 124, 141, 250, 251, 253, 369,
    463, 468, 854, 865
Chertsey (Cherteseye), abbey, Surrey,
    24, 98, 99, 152, 270, 306, 367, 369, 396,
    401, 439, 493, 569, 643, 683, 698, 716,
    777, 778, 782, 814, 817, 926, 928, 971,
    991, 1022, 1051, 1087, 1220, 1324,
    1355, 1369, 1434, 1502, 1529, 1595,
    1688, 1711
    , elections, 157–162,
    1476–1479, 1489
    , place, 138, 306, 367
Chertseye, John de, 1063
Cherwere, 1636
Chester le Street (Chesterstrete), Durh,
    981
Chesterton, William de, 1195
Chetfield, William de, 835
Cheverdich', Matildis de, 1033
Chevere, Chuvere, William, 203, 204,
    1084
Cheyneston, Hugh de, 1163
Chichester, Sussex, archd., 971
    , dean and chap., 399
    , dioc., ix, 181, 809, 1035,
    1131, 1162, 1177, 1195, 1205, 1206,
    1522, 1669, 1703
    , Robert, bp., 181, 274, 697,
    788, 869, 887, 971, 995, 1002, 1080,
    1131, 1162, 1195, 1205, 1206
    , William, bp., 1703
Chichester', William, 1507
Chiddarne, Madoc de, 462
Chidden (Chidesden), Hants, 796
Chiddingfold (Chidyngfold'), Surrey,
    1038, 1176, 1370, 1662, 1703
Chigwell (Chikewelle), Essex, 1744

Chikkewell', Hamund de, Hamo de, 69, 88, 106, 107
Chilberton, Robert de, 195, 196
Chilbolton (Chabeghton), Hants, 155, 879, 1176, 1316
Chilcombe (Chiltecombe), Hants, 26, 275, 1357
Childecote, Robert de, 546
Childenull', John de, 423
Chilewell', Richard de, 259
Chilington (Chiltyngton), Sussex, 1703
Chilton Candover (Chilton Candevere), Hants, 520
Chilworth (Chelworth), Hants, 1154 *and see* St Martha.
Chippenham', Henry de, 469
Chipstead (Scheptede), Surrey, 129, 173, 224, 1187
Chirdestok', Edward de, 813, 897
Chiriton, Richard de, 151
Chisenhale, Robert de 1038
, Thurstan de, 1516
Chitterne, John de, 63–65, 95, 152
Chobham (Chabeham), Surrey, 643
Christchurch Twynham (Christechirche T), Hants, 175, 235, 265, 412, 425,–429, 868, 1146, 1173
Chuddene, William de, 30
Chuert, William, 657
Church', Robert atte, 524
Churchdown (Cerchidon), Glos, 966
Church Knowle (Knolle), Dorset, 1056
Church Oakley (Chicheoklee, Chichocle), Hants, 595, 660, 831, 942n.
Chynham, Edmund de, 255
, John, 1363
Chyntynge, William, 1080, 1215
Cirencestr', John de, 1049
Cissor, Adam, 203
, Henry dictus, 998
Clamorgan, Ann de, 1620n.
, John de, 1503n.
, Nicholas de, 759
Clamvile, Thomas, 1236
Clandon, East, Abbots (Clendon), Surrey, 368, 401, 458, 814, 817
, West, Surrey, 398, 450, 508, 546, 1220, 1636
Clanfield (Clanefeld), Hants, 510, 935, 1017, 1093, 1113, 1750
Clapham (Clopham), Hants, 178, 179, 345, 392n., 788, 789, 820, 1649, 1706
Clapton, Thomas de, 1097
Clare, Gilbert de, 1187n.
, Maud de, 1739n.

Clatford, Hants, 597
, Upper, 738
, Goodworth, 375, 738
Claver, John, 68
Claverle, William de, 1391
Clawe, Walter, 1072
Claybrooke (Cleybrok'), Leics, 1710
Clee, Leics, Lincs, 1590
Cleeve, Glos, 1165
Clement VI, 269n.
Clement VII, 47n.
Clerc, John, 715, 801
, Richard le, 499, 1021, 1175
, Robert le, 249, 461
, William le, 1636
Clere, John, 1581
, William de, 1356
Clerkenwell (Clerkenwelle), 1742n.
Clestorp', John de, 1548
Cleygh, William, 830
Cliddesden (Cludesden'), Hants, 260, 307, 402, 664, 851
Cliff (Glyve), Kent, 959
Clifford, John, 21
, Roger de, earl of Westmoreland, 1558
Cliston, John de, 1035
Clive, Robert atte, 906
Clopton, Thomas de, 540, 712
Cluny, abbot of, xiv
Clynton, William de, earl of Huntingdon, 127, 973
Clyve, Thomas de, 953
, William, 1476–1479
Cobbild, Thomas, 1162, 1206
Cobeham, John de, knt., 538, 657, 1215n.
, Reginald de, 1268
Cobham (Coveham), Surrey, 425, 614, 1595
Codeford', John de, 1338
, Philip de, 1246
Codford (Codeford), Wilts, 1152, 1226
Codnor (Codenore), Derb, 259, 377, 483, 702, 828
Codynton', John de, 1248
Cohone, Richard, 1127
Coigny, Robert, 1253, 1633
Cok', *see* Couk.
Cokeham, John de, knt., 1080
Cokerel, Joan, nun, 1480–1483
Cole, John, 1618
Colehurch, St Mary, London, 1141
Coleman, John, 64, 65, 95, 96

Colemore (Colemere, Connere), Hants, 600, 822
Coleshull', Ranulf de, 116,
, Thomas de, 79
Coleton', William de, 554, 555
Collingbourne (Colyngborne), Wilts, 1157
Colyngborne, Henry, 1246–1248
Colmworth, Beds, 790
Colonia, John de, 404
Colput, Richard, 1173, 1192, 1196
Colreche, Roger de, 1471
Colthrop (Culesthorp), Berks, 1046
Colton, William de, 260
Colyngburn, Colynborne, Henry de, 1120
, Katerina, nun, 1471
, Robert de, 798, 1042
Combare, John, 1749
Combe, Hants, 1099
Combe Prima, Som, 1728n.
Commere, Thomas de, 600
Compton (Cumeton, Cumpton'), near Guildford, 863, 1131, 1291, 1656
, near Winchester, 81, 176, 177, 187, 478, 689, 1002, 1354, 1417, 1592
, Walter de, 217, 218
Comyn, John, 787
Condam, Walter, 1526
Conert, John de, knt., 536
, Margaret de, 1567
Conrreour, Thomas, 1370
Consande, Consonde, Richard, 181, 182, 1151
Constasthorp', Thomas de, 1715, 1717
Coombe Warren (Combe), Surrey, 896
Corbel, Robert, ben., 695
Corf', John de, 1262, 1296, 1300, 1438, 1491, 1542, 1607, 1635–1637, 1679, 1726, 1728, 1733, 1751, 1752
Cormailles, Joan de, nun, 273
, John de, 273n.
, Michael, 599
Corn, John, 635
Cornhampton, William de, 1108
Corsham, Wilts, 1712
Corston, Thomas de, 1738
Corteys, Hugh, 408
, John, 913, 947
Cosgrave, Stephen de, 847
Cottered (Codereth), Herts, 1669
Coucy, Ingelram de, 1676n.
Coudray, Fulk de, 595
, Thomas de, 1046, 1550

Couer, John de, knt., 134
Cougham, Robert de, 733, 756
Couk, Thomas, 52, 72, 73
, William le, 1241
Coule, Henry, 1628
Coulsdon (Colesdon'), Surrey, 68, 971, 1034
Coupere, William le, 180
Courneys, 1366
Coutances (Constanc'), dioc. 242, 1304
Coventry and Lichfield, archd., 1735
, dioc., 50, 84, 121, 1735
, dean and chap., 996
, Robert bp., 1735
, Roger bp., 121, 1039
Cowden (Couden), Kent, 1633
Cowley (Couele), Mdx, Oxon, 1449
Coxford (Cokesford), priory, Norf, 797
Coyne, Henry, 118
Crabbe, John, 1514
Craft, Hugh, 1418, 1557, 1605, 1661, 1671
Craneborne, John de, 523, 651, 676, 677
Craneslee, Simon de, 436
Craneslegh', William de, 741
Cranford', Robert, 1455
Cranleigh (Cranelegh'), Surrey, 1148, 1376, 1530, 1558, 1573, 1670
Cras, Richard le, 1014
Crascombe, Nicholas de, 1446
Crawley (Craule), Hants, 135, 148n., 208, 278, 603, 611, 651, 1329
Crecy, battle of, 224n., 244n., 256nn.
Creue, Thomas 133, 290
Cristyan, Richard, 349
Crondal (Crondale), Hants, ix, 376, 899–901, 928, 1050, 1052, 1290, 1308
Crondale, John de, fm. 43
Crosse, Thomas de, 165
Crok', William, 1334
Crook', Thomas, 1300, 1435
Crouchback, Edmund, 209n.
Crouche, John atte, 33, 43
Crowland, (Croyland), abbey, Lincs. 1390
Croxford, Thomas de, 303, 304
Croydon (Croyndon), Surrey, 11, 39, 89, 195, 662
, dean, 899
Croyndon, Peter de, 662
, Stephen de, 1197
, Thomas de, 32
Croyser, Croisszer, William, 1155, 1306, 1333

Crux Easton (Crokeseston, Eston' Crok), Hants, 637, 1275
Cubblesdon (Cublesdon), Staffs, 18, 93, 118, 229
Cuckfield (Cokefeld), Sussex, 1080
Cuddington (Codynton'), 68, 142, 551
Cumberton, 715
Cuntasthorp', Thomas de, 1676
Cupping, Thomas, 1015
Curry Rivel, Som, xv
Curteye, William, 889
Curteys, Curtoys, John, 1657
———, Robert, 791
Cusancia, Peter de, 972, 1279
———, William de, xi, 216, 548, 728, 940
Cutel, Walter, 1299

Dabernon, John, 533
———, William, knt., 490, 535
Dagworth, Thomas de, knt., 581
Dallynge, John de, 346
Dalston, Thomas, 1416
Dalton, Robert, 1690
Danhurst, Robert, 1744n.
Daniel, Thomas, 342
Danndely, William, 415
Danvers, Agnes, 622n.
Darcy, John, 244, 301
Dartford (Derteford'), Kent, dominican nuns, 1200
———, Joan, prioress, 1200
Daubeneye, William, ben., 1734
Daulyn, Simon, 945, 973
Daventree, Davyntree, Peter de, 894
David, Thomas, 907, 936, 964, 1222, 1223
———, Walter, 1617
Dean, West (Westdone), Hants, 294, 517, 1450
———, Maudut (Dene), 786
de la Chapell, William, 126
de la Mare, Elizabeth and Peter, 148
de la Pré, abbey, Herts, 718, 826
de la Vyne, John, 134, 144, 222
Denham, Donham, John de, 1226, 1238, 1326
Dennyngworth, Bartholomew de, 1642
Denton, ? Sussex, 1567
———, Thomas de, 1599
Depedene, Dupedene, Nicholas de, 573, 1119
Depham, John de, 180
———, Walter de, 77, 180
Derby, Edmund de, 929n.
———, Richard de, 261

Derneford', Adam de, 314
———, Henry de, 1414
de Sancto Albano, Elias, 153
de Sancto Johanne, Edmund son of Hugh, 18, 19, 93, 118
Descote, Margaret, d. of Hugh, 744
Devenish, Nicholas, viii, 217, 371, 1103n.
———, Thomas, 1070, 1653
Devercy, John, 316
Diare, John le, 355
Dibden (Dupedene), Hants, 573, 1114, 1119, 1685
Dissee, Disse, Thomas, 944, 1135
Ditton, Kent, 896, 1655
———, Long (Longeditton'), Surrey, 68, 98, 411, 951, 1064
———, Thomas de, 1505
Doddington (Dodyngton), Lincs/Northants, 104, 106
Dodeford, John de, 1535
Dodenham, Thomas de, 1158
Dodlesfold, Ralph de, 1703
Dodyngton, William de, carm., 539
Doget, Robert, 169, 170
Dogmersfield (Dogmersfeld), Hants, 92, 116, 1023, 1403, 1686, 1687
Dolby, Roger de, 986
Donhead St Mary (Donheved Marie), Wilts, 792
Donmowe, William, 602
Donniton, Ralph de, ben., 29
Donnyngworth', Bartholomew de, 840
Dorchester (Dorkacestr'), Oxon/Dorset, 960, 1004
Dorkecestria, John de, 370
Dorking (Dorkynge), Surrey, 305, 532, 1636
Dorset, archd., 1032
Dorsete, Richard de, 203, 489
———, William, 709
Doublel, Blaise, ben., 262
Douk', Walter, 264
Down (Doun) in Odiham, Hants, 142
Downton (Dounton'), Wilts, x, 660, 994–996, 1646, 1647
Draghton', Robert de 1084
Draicote, William de, 435
Draper, Thomas, 613
Drax, Richard, 230
Draynford, in Kingston, Surrey, 896
Drayton, Richard de, 1491
Drexthorp, Lincs, 147
Drogheda (Droghda), Ireland, 929
Drokenford, Thomas de, knt., 637

Droxford (Drokenesford'), Hants, 461, 1148, 1343, 1344, 1428
, dean of, 818, 1424, 1710
Drungewick (Duryngwik'), in Wisborough Green, Sussex, 181
Dublin, John, archbp., x, 995, 1011
, dioc., 1649
Duddelee, John, 673
Dukebrigg', William de, 1117
Dumbeliton', Richard de, ben., 158
Dummer (Dummere), Hants, 1650
Dunham, 720, 839
Dunheved, Michael, 1417, 1643
Dunsfold (Duntesfold), Surrey, 722, 1195, 1439, 1523, 1603, 1648
Dunsteple, John, 98
Dunton Waylett (Dounton Waylate), Essex, 192, 212
Dupedene, *see* Depedene.
Durbath', William de, 606
Durford, abbey, Sussex, 863, 1131, 1291
Durham, dioc., 981, 1186
Durlee, Thomas de, 63, 268, 661, 770, 775, 832, 860, 1214
Durnham, John de, 1246
Duryval, Thomas, 112, 972
Dyare, Dyer, John le, of Wight, 46, 220, 221
Dymmok', William de, 215

Eastbourne (Eseborne), Sussex, 1522
East Claydon, Bucks, xv
East Kirkley (Estirkele), Lincs, 978
Eastnor (Estenore), Heref, 238, 239
East Orchard (Orchard'), Dorset, 277
East Parley (Estpirlee), Hants, 456
East Riding (Est Ridinge), Yorks, archd. 894
Eastrop (Esthrop'), near Basingstoke, 839, 1326
Eccleshale, Richard de, 815, 870
, Thomas de, 870, 954, 955, 1010, 1014
Edenef', William, 1017, 1122, 1127
Ederosi, i.e. Ivychurch in Alderbury, Wilts, 43
Edington (Edyndon), Wilts, vii, 400, 461, 834, 1142, 1275-1277, 1279, 1280, 1516, 1612
Edith', John, 1046
, Geoffrey, 1531
Edmerthorp (Thorp Edemere), Leics, 1572
Edmund, 929,
, Roger, 740

Edrith', John, 1117, 1144
Edward II, 1200
III, viii, xiii, 3, 39, 45, 48, 139, 142, 162, 169, 212, 214, 227, 234, 353, 364, 373, 385, 420, 432, 436, 438, 476, 482, 484, 488, 512, 548, 549, 592, 596, 597, 616, 718, 728, 733, 734, 741, 759, 761, 785, 788, 805, 808, 810, 831, 877, 921, 931, 985, 992, 995, 1001, 1010, 1014, 1032, 1039, 1040, 1081, 1130, 1162, 1206, 1207, 1289, 1347, 1368, 1371, 1374, 1375, 1385, 1388, 1404, 1413, 1430, 1440, 1452, 1463, 1470, 1479, 1480, 1505, 1528, 1607, 1655, 1677, 1698, 1699
Edward, prince, the Black Prince, 69, 107, 120, 528, 529, 672, 693, 986, 1034, 1233, 1497, 1539, 1564, 1626
Edyndon, William de, treasurer of England, 1
, provided to Winchester, 1-11
, consecration, 86
, John de, ix, xi, 249-252, 369, 395, 463, 464, 690, 807, 812, 814, 815, 817, 834, 854, 855, 860, 1062, 1200, 1267
, Thomas de, ix, 725, 860, 882, 975, 976, 1751
, Walter de, 341
, William, not the bishop, 406, 1608
Effingham (Effyngham'), Surrey, 474, 1143, 1271, 1396
Egham (Egeham), Surrey, 367, 396, 781, 782, 1502
Elden (Elleden), Hants, 77, 180, 315, 1244, 1515
Elemosina, Peter de, ben., 1240
Elen, Roger de, called Pope, 531
Elfeton', Richard de, 862
Eling (Elynge), Hants, 629
Elingdon (Elyndon'), Wilts, 457, 730
Ellingham (Elyngham), Hants, priory, 175, 242, 1304, 1734
, church, 1566, 1647, 1734
Ellisfield (Ulsefeld'), Hants, 646, 1521, 1723
Elstead (Elnestede), Sussex, 1206
Eltesle, Thomas de, 404, 1118 (junior and senior), 1123, 1172 (junior)
Ely, dioc., x, 305, 1118, 1322
, Thomas de Lisle, bp., 104, 138, 139, 1118
, Richard de, 1349

Elyndon, dioc. Salisbury, *see* Wroughton.
, Nicholas de, 1357
Elyng', Richard de, 522, 570, 1277
Elyot, Richard, 1650
, William, xi, 402, 654, 791
Elys, Richard, 934, 1106
Empshot (Imbeschete, Imbeschute), Hants, 857, 1399, 1522
Emsworth, Hants, 217n.
Engleys, John, knt., 934
Englishe, Thomas, 1283, 1570
Engulby, William de, 298
Enham, Hants, *see* Knights Enham
, Thomas de, ix, 154, 158, 171, 205, 268, 516, 626, 627, 681, 855, 882, 974, 976, 1008, 1017, 1020, 1028, 1084, 1111, 1127, 1137, 1192, 1227, 1229–1231, 1238, 1242, 1245, 1246, 1248, 1252, 1264
Eorl, John, 1020
Epsom (Ebesham), Surrey, 68, 269, 270, 1369
Ercheffonte, William de, 476
Ermynne, William, 1567
Ernesby, John de, 1378, 1513
Escote, Hugh de, 344
, Thomas de, 344
Esher (Essere), Surrey, 166, 265, 271, 272, 322–324, 331, 332, 336–339, 354–388, 397, 430f, 512–519, 525–555, 568–574, 577–593, 614, 724, 738–742, 763, 767, 774, 775, 802, 803, 825f, 831–833, 855, 863–865, 878, 882, 896, 929, 930, 942, 948, 980, 1023–1026, 1067–1072, 1086, 1143–1147, 1168, 1256, 1260, 1269–1072, 1086, 1143–1147, 1168, 1256, 1260, 1269–1271, 1514, 1515, 1524–1528, 1555, 1562–1573, 1575, 1590, 1594, 1602, 1603, 1611, 1738, 1739
Essex, archd., 212
, John de, 1081, 1084, 1242, 1245–1248
Estbury, Walter de, 1558
Estham', Walter de, 1573, 1670
Eston, ? Crux Eston, 353, 1441
, Roger de, 153, 1087
Eton, Beds, 848
Everard, Robert, 506
Everdon, John de, 1291, 1656
Eversden', Robert de, 759
Eversley (Everdeslegh, Evereslegh), Hants, 41, 307, 750, 960, 1004, 1121, 1253, 1633

Evreux, dioc., France, 263 and *see* Lyre.
Ewell (Ewelle), Surrey, dean, 16, 67, 68, 84n., 411, 714, 715, 950, 978, 982, 1051, 1431
, church, 98–100, 108, 145, 152, 926–928, 1050, 1051, 1078, 1087, 1342, 1434, 1529
Ewhurst (Iwehurst), Surrey, 760, 781, 782, 888, 1094, 1216, 1535, 1629, 1636
Exeter, dioc., 63n., 413n., 1572n.
, canon, 1728
, bishop, 986
, John, bp., 413
Exon', John de, 765, 931, 992
, Roger de, 923
Exton, Hants, 666
Eye, priory (Eya), Norf, 169
Eykeryng', Thomas de, 351, 449
Eyland, Adam, 1364
Eymer, Edith, ben., 916
Eyr, William, 43
Eyton, John de, 1310

Fabri, Walter, xi
Fabyan, John, 1374
Faccombe, Hants, 1057, 1440, 1517
Fadir, Thomas le, 721
Fairford, John de, 1685
Fairforth, William de, 390
Fakenhamdam, John de, 1037
Falewell, Peter de, 1608
Falk', Peter de, 740, 894, 1099
Fallecis, Saludun de, 1252, 1262
Falloe, William de, 1318
Fareham (Farham), Hants, 656, 1105, 1323
Farendon', John, 1104
Farham, Richard de, 639
Faringdon (Farendon'), Hants, 413, 661, 1572
Farleigh Wallop (Ferlee), Hants, xi, 68, 98, 238, 239, 489, 654, 791, 1117, 1336, 1377
Farley Chamberlayne (Farlee), Hants, 384, 605, 1144, 1234, 1445, 1520, 1594, 1654, 1707, 1747
Farley (Ferlegh, Farlee), Surrey, 663, 827, 944, 1135, 1563
Farley, West (Westfarlegh), Kent, 779, 780
Farlee, Henry de, 1336n.
, William de, 136, 321, 322, 324, 611, 874, 1534
Farlington (Farlyngton), Hants, 1030, 1674

Farnborough (Farnebergh'), Hants, xi, 53, 94, 164, 729, 1201, 1398, 1419, 1499, 1651, 1658

Farndale, Farnedale, Walter de, 274, 286, 540

Farnham (Farham), Hants, dean, 16, 336, 541

———, castle, vii, x, 287, 315–320, 325–330, 333–335, 399–424, to 468, 480–482, 516, 541, 543, 561–563, 716–723, 854, 891, 956–957, 960–962, 973–975, 982–984, 1041–1043, 1092, 1165–1167, 1225, 1236, 1237, 1257–1259, 1260, 1267, 1304–1318, 1321–1323, 1448, 1458, 1498, 1499, 1521–1523, 1549–1552, 1585–1588, 1607, 1624, 1653, 1658, 1660–1664, 1668, 1680–1683, 1703, 1710, 1711

Faryndon', John de, 500

Faukes, Thomas, 1607

———, William, 1197

Fawley (Fallee), Hants, 133, 290

Fehew, Fehw, James, 1649

Felawe, John, 1165

Fengate, Adam atte, 1284

Fenglesham, John carm., 43

Fenny Stratford (Fennystrettford), Berks, 264, 280

Fernham (Fyrnham), Berks, 769

———, Ralph de, 385

Ferre, Eleanor and Guy, 246

Ferrour, John, 551

Ferring, Susex, 274, 869

Fescamp', John de, ben., 1031

Fetcham (Fecham), Surrey, 533, 902, 937, 1333, 1442

Fifehead (Fyfhyde), Dorset, 718, 825, 826, 972, 1272, 1449

Fifehead Skydmore, dioc. Salisbury, 972

Fifhide, William de, 705, 1046, 1057, 1440, 1550

Fil' Theobaldi, Geoffrey, 932

Finchampstead (Fynchampstede), Berks, 261

Fingest (Tyngehurst), Bucks, 357, 1029

Finsbury (Fynesbury), Midd, 238

Fitelton, Thomas de, 1246

Fitlynge, Amand de, 724

Fittleworth (Fitelworth), Sussex, 1669

Fitz Herbert, Matthew, knt., 110, 933, 1005

Fitz Hugh, James, 1706

———, Roger, 142

Fitz Peter, 1042

Fleet Marston (Fletemerston), Bucks, 95

Flemmyng', Walter, 604

Flintham (Flyntham), Notts, 1130

Florenc', John de, 879

Fogor', William, 1625, 1660

Folefenne, Richard de, 418

Folevyle, William, fm., 43

Folk, Thomas, 525, 550, 853, 854, 865

Folyot, Roger, 1189

Foncel, Richard de, 348

———, Roger de, 1266

Fontevrault (Fontis Ebrardi), order, 50, 451, 510, 818

Fonthill Bishop (Fontel Episcopi), Wilts, 88, 106, 107, 1152

Ford, la, 853

Forde, Henry de, 322, 323, 355, 369, 393, 394, 400, 406, 409, 930

———, Thomas de, ben., 29

Fordingbridge (Fordyngbrugg, Forde), Hants, 309, 359, 416, 539, 1716, 1722

———, dean, 261, 815

———, Hospital of St John, 261, 416, 1507

Franceys, William, 1175

Frannk', Robert, 1383, 1600

Fredryngeye, John de, 1683

Freefolk (Fryfolk Syfrewast), Hants, 366, 624, 697, 904, 1109, 1432

Freland' Walter de, 1365, 1735, 1736

Frenssh', John le, 496

Frere, Geoffrey, 1578

Freshwater (Fresshewatere), I. Wight, 63n., 393, 400, 409, 930, 1713

Freston', William de, 1458

Freton', Richard de, 1197

Friland, Walter de, 405, 582, 994

Fritwell (Fretewell'), Oxon, 838

Frobury (Frollebury), in Kingsclere, Hants, 308, 841

Frollebury, John de, 247, 1579 *and see* Marschal.

Frome, William, ben., 24

Fromond, Robert, 384, 934

Frowbury, John de, 749

Froyle (Froille), Hants, 30, 154, 171, 205, 516, 626, 681, 855, 882, 1008, 1230, 1371

Frye, John le, 382

Frylond, William, 886, 891

Fulford, John de, 626, 627, 682, 1128

———, Roger de, 157, 574, 576, 618, 626, 627, 651, 661, 681, 682, 726, 916, 1009

Fulham, Henry de, 348
Fyfhyde, Walter de, ben., 1526
Fynacourt, Walter, 658
Fynamore, Walter, 1279
Fyndon, Peter de, 113, 114, 217, 218

Gainsborough (Geynesburg), Lincs, 945
Galobre, Thomas de, ben., 229, 234
Gamene, Robert le, 696
Gardyner, William, 1716
Gary, John, 1274
Gasturia, Robert de, ben., 1456
Gatacre, Philip de, 612
Gatcombe (Gatecombe), I. Wight, 22,
635, 1107, 1207, 1404, 1601
Gate, Robert atte, 291, 292
Gaterugg', William de, 337, 1147
Gatesbury, Ralph de, 310, 405
Gatton, Surrey, 699, 1025, 1237
Gaucelin de Eauze, card. bp. of
Albano, 111
Gaugire, Nicholas, ben., 1240
Gaundevill', John de, 1316
Gaydone, Robert de, 1068
Geardyn, John, 1092
Gerard', Richard, 1545
Gerberd', Robert 934
Gerlethorp', John de, 1034
, Thomas de, 971
Gernon, Hugh, 223
Gernoun, John, 1738
Gervais, Roger and Isabella, 289
Gervaise, Couma, prioress Wintney,
632
Gervays, Joan, abbess, Romsey, 514,
544, 916
, William, 982, 1451, 1552,
1587
Geynesburg, Simon de, 127
Giffard, Gifferd, Gyffard, John, 1742
, Nicholas, 151
Gilbert, dean of London, 81
, John, 1390
Gillingham (Gyllyngham), Dorset,
166–168
Girchet, Thomas, 1625
Gladyere, Richard, 761
Glanvule, Thomas, 1742
Glatton, Hunts, 1075
Glemesford', John and Beatrice de,
1546
Gleobury, John, 1493
Glouc', 1107
Gloucestr', John de, 726
Gloucester, abbey, 63n., 485, 703,
1263, 1429

Gnowshale, Edmund de, 1187
Godalming (Godalmynge), Surrey, 572,
954, 955, 1010
Godard, John, 842, 1547
Gode, Henry, 1647
Goderynton', Reginald de, 388
Godman, John, 20, 491, 1665
Godshill (Godeshull'), I. Wight, 420
Godstone, *see* Wolkhampstead.
Godwyne, John, 853
Gogh, John junior, 493, 698, 869
Gold, Golde, Peter, 1511, 1746
, Roger, 1606
Goldesburgh', Antony de, 1572
Goldeston, Thomas de, 707, 890, 1047
Goldhill, Dorset, 276
Golegh, John, 1271
Goodworth Clatford (Godeworth),
Hants, 375, 738, 1625, 1660
Goudman, John, 642, 905, 1502
, William, 569
Gorges, Theobald de, 302, 349, 736,
1664
Gormecestre, Thomas de, 27, 43
Gosselyn, John, 999
Gotes, John de, 1703
Gotham, Roger de, 269, 270
Gourda, Walter, 1387, 1666
Gover, John de, knt., 134
Grandisson, Otho and Beatrice, 1422
, William, 428n.
Grandmesnil, Hugh de, 1614n.
Graspays, Graspeis, William, 88, 106,
107, 108
Grately, Hants, 1280, 1580
, Walter, 1488
Gravesend (Graveshende), Kent, 1198
Great Bookham, *see* Bookham.
Great Eversden (Everesdon' Magna)'
Camb, 138
Greatham (Gretham), Hants, 217n.,
371, 1070, 1653
Great Shefford (Schifford Magna),
Berks, 858
Great Warley (Warle Abbesse), Essex,
1113
Gregory IX, pope, 1491n.
X, 92, 1424
, Richard, 1205
Grene, Richard atte, 1644
, Robert atte, 1224
Grenehurst', John de, 1192
Grenet, Peter, 995, 1011
Grenhull', Robert, 601
Grestain, abbey (Eure), France, 1181n.

Gretton, Richard de, 1289
Grey, Henry, earl of Rotherfield, 894
        , John de, knt., 259, 377, 383,
702, 828, 894
        , Robert, 1568
Greyne, John le, xi
        , Richard atte, 984
Greyneweye, John, 1636
Groseur, John, 1184
Grove, Berks, 1300, 1435
Groyn, John, 381
Grugg', John, 1454
Grymesby, John de, 1141
Gugwell, Reginald de, 1606
Guildford (Guldeford), Surrey, 863,
965, 1079, 1291
        , dean, 16, 84n., 368, 552,
716, 816, 817, 1010, 1198, 1273, 1636
        , Dominican convent, 22
        , H. Trinity, 16, 779, 780,
1143, 1278, 1349, 1384
        , St Mary, 499, 731
        , St Nicholas, 771
Gukke, John, 1642
Guldeforde, Henry de, 365
        , John de, 1458, 1490
        , Richard de, 22, 391
Gurgan, William, 366
Gurnel, John, 1577, 1611
Gyles, John, 1623, 1644

Habbegod', Richard, 640, 689
Hadham (Hedham), Herts, 57, 138, 961
Haghman, Hagheman, Nicholas, 41,
307, 414, 650, 750
Halghton, Thomas de, 571
Hakat, William, 151, 1742
Haket, Thomas, 137, 150, 751, 903,
1159, 1715
Hakker, Walter, 1636
Halle, Richard atte, 1233
Halling (Hallyng), Kent, 676
Halterwort', Thomas le, 791
Halterwrighte, Thomas le, 664
Halton, Berks, 1712
Ham (Hamme), Surrey, 896
        , dioc. Salisbury, 1372
Hambeya, Galvanus de, 242
Hamble (Hamele), priory, Hants, 436,
741, 1487
Hambledon (Hameldon), Surrey, 131,
209, 300, 319, 320, 462, 693, 1020,
1105, 1238, 1341, 1356, 1744
Hameldon, John de, cist., 830
Hamme, Richard de, 622, 1653
Hammush', Nicholas, 1321

Hamo, bp. Rochester, 676, 779
Hampton, Richard de, 329, 330, 878,
1428
        , Robert de, 378
        , Thomas de, 1257, 1634
Handborough (Hanerberghe), Oxon,
972
Handesone, John, 1199
Handlo, John de, knt., 163
Hangelton', Ralph de, 1191
Hangre, Richard de, 1685
Hanleye, William de, 1645
Hanmull', John, 1079
Hannington (Hanyton), Hants, 678,
1192
Hardewyn, Robert, 1294
Hardres (Hargh'), Kent, 444
Hardwayne, Robert, 1750, 1752
Hardwick (Herdewyk), Lincs/Leics,
1117
Hardyng', Thomas, 534
Harple, Harpele, William de, 66, 75,
225, 226
Harpour, John, 972
Harrington (Haveryndun), Lincs, 956,
958
Harrow (Haregh), 809, 899-901
Harthorp, Thomas de, 1132
Harting (Hartynge), Sussex, 697
Hartley Mauditt (Hertele Mauduyt),
Hants, 267, 636, 1337
                Wespall (Hertele Waspail),
Hants, 410, 447, 612, 686, 1052, 1345,
1740
                Wintney (Herteleye Wint', H.
monialium), Hants, 498, 648, 710, 852,
913, 952, 1122, 1292, 1702
Harwedon', Henry de, 1490
Hascombe, William de, 802
Haselbech', Richard de, 1710
Hasthorp, Thomas de, 1575
Hatch (Hacche), Hants, 692, 806, 1212
        , Surrey, 896
Hatch Beauchamp, Som, 825, 826
Hattere, Peter, 1632
Haulo, Walter de, 277
Havant (Havonte), Hants, 139, 140,
1029, 1030
Haverbergh', John de, 1153
Havydon', Roger de, 1069
Haydon', John de, 145
        , Thomas de, 145
Hawkley (Haukele), Hants, 1748
Hayes (Hese), Kent, 1582

Hayling (Haylinge), Hants, 373, 1424, 1452, 1453
, priory, 373
Hayton, William de, 422
Haywode, John de, ben., 987
, Nicholas de, 347
, Walter de, 679, 848
Haywood (Hewode), ? Staffs, 1039
Headbourne Worthy (Worthy comitis), Hants, 1024, 1182
Headley (Hethleigh', Hedlee), Surrey, 509, 575, 967, 996, 1012, 1185
Heath, Kent, 853n.
Heckfield (Heighfeld'), Hants, 511, 942n., 947, 1307, 1616, 1657
Hegham, knt., 1174
, John de, 128
Heighton, Sussex, 1035
Helm, Roger, 1669
Helmenden, Thomas de, 1063
Hemmesby, Richard de, 1276
Hemmisch', Nicholas, 1607
Hempston Cantilupe, Devon, 767n.
Hemyngby, Thomas de, 888
Hendeman, John, 805, 1657
Hengham, John de, 188, 295
Henley, Cold, (Henlee), in Whitchurch, Hants, 501, 1095, 1555
Hennte, Henry, 1611
Henton, Adam de, 1433
, Nicholas de, 902, 937
Hepworth, Stephen de, 1659
Herdeby, William, 1367
Hereford, 1018, 1084
, dean, 215, 1678
, dioc. 809, 1678
, bp. John, 238, 275, 276
, bp. Louis, 1678
, ch. St Andrew, 215
Hereyndon', Adam de, 1307
Herierde, Alexander de, 556
Herin, Richard, 1510
Hering, *see* Heryng.
Herinthorp', John de, 1735, 1736
Herman, Roger, 1252, 1267
    Walter, 1420
Henry, William son of, 1197
Herriard (Herierde), Hants, 578
Hert, Thomas, 518
Herteshorne, Thomas de, 1130
Hertford, 103n.
, archd., 990
, dean, 988, 990
, John de, carm., 43
Hertyngdon, Adam de, 1616

Hervy, Richard, 1325
Heryng, John, 175, 712
Heselerton, Richard de, 373
Heyford, Thomas de, 356, 793
Heynote, John, 50, 51, 74, 155, 254, 284, 794
Heytesbury (Heightredebury), Wilts, 752, 753
Heyton', Thomas de, 98-100, 102
'Heywode', 1735 *and see* Haywode.
Higham Gobion (Hegham Gobyon), Beds, 1153
Highclere (Alta Clera), Hants, x, 252, 530, 617f, 633f, 764, 769, 772, 1044, 1192, 1202, 1218, 1281-1286, 1407, 1485, 1517-1520, 1576-1579, 1584, 1605-1610, 1641, 1642, 1672 1676-1679, 1712-1715, 1718a & b, 1744
Highworth (Heyworth), Wilts, 1702
High Wycombe, Bucks, dean, 958
Hilton, Adam de, 1071, 1075
Hinton Ampner (Heneton), Hants, 658, 705, 915
, Little (Hyneton), Wilts, 1406, 1559, 1675-1687
Hobbes, John, 1171
Hobyn, Robert, 1221
Hogham', Robert, 916
Hogenorton, John de, 1058, 1285, 1631
, Robert de, 1583
Holbeach (Holbech'), Lincs, 985
Holewale, John, 491
Holland, William count of, 1337n.
Holm, Roger, 1650
Hoo, John de, 762, 846, 1178, 1229
, Philip de, 443
, Richard, carm., 43
, Thomas de, 356
Hood, Robert, 1689
Hook (la Hoke), Surrey, 896
Hope, Peter de, 133, 770
Hore, William le, 1299, 1436
Horley (Horle), Surrey, 68, 683, 777, 991
Horman, Walter, 1373
Horsebridge, in Kings Somborne, 1244n.
Horsman, John le, 674
Horstead (Horstede), Norf. 1130
Horwode, Fulk de, 1215
, John, 98
Hosclore, Richard, 629
Hospitallers, 539, 813, 978, 1042, 1177
Hoton or Hocon, Adam, 1098
Houghem', Nicholas de, 903

Houghton (Haughton), Hants, 176, 321, 322, 323, 369, 393, 394, 406, 481, 807, 812, 814, 881, 1001, 1009, 1142, 1183, 1193, 1194, 1328
, Adam de, 642
, Nicholas de, 1159
Houleston, Thomas de, 321–324
Hound (Houne), Hants, 436, 741, 1562
Houston, Isabella, 1503, 1715, 1717
Hugeman, Richard, 714
Huggate, Thomas de, 1166
Hugh, James son of, 1706
Hugheyn, John, 1094, 1095
Hull, xv
Hulle, Walter atte, 332, 512, 788, 789
, William de, 1207, 1720
Humfray, Richard, 717
Hungerforde, Thomas de, viii
Huntingfield, Henry de, 904n.
Huntington, 1677
, archd., 139, 1075
, earl of, 127
, Juliana, countess of, 1423
, John de, 291, 292
Hurle, William de, 279n.
Hurlee, John de, ben., 158
, William de, 279n.
Hursele, John de, 387
Hursley (Hursele), Hants, 311, 324, 611, 646–649, 768, 874, 1598, 1691, 1698, 1701, 1704, 1705, 1733, 1735n.
Hurstbourne Tarrant (Husseburne Regis, H. Tarente), Hants, 121, 122, 297, 496, 1188, 1252, 1262
Husee, John, 419
, Henry, knt., 366, 624
, Katherine, 624
Husseborne, Henry de, 1243, 1644
Hustane, Geoffrey de, 1715n.
Hybury, Richard, 1176
Hyde, abbey, Hants, 241, 330, 337, 343, 351, 372, 378, 446, 475, 494, 515, 534, 553, 574, 576, 579, 605, 610, 631, 656, 682, 696, 720, 721, 727, 757, 772, 830, 1088, 1161, 1221, 1226, 1241, 1325, 1360, 1362, 1363, 1366, 1386, 1387, 1501, 1510, 1513, 1526–1528, 1585, 1632,
, abbot, 39
, ch. St Bartholomew, 342, 534
, Richard de, 63
Hyda, Hyde, John de, 115
, Ralph de, 595
Hyle, William en le, 517
Hynkele, Robert de, 711, 896, 978

, William de, 951, 1063
Hylton, *see* Hilton.

Ichenstok', John de, 80
Icklesham (Iklesham), Sussex, 1195
Iddebury, Henry de, 1596
Ilkeston, William de, 193
Imber (Inmere), Wilts, 619, 1553
Imworth, Gilbert de, knt., 257
Inge, William, archd., viii, 63, 84
Ingepenn, John de, 642, 890, 1048
, Peter de, 123, 124, 141, 250
, Robert de, 491, 492
Ingram, Peter, 894
Ingulby, Ingylby, William de, 961, 962
Innocent VI, pope, xiv
Insula (del Isle), Bartholomew, 963, 1623
, Elizabeth, 441, 758, 963, 1623
, Gerard, 639
, John de, 635, 1207
, Thomas de, 325, 1045
Irford, John de, 43
Irmongere, Thomas le, 633
Irtlyngburgh', Nicholas de, 978, 1066
Isabella, queen, 756
, the king's daughter, 1163, 1676
, de Lancaster, prioress, 209, 228, 300
Isendyk', Judaeus de, carm., 43
Isfield (Isefeld), Sussex, 1659
Isle, del, *see* Insula.
Isleworth (Istelworth), Mdx, 1104
Islip, Islep, Simon, archbp., 813, 853, 899, 1079, 1118, 1176, 1401, 1560, 1582, 1632, 1673
Istele, Nicholas de, 1582
Itchen Abbas (Ichene), Hants, 70, 190, 472, 523, 1086, 1110, 1388
Itchenstoke (Ichenstok'), Hants, 115, 599, 651, 676, 939, 1108, 1378, 1518, 1646
Ivingho, John de, 914, 943
Ivinghoe (Ivyngho), priory, Berks, 470, 608, 1033, 1342, 1743
Ivychurch (monasterium ederosi), priory, in Alderbury, Wilts, 43, 1607
Iwerne Minster (Iwerneminstre), Dorset, 1347
Iwon, Roger, 372
Ixnynge, Thomas de, 1229

Jardyn, John, 1133, 1139, 1140

Jarpenville, Giles de, 1635–1638
, Thomas de, 417, 1383
, William de, 417
Jarom, Robert de, 506, 537, 679
Joce, William, 135, 208, 278
John, king of England, 1659n.
, king of France, xiii, xiv
, the king's son (of Gaunt), 1572
, XXI, pope, 190
, archbp., see Stratford.
, earl of Kent, 708
, earl of Warenne, 170
Jolyf, William, 192, 203, 409
Joskyn, Thomas, 1744
Jumièges (Gemitico), abbey, France, 1453
Jurdan, Thomas, 1745

Kaerwent, Kerwent, Kerewent, Nicholas de, 774, 812, 969, 1084, 1114, 1115, 1248, 1308, 1313, 1607, 1733
Kaygnes, Kaynes, Thomas de, 1050, 1051
Kedyngton', Kedyton', Geoffrey de, 109, 110, 932
Keevil (Kyvele), Wilts, 1574
Kelleseye, Robert de, 515
Kelly, Ralph, carm., archbp. Cashel, 42, 44
Kemeseye, Henry de, 748, 1145
, Walter de, 235
Kempshot (Kempshute), in Winslade, Hants, 1186
Kempston, 587
Kendale, Edward de, knt., 103, 186, 296, 856
, John de, 508, 533, 902
Kenesworth', John de, 608
Kenilworth (Kenylworth), priory, 121
Kene, John de, 622
Kent, Edmund, earl of, 139, 364
, John, earl, 708
, Margaret, countess, 143
, Adam, 1675
, John de, 440, 896
Kenyngton, John de, 694, 995
Kerolston', John de, 1025, 1237
Kerselawe, Kerselewe, Richard de, 1233
, Roger de, 396, 781, 782, 1216
Keteryng', Roger de, 498
Keteryngham, John de, 940
Kettelby, John de, 1293
Kibblesworth (Kybleworth), ? Durhm, 988

Kimpton (Cumeton'), Hants, 395, 861, 866
Kingsclere (Clera Regis, Kingescrere), Hants, xv, 46, 189, 220, 221, 247, 355, 391, 607, 1617, 1629, 1702
Kings Cliff (Kyngesclyve), Northants, 1160
Kings Somborne, Hants, 394, 459, 1244n.
Kings Worthy (Worthy Regis), Hants, 696, 1362
Kingston-on-Thames (Kyngeston super Thamis'), Surrey, 16, 54, 71, 98, 190, 201, 303, 304, 440, 614, 711, 987, 1066, 1678, chapel St M. Magdalen, 264, 280, 478, 896, 951, 1063, 1064, 1179, 1180
Kingston (Kyngston'), I. Wight, 442, 840, 896, 1642
Kirk Merrington (Westmeryngton), Durhm, 1186
Kirketon' William de, 648
Kirton in Lindsey, Lincs, 1017
Kislingbury (Kyslingbury), Northants, 1205
Knaith (Knayth'), Lincs, 244, 301
Knighton (Knyghteton'), I. Wight, chapel of H. Trinity, 302, 349, 736, 864, 1664
Knights Enham (Enham militis), Hants, 163, 1455
Knot, Walter, 1650
Knut, king, 613n.
Knyght, Ralph, 502, 760, 781, 782, 1491, 1497, 1499, 1502, 1533
, Roger, 887
, William, 191, 279
Knyghtecote, Peter de, 1281, 1285
Kyfthill, William de, 244, 301
Kyllum, Geoffrey de, 139, 140, 1029, 1030
, Robert de, 139, 140
Kymberlee, John de, 1002
Kynebell', Robert de, 347
Kyng, John, 420, 1713
Kyngesfold, John de, 1635, 1636
Kyngeston', John de, 442, 835, 1642
, Nicholas de, 466, 467, 1102, 1119, 1685
Kyonus, John, 1341
Kyrkeby, Roger de, 961, 962

Ladde, Amicia, 1464
, Thomas, 293
Lainston (Leyneston'), Hants, 207, 640, 717, 1436

Lambeth (Lamheth'), Surrey, 96n.,
225, 302, 404, 813, 1118, 1123, 1172,
1401, William de, 1172
Lambyn, Thomas, 1404, 1601
Lamphey, Dyfed, 1222n.
Lamport, William, 1726
Lancaster, Henry, earl of, 172, 209n.,
267, 498, 636, 710
   , Isabella, 209n.
   , John duke of , 866, 909,
1726, 1732
   , Matilda, countess, 1337
Lancing (Launcing), Sussex, 1703
Landeilo, Carmarthen, 1669
Lane, Richard in the, 904
   , William in le, 1109, 1331
   , John atte, 1230, 1360, 1432
Langedon, John de, 332
Langeford, Edmund de, 832, 1350
   , Nicholas de, 76, 132, 876
   , Richard de, 89–91
Langford (Langeford), Oxon, 191
Langley Marsh (Langele Mareys),
Bucks, 420
Langressch', Mary de, 384
Langton (Langeton), 309
Lantefey = Lamphey, Dyfed, 1222
Lanynton', Robert de, 494
   , Thomas de, 701, 728, 740
Laser, Richard, 746
Lasham, Hants, 473
Latimer, William, knt., 298, 1088,
1191, 1690
   , Thomas de, 962
Launceston (Lanceston'), Corn, xii
Laurence, John, 1407, 1519, 1636,
1672, 1714
   , Richard, 1320
Lavendon', Robert, 1415
Laverstoke (Laverkestok', Larkstok'),
Hants, 255, 579, 631, 634, 772, 1088,
1221
Lavington (Levynton), Sussex, 972
Laweles, Richard, 1238
Leach, North, Glos, 809n.
Leatherhead (Ledrede), Surrey, 66–68,
75, 98, 225, 226, 388, 423, 571, 746
Leaveland (Lavelonde), Kent, 353
Lecchelade, John de, ben., 60
Lech', John de, ix, 151, 444, 445, 562,
564, 809, 810, 899–901, 916, 917, 926,
928, 1035, 1050, 1051, 1052, 1308
Leckford (Lekford), Hants, 836, 1065,
1368
Ledebury, Thomas de, 887, 983

Ledwell', Henry, 838
Leeds (Ledes), priory, Kent, 43, 66, 75,
225, 226, 388, 423, 571, 779
Le Fleure, Richard, 352
Legh', Robert de, 426
   , Thomas de, 1273
Leicester (Leycester), abbey, 909
   , archd., 1710
   , Robert, earl of, 50n.
Leigh (Northlegh'), Oxon, 357
Leighlin, Ireland, 42
Leighton Buzzard (Leghton 'Busard),
Beds, 633
Leghton, Reginald de, 199
Lekford, Stephen de, 362
Lemyngton, Robert de, 1138, 1144,
1146, 1234, 1437, 1445, 1498, 1726
Lent', John, 931
Leominstr', John de, 1197
Lesnes, abbey, Kent, 43, 762, 1178,
1659
Leth', John de, 803
Lever, William, 597
Leverington, William de, 1173
Lewedham, John de, 699
Lewes (Lewen'), Sussex, 699, 1025,
1028, 1237, 1349, 1359, 1575, 1590
   , John de, 1603, 1648
Leyburn, Thomas and Juliana, 1423n.
Leycestr', John de, 267
Leye, Geoffrey de la, 43
Leyre, Robert, carm., 43
Lich', Robert de, 996
Lichefeld, Adam de, 636
Lichfield, Staffs, 967, 1010, 1038
Liddington (Lidyngton), Wilts, 1081
Limerstone (Lymerston'), in
Brighstone, I. Wight, 41
Limpsfield (Lymenesfeld), Surrey, 199,
940
Lincoln, Thomas, bp., 95, 139, 140
   , John, bp., 191, 240, 303, 357,
790, 870, 958, 966, 973, 980, 982, 985,
988, 1029, 1066, 1075, 1081, 1083,
1117, 1153, 1160, 1172, 1216, 1454,
1590, 1604, 1645, 1669, 1710
   , dioc., 63n., 147, 152, 180, 191,
303, 306, 309, 334, 389, 790, 816, 870,
956, 989, 990, 1029, 1066, 1075, 1081,
1117, 1153, 1189, 1216, 1493, 1572,
1590, 1645, 1710
   , Robert de, 1317, 1323, 1751
Linkenholt (Lynkenholte), Hants, 485,
703, 1210, 1263, 1429

Lisle, John de, 1395, 1404, *see also* de Insula.
Listolgh', Walter de, 1120
Litchfield (Ludeschulve, Lynchesford), Hants, 749, 1339, 1579
Litherere, John le, 520
Little Berkhamstead, *see* Berkhamstead.
Little Bookham, *see* Bookham.
Little Hinton, *see* Hinton.
Little Fobby (Parva Fobbyour), 1073
Little Yarmouth (Parva Jernemuthe), Norf, 297
Llandaff, dioc., ix, 63
Llansanffraid (Lansanfred), 956, 959
Llanthony (Lanthon), Glos, 604, 1332
Lockeridge (Lokerugg) in Overton, Wilts, 1072
Lodesworth, Sussex, 1331
Lok', John, 497, 1002
Loksele, Henry de, 308
Lokynton', Roger de, 471
Lombard, John, 1023, 1315
——, Thomas, 1332
Lomis, Nicholas de, 54
Lonaigne, Nicholas, knt., 1689
London, John de, 166–168, 178, 614, 817, 915, 1220
——, city, 12–19, 223, 277, 353, 752, 809, 834, 1035, 1449, 1626
——, dioc. 192, 280, 444, 724, 745, 842, 899, 1104, 1113, 1229, 1682, 1744
——, bp., *see* Northburgh, Stratford, Sudbury.
——, Arches, deanery of, 853, 1079
——, palace, 540
——, Old Temple, 240, 303
——, Temple, 1216
——, Corpus Christi chapel, *see* St Lawrence, Candlewick Street.
—— churches: All Hallows, Barking, 1708
——, St Alphege, 940
——, St Andrew, Holburn, 1237
——, St Andrew, Cornhill, 1689
——, St Bride, 1523
——, St Dunstan, 933, 934
——, St John, Friday Street, 1079
——, St Lawrence, Candlewick Street, 547, 1076, 1457
——, St Lawrence, Jewry, 961
——, St Margaret, Pattens Lane, 968, 1253
——, St Martin-le-Grand, 940, 1347
——, St Mary Abchurch, 1595
——, St Mary without Bishopsgate, 383, 389, 623, 685, 722, 1079, 1111, 1177, 1195, 1204, 1231, 1439, 1523, 1531
——, St Mary Colechurch, 1141
——, St Mary Magdalen in Guildhall, 1025
——, St Mary, Staining Lane, 1516, 1545
——, St Michael, Wood Street, 1215
——, St Nicholas Cold Abbey, 199
——, St Nicholas Shambles, 1169
——, St Olave near the Tower, 345, 1006
——, St Pancras, 853
——, St Paul's cathedral, ix, x, xiv, 57, 809, 1689
——, dean, 39, 40, 81
——, chancellor, 334
——, archd., 1523
——, St Thomas, 178
Longe, Henry le, 1164
Long Ditton, *see* Ditton.
Longparish (Middleton'), Hants, 370
Long Stanton (Staunton longa), Cambs, 1118
Lorens, John, 1636
Lorkyn, John, 1673
Loudham, John de, 1025
Louth, Richard de, 319, 320
Loveday, Hugh, 505
Lovekyn, John, 264, 280, 478, 951, 1063, 1064, 1179
Lovel, John, lord, 163n.
——, William, 661, 813, 1415
Loxle, Henry de, 841
——, Robert de, 1744
Lucas, Walter, 1269
Lucy, Peter de, 803
Ludeford, Geoffrey de, 718, 825, 826
Ludeshull', Richard de, 675
Ludespade, Edmund de, 1235, 1408, 1724
Ludgarshall (Lutegarshale), Glos, 666
Lumbard, John, 509, 575
Lunt, W.E., xiv
Lusteshull, Richard de, 166–168, 268, 464n., 611; cf. Ludeshull.
Lutegarshale, Henry de, 374
Lutespade, *see* Ludespade.
Lychett Maltravers, Dorset, 1032n.
Lyncoln', Robert de, 1323
Lynchesford, Lyntesford, Richard de, 1060, 1061, 1077, 1219, 1339, 1493
Lyndhurst, Hants, 767n.

Lynne, William de, bp., 1703n.
Lynn, 1450
Lyons, councils of, 92, 190, 1078, 1424
Lyre, abbey (Eure), France, 263, 393,
420, 808, 1240, 1266, 1302, 1312, 1338,
1389, 1397, 1437, 1456, 1508, 1509,
1574, 1619, 1713, 1718b, 1720
Lysewey, Hugh, 349
Lysle, John de *and see* de Insula.
Lyste, John atte, 672
Lythe, Adam atte, 367

Mackenlagh', Michael, bp. x
Madhurst, John, 1570
Maghe, Philip, 1303n.
Magote, John, 1266
Magreyn, *see* Mygreyn.
Maideston', Adam de, John de,
William de, all carm., 43
Maidstone, Kent, chapel, 84
Maiheu, *see* Mayheu.
Malemayne, Nicholas de, 1422n.
Malling, East abbey, Sussex, 1673
         , South (Suthmallynge), Sussex,
195, 197
Malden (Maldon), Surrey, 68, 620, 800,
927
Malmesbury, John de, 1246
         , William de, 163, 1464,
1480
Malwayn, John, 42
Man (Maan), Isle of, 1223
Mandeville, Thomas de, 235, 236
Mauncel, Henry, 647
Manningford (Manyngford), Wilts,
1026
Mapledurham (Mapulderham), Hants,
104, 198, 206, 763, 965–969, 1411
Marcaunt, Nicholas, 1111
Marcle, William de, 239
Mare, Alice de la, nun, 1471, 1694
         , Thomas de la, 109
Markannt, Nicholas, 1177
Market Overton, Rutland, 1029
Marlebergh', Thomas de, 909 Hugh de,
1529
         , Thomas de, 909
Marmynton', John de, 836
Marmyon, Henry, 1546, 1565, 1627
Marston (Mershton), prob. N.
Marston, Bucks, 152
Martini, Peter, carm., 43
Martyn, Richard, called of
Chippenham, 487
Marwell (Merewelle), Hants, 198, 199,
400, 406, 409, 608, 638f., 649, 650,

768, 873, 1116, 1224, 1340, 1447, 1590,
1591
Mason, Masson, Geoffrey le, 655
         , John, 1544, 1562
         , Richard son of William le, 741
         , Stephen le, 1341, 1744
Matheu, Richard, 703
Mauduyt, Bugonus, 294, 786
         , John, 1280, 1580
Mautravers, John and Wancilina, 1032
Maydeneford', John de, 743
Maydene Wynterborne, Walter de, 516
Maydewell', John de, 1342
Maydenwelles, Robert de, 214
Mayfield (Maghefeld), Sussex, 899
Maygn', 183, 258
Mayheu, John, 614, 724
Maylok, Ralph, 1718b
Mayn, Robert, 1399, 1522n.
Mayner, Henry, 83
Mayson, *see* Mason.
Maythland, Richard de, 1262, 1263
Maxfeld, John de, 449
Meath (Miden'), Ireland, 898–901, 929
Mede, Walter atte, 1636
Melburn, John de, 996
Meleward', Thomas, 1053
Melkesham, Robert de, ben., 29
Melton', William de, 403, 1141n.
Menevia, i.e. St Davids, Wales, ix, x,
227n., 809, 956, 959, 1222, 1669
         , Thomas, bp., 1222
Meon, East, (Estminnes, Estmeon'),
Hants, 217n., 1408, 1645, 1724
         , West (Westminnes), Hants, 694,
995, 1011, 1124, 1170
Meone, William de, 81, 176, 177, 321
Meonstoke (Munestok', Mynnestok'),
Hants, 249, 320, 461, 1148
Mere, Robert atte, 731
         , Thomas de, 780, 1143
         , William de, 843
Merewelle, Richard de, 1490
Merlawe, John de, 477, 556–567, 1200,
1227, 1240
         , Walter de, 563, 645, 914,
1490
Merowe, John de, 327, 1010
Merrow (Merewe), Surrey, 470, 608,
1342
Merstham, Walter de, 199, 200, 940
Merston, Mershton, Henry de, 991
         , John de, 1188
Merton, priory, Surrey, 27, 54, 142,
201, 304, 334, 345, 411, 440, 448, 474,

499, 551, 711, 731, 760, 780, 781, 820, 824, 896, 978, 1066, 1143, 1160, 1216, 1230, 1269, 1271, 1278, 1289, 1349, 1380, 1384, 1396, 1458-1463, 1535, 1649, 1678
, college, *see* Oxford.
Merwe, John de, 726
Merwelle, Richard de, ben. 29, 563
Messyngham, Massyngham, Robert de, 52, 72, 73
Michael, John, 1566
Michaelstow (Stowe seynt Michael), Corn, 986
Michel, Robert, 1507
, Simon, 373
Micheldever (Micheldevere), Hants, 446, 906, 1363
Michelmersh (Muchelmersh), Hants, 681, 774, 1114, 1115, 1234, 1239, 1500, 1569, 1621, 1682
Mickleham (Mikelham), Surrey, 23, 698, 869, 1000, 1027, 1402, 1741
Middleton (Middelton), Hants, or Longparish, 123, 124, 141, 370, 776, 861, 1039
Middelton, John de, 276, 1074, 1359
, William de, 986, 1598
Midewynter, William, 757
Mignot, Guillaume, 1574
Mildenhale, Robert de, 1198, 1690
Milford (Mulleford), Hants, 235, 412, 1138, 1146, 1173
Millbrook (Mullebrok'), Hants, 128, 188, 295, 628, 922, 1319, 1367
Minstead (Mynstede), Hants, 178, 1298, 1413
Minterne (Mynterne), Dorset, 527
Missenden (Mussynden'), abbey, Bucks, 241, 1075
, Thomas de, 1445
Mitcham (Micham), Surrey, 68, 98, 524, 1120, 1261
Mitford, Robert de, 922
Mohann, Baldwin de, 309
Mohant, Mohaut, Roger, 1489
Molesey (Moleseye), Surrey, 896
Molyneux, Margaret de, ben., 577, 588-593
Molyns, *see* Molyneux.
Monasteriis, William de, 1456n., 1487
Monasterio, William de, ben., 1302, 1312, 1338, 1389, 1397, 1437
Monch', Richard, 1282
Monk, John, 1579
, Nicholas, 1375

Mongroye, John, 864
Monks Kirby (Kyrkeby monachorum), Warw, 1735
Monk Sherborne (Shireburne), Hants, 229-234, 385, 596, 653, 805, 831, 1374, 1385, 1485, 1506, 1583
Monlisch', John de, 380
Monnle', Nicholas called le, 1263
Monstede, John de, 663
Monte, Robert de, 967
, Thomas de, 1588
Monteacuto, Catherine de, 428
, Edward de, xv
, William, earl of Salisbury, xv, 46n., 194, 227, 907, 1223, 1416, 1542, 1613
Montegomeri, John and Rose, 55
Monuz, Nicholas, 1024
Monxton (Anne de Beck'), Hants, 352, 1614, 1625
Mora, Richard de, 261
Mordak, Robert, 1633
Morden (Mordon'), Surrey, 68, 98, 1199, 1425, 1589
Moure, Robert de la, 261
More, Robert atte, 1617
, Thomas de la, 261
Morestead (Morstede), Hants, 275, 276, 845, 853-855, 939, 974, 1100
Morle, John, 98
Mortestrete, Walter de, 734
Morteyn, Edmund, 309, 359
, Peter, 364
Mortimer, earl of Salisbury, 194n.
, Roger de, 1336n.
Morton', Hugh de, 1131
, William de, 650
Morwy, John, 1076, 1185
Mot, John, 1713
Mottesfonte, John de, 1641
Mottisfont, priory, (Motesfonte), Hants, 146, 459, 460, 497, 543, 629, 792, 892, 909-912, 1726-1732
Mottistone (Moteston), I. Wight, 228, 832, 1350, 1620, 1641, 1724
Mottynge, Thomas de, 968, 1540
Mountayne, William, 1735, 1736, 1739
Mountpeller, Thomas, 1224, 1248, 1262, 1263, 1355, 1421, 1434, 1491, 1499, 1532, 1533, 1542
Mucheldevere, Thomas de, 1641
Muchelmor, Peter, 1667
Muleward, John, 1385
, William le, 1636
Mulle, Gilbert atte, 307

Mulle, Richard atte, 1555, 1688
Murdac, Robert, 1253
Mursele, Hugh de, 327
Mussenden, Thomas de, 1144
Mygreyn, John, 501, 1095

Nasscroft, Walter atte, 641
Nasshe, Richard atte, 1659
Nassington, Philip de, 413, 1572
Nately Scures (Natele Scures), Hants, 526, 1295
Natton', William de, 783, 1244
Neel, Gilbert, 1439, 1523
Neeuton, Hugh de, 275, 276
Neirunt, John, 95
Neovill, Hugh de, knt., 261
Netheravon (Netherhavene), Hants, 776
Netherbury-Ecclesia, Dorset, 954n.
Netherhavene, John de, 909, 1726–1732, 1737
Nether Wallop (Wallop inferior), Hants, 348, 1071, 1096, 1400, 1650, 1669
Netley (Lettele, loci S.Edwardi), abbey, Hants, 387, 1059–1061, 1077, 1270
Nettelworth, Netilworth, Henry de, 1430, 1454
Neubolt, Robert de, 1361, 1546
Neuman, Walter, 1135
Neuport, John de, 383
Nevile, Alesia de, 1523
      , Hugh de, knt., 1007, 1055, 1089
      , John de, 1140, 1141, *and see* Neovill.
Newark (Novo Loco), Surrey, xi, 158, 502, 552, 687, 1021, 1175, 1184, 1209, 1287, 1392, 1393, 1504, 1533, 1551
Newborgh, Robert, 1457
Newchurch (Newecherche), I. Wight, 318, 808, 809, 810, 900, 926–929, 1509, 1574, 1720
Newenham, John de, 1112, 1559, 1686, 1687
      , Robert de, 1245, 1266
      , William de, 581
Newynton, Neweton, Martin de, 1211, 1282
Newnham (Newenham), Hants, 171n., 653, 942n.
Newport, John de, ben., 43
Newstead (Neustede), Kent, 809
Newton (Newynton), Hants, 837, 1147, 1608
Newton Toney (Neweton Tony), Wilts, 115

Newton Valence (Nieweton), Hants, vii, 688, 767, 1608, 1612, 1748, 1749
Nichol, Silvester, 1370
Nicholas, archbp. Ravenna, legate, 39, 81
Nigris, Laurence de, 1703
Niton (Neutone), I. Wight, 214, 616, 877, 1302, 1389
Noble, William, 966
Noht, Noght, Nhot, Walter, 207, 573, 1114, 1115, 1224, 1234
No'm', John, 1091
Noionn, John de, 1081, 1082
Nok', James atte, 785
Norbiton (Norbelton), Surrey, 896, 1179, 1180
Normanby, Peter de, 281, 282
Normand, Roger, knt., 374, 1381
Northampton, 718, 826
      , archd., 980, 985, 1029, 1082
      , St Mary de Pratis, 1272, 1449
Northanger, *see* Nuthanger.
Northavene, Henry de, 1709
Northburgh', Michael, bp. London, x, 999, 1006, 1025, 1073, 1076, 1104, 1106, 1113, 1141, 1169, 1215, 1237, 1253
North Charford, *see* Charford.
North Stoneham, *see* Stoneham.
North Waltham, *see* Waltham.
Northon', John de, 827
Northstok', William de, 495
Northwode, John de, 1368, 1574
      , Simon de, 790, 1347
Norton ? Kent, 1176
      , Agnes de, 1546n.
      , Geoffrey de, 1286
Norwich, dioc., 70n., 297, 1018, 1130
      , bp., 169, 170, 1018, 1130
      , archd., 1130
Norwico, Richard de, 174, 192, 212, 213, 282, 549, 836, 1065
Notyngham, Alan de, 376, 1052
      , Thomas de, 1036
Novo Loco, *see* Newark, or New Place, or Aldebury, or St Mary without Bishopsgate.
Nubbeleye, Nubbelegh, John de, 3, 37, 463, 464, 467, 609, 611, 649, 663, 865, 872, 873, 883–885, 898, 948, 975, 1044, 1116, 1235, 1259, 1327, 1692
Nuggh', Henry, 344

Nuneaton (Eton monialium, Nonneston'), Warw, 50, 451, 510, 818, 935, 1265, 1294, 1343, 1710, 1750, 1752
Nunnaminster, i.e. St Mary, abbey, Winchester, 117, 326, 341, 472, 491, 492, 523, 549, 577, 588–593, 626, 641, 681, 836, 939, 1008, 1058, 1065, 1086, 1334, 1368, 1371, 1388, 1471–1474, 1536, 1666, 1694–1701
, cemetery chantry, 642, 890, 1048
Nursling (Nusshelyng'), Hants, 813
Nutfield (Notfeld, Nothfeld), Surrey, 305, 1080, 1215, 1689
Nuthanger (Northangre), in Kingsclere, Hants, 860, 941, 1218
Nutley (Nouthlegh', Nutlegh, Nuteschullinge), Hants, 625, 1134, 1514

Oakley (Oclee), Hants, 1374
Oakwood (Ocwode), Surrey, 1191
Oare (Ore), Wilts, 1077
Ockham (Ogeham, Okesham, Okam), Surrey, 306, 310, 405, 569, 582, 778, 994, 1208, 1284
Ockley (Ockle), Surrey, 1106, 1422, 1636
Ocle, Thomas de, 1509, 1574
Oddingley (Oddynglegh), Worcs, 43
Odiham (Odyham), Hants, 142n., 153, 587, 621, 1276, 1382, 1438
Offham, Adam de, 399, 1018
Offord, John de, bp., 404, 662n.
Offynton, Robert de, 407
Ogbourne (Okeburn), Wilts, 112, 212, 352, 403, 476, 615, 684, 740, 983, 1099, 1614
Ogbourne St George, Wilts, 112, 894
Ok', Edward atte, 35
, James atte, 931, 963
Okham, Thomas de, 109, 110
Oldhale, William de, 621
Old Temple, *see* London.
Olneye, Thomas de, 849, 982, 1104, 1679
Orchard, Dorset, 725
, Thomas de, 277, 725
Orcheston', Richard de, 999
Orewell', Thomas de, 1205
Orleton, Adam, bp., vii, viii, xv, 3, 54, 135, 334, 343, 389, 626n., 1008
Orpington, Kent, 1582
Orsett (Orsete), Essex, 212
Orton (Oreton), Leics, 306
Orwell (Orewell'), Cambs, 1167
Osbereton, William de, 738

Osberston', William de, 1222, 1223, 1274, 1297
Osborne, I. Wight, 842n.
Osmencon, John de, ben., 29
Otery, John de, ben., 24
Oteryngham, Alan de, 615
Otford, Kent, 86
Othyn, William, 1655, 1693
Otryngham, Peter de, 684, 894
Otterbourne (Oterbourne), Hants, 1691
Otto and Ottobon, xi, *see note to* 96.
Oundle (Undele), Northants, 1160, 1563
Overton, Hants, 513, 678, 790, 863, 867, 907, 1410, 1505, 1609, 1668
, John de, 433–435, 865
, William de, 1321
Over Wallop (Wallop superior), Hants, 419, 1311, 1592, 1723
, Thomas de, 1592
Ovington (Ovyngton), Hants, 739, 1112
Oweyn, John, 1275
Owslebury (Oselbury), Hants, 400n.
Oxewvk, John, fm., 43
Oxford, archd., 966
, university, viii, x, xvi, 1718a
, chancellor, 389
, Balliol, 961
, Merton, 620, 633, 800, 827, 944, 1135
, Queens, 163n., 1455
Oxted (Okstede, Ocstede), Surrey, 487, 521, 1268

Paddington (Padynton), 1636
Page, Robert, 1288, 1708, 1709, 1791
Pagham (Pageham), Sussex, dean, 111
Pakenham, Simon Tony, 771
Palfreour, John, 260
Palmer, Palmere, John, 1103
, Maud, nun, 117
, Richard, 439, 1103
Pampilou, Ralph de, 1490
Pante, Richard, 1336
Papham, Richard de, 705
Parham (Perham), Sussex, 1205
Parson, Thomas, 1517
Parsones, John, 1614, 1625
Parva Sandal, Yorks, 1349
Parye, Thomas, 1740
Pasquerii, Pasquier, ben., 1487
Passelewe, Walter, 350, 359
Patney (Pateneye), Wilts, 1101, 1330
Patryngton', Hugh de, 1202
Paulesholte, Lambert de, 1213
Pavely, John, prior, 1042, 1177

Paxton, Thomas de, 25, 97, 185, 266
Payn, Adam, 691
, John, 37, 61, 101, 313, 424, 519, 659, 770, 860, 872, 1149, 1190, 1254, 1296
, Henry, 659
, Philip, 340
, William, 1280
Payto, William, 993
Pebworth, Glos, 268, 281, 814
Pecham, John de, 583, 661, 1036, 1120, 1245, 1246
Pedirton, Thomas de, 1475, 1488
Peender, William son of, 64
Pekke, Peter, 1127, 1173, 1242, 1248
Pelegrini, Hugh, 954, 1010, 1038
, Raymond, 111, 166–168, 269, 376, 899–901
Pellitoft, Philip, knt., 988
Pembrok, John de, 143, 1056, 1271
Pembroke, Laurence, earl of, 183
Peniton Mewsey (Penyton), Hants, 314
Pennington (Penyton'), Hants, 1375
Penrech', John, 1590
Pentelewe, Thomas de, 1192
Penton Grafton, 1181n.
Penynton', William de, 1212
Penyton, Walter de, 1429
Peper Harrow (Piperharewe), Surrey, 327, 1010, 1014, 1126, 1206, 1236, 1742
Pepyn, John, ben., 263
Percy, Henry de, knt., 1050
, Thomas de, bp., x
Pernycote, Robert de, 23, 555, 645, 698, 1636
Pershore (Perschore), Worcs, 672
Person, Thomas, 1440
Persons, John, 738
Persyval', John, 1299
Pesshon, Robert, 1303
Petersham (Petrichesham), Surrey, 896
Pethereth, John de, 1575
Pethy, Thomas, ben., 1526
Petir, William, 1740
Petworth (Putteworth), Sussex, 1050, 1051
Petyt, John, 956–959, 1504, 1539, 1551, 1626
Peuseys, John, 1367
Peveseye, William de, 112, 211, 1140
Peverel, Andrew, knt., 904, 1109, 1432
, Henry, knt., 1154
Peyce, William de, 246, 1208
Peyto, William de, junior and senior, 1242, 1365

Philip, prior of Andover, 1303
, John, 309
Philippa, queen, 128, 163n., 193, 298, 397, 767n., 816, 955
Piers, Robert, 1631
Pilham, Lincs, 973
Pipard, Laurens, 1395, 1630, 1642
Piper Harrow, see Peper Harrow.
Pirie, Purie, John, 609, 1521, 1723
Pittleworth (Puttleworth), Hants, 347, 622
Placy, Nicholas, knt, 509, 761
Plain, Plan, Robert, 1563
Pleshete, Adam atte, 1422
Plomer, Thomas, 225, 226
Podenhale, John and Joan de, 1326
Poitiers, xiii
Pole, Michael de la, 1454
, Thomas de la, knt., 1181, 1430
, William de la, knt., xv
Poleyn, Nicholas, 938, 966
Polinorva, William de, 397, 454
Polyngfold, Richard de, 417
Ponchardon, Oliver de, 1057
Pontiliaco, Ponterliaco, Almaric de, xi, 216, 706, 791, 878, 880
Pontissara, John de, bp., 113, 218, 355, 435, 658, 707, 787, 948, 970, 1041, 1072, 1235, 1299, 1524, 1618, 1667, 1691
Poor, Richard le, bp., 399n.
Popham, Edmund de, 618
, Richard de, 891
, Robert de, ben., 556, 559, 560
Poplar (Popelere), 547
Port, Adam de, 399n.
Portchester (Portchestria), Hants, 365, 977
Porter, Richard, 1261
Portland, Dorset, 123, 141, 1683
Portsea (Porteseye), 415, 1016
Portsmouth (Portesmuth'), 127n.
, St Nicholas hospital, ix, 249, 860, 1751
, St Thomas of Canterbury, 486, 1019, 1037, 1364
Potente, William, 1572
Potton, Beds, 870
Pratellis, Everard de, 362, 1555
Pravis, John, 31
Preston, Kent, 1632
, John de, 1273
, William de, 1141

Preston Candover (Preston Candevere), Hants, 743
Priors Hurstbourne (Hussebourne), Hants, 350, 359, 360
Prioru, Richard, 1498
Prosenhurst, Nicholas, 1377
Pruec, Richard, 1351
Pultenoie, Pulteneye, John, knt., 547, 1457
Punamit, Walter, 722
Puppe, John, 257, 383
Putte, John atte, 1152
Putlye, Henry de, 1752
Puttenham (Potenham), Surrey, 257, 383
Pydefer', Robert, 1718a
Pyk', Robert, 1506
Pyl, William le, 1491
Pylkes, Thomas knt., 1708
Pyrford (Piriford), Surrey, 158n.

Quarley (Querlee), Hants, 112, 740, 887, 983
Quarr (Quarrer'), abbey, I. Wight, 316, 669, 893
Queor, Quarreor, Qeor, Quarrer', John le, 361, 867, 1544, 1662, 1703
Querle, Thomas de, 727
Queynton', John de, 1371

Radclive, William de, 623
Radipole (Rappole), Dorset, 1296
Radynge, *see* Redynge.
Ragebas, John, 1126
Ralph, bp. of London, *see* Stratford.
, of Shrewsbury, bp. Bath and Wells, 72, 73, 116
Ramridge (Remeryng), Hants, 1181, 1430
Ramsbury (Remesbur'), Wilts, 141, 166, 217, 235, 321
Ranby, William de, 653
Randulf, William, 92
Rannvill', Geoffrey de, 646
, Nicholas, 151
Rasen, Roger de, 1355, 1434
, Thomas de, 1324, 1355, 1434, 1592
Raunds, Northants, 708
Raunvil, *see* Rannvil.
Ravenesere, Richard de, 1309
Raveneston', Nicholas de, 1036, 1246, 1248
, Ralph de, 877
Ravenna, Nicholas archbp., 39

Recher, Thomas, knt., 356
Redenesse, William, 1389
Rede, John le, 269, 270
, William de, 1337
Redegrave, Richard de, 95, 96, 181, 182
Redeman, Matthew, 1061
Redynge, William de, 1629
Reigate (Reygate), Surrey, church, 64, 65, 95, 96, 181, 182, 1157, 1167, 1205, 1288, 1708, 1709
, priory, 305, 532, 644, 698, 699, 1402, 1741
Remmesbury, John de, 1298, 1631
, Richard de, 1382
Remston', Rempston', Richard de, 1512, 1738
Renald, John, 1226, 1501
Renfeld, John de, 478
Repplynham, Thomas de, 816
Restwold, Thomas, 1272, 1449
Retherfeld, John de, 1067
Retherick, Griffin and Thomas, 1394n.
Retherwyk, John de, ben., 157
Reymundi, Peter, 269
Reynald, cardinal deacon, 1010, 1038, 1176, 1703
Reynolds, Walter, archbp. Canterbury, 178
Ricarii, Gerald, 1237
Richard, son of John, 729
, *natus Walterus Edith'*, 863
Richeman, William, 538
Richer, William, 908, 965, 1006
Richmond (Richemund), Yorks, archd., 710
Richon, Walter, 705
Ridere, John called, 579
Rimpton (Rympton), Som, 773, 897
Ringwood (Ryngewode), Hants, xi, 43, 815, 1062
Ripley (Rippeleye), Surrey, 1287
Risyngdon', John de, 697
Robert, prior of Christchurch, Canterbury, 662
Rochester (Roffen'), Kent x
, castle, 256n.
, dioc., 43, 676, 677, 779, 780, 959, 967, 1176, 1198, 1200, 1576, 1633
, John, bp., 1176, 1198
, William, bp., 1576, 1633
Rode, William, 1542, 1613
, William atte, 1712
Rodeston', Elias de, 1064, 1179
Romayn, Juliana, 178

Romayn, Thomas, 178, 179, 392
Rombrigge, Robert de, 77
Rome, ch. of St Adrian, 954, 1010, 1038, 1176
Romsey (Romeseye), abbey, Hants, 28, 115, 125, 273, 514, 544, 599, 611, 619, 663, 744, 834, 916–921, 1378, 1518, 1534, 1553, 1646
———, portion of St Laurence, 611, 619, 663, 1534, 1553
Ronceby, John de, 1599
Rondulf, Margaret, 746
Rontyng, John, 983
Ronz, Richard, 1503, 1532
Roo, John, 1690
Ropistagno, 269
Rotherfield (Rothersfeld'), Oxon, 894
Rotherhithe (Retherhuth), Hants, 89, 91, 1256
Rothewelle, Hugh de, 190
Rouclee, Geoffrey, 1074, 1532
Roughborn', John atte, 1090
Roughton (Rusheton), Lincs, 1645
Rouz, Thomas de, 482
Rowner (Roughhenore), Hants, 319, 320, 408, 1351
Russel, Alianora, widow of Theobald, 126, 382, 507, 713, 754, 1047
———, John, 240, 241, 302
Rutherfeld, John de, 1211, 1282
Ruwe, Rue, Robert de, 333, 359, 360
Rydden', John fm., 43
Rye, Sussex, 995
Rympton, John de, 507, 713

St Cross, Winchester, vii, ix, 166–168, 268, 464
———, I. Wight, 166–168, 268, 464
St Davids, *see* Menevia.
St Denys, priory, Southampton, 62, 386, 421, 431, 432, 469, 471, 522, 570, 638, 667, 671, 829, 930, 938, 966, 1277, 1281, 1285, 1305, 1631, 1684
St Elizabeth, chapel, Winchester, 113, 114, 168, 217–221, 268, 322, 323, 355, 357, 361, 433–435, 465, 480, 603, 649, 652, 655, 658, 683, 694, 707, 768, 787, 818, 872, 883, 898, 948, 970, 998, 1003, 1035, 1041, 1043, 1044, 1072, 1116, 1235, 1259, 1299, 1524, 1533, 1544, 1598, 1618, 1628, 1667, 1691, 1692
St Florent, abbey, near Saumur, France, 1556
———, William, abbot, 1556
St Helens, priory, I. Wight, 1031
St John of Jerusalem, *see* Hospitallers.

St Lawrence (Wathe Sancti Laurencii), I. Wight, 507, 754, 781
St Martha, i.e. Chilworth, Surrey, 552, 687, 1392
St Mary Bourne (Baurne), Hants, 350, 359, 360, 496, 1188
St Neots, priory, Hunts, 1081
St Sauveur-le-Vicomte (sancti Salvatoris vicecomitis), Manche, France, 242, 1304
St Vigor de Cérisy, abbey, France, 229n., 695, 1485
Sacombe, John, 1441, 1576
Sadelere, John, 1224
Sadok', 208
Sadyngton, R' de, 49
Saling (Salynge), Essex, 655
Salisbury, chancellor, 153, 587, 1382, 1438
———, official, 1737
———, canons, 3, 11, 562, 572, 583, 611, 621, 726, 1010, 1038, 1252
———, bp., *see* Wyville,
———, earl of, *see* Monteacuto.
———, dioc., 730, 739, 752, 769, 807, 809–812, 834, 858, 954, 960, 972, 1026, 1032, 1056, 1077, 1101, 1108, 1110, 1112, 1148, 1165, 1213, 1214, 1226, 1258, 1276, 1296, 1313, 1330, 1346, 1347, 1372, 1406, 1536, 1559, 1574, 1612, 1650, 1657, 1675, 1683, 1686, 1687, 1702, 1712
Sallyng', Sallung', Geoffrey de, 935, 1017, 1093, 1113
———, John de, 146, 892
Salom, John, 1019
Salopia, Ralph de, 1606n.
Saltemersh', William de, 1583
Sampson, Nicholas, 691
Sancta Ecclesia, John de, 605
Sancto Albano, Elyas de, 587, 621
———, Roger de, 537
Sancto Johanne, Eva de, 749, 1094, 1579
———, Edward de, 679n., 1586, 1629, 1662, 1702, 1737
———, Elizabeth de, 639n.
———, Hugh de, 1310
Sancto Manifeo (Sant Manifee), Robert de, 942, 1309
Sancto Martino, Laurence de, 517, 1450
Sancto Neoto, John de, 1059, 1077, 1245
Sancto Philiberto, John de, knt., 679, 848

Sancto Stephano, 684
Sanderstead (Sandrestede, Saundrestede), Surrey, 68, 98, 240, 241, 662, 1632
Sandford, John de, 1592, 1597, 1723
, William de, 1411
Sandon, hospital, Surrey, 554, 555, 949
Sandon, Berks, 889
Sandrestede, John de, 1246
Sandyacre, William de, 732
Sankevill', Matilda, 1216
Sannford', John de, 630, 1137
Sansted', Thomas de, fm., 43
Sardis (Cardicensis), bp. of, x, 71
Sare, Adam, 396
Sarum, John de, 752, 753
, Robert de, 219
Saumon, John, 987
Saumur, France, 1303n., 1556
Saundely, Philip de, knt., 520
Saunderstede, see Sandrestede.
Savage, William, 1410, 1609
Saxlingham, Richard de, 981
, Thomas and Cecilia, 118
Say, — de, 793
, John, 1022, 1168
Scamayle, John, 1636
Scarle, William, 43
Scarlet, Walter, 1142, 1183
Scherston, John, 625
Schetelyngton', Richard de, 1402
Schipton, John, 1524
Schirborne, Schirburn', John de, 729
, Walter de, 527
Schire, Robert de, 368
Schirefeld', Stephen de, 453
Schirford, Robert de, 1424
Schitlyngton, Henry de, 358
, Robert de, 932, 933
Schog', John, 1515
Schoreham', Richard de, 1522
Sclatter', John, 1058
Scoteney, Robert de, 644
Scryveyn, John, 960, 1004
Sculcoates (Sculcotes), Yorks, 894
Scures, John de, knt., 517n., 526, 886, 1295
Séez, abbey, France, 788n.
Seffold, Richard de, 181
Seint Leger, Thomas, knt., 1307
Selborne, priory, Hants, 31, 437, 496, 568, 618, 844, 1017, 1127, 1379, 1484
Selde, Thomas, 1238, 1248
Sele, priory, Sussex, 1162
Selling (Sellynge), Hants, 89-91

Selot, Walter, 687
Sely, Thomas, 587
Send (Sende), Surrey, 1184, 1636
Seneschal, Peter le, ben., 262, 263
Serle, William, 84, 1070
Sevenhampton, Walter de, viii, 328-330, 720, 773, 815, 860, 881, 1009, 1142, 1150, 1258, 1264, 1327, 1329, 1340, 1525, 1534, 1553, 1618, 1666, 1751
Seymor, Isabella, d. of Margery, 125
Seys, John, 227, 245, 598, 802, 907
Shaftesbury (Shafton'), abbey, Dorset, 166, 167, 1347, 1574
, John de, 375
Shalden, Hants, 111, 338, 339, 821, 1421
Shalfleet (Schaldeflete), I. Wight, 194, 227, 245, 598, 802, 907, 936, 964, 1222, 1223, 1416, 1542, 1613
Shalford (Schaldeford), Surrey, 623, 685, 1111, 1177, 1531
Sheen (Schene), Surrey, 896
Sherborne, castle, 1032, 1347
, priory, see Monk Sherborne.
Sherborne Coudray (Schireborne Coudray), Hants, 595, 1046, 1550, 1719
Sherborne St John, Hants, 506, 537, 679, 695, 895, 1046, 1548, 1719
Shere (Shire), Surrey, 1059-1061, 1077
Shere Vachery (Shiere Vachery), Surrey, 581
Sherfield English, Hants, 934
Shetlyndon', Roger de, 1741
Shifford, Thomas de, 1056
Shipton (Schipton), Hants, 1287
, John de, 1533
, Thomas de, 1173, 1202, 1203, 1249
Shirborne, see Schireborne.
Shirburn, Oxon, 180
Shoreham, Sussex/Kent, 1021, 1175, 1582 (Kent)
Shorne (Schorn'), Kent, 1576
Shorwell (Schorewelle), I. Wight, 380, 580, 1045, 1395, 1630
Shrewsbury, Ralph de, bp. Bath and Wells, 92, 277, 773, 825, 1023, 1403, 1488
Shyford', Thomas, 1137
Sidebrok, John de, 357
Silchester (Sylchestre, Cylchestre), Hants, 548, 728, 972, 1153, 1279, 1352
Skeryngton', John son of Roger de, 736

Skilling, Walter, 1329
Skinnand (Skynnand), Lincs, 43
Skiryngton, John *natus* Roger, 1054
Skot', John 1523
Skyngton, John de, 150
Sladdok', John de, 1209
Slonghore, Roger de, 1660
Sloughtre, Roger de, 1340
Sluys, battle of, 18n., 127n.
Smogg', John, 796
Smythe, Smithe, John, 624
    , Walter, 1435
    , William, 172, 1443
Snodeham, Richard, 1162
Snodenham, Richard de, 1014
Snokeshull', Robert de, 581, 1624, 1636–1639
Solde, *see* Selde.
Solere, Hamond de la, 1125, 1312
Solle, Thomas, 1550, 1719
Somborne, John de, 628, 922
    , Robert de, 923, 925
    , William de, 526
Somerford Mauduit, 1253, 1633
Somerton, Oxon/Som, 741
Sonning (Sonnyng), Berks, 194, 198
Sopley (Soppeleye), Hants, 175, 1154
Souky, Robert de, 18, 19, 93
Southampton, 49, 217n., 691
    , dean, 313, 431, 656, 667
    , All Saints, 156, 248, 299, 638, 671
    , St Denys, *see* St Denys.
    , Holy Cross, 386, 469, 667, 1305
    , St John Baptist, 1397
    , St Laurence, 421, 938, 966, 1684
    , St Mary, 165, 292, 313, 424, 519, 659, 770, 872, 1149, 1150, 1190, 1193, 1194
    , St Michael, 1154
South Malling, *see* Malling.
South Stoneham, *see* Stoneham.
South Tidworth, *see* Tidworth.
South Waltham, *see* Waltham.
South Warnborough, *see* Warnborough.
Southrop, Glos, 1171
Southwark, manor and chapel not indexed.
    , dean, 16, 801, 838, 1512
    , St George, 363, 1540
    , St Margaret, 16, 583
    , St Mary, priory, x, 43, 60, 96, 158, 182, 229, 230, 237, 334, 339, 358, 390, 431, 432, 545, 583, 661, 700, 714, 716, 732, 735, 799, 838, 847, 1036, 1120, 1157, 1164, 1167, 1245–1251, 1261, 1283, 1288, 1301, 1415, 1421, 1464, 1471, 1522, 1570, 1595, 1706, 1708, 1738
    , prior, 64, 65, 346, 392, 407, 524, 583, 645
    , St Olave, 392, 1132, 1575, 1590
    , St Thomas hospital, xii, 645, 914, 943, 969, 1084, 1426
Southwick (Suthwerk), priory, Hants, 111, 151, 362, 365, 415, 486, 518, 625, 674, 709, 726, 743, 748, 821, 946, 977, 1015, 1016, 1019, 1031, 1037, 1134, 1145, 1166, 1364, 1399, 1444, 1674
Sparkford (Sparkeford), Hants, 663, 682
Sparsholte, William de, ben., 563
Spencer, Thomas, 1632
Spervan, Bartholomew, 758, 963, 1105
Spirk', John, fm., 43
Spridhanton, Richard and William, 1398, 1499
    , Walter de, 1201
Spring, John atte (ad fontem) and Peter, 345
Sprocford, William de, 1231
Sprynget, Robert, 1369
Spyne, Matilda de, 589
Spyng', William, 1111
Squyer, Robert le, 769
Stafford, 617,
    , Ralph, earl of, 244, 309, 405, 617, 850, 994, 1012, 1073, 1156, 1169, 1187, 1196, 1208, 1255, 1284, 1356, 1716, 1735, 1736
    , Thomas de, 1716, 1722
    , William de, 1716, 1722
Stake, John, 726
Stammpes, John de, carm., 43
Stanbridge Earls, Hants, 622n.
Standen, East (Estandon, Staunden), chapel of St Leonard, I. Wight, 137, 150, 316n., 751, 903, 1159, 1715, 1717
Stanes, Thomas de, 971
Stanesmoor, Thomas de, 265
Stanfeld', John de, 240, 241, 662
    , Richard de, 431, 432
Stanford in the Vale, Berks, 353, 1657
Stanford Rivers, Essex, 994
Stanmer, Sussex, 195n.

Stannford, Robert de, 596
, Roger de, 660
, Thomas de, 317, 452
Stangrave, Robert de, knt., 487, 521, 1268
Stanton, John, 972
Stapenhull', Ralph de, 421, 938
Staunden, William de, 137
Staunton, Glos, 1702, 1711
, John de, 1194, 1244, 1515, 1634, 1640
Staverne, John de, 1153
Stedeham, John de, 909
, William de, 339
Stedemersh', William de, 895
Steeple Langford (Stepel Langeford), Wilts, 321
Steeple Morden (Stepelmordon'), Cambs, 1322
Stenynge, John de, 1238
Stepney (Stebenheth), 932
Stepyng, Robert de, 1206, 1236
Stertere, John le, 1017
Steventon (Styvynton), Hants, 325
Stibb, Geoffrey, 336, 338, 339
Stockbridge (Stokebrugg'), Hants, 1618
Stockerston (Stokefaston), Leics, 1604
Stodeye, John de, 981, 1159, 1676, 1717
Stodmersh, William de, 1038, 1176
Stoke by Nayland ? 'Stokeneylond', Suff, 1675
Stoke next Guildford, Surrey, 908, 965, 1006, 1007, 1028, 1055, 1089, 1136, 1174, 1225, 1359
Stoke Charity (Eldestoke), Hants, 1257, 1634
Stoke d'Abernon, Surrey, 1068
, William de, 1068
Stoke Goldington (Stoke Goldyngton'), Berks, 1315
Stok', Stoke, Stokes, John de, 975
, Nicholas, 1689
, Richard, 661, 1201, 1246, 1398
, Richard atte, 485
, William de, 20
Stokebrugg', Gregory de, 437
Stokebysshop, Nicholas de, 306
Stonch, Robert de, 138
Stoneham, South (Stanham episcopi), Hants, 291, 292, 519
, North (Stoneham abbatis), Hants, 515, 656, 680, 784, 871, 1387
Stonore, John de, knt., 966, 1092, 1139, 1505
Stortford (Storteford), Herts, 613

Stoughton, Henry, 327n.
Stow (Stowe), 139, 193
Stow Park, Lincs, 958
Stow on the Wold (Stowe sancti Edwardi), Glos, 614, 724
Stowell', William de, 572, 954, 955
Stowyng', Robert, 666
Stracton', Walter de, 1195
Stratfieldsaye (Stratfeld Say), Hants, 285, 723, 848n., 942, 987
Stratfield Turgis (Stratfeld Tourgys), Hants, 293
Stratford, John archbp. Canterbury, 4, 11, 39, 48, 57, 59, 66, 68, 81, 84–86, 89, 111, 178, 195, 225, 353, 392, 662n.
, Ralph, bp. London, 57, 59, 86, 199, 206, 212, 286, 540, 763, 932, 940, 961, 968
, Robert, bp. Chichester, 86, 508
Stratford on Avon, 86n.
Stratton, 722
, John de, 115, 345
Straunge, Simon le, 486, 1016, 1019
Streatham (Stretham), Surrey, 403, 615, 684, 894, 979
Stretton, Salop, 1641
, Robert, bp., 1735n.
Subbay, Thomas de, 353, 354
Sudburye, Simon de, bp. London, archbp. Canterbury, 1276, 1382, 1438, 1457, 1516, 1523, 1545, 1560, 1595, 1596, 1689, 1708, 1744
, Thomas de, 929
Suffolk, archd., 169
Sulthorn, 502, 781, 782
, Ralph de, 760
Sunbury (Sonnyngby), Mdx, 1229
Sunnynges, Adam de, 386
Surbiton (Sorbelton), Surrey, 896
Surrey, archd., viii, 16, 22, 48, 60, 63, 68, 69, 75, 84, 85, 91, 97, 98, 100, 108, 120, 134, 138, 142, 152, 161, 170, 182, 190, 193
, vacancy, 197, 199, 201
, new archdn., 202, 204, 226, 241, 246, 270, 280, 287, 298, 304, 327, 331, 336, 338, 346, 354, 356, 358, 363, 383, 388, 390, 396, 397, 399, 401, 403–407, 417, 418, 422, 423, 439, 440, 455, 470, 471, 474, 478, 487, 490, 493, 495, 499–502, 508, 509, 512, 521, 524, 525, 528, 529, 532, 533, 535, 536, 538, 541, 546, 551, 552, 569, 571, 572, 575, 581, 602, 613, 615, 617, 619, 620, 623,

633, 643-647, 658, 662, 665, 672, 684, 685, 687, 693, 698-700, 704, 711, 714-716, 719, 722, 731, 732, 735, 760-762, 777, 780-782, 789, 799-801, 804, 814, 816, 817, 820, 827, 835, 838, 846-850, 863, 869, 870, 876, 878, 889, 894, 902, 927, 929, 940, 944, 951, 954, 955, 962, 967, 969, 971, 978, 982, 986, 991, 994, 996, 1010, 1014, 1020-1022, 1025, 1036, 1038, 1051, 1061, 1066, 1068, 1073, 1076, 1077, 1079, 1080, 1087, 1088, 1090, 1098, 1103, 1106, 1118, 1120, 1131, 1135, 1143, 1162, 1164, 1167, 1169, 1172, 1175-1179, 1185, 1191, 1196, 1198-1200, 1204, 1205, 1208, 1209, 1215, 1216, 1220, 1229, 1231, 1233, 1236-1238, 1242, 1255, 1256, 1261, 1265, 1267-1269, 1271, 1273, 1278, 1284, 1286, 1288, 1289, 1291, 1293, 1301, 1324, 1333, 1335, 1341, 1342, 1349, 1355, 1359, 1365, 1369, 1370, 1376, 1383, 1384, 1392, 1394, 1396, 1401, 1402, 1415, 1422, 1425, 1431, 1433, 1434, 1439, 1441, 1442, 1458, 1462, 1476, 1479, 1489, 1497, 1502, 1504, 1512, 1516, 1523, 1529, 1531, 1533, 1535, 1539, 1540, 1551, 1555, 1558, 1563, 1564, 1567, 1570, 1575, 1576, 1582, 1589, 1590, 1596, 1604, 1624, 1626, 1632, 1635, 1639, 1645, 1673, 1677-1679, 1688-1691, 1703, 1708, 1711, 1736, 1738, 1742, 1744

Surr', Robert de, 868
Suthbrok', John, 1636
Suthfeld, Ralph de, 281, 282
Sutton, Geoffrey de, fm., 43
, John de, 1549
, Richard de, 302, 1197
, Thomas de, 831, 1290
Suyng', John, 1295
Swallowcliff (Swaleclyve), Wilts, 752, 753
Swanebourne, William de, 131, 209, 300
Swarraton (Swareton), Hants, 798, 1042
Swayn, Nicholas, 1005
Swenlond, Robert de, 193, 256, 298
Sweyn, John, 1723
Swyneborne, Adam and Alice de, 533, 902
Swyniton, John de, 1193
Sydenham (Cydenham), 1397
Sygleschore, John de, 1182

Symond, John, 1532, 1641, 1724
, Richard, 1145
Synbon, John, 808
Syndlesham, Thomas de, 418

Talleyrand de Périgord, xiv, xv
Talemache, Nicholas, 184, 247, 340
Tamerton, John de, 1616, 1657
Tamworth', William de, 548
Tandridge (Tanrugge, Tanrigg), priory, Surrey, 32, 196, 644, 846, 1229
Tannere, Edward, 1107
, John le, 441
Tatsfield (Tachefeld, Tattlesfeld), Surrey, 356, 793, 1394
Taunton, Som, x
, constable, 38
, archd., 825
, St Peter, priory, 52, 72, 73, 1475
, William de, 527
Taylour, John, 1134
Telscombe (Tetelescombe), Sussex, 1002
Terneye, ? Turvey, Beds, 1111
Testede, William de, 863
Thame, Philip de, prior of Hospitallers, 539, 813
Thames (Tamisia), weirs and mills, 896
Thatcham (Thacham), Berks, 1152
Thiron, Tiron, abbey, Eure et Loir, France, 1487
Tholomeis, Luke de, xv
Thomas, bp. Lincoln, 95
, prior, St Denys, Southampton, 62
, John (Lecest' de Thresk), 70
, William, 719
Thony, Simon, 683, 1090
Thorald, John, 1043
, Walter, 1041
Thorleston, Ralph de, 909, 1726
Thorley (Thorlee), I. Wight, 265, 843, 868
Thorne, William de, 89, 90
Thorneye, Walter, 1246
Thorp, Surrey, 1233
Thorpe, Adam de, 93
, John de, 988-990
Thorverton, John de, 951
Throkenesford, Nicholas de, 727
Thruxton (Throkleston, Thurleston), Hants, 143, 273n., 1056, 1137, 1597
Thrykingham, Lambert de, 1191
Thudden', William de, ben., 1490
Thurnby (Tirneby), Leics, 735

Thursteyn, John, 1118
, Robert, ben., 357, 1235
Tibetot, John, 1196
Ticheborne, Roger de, 41, 468
Tichemersh, John de, 1576, 1604
Ticynge, Henry de, 552
Tidpit (Todeput') in Martin, Wilts, 1650
Tidworth, South (Tudeworth', Todeworth'), Hants, 374, 691, 1381, 1546, 1565, 1627
Tillington (Tolyton), Sussex, 1131
Timsbury (Tymberbury), Hants, 619, 1553
, (Tymbresbergh), Som, 742, 745, 1446
Tirwhit, William, 169, 170, 1674, 1677
Tiryngham', John de, 710
Tisted, East (Estistede), Hants, 1067, 1211, 1282, 1581, 1663
Titchfield (Tichfeld), Hants, 271, 1314
, abbey, 271, 272, 670, 1314, 1391
Titsey (Ticheseye), Surrey, 647, 1335, 1516
Titynge, Henry de, 685
Todysterne, Nicholas de, 484
Togond, John, 1449
Tolyton', John de, 697
Tonbridge (Tonnebrugge), 43, 1208
Toneford, John de, 662
Toneton, John de, 377
, Roger de, 259, 283, 377
Tonge, Robert de, 438
Tonk, Walter, 280
Tonner, Laurence de, 977
Tooting (Totynge), Surrey, 715, 735, 838, 1512, 1738
Tortington (Tratynton), priory, Sussex, 971
Totteford', John de, 411, 951, 1655
Toucestre, John de, 179
Tourgys, John and Thomas, 293
Travers, Peter, 264
, Richard, 1343
Trelowargh, 830
Trencham, Henry de, 54, 825, 826
Tresham, Richard de, 1406, 1559
Trewelove, William, 43
Trigontras, John, 364
Trillek, John, bp. Hereford, 276n.
Tristram, Ralph, 371, 1067, 1211
Trottiscliffe (Trottesclyve), Kent, 676, 677, 779
Trowbridge (Troubrigge), Wilts, 609

Trussel, William, knt., 18, 93, 118, 229
Tuderlee, William de, 1591
Tudeworth, John de, 656, 680, 784, 871
Tugford (Toggeford), Salop, 275, 276
Tunnbregg', John de, 521
Tunworth (Toneworth), Hants, 259, 283, 377, 383, 702, 828, 1588
Turk, John de, 1234, 1239, 1500, 1569, 1621, 1682
Twyford, Hants, 480, 655, 935, 1086, 1318
, John de, 1709, 1738, 1752
, William de, 223, 832
Tybotes, John, 1551
Tydd St Giles (Tyd' sancti Egidii), Cambs, 104
Tydynge, Henry de, 1078
Tygehale, John de, 130, 210, 274
Tymberlake, Richard de, 276
Tyntagel, Severin de, xii
Tyrenache, 425–429
Tyrinton, William de, 79
Tyrwyt, *see* Tirwhit.
Tyshe, Richard de, 967
Tysour', William, 474, 1143
Tysslebury, John de, 1358
Tytherley, (West) (Westunderlee), Hants, 344, 517, 1321, 1607
Tytho, 761

Ultra Aquam, Peter de, ben., 1619
Umframvile, William de, 243
Upfeld, Thomas, 1636
Upham, Hants, 433, 434, 652
Uphavene, Richard de, 1413
Uphull', Richard, 1099
Upmarden (Upmerdon'), Sussex, 274
Uppingham', John de, 1160, 1161, 1210
Upton, John de, 519, 638, 667, 671, 1636
, Philip de, 931, 941
, Richard de, 380
Upwell, 762, 1229
Ursinus, Raynald de, cardinal deacon, 572, 752
Usk, Monm, 318, 335, 462
Usk, John de, ix, 63, 78, 79, 82, 84, 135, 149, 157, 203, 204, 230, 251, 252, 253, 262, 268, 369, 425
, John, ben., 1477
Usuflet, John, 1169
Uvedale, Thomas de, knt., 647, 1335, 1516
, John de, 647n.

Vacherie, la, chapel in Cranleigh, Surrey, 581
Vaghan, Vachan, Richard, viii, ix, 84, 202–204, 287, 336, 338, 525, 541, 550, 719, 804, 855
Valence, Valeys', John de, 260, 794, 806
Valevan, William, 1626
Valois, Philip de, IV of France, 47
Valoyns, John de, 307, 402, 664, 692, 851
Vannes, Brittany, 47n.
Vanceye, Vauxeio, Denis de, ben., 695, 1485
Veer, John, earl of Oxford, 1029
Veysi, Robert le, 370
Villeneuve-les-Avignon, 883
Vincent, George, 78
Virley, John, 1564
Voirdire, Nicholas, 1073, 1169
Volet, Everard, 1540
Vyne, *see* de la Vyne.
        , Thomas atte, 158

Wadden', 1311
Wadenest, Thomas, 649
Wadenhoe (Wadenho), Northants, 1066
Wager, Robert, 1721, 1733, 1734
Wake, John, 1297
Wakefeld', Humphrey de, 54
Waker, John, 858, 1420
Wakerley (Wakerlee), Northants, 1454
Walcote, William de, 372
Waleys, John, 800
        , Nicholas, 1595
        , Walter, 194, 1213
Walkhamstead (Wolknestede) i.e.
Godstone, Surrey, 195–197, 762, 846, 1178, 1229, 1659
Wallop, Thomas de, 1311
Walsshe, Adam le, 264, 280
Walter, Geoffrey son of, 1420
Waltham, Bishops, i.e. South
Waltham, 101, 289, 651, 765, 766, 771, 997, 1009, 1015, 1016, 1287–1303, 1418, 1445, 1446, 1449, 1454, 1557, 1605, 1615, 1618–1623, 1643, 1644, 1661, 1671, 1744–1752
        , North, 444, 453, 503, 630, 1137, 1448
Walton-on-Thames (Waleton, Wauton), Surrey, 103, 186, 296, 856, 1273, 1677
Walton', Waleton', Henry de, 710
        , John de, 1222, 1223
        , William de, 1679

Walyngford, William de, 129, 173, 224, 1187
Wamberghe, Adam de, ix, 12, 13, 17, 70, 140, 168, 176, 177
Wanborough (Wanebergh'), Wilts, 455
Wandsworth (Wandlesworth), Surrey, 332, 512, 788, 789, 1197, 1545, 1596
Wanstead (Wanstede), Hants, 748, 1166
Wantynge, Richard de, 1287, 1392
        , William de, 98, 1090
Wanynden', Wanydon', Walter de, 620, 777
Wapford, Robert de, 722
Wappenbury (Warpyngbury), Warw, 1735
Warblington (Warblynton), Hants, 1424, 1636
Ware, John, John de, 1147, 1183, 1188, 1190, 1193, 1257, 1259, 1264, 1275–1277, 1279–1282, 1285, 1287, 1290, 1292, 1294–1298, 1300, 1302–1307, 1309–1312, 1314–1321, 1323–1328, 1331, 1332, 1334, 1336–1338, 1343–1345, 1350–1354, 1356–1358, 1448, 1464, 1484, 1487, 1507
Wareham, Dorset, 1110
Warenne (Garenn'), John earl of, 1677n.
Wargrave (Weregrave), Berks, 773, 1272, 1324–1343, 1580–1584, 1629–1633, 1635, 1669, 1684, 1685, 1687–1689, 1694, 1740–1742
Warham, William de, 432
Warin', Waren', Gilbert, 1032
        , John, 837, 1448
Warley Abbess, i.e. Great Warley, Essex, 1113
Warlingham (Warlyngham), Surrey, 500, 617, 850, 1104, 1196, 1679
Warmer, John, 767, 1608
Warmynton, John de, 1057, 1065
        , Richard de, 1180
Warner, Peter, 1292
        , Thomas, 1147
Warnford (Warneford'), Hants, 752, 753, 823, 895, 1652
Warnborough, South (Werneborne), Hants, 208, 1390
Warwick, Thomas, earl of (Warrewik), 105, 1376, 1530, 1541, 1573
Waspail, John, 410, 612, 686, 1052, 1345
        , Nicholas, 410, 447

Waspail, William, 1740
Watele, Simon de, 693
Wateley, ? Whatley (Som), Wheatley in Binstead (Hants), 814
Waterfall', John de, 1425
Watesford, Peter de, 1095
Watford (Whatford), Herts, 1551
   , Robert de, 48
Watton-at-Stone, Herts, 988-990
Waverlee, *see* Cevere.
Waverley, abbey, Surrey, x, 455, 602
Waverleye, William de, 135, 137, 926-928
Welde, John, 1116
Welewyk, Hugh de, 324
   , John de, 578
Welleford, Alan de, 1054
   , Hugh de, 1350
Welles, Henry de, 1549
   , Robert de, 545, 583
Wellesburn', Richard de, 850, 1196
Wellow (Welewe), Hants, 1270
   , East, 387
Wells, 846, 1635
   , archd., 34
   , canon 1728
Wellsworth (Walesworth), in Idsworth, Hants, 362, 518, 1444
Wellys, John, 1450
Welyngton', Reginald de, 580
Wendye, Geoffrey, 1633
Wengrave, John, 1216, 1532
Werdon', John de, 134
Wesbury, John de, 766
Wesenham, Gidfrey de, 1689
West, Thomas, knt., 767, 1612n.
   , Thomas, priest, 1066, 1382, 1423
West Boarhunt (Westborhunte), Hants, 946, 1145
Westbury, John de, 1254
West Clandon, *see* Clandon.
West Dean, *see* Dean.
West Horsley, *see* Horsley.
West Meon, *see* Meon.
West Molesey, *see* Molesey.
West Titherley, *see* Titherley.
West Woodhay, *see* Woodhay.
Westclendon', John de, 450
Westcote, Thomas de, 822
West Horsley (Westhorsele), Surrey, 1103
Westminster, royal palace, 1039, 1542
   , abbey, 509n., 512, 761, 789, 967, 1076, 1093, 1197, 1199, 1286,

1425, 1441, 1545, 1576, 1589, 1596, 1604, 1645
   , Simon, abbot, 1093
Weston Colville, Cambs, 305
Weston Corbett (Weston Corbett), Hants, 755, 1053, 1171
Weston, John, 1301
   , Geoffrey de, 1216
   , Henry de, 1452, 1453
   , Philip de, 123, 124, 141, 147, 370, 776, 1039
   , Richard de, 398, 458, 490
   , William and Margery, 398, 508, 546
West Stratton (Westratton'), 906
Weststratton, William de, 873
Weybridge (Waybrugg'), Surrey, 306, 502, 889, 1021, 1175, 1209, 1504, 1551
Weycombe, John de, 1735
Weye, Robert atte, 1643
   , Thomas, 1127
Weyhill, *see* Woe.
Whattford, Peter de, 501
Whelere, Robert le, 692, 1326
Wherwell, abbey, Hants, 20, 260, 905, 1297
   , abbess, 148, 1464-1470, 1480-1483
   , conventual church, 123, 124, 141, 184, 247, 370, 1297
   , prebendal church, 260, 340, 375, 776, 1039, 1274, 1297, 1420
Wheston, John de, 1302
Whippingham (Wyppyngham), I. Wight, 482, 733, 756, 765, 785, 931, 992, 1032, 1312, 1508, 1543, 1622, 1681, 1718b
Whipstrode (Whippestrede), In Fareham, Hants, 443, 1511, 1746
Whitcherche, John de, 122, 297
   , Thomas de, 120
Whitchurch (Whitchirch'), Hants, 350, 360, 366n., 496, 501n., 530, 624, 904, 1095, 1331
White, Thomas le, 28
Whitecroft, Thomas de, 678, 1001, 1192
Whitefield (Whitefeld), chapel of St Nicholas, I. Wight, 981, 1676
Whiterik', John, 353
Whitewell', John de, 960
Whiteweye, John de, 1006, 1007, 1028, 1055, 1089, 1136, 1174, 1225
Whithorn, bp. of, x
Whithors, Nicholas, 751, 903

Whithors, Walter, 1517

Whitsbury (Wycchebury), Hants, 381, 601, 1049

Whytberd', William, 1074

Wich', Robert, 1686

Wichebury, John de, 607

Wichford, John de, 1101

Wickham (Wykham'), Hants, 886, 891

Wickham Bishops (Wycham), Essex, 940

Wideman, Richard, 473

Widley (Wydelegh'), Hants, 674, 709, 1202, 1249

Wield (Weld), Hants, 184, 260n.

Wight, Isle of, 46, 84, 126, 137, 150, 174, 192, 194, 211, 213, 220, 228, 243, 245, 262, 263, 265, 268, 281, 282, 291, 302, 316, 318, 349, 380, 382, 393, 420, 441–445, 482, 484, 507, 531, 580, 598, 635, 669, 673, 713, 733–736, 747, 751, 754, 756, 758, 759, 765, 774, 785, 802, 803, 808–810, 832, 840, 843, 861–864, 868, 876, 877, 900, 903, 907, 923, 926, 927, 930, 931, 936, 953, 981, 984, 992, 1031, 1032, 1045, 1047, 1054, 1074, 1107, 1159, 1163, 1207, 1219–1223, 1240, 1243, 1258, 1266, 1302, 1312, 1338, 1350, 1354, 1389, 1395, 1404, 1416, 1437, 1443, 1456, 1498, 1503, 1508, 1509, 1532, 1542, 1543, 1574, 1601, 1611, 1613, 1619–1623, 1630, 1641–1644, 1664, 1676, 1681, 1713, 1715–1721, 1724, 1733

 , dean of, 318, 393, 669, 733, 734, 744, 751, 754, 758, 759, 765, 802, 803, 808–810, 832, 840, 861–864, 893, 925, 927, 931, 953, 963, 964, 984, 992, 1032, 1045, 1047, 1107, 1111, 1159, 1266, 1350, 1354, 1404, 1416, 1509, 1532, 1542, 1611, 1620, 1623, 1641, 1642, 1713, 1717, 1720, 1721

Wigton (Wighton), Yorks, 109, 110

Wikewane, Nicholas de, 790

Wilford, Robert de, 214

Williamesthrop' William de, 480

Williamstate, John de, 1124

Winchester, city, 7, 9, 47, 798

 , bishops, unnamed, 68, 73, 136, 379

 , dean, 550, 727, 804, 1008, 1127, 1351, 1528, 1745

 , chapter, 6, 85, 1008, 1200

 , official, 389, 431, 448, 452, 453, 479, 481, 482, 492, 542, 1002, 1030, 1395, 1501

 , archdeacon, 14, 19, 48, 50, 77, 92, 93, 101, 111, 112, 116, 118, 122, 124, 126, 137, 141, 150, 153, 154, 171, 180, 184, 214, 215, 220, 227, 229, 230, 233, 235, 239, 242, 259, 260, 263, 265, 271, 274, 291, 293, 297, 302, 307–309, 315, 316, 319, 325, 326, 330, 335, 339, 340, 342, 344, 347–349, 351, 352, 359, 361, 364–366, 370–378, 380–387, 391, 393–395, 399, 402, 498, 410, 412–415, 419, 420, 422, 429, 436–438, 441–446, 451, 456, 459, 469, 472, 473, 476, 477, 483–489, 494, 496–498, 501, 503, 506, 507, 510, 511, 515–518, 520, 522–526, 534, 537, 539, 540, 548, 550, 553, 568, 570, 573, 577–580, 587, 591, 595–601, 603–608, 610, 612, 616, 619, 621–631, 635–642, 646, 648, 650, 653, 654, 656, 663, 664, 667, 669–674, 676, 679, 686, 688, 691, 692, 694, 696, 697, 701–703, 705, 708–710, 713, 717–721, 726–729, 733, 734, 736–738, 740, 741, 743, 747–751, 753, 754, 757–759, 764–767, 772, 776, 783, 785, 791, 792, 796, 798, 802–806, 808, 810, 815, 818, 821, 822, 824, 826, 828–833, 839–841, 843, 844, 848, 851, 852, 857, 861, 862, 864–868, 877, 881, 886–888, 891, 895, 901, 903–907, 912, 913, 920, 925, 927, 931, 933–935, 938, 939, 946, 947, 952, 953, 957, 963, 966, 972, 973, 977, 983, 984, 987, 992, 997, 999, 1005, 1008, 1009, 1015–1019, 1024, 1026, 1032, 1037, 1039, 1042, 1045–1049, 1052–1054, 1057, 1058, 1067, 1069–1071, 1074, 1075, 1086, 1091, 1092, 1094, 1095, 1099, 1100, 1107–1109, 1110, 1113–1115, 1119, 1121, 1122, 1125, 1127, 1134, 1137, 1140–1142, 1144–1146, 1150—1153, 1158, 1159, 1166, 1171, 1173, 1181, 1183, 1186, 1188, 1190, 1192–1194, 1201, 1202, 1207, 1211, 1212, 1221, 1223, 1226, 1230, 1240–1244, 1252–1254, 1257, 1259, 1262, 1263, 1270, 1272, 1274, 1275, 1360–1368, 1371, 1373–1375, 1377–1382, 1385–1391, 1393, 1397, 1400, 1403, 1404, 1408–1414, 1416, 1417, 1420–1424, 1426, 1428–1430, 1432, 1435–1438, 1440, 1443–1445, 1448–1452, 1454–1456, 1468, 1483, 1486, 1487, 1496, 1498, 1499, 1501, 1503, 1505–1515, 1518, 1521–1524, 1531, 1532, 1534, 1538, 1542, 1544–1546, 1548–1550, 1552, 1553,

1556, 1566, 1568, 1571–1574, 1578–1580, 1583, 1585, 1586, 1588, 1591, 1592, 1597, 1598, 1602, 1607, 1608, 1611, 1612, 1614, 1616, 1619, 1620, 1625, 1631–1634, 1646, 1650, 1651, 1653, 1657, 1660, 1664, 1665, 1669, 1674, 1676, 1684, 1685, 1687, 1696, 1702, 1710, 1713, 1716, 1718–1721, 1723, 1724, 1730, 1734, 1737, 1740, 1743, 1745, 1746, 1749, 1750, 1752

, sacrist, 84

, St Swithuns, cathedral priory, prior, 343, 477, 543, 544, 556f, 855, 1490f,

, St Mary, abbey, *see* Nunnaminster.

, St Cross, Hospital, *see* St Cross.

, St Elizabeth, chapel, *see* St Elizabeth.

, Hyde abbey, *see* Hyde.

, Winchester College, 289n., 436n.

, churches,
 All saints in the Vineyard, 326
 St Anastasius, 215, 737, 1158
 St Bartholomew, Hyde, 342, 534
 St Faith, 268, 467, 1102, 1126, 1320
 St George, 372, 475, 606, 727, 757, 798, 803
 St James, 542, 949, 1409, 1745
 St John of the Hills, 975, 1277
 St Laurence, 378, 1241
 St Martin, Parchment Street, 20, 335, 542, 905, 1665
 St Martin, outside Westgate, 1412
 St Mary Kalendar, xii
 St Mary in the forecourt of St Swithuns, 1003, 1285 (?)
 St Mary, over Northgate, 997, 1578
 St Mary, in the Vale, 452, 766, 1254, 1296, 1300, 1435

St Maurice, 275, 317, 321, 322
St Michael, 522, 553, 829, 830
St Nicholas, Kingsgate Street, 525, 550, 719, 804, 845
St Peter in Jewry, 1366
St Peter, on Cheshill, 471, 570, 1281, 1631
St Peter, Colebrook, 641, 1058, 1334
St Peter outside Southgate, 1138
St Peter, Whitebread, *de albo pane*, 241, 301, 721, 1510
St Peter, fraternity of, xii

, bishops, *see* Pontissara, Orleton.
Winchfield (Wynchefeld), Hants, 127, 632, 945, 973, 1423, 1743
Windesore, Robert de, 1458
Windsor (Windesore), 1214
Winnall (Wynhale), Hants, 1035
Winslade (Wyneslade), 414, 650, 1186n.
Winter, Joan de, 1375
Winterbourne, Wilts/Glos, 1253, 1633
Winterburn', Emma de, cist., 632
Wintney (Wynteneye) priory, Hants, 289, 578, 632, 1292
Wircestre, Robert, 1157
Wisborough Green, Sussex, 181n.
Wisley (Whisshele), Surrey, 69, 88, 106, 107, 120, 529, 1564
Witchampton (Wychampton), Dorset, 1032
Witchford (Wychford), Cambs, 1550
Withened', William 1743
Witley (Wittele), Surrey, 397, 454, 816, 870, 954, 955, 1200
Witney (Wytteneye), Oxon, x, 1189, 1493, 1516, 1689, 1690
Wiveliscombe (Wyvelescomb), Som, 825
Woburn (Wouborne), Beds, 982
Wodeford, John de, 1204
, William de, 1173, 1531
Wodeham, Milo de, 643
Wodelok', John son of William, 433, 434, 1526
, Melchior, 1501, 1585
, Robert, 1490
Wodelond', Richard de, 616, 877, 1401
Wodenvyle, Richard, 1632

Woderoue, Robert, 1420, 1421, 1532, 1533
Woe (Wee), i.e. Weyhill, Hants, 1181, 1430, 1454
Woking (Wokkynge), Surrey, 1533
Wolde, Andrew de, 1710, 1718a
Woldingham, ? Warlingham, 1255
Wolf', William, 400; called Wolf, 461
Wolknestead, see Walkhamstead,
Wollop, Richard de, 419
, William de, 271
Wollors, David, 1248
Wolmongere, Richard, 1490
Wolsche, William de, 1100
Wolveleye, John de, 3, 34, 84, 157, 197, 199, 262, 263, 268, 432–434, 444, 445, 457, 562, 583, 586, 661, 668, 681, 695, 705, 726, 774, 775, 914, 931, 969, 1020, 1045, 1086, 1175, 1259
, John junior, 939
Wolverton (Wolferton, Wonfyngton), Hants, 109, 110, 882, 932, 933, 1005, 1586, 1702, 1725, 1737
, Robert de, 41
, Thomas de, 652
Wolvesey (Wolves'), castle, ix, x, 202, 207, 463, 479, 649, 663, 873, 905, 906, 1008, 1224, 1327, 1340, 1525, 1589, 1590, 1618, 1628, 1665–1667, 1719–1725, 1751
, Thomas de, 609
Wolveston', William de, 1529
Wondeye, Geoffrey de, 1253
Wonersh (Wonnersh', Wohghnersh), Hants, 1204, 1231
Wonham, John de, 700
Wonston (Wonsyngton), Hants, 217n., 975, 1327, 1484
Woodeford (Wodeford'), Essex, 1596
, Wilts, 739, 812
Woodhay (Wodehay), Hants, 1405
, East, 35, 252
Woodland (Wodelonde), Kent, 1236
Woodmancote (Wodemancote), Sussex, 1177
Woodmansterne (Wodemersthorne), Surrey, 98, 346, 799
Wootton (Wodyton), I. Wight, 747, 758, 963, 1054, 1623, 1630
Wootton St Laurence, Surrey, 1129n.
Worcester, x, xi, dioc. 78, 194, 1535
, John bp., 1535
Worldham, East (Worldham magna), Hants, 1017, 1127

Worlingworth (Wyrlyngworth), Suff, 1018
Wormenhale, John de, 1353, 1641, 1679, 1726, 1751
Wormleighton (Wylmeleghton), Warw, 121
Worplesdon, Surrey, 83, 183, 258, 538, 657, 1636
Worston', Hugh de, 1702, 1725, 1737
Worting (Wortynge), Hants, 329, 330, 720, 1226, 1325, 1501, 1585
Wortynge, William de, 362
Wotton (Wodyngton, Wotton'), Hants, 193, 256, 298, 477, 961, 962, 1088
, Surrey, 1198, 1690
, John de, 895
, William de, 752, 753, 823, 895, 1548
Wranby, William de, 326
Wranghby, Walter de, 515
Wrangle, Lincs, 1113
Wreford, William de, 1177
Wroughton (Elyndon'), Wilts, 457n., 675, 783, 1313, 1346
Wycham, John de, 1146
Wyche, Robert atte, 1403
Wychford, John de, 1328
, Robert de, 1183, 1193, 1194
Wycombe (Wycambe), dean, 1216
, John de, 32
, Richard de, 1742
Wygynton', William de, 249
Wyhamescote, John de, 1170
Wyke, Roger de, 390
Wyke Regis, Dorset, 527
Wykam, John de, 1173
Wykeham, William de, 289n., 436n., 1307, 1347, 1598n., 1616
Wykewane, Nicholas de, 513
Wykford, Robert de, 1361, 1602, 1743
, Roland, ben., 563
Wyle, Henry atte, 1092
Wylie, Wyli, John de, 103, 186, 296, 856, 1678
Wylinton, Reginald de, 380
Wylkham, Thomas de, carm., 43
Wylons, Robert, 1636
Wylton, John de, ben., 158
, Peter de, ben., 1490
Wylughby, Richard, 1433n.
Wymering (Wymeringe), Hants, 362
Wymondham, Roger de, 1651, 1658
Wyn, John, 342, 542
Wyncestre, John de, knt., 717
Wynchester, John, 1253, 1633

Wynchyndon, Adam de, 297
Wyneford, Nicholas de, 1319
Wynewyk, John de, 1071, 1075
    , Richard de, 1075
    , William son of Richard, 334
Wyngreworth, Giles de, 1400, 1669
Wynhale, John, 737, 1412
Wynkeleye, John de, 194, 227
Wynnecote, Bartholomew de, 1257
Wynton, John de, 314, 640
    , Nicholas de, 176, 177, 187, 1484
    , Peter de, 271, 272
    , Richard de, 1436
    , Thomas de, 618, 909
Wyntreshull, Constance de, 1464–1470, 1480
Wyot, Stephen, 806, 1345, 1740
Wyrecestr', Thomas de, 238, 239
Wyrkynton', William de, 261
Wyschalde, Richard de, 448
Wyschawe, Richard de, 456
Wyse, John le, 398
    , William, 416
Wysman, Roger, 1088
Wyssyndon', Robert de, 1215
Wythchurch, John de, 1252n.
Wythewelle, John de, 750
Wyville, Robert de, bp. Salisbury, xv, 61, 88, 106, 123, 124, 136, 141, 147, 166, 194, 198, 217, 235, 269, 321, 739, 812, 834, 960, 972, 1026, 1032, 1050, 1056, 1077, 1108, 1110, 1112, 1142, 1148, 1165, 1177, 1347, 1537, 1554, 1559, 1574, 1650, 1657, 1687, 1742
Wyville, Walter de, xv
Wyxenhale, ? Wixhill, Salop, 1390

Yakeslee, Henry de, 1426
Yale (Yal), 170
Yarmouth (Eremuth), I.Wight, 734, 1163, 1721, 1733
Yaverland (Everlond), I.Wight, 126, 382, 713, 1047
Yfeelle, Nicholas de, 85
Yonge, John le, 192, 212, 213
    , Thomas le, 1260, 1313, 1346, 1449, 1457, 1458, 1490, 1626, 1666
Yongwyne, John, cf. John de Boxgrave, 219–221
York, dioc., 109, 894, 1130, 1349, 1575
    , treasurer, 1071, 1075, 1309, 1400, 1669
    , chapter, 109
    , abbey, 1575
    , W', archbp., 894

    , John, archbp., 1349, 1575

Zelot, Walter, 1384
Zouche, Robert la, 239, 489, 605, 654, 791, 1336, 1377
    , William la, 239n.